The World and Darfur

Arts Insights showcases current research in the social sciences, humanities, and social work.

An initiative of McGill's Faculty of Arts, Arts Insights brings together research in the Social Sciences, Humanities, and Social Work. Reflective of the range of expertise and interests represented by the Faculty of Arts at McGill, Arts Insights seeks manuscripts that bring an interdisciplinary perspective to the discussion of ideas, issues, and debates that deepen and expand our understanding of human interaction, such as works dealing with society and change, or languages, literatures, and cultures and the relationships among them. Of particular interest are manuscripts that reflect the work of research collaborations involving McGill faculty and their colleagues in universities that are part of McGill's international affiliation network.

Arts Insights will publish two titles a year in English. The editors prefer original manuscripts but may consider the English-language translation of works that have already appeared in another language.

Series editors: Nathalie Cooke, Richard Schultz, Wendy Thomson

1   *Projecting Canada*
    Government Policy and Documentary Film at the National Film Board
    Zoë Druick

2   *Beyond Wilderness*
    The Group of Seven, Canadian Identity, and Contemporary Art
    Edited by John O'Brian and Peter White

3   *Mordecai Richler*
    Leaving St. Urbain
    Reinhold Kramer

4   *Women in Power*
    The Personalities and Leadership Styles of Indira Gandhi, Golda Meir, and Margaret Thatcher
    Blema Steinberg

5   *The World and Darfur*
    International Response to Crimes Against Humanity in Western Sudan
    Edited by Amanda F. Grzyb

The World and Darfur

INTERNATIONAL RESPONSE TO CRIMES
AGAINST HUMANITY IN WESTERN SUDAN

Edited by Amanda F. Grzyb

McGill-Queen's University Press
Montreal & Kingston | London | Ithaca

© McGill-Queen's University Press 2009
ISBN 978-0-7735-3535-0

Legal deposit first quarter 2009
Bibliothèque nationale du Québec

Printed in Canada on acid-free paper that is 100% ancient forest
free (100% post-consumer recycled), processed chlorine free

McGill-Queen's University Press acknowledges the support of the
Canada Council for the Arts for our publishing program. We also
acknowledge the financial support of the Government of Canada
through the Book Publishing Industry Development Program
(BPIDP) for our publishing activities.

LIBRARY AND ARCHIVES CANADA CATALOGUING IN
PUBLICATION

The world and Darfur : international response to crimes
against humanity in western Sudan / edited by Amanda F. Grzyb.

(Arts insights ; 5)
Includes bibliographical references and index.
ISBN 978-0-7735-3535-0

1. Crimes against humanity – Sudan – Darfur.   2. Genocide
– Sudan – Darfur – Prevention – International cooperation.
3. Sudan – History – Darfur Conflict, 2003– – Civilian relief.
4. Humanitarian intervention – Sudan – Darfur.   5. Sudan
– History – Darfur Conflict, 2003– – Mass media and
the conflict.   6. Conflict management – Sudan – Darfur
– International cooperation.   7. United Nations – Peacekeeping
forces – Sudan – Darfur.

I. Grzyb, Amanda F., 1970– II. Series: Arts insights 5

DT159.6.D27W67 2009   962.404'3   C2008-907685-0

Set in 10.5/13 Warnock with Neue Helvetica Extended
Book design and typesetting by Garet Markvoort, zijn digital

In memory of Eric Markusen

Contents

Acknowledgments

In late 2005 the University of Western Ontario's Holocaust Literature Research Institute (HLRI) brought together genocide scholars and activists from across North America for a three-day conference to discuss the political and humanitarian crisis in Darfur. Hundreds of students, faculty members, and concerned members of the community attended the gathering to hear presentations about the history of Sudan, reports about the atrocities in Darfur, the international response to crimes against humanity, and the parallels between Darfur and the 1994 Rwandan genocide. This collection of essays was inspired by the conference proceedings, and most of the book's contributors presented an early version of their chapters there. I am grateful to Rich Hitchens of the Canadian Centre for Genocide and Human Rights Education for initiating, planning, and organizing the Darfur conference with the dedication and enthusiasm that he lends to all of his community-education initiatives. I would also like to acknowledge my friend and colleague, Professor Alain Goldschläger, director of the HLRI, who generously hosted the Darfur conference.

I offer thanks, as well, to Kyla Madden and Joan McGilvray at McGill-Queen's University Press for their steadfast support, enthusiasm, and encouragement during the preparation of *The World and Darfur* manuscript, and to my excellent students and research assistants, Amy Avis, Samantha Burton, Andrew de Waard, Erik Stackelberg, and Chris Richardson, who provided me with invaluable help at various stages of this project. I was extremely fortunate to work with a brilliant copy editor, Curtis Fahey, whose professionalism, commitment, and eye for detail are unparalleled. And I was also lucky to work with an excellent indexer, Noeline Bridge, who prepared the index on a very tight schedule.

I would like to thank Human Rights Watch for permission to reproduce Abd al-Rahman's drawing from *The Smallest Witnesses* exhibition, C. Peter Morgan for permission to reproduce his photo of the *Darfur/Darfur* exhibit at the Royal Ontario Museum, and Ron Haviv / VII for permission to reproduce his photograph, "Young girls leave camp for internally displaced persons to gather firewood." Additional thanks to Ron Haviv / VII for granting the Press permission to use the cover photo; it is an image that perfectly captures the ambivalent response to Darfur by the international community.

I gratefully acknowledge my parents, their partners, my parents-in-law – Bernie Grzyb, Betsy Reilly, Richard Shroyer, Susan Mockler, Janelle Reed, and Richard Reed – and my wonderful sister, Emily Grzyb, for their support. Finally, I am deeply indebted to my husband, John Reed, and our young daughters, Charlotte and Lucy Grzyb-Reed, for their love, inspiration, and understanding throughout the duration of this project. Charlotte and Lucy: by the time you read this volume, I hope we are living in a much more peaceful time.

Amanda F. Grzyb
London, Ontario
December 2008

Contributors

MAJOR BRENT BEARDSLEY is a serving infantry officer in the Royal
Canadian Regiment of the Canadian Army. He has served for twenty-
eight years in a wide variety of field force and staff appointments
including four tours of regimental duty with all three battalions of his
regiment in London, Ontario, Winnipeg, Germany, and Gagetown,
New Brunswick. On extra-regimental employment he has instructed
at the Canadian Forces Officer Candidate School, served as a staff officer on the Army Doctrine and Training staffs, and acted as the chief
instructor of the Canadian Forces Peace Support Training Centre.
He is currently employed as a research officer at the Canadian Forces
Leadership Institute. Major Beardsley's operational tours include duty
in Cyprus, Germany, Norway, UN headquarters in New York, and
Rwanda. During the latter mission, he was employed as the personal
staff officer to Canadian General Romeo Dallaire, the commander of
the UN peacekeeping force in Rwanda, before and during the genocide
in 1994. Major Beardsley is a graduate of the Canadian Forces Staff
School, the Canadian Land Forces Command and Staff College, and
the Land Force Technical Staff Program. Academically, Major Beardsley is a graduate of Sir George Williams University with a pre-arts
diploma (1974), Concordia University with a BA in history (1977),
McGill University with a post-graduate diploma in education (1978),
and the Royal Military College of Canada with a master's degree in
applied military science in management (1999). He is currently com-
pleting a second master's degree in war studies, where the focus of
his research is on genocide, human security, and humanitarian inter-

vention. Major Beardsley was the co-author with General Dallaire of the award-winning and best-selling non-fiction book *Shake Hands with the Devil: The Failure of Humanity in Rwanda* (Toronto: Random House Canada 2003). He has also consulted on several documentaries, participated in numerous conferences, and spoken widely in North America to audiences on the Rwandan genocide. He resides in Kingston, Ontario, with his wife, the former Margaret Esau, his children Jessica, Joshua, and Jackson, his mother, Dorcas Beardsley, and their incredible poodle Rambo.

DR GERALD CAPLAN has an MA in Canadian history from the University of Toronto and a PHD in African history from the School of Oriental and African Studies at the University of London. Once an associate professor in the Department of History and Philosophy of Education at the Ontario Institute for Studies in Education (OISE/University of Toronto), he is the author of two scholarly history books, two UNICEF reports (child labour and children in conflict), two major Canadian public-policy studies (broadcasting and education), and many articles and book reviews in newspapers, magazines, and academic journals; a collection of his newspaper articles has been published. His most recent major publications are the book-length study *Betrayal in Africa* (Toronto: House of Anansi 2008), essays on genocide and Africa for *Walrus* magazine, and a comprehensive report called *Rwanda: The Preventable Genocide* for the International Panel of Eminent Personalities established by the Organization of African Unity to Investigate the 1994 Genocide in Rwanda. In recent years, Gerald Caplan has been a member of the senior experts' team undertaking an evaluation of the United Nations' African development agenda on behalf of the UN's special coordinator for Africa; a senior consultant for the UN's Economic Commission for Africa, based in Addis Ababa; a senior consultant for the United Nations Development Program; and a senior consultant for UNICEF, the World Health Organization, and the African Union in preparing an action plan for improving the well-being of African children that was presented to the 2005 Summit of African Heads of State. His major preoccupations today are African development, AIDS, and genocide. He has developed a course on the Rwandan genocide which he teaches for the University for Peace and advises solidarity groups on genocide prevention and the crises in Darfur (Sudan) and northern Uganda (the children of Gulu). For several years he was adviser to Stephen Lewis, then special UN envoy for HIV/AIDS in Africa, and in 2008 he joined Mr Lewis's new NGO, Aids-Free World, as senior adviser. He continues to provide public commentary on African development and on genocide prevention and speaks widely on both issues.

DR FRANK CHALK is professor of history at Concordia University, Montreal, and is the co-author, with Professor Kurt Jonassohn, of *The History and Sociology of Genocide: Analyses and Case Studies* (New Haven, Conn.: Yale University Press 1990). Professor Chalk's chapters and articles have appeared in a number of books and journals, including *Holocaust and Genocide Studies*. He has lectured and presented papers on genocide at conferences and universities around the world and before the Prosecution Staff of the International Criminal Tribunal on the Former Yugoslavia and Rwanda at The Hague. Professor Chalk served as president of the International Association of Genocide Scholars (June 1999–June 2001) and is a past president of the Canadian Association of African Studies. He is director of the Montreal Institute for Genocide and Human Rights Studies (MIGS) at Concordia University, where he teaches undergraduate and graduate courses on the history and sociology of genocide, the Holocaust, and the history of United States foreign relations. During his sabbatical leave in the academic year 2000–01, Professor Chalk was a fellow of the Center for Advanced Holocaust Studies of the U.S. Holocaust Memorial Museum, Washington, D.C. His current research focuses on two areas: radio broadcasting in the incitement and prevention of gross violations of human rights, including genocide, and the history of the domestic laws on genocide developed by nations that seek to implement through their national legislation the United Nations Convention for the Prevention and Punishment of the Crime of Genocide. He expects both research projects to result in books. Professor Chalk is the co-director, with General Romeo Dallaire, MIGS senior fellow, of the *Will to Intervene (W2I)* project at Concordia's MIGS and a participant in *Life Stories of Montrealers Displaced by War, Genocide, and Other Human Rights Violations*, a five-year project involving forty researchers and nineteen community organizations with funding from the Social Sciences and Humanities Research Council of Canada and Concordia. His most recent publications include chapters on "Hate Radio in Rwanda," in Howard Adelman and Astri Suhrke, eds., *The Path of a Genocide: The Rwanda Crisis from Uganda to Zaire* (New Brunswick, N.J.: Transaction Press 1999), and "Radio Broadcasting in the Incitement and Interdiction of Gross Violations of Human Rights, including Genocide," in Roger Smith, ed., *Genocide: Essays toward Understanding, Early Warning, and Prevention* (Williamsburg, Va.: Association of Genocide Scholars 1999). Together with Dinah Shelton, Howard Adelman, Alexander Kiss, and William Schabas, he was an editor of the three-volume Macmillan USA (Detroit: Thomson Gale) *Encyclopedia of Genocide and Crimes against Humanity*, which was published in November 2004. He holds a PHD in history from the University of Wisconsin.

DR AMANDA GRZYB is assistant professor in the Faculty of Information and Media Studies and associate scholar at the Holocaust Literature Research Institute at the University of Western Ontario. Her research and teaching interests include Holocaust and genocide studies, homelessness, social movements and media, and American and African-American literature and cultural studies. Grzyb gives frequent public lectures on genocide and the media, and she has led several workshops on teaching the Holocaust with film and video. She is currently doing research on the representation of homelessness and diversity in Canadian newspapers with the support of a strategic research grant from the Social Sciences and Humanities Research Council of Canada. From 1997 to 2001, Grzyb was the director of a residential summer-camp program for children, aged eight to thirteen, living in New York City homeless shelters. She remains active with local homeless shelters and affordable-housing advocacy initiatives, serving on the board of directors of the Unity Project shelter in London, Ontario, since 2005. She holds a PHD in English from Duke University and an MA in theory and criticism from the University of Western Ontario. She lives in London, Ontario, with her husband, John Reed, and their daughters, Charlotte and Lucy.

DANIELLE KELTON is currently enrolled in the Master of Public Diplomacy Program at the University of Southern California, bringing together her interests in media, conflict resolution, and international relations. She is serving as the business manager of a research project on Alhurra TV, which evaluates the effectiveness of the United States media outlet in the Middle East at the USC Center on Public Diplomacy. Prior to enrolling in the program, Kelton worked as a research intern at the Montreal Institute for Genocide and Human Rights Studies, where she was charged with monitoring and analysing Sudanese state-sponsored media outlets including radio, television, print, and web. Kelton graduated from McGill University in 2006, earning her BA in political science and psychology.

DR H. PETER LANGILLE is director of "Global Common Security i3" in London, Ontario, where he specializes in peace and conflict studies, UN peace operations, emergency responses, global politics, and Canadian defence policy. Langille is currently assessing the UN's surveillance and monitoring requirements in UNAMID (Darfur) as part of an official report for the UN Special Committee on Peacekeeping Operations. He also supervises officers in the Masters in Defence Studies Program at the Canadian Forces College in Toronto. Near the conclusion of the Cold War, he initiated discussions on revising NATO and Warsaw Pact military doctrine and deployments to a more defensive orientation. In the early 1990s, his proposal and plans to convert CFB Cornwallis into a Canadian Multinational Peacekeeping Training Centre were solicited by numerous governments and subsequently prompted the development of the Pearson Peacekeeping Training Centre. Following the genocide in Rwanda, he served on the core working group of the government of Canada study *Towards a Rapid Reaction Capability for the United Nations*. Langille's book *Bridging the Commitment Capacity Gap: Existing Arrangements and Options for Enhancing UN Rapid Deployment* (Wayne, N.J.: Center for UN Reform Education 2002), developed the concept, case, model, and plans for a permanent UN Emergency Service. His fourth book, *Urgent* (forthcoming), will elaborate on the diverse requirements of this service. Langille has taught at seven Canadian universities. His MA (conflict analysis) is from the Norman Paterson School of International Relations, Carleton University. His PHD (peace studies) is from the University of Bradford (UK). He has been the recipient of a Human Security Fellowship and a SSHRCC post-doctoral fellowship, and he was the second person to receive the World Federalist Movement-Canada's "Hanna Newcombe Award" for his various efforts in support of more effective United Nations Peace Operations. Langille has worked with various levels of government and he remains active on the board of four civil society organizations. Aside from research and teaching, he has six years of practical experience in the prevention, management, and transformation of violent conflict.

DR DANIEL LISTOE is a lecturer in the departments of English and Hebrew Studies at the University of Wisconsin-Milwaukee. He teaches courses on the politics of Holocaust memory and the intersection of rhetoric and human rights. Listoe has published articles and book chapters about the Holocaust, public memory, and American literature, and he is currently working on a book-length project entitled 'Translating Catastrophe: The Aesthetics of History and Modern Literature.' Listoe holds a PHD in Modern Studies from the University of Wisconsin-Milwaukee.

DR ERIC MARKUSEN was professor of sociology and social work at Southwest Minnesota State University and a senior researcher with the Department of Holocaust and Genocide Studies of the Danish Institute for International Studies. Before his untimely death in January 2007, he was a co-editor of *Genocide Studies and Prevention*, the official journal of the International Association of Genocide Scholars, and he served as associate editor for the two-volume *Encyclopedia of Genocide* (Santa Barbara, Calif.: ABC-Clio 1999). Marksen was co-editor with Samuel Totten of *Genocide in Darfur: Investigating Atrocities in the Sudan* (New York: Routledge 2006), and also wrote about nuclear-weapons policy, the nature of modern war, the Holocaust, and the genocides in Bosnia, Rwanda, and Sudan. He travelled extensively in the former Yugoslavia during and after the wars of the 1990s and made many visits to meet with officials at the International Criminal Tribunal for the Former Yugoslavia. Markusen served as an investigator on the Atrocities Documentation Team sent in July and August 2004 to the Chad-Sudan border to interview refugees from Darfur. He obtained an MSW from the University of Washington and a PHD from the University of Minnesota. *The World and Darfur* is dedicated to his memory.

DR ERIC REEVES is professor of English language and literature at Smith College in Northampton, Massachusetts. He has spent the past nine years working full-time as a Sudan researcher and analyst, publishing extensively both in the United States and internationally. He has testified several times before the Congress, has lectured in a range of academic settings, and has served as a consultant to a number of human rights and humanitarian organizations operating in Sudan. He has published extensively on all aspects of Sudan's recent history, both nationally and internationally. He is author of the recently published *A Long Day's Dying: Critical Moments in the Darfur Genocide* (Toronto: Key Publishing House, 2007). Reeves holds a PHD in English from the University of Pennsylvania.

DR CARLA ROSE SHAPIRO is a Social Sciences and Humanities Research Council of Canada post-doctoral fellow in the Department of History at the University of Toronto. She is an independent curator whose research focuses on artistic and museological approaches to visualizing the experiences of Holocaust survivors. She has also worked with the Rwandan, Cambodian, and Armenian communities to create exhibitions about genocide survivors in their communities. In broader contexts, Shapiro has applied approaches to exploring historical events through the prism of photographic portraiture and (auto)biography. Her curatorial work includes the exhibitions *Portraits from the 100 Days*; *Portraits of Survival: Life Journeys during the Holocaust and Beyond*; and *"We Who Survived ..."*. Shapiro holds an MA in museum studies from the University of Toronto and a PHD in media and cultural studies from the University of Sussex.

DR SAMUEL TOTTEN is a senior researcher at the Centre for Conflict Management, National University of Rwanda. He is the author of several books, including *Dictionary of Genocide*, with Dr Paul Bartrop, Deakin University, Victoria, Australia (Westport, Conn.: Greenwood Publishers 2009), and *The Prevention and Intervention of Genocide: An Annotated Bibliography* (New York: Routledge 2006). He is the co-editor of numerous works on genocide, including *Century of Genocide: Critical Essays and Eyewitness Testimony*, with William S. Parsons (New York: Routledge 2009); *The Fate and Plight of Females during and following Genocide* (New Brunswick, N.J.: Transaction Publishers 2009); and *Genocide in Darfur: Investigating Atrocities in the Sudan* (New York: Routledge 2006), with Eric Markusen. Totten is a co-founding editor of *Genocide Studies and Prevention: An International Journal* (University of Toronto Press). He is also the series editor on genocide for Transaction Publishers and the managing editor of its series entitled *Genocide: Critical Bibliographic Review*. During the summer of 2004, Totten served as one of the twenty-four investigators with the US State Department's Atrocities Documentation Project interviewing Darfurian refugees along the Chad/Sudan border in order to collect data for the express purpose of ascertaining whether genocide had been perpetrated in Darfur. From January 2008 through July 2008, Totten was a Fulbright Scholar at the Centre for Conflict Management, National University of Rwanda. Totten holds an EdD from Columbia University.

Foreword

It is a great privilege to be asked to write the foreword to this multidimensional and scholarly work on the genocide in Darfur. As the force commander of the United Nations Assistance Mission in Rwanda (UNAMIR) in 1993–94, before, during, and after the Rwandan genocide, I witnessed one of the fastest and deadliest genocides in the closing years of the twentieth century. Approximately fifty years after the largest and deadliest genocide in history, the Holocaust, after humanity pledged "Never Again" and after the United Nations and the international community placed the Genocide Convention into international law to prevent, suppress, and punish the crime, the world once again confronted a genocide in Rwanda in April 1994. In response, humanity once again, as it has done too often in the past – in Armenia, the Ukraine, Burundi, Bangladesh, and too many other locations – watched and witnessed yet another genocide sweep a nation and murder a people without an effective response to prevent the preventable, to stop the horrendous, and to punish justly the key perpetrators. Unfortunately, "Never Again" remained "Yet Again."

In January 2004 I testified for the prosecution against Colonel Theoneste Bagasora, one of the alleged leaders of the Rwandan genocide, at the International Criminal Tribunal for Rwanda. I considered this testimony to be a continuation of my mission to Rwanda. Since returning from Rwanda in 1994, I had never gone back to that country, which in my heart and mind I knew I had to do at some point in my life in order to achieve some degree of closure for myself and for my own sanity. With my testimony at Arusha complete, I decided to travel to Rwanda with my wife and, to record the visit, a Canadian documentary film crew. My purpose in doing so was to bear witness once again, before the Rwandan people and any others who would listen, to the preventable catastrophe Rwandans suffered in 1994 and to glimpse into the heart of Rwanda ten years later.

While the commemoration events on 7 April were well attended by representatives of the international community, I was greatly disappointed that most heads of state from the Western, northern, and developed world had failed to take the time to come to Rwanda and to apologize for their failure and the failure of their nations to prevent or stop the genocide. Instead, their representatives, many of whom were low-level officials, failed to take direct responsibility. They tended to talk about "our" failure as if by accepting some vague collective responsibility they could absolve themselves of individual responsibility and, more important, accountability for our failure in Rwanda. In addition, these representatives repeatedly and unconvincingly pronounced "Never Again" as the words "Yet Again and Again" rang through my mind.

I was also concerned that the Western media circus that arrived in Rwanda to cover the commemoration events seemed to be more focused on a few photo-ops, a byline, a too brief and too superficial evening news clip than on actually explaining and clarifying the Rwandan genocide and raising it to where it needs to be in the memory and the conscience of humanity's leadership. This concern was reinforced when, at the end of the commemoration events in Rwanda, the Western media deserted the country and "the story" as rapidly as they had in 1994 and the coverage of this important event was relegated to the backburner, just as had happened in 1994 when the O.J. Simpson trial, the Tonya Harding case, and other irrelevant stories knocked the Rwandan genocide out of the news at the height of the slaughter of the innocents.

I was also disappointed once again with the non-governmental organizations (NGOs), whose representatives arrived in force for the commemoration events and took every opportunity in front of a camera, at a conference, or when speaking to a reporter to point the finger of failure and responsibility at everyone but themselves. They forgot the old saying that when you point the finger at another you have three fingers pointed at yourself. How conveniently they have forgotten (with a few notable exceptions like the International Committee of the Red Cross) how they scrambled over the bodies of the living and the dead to fly out of Rwanda to safety in the early days of the genocide while abandoning their local staff and operations to ensure their own survival. They then had the gall to rain criticisms upon everyone else (and even the few like Care International and UNICEF who remained), but I saw precious few of them return to Rwanda in its hour of greatest need until the situation was "safe." A little humility and a review of the limits of their actual commitment to humanity in war zones would provide greater credibility in such discussions.

In April 2004, while the so-called representatives of the international community were pledging "Never Again" in Kigali, yet another genocide was in full swing a few thousand kilometres to the north of Rwanda, in the area of Darfur in Sudan. Observing the events in Darfur unfold was, for me, in many ways like having a flashback to the failed response to the Rwandan genocide in the spring and summer of 1994. Two teams of inquiry were dispatched. The US-sponsored team concluded that genocide was in fact taking place in Darfur. US Secretary of State Colin Powell presented the findings to the US Congress, which resulted in a unanimous vote in support of the conclusion that genocide was occurring, yet again, in Africa and more specifically in Sudan. However, when asked if there would be a significant policy change in the form of a major US-sponsored or -led intervention to stop the genocide, the US administration clearly stated No and the genocide continued.

In 1994 the United States refused to acknowledge, until it was too late, that the events in Rwanda constituted a genocide. Such an acknowledgment, in accordance with the Genocide Convention, would have obliged the United States and the other contracting parties of the international community to intervene to stop the genocide. But in 1994 the United States, among others, would acknowledge only that "Acts of Genocide" were taking place and would not define how many acts it took to constitute a genocide. Then, it did nothing to stop the genocide and in fact did all in its power to prevent others from doing anything effective.

In 2004 the United States acknowledged that the atrocities in Darfur constituted genocide, and then again it chose to do little to stop the violence. A poorly trained and equipped, inadequately funded, and weakly mandated African Union force called AMIS, which, like UNAMIR in Rwanda, was able to do little more than deliver some humanitarian aid, facilitate fruitless negotiations, and bear witness to the genocide, was the best the international community could manage.

The only difference between the two US responses is that the response to Darfur, in fact, set the dangerous precedent that the government can acknowledge a genocide and then get away, immorally, with providing no response to suppress it as is required by the Genocide Convention. Yes, billions in aid have been sent to Darfur, but one wonders if this is not a business in itself.

In essence, the Genocide Convention has been castrated into impotence. How will we ever achieve "Never Again" if we have no intention of making effective and meaningful commitments in support of international law, fundamental human rights, and basic human dignity? Where is the will to intervene at the political levels?

A second commission of inquiry into the Darfur genocide was sponsored by the United Nations. While it contained a number of the same investigators and while the evidence that it gathered was even more damning and added to the proof of yet another genocide, the political decision in New York was to conclude that while "acts of Genocide, crimes against humanity and war crimes" were taking place in Darfur, they did not prove that a genocide was in fact taking place. Again, as had occurred in Rwanda, the debate turned into an academic and legal exercise while thousands, then tens of thousands, and to date hundreds of thousands of human beings died in Darfur, most by murder but also as a result of thirst, starvation, disease, and a torture against women called rape. One could almost hear the collective sigh of relief by the great powers and by all member states in the international community: "Oh, thank God it is not a genocide, just *gross violations of human rights, crimes against humanity, and war crimes* and therefore we can do little or nothing." As if murder, rape, systematic massacres, ethnic cleansing, and destruction of way of life are not enough to warrant a determined humanitarian response. What does "Never Again" mean in Darfur?

This book is important and I encourage everyone to read it, talk about it, think about it, and, most important, do something about it. If you as individuals are waiting for the United Nations, governments, including our own, or any other group in the international community to take the lead, then you will only be disappointed by their failure and lack of will to intervene. My concern is that you could end up inexcusably absolving yourself, as a member of humanity, from your personal responsibility to human rights and especially to the human rights of others in danger. It will take each one of us turning a page on the past and committing ourselves to action in support of human rights with our time, our money, and our efforts to ensure that "Yet Again" becomes "Never Again." We cannot continue to fail to prevent, to stop, and to punish the crime of genocide, massive crimes against humanity, and war crimes and then claim that we believe in human rights and human dignity. Even worse, we continue to suggest that our country is a model for the world to follow when the majority of humanity does not even enjoy the simple right to life.

While this book is focused exclusively on Darfur, it also teaches us about how to build an effective response to genocide, massive crimes against humanity, and war crimes. In his millennium address, then Secretary General of the United Nations Kofi Annan challenged the international community to examine the balance between state sovereignty, the dominant paradigm since the Treaty of Westphalia, and the requirement of the international community to protect human rights. Canada, led by our then foreign affairs minister, Lloyd Axworthy, accepted the challenge and supported an international commission to examine this dilemma and to make achievable recommendations on how we can respect state sovereignty while still protecting human rights, especially when the violator is the state in question. The panel of eminent personalities included our own Michael Ignatieff, and its report formulated a doctrine entitled the Responsibility to Protect or R2P. Canada accepted this doctrine and over the next few years was able to gather widespread international support for it, resulting in its eventual endorsement by the General Assembly and the Security Council of the United Nations. This doctrine is based on the fundamental belief that the primary responsibility of any state is to protect the human rights of its citizens and that, if a government is unable or unwilling to do so or is the perpetrator of gross violations of human rights, crimes against humanity, and war crimes and/or genocide, that responsibility passes to the international community. The doctrine then goes on to articulate the methods that can be used, including, as a last resort and with international sanction, the use of force to protect the rights of human beings. R2P has been a major Canadian contribution to the whole subject of how we respond to catastrophic crimes like those in Rwanda and Darfur. But R2P is only a doctrine or a methodology; what is required is actually doing it, that is, operationalizing it. I believe that R2P provides each and every one of us with a roadmap that we should individually advocate and use to pressure our political leaders in Canada and beyond to implement the doctrine in the twenty-first century.

When I returned from Rwanda and spent years reflecting upon that experience, I came to a simple conclusion that I have articulated on numerous occasions with the phrase "Are all humans human, or are some more human than others?" If as Canadians we agree that all human beings are equal and must possess the same human rights, then we have to start demonstrating it by taking action to ensure that, for example, the life of a Rwandan child or a Darfurian child is as precious and important to us as the life of a Canadian child. Not until we get to this level of humanity within our political leadership will we find the will, the means, and the strength to sustain the sacrifices essential to ensuring that the same human rights will be established and respected for all humanity. If the twentieth century was, as many scholars claim, the "century of genocide," then let the twenty-first century be the century of humanity, when we as human beings rise above race, gender, ethnicity, religion, ignorance, apathy, greed, and hypocrisy, set aside national and personal self-interest, and instead create a new world order where all humanity will enjoy the same human rights. Only then will "Yet Again" truly become "Never Again."

Lt.-Gen. (Ret.) Roméo Dallaire
February 2009

The World and Darfur

Introduction: The International Response to Darfur

AMANDA F. GRZYB

On 2 April 2004 Jan Egeland, the United Nations under-secretary general of humanitarian affairs and emergency relief coordinator, declared Darfur, Sudan, to be "one of the most forgotten and neglected humanitarian crises in the world."[1] The primary target of Egeland's remark was not the Government of Sudan (GOS) or the Janjaweed militia – who together have raped and killed hundreds of thousands of Darfurian civilians[2] and forcibly displaced millions more since 2003 – but the "international community," the nations of bystanders whose neglect of Darfur, like Rwanda before it, appears to happen by force of habit. After five years of civilian bloodshed and multiple UN resolutions to address it, the situation in Darfur remains unresolved and, by some accounts, continues to deteriorate. The crisis has compelled the international community to re-examine its collective responsibility to prevent and punish the crime of genocide, and reinvigorated discussions about the potential of the recently endorsed UN Responsibility to Protect (R2P) doctrine, which obligates the international community to protect civilians from genocide, war crimes, ethnic cleansing, and crimes against humanity in cases where the violence is committed by the victims' government or where the victims' government is unable to protect them from such violence.[3]

Since 2004, many of the international debates about Darfur can be reduced to two central questions. First, do the atrocities committed against non-Arab Darfurians constitute genocide, crimes against humanity, ethnic cleansing, a counter-insurgency campaign, or some combination of all four? And, secondly, how and when should the international community intervene – or not – to quell the killing, raping, and forced displacement of civilians? Almost all of the scholars, activists, and civil society organizations concerned with Sudan agree that the international community has not fulfilled its political and humanitarian obligations in Darfur over the last five years, failing, once more, to mitigate a preventable, human-wrought disaster. Nsongurua J. Udombana, director of the Center for Human Rights at Central European University, goes so far as to claim that the international community's inability or unwillingness to act in Darfur is tantamount to complicity in the crimes that are committed there, that "powerful states and institutions that could have stepped in to make a difference ... became accessories to acts of genocide."[4]

While there is general agreement about the neglect of Darfur by the international community, there is not a consensus about how to rectify this negligence. Many genocide scholars and Darfur aid organizations – particularly those based in North America – have advocated a UN peacekeeping force in Darfur with a strong Chapter VII mandate to protect civilians.[5] In May 2007 John Prendergast and Colin Thomas-Jensen of the International Crisis Group and the Enough project argued that there are two necessary components for a solution to the crisis: "a peace agreement that addresses the remaining issues of the non-signatory rebels and broader Darfurian society" and "an effective civilian protection force, the starting point for which is the 'hybrid' UN-AU [African Union] force mandated by the international community but rejected by Khartoum."[6] While the UN Security Council authorized such a hybrid UN-AU force in July 2007, the mission remains understaffed and ill-equipped, and civilians remain vulnerable to attack. In a September 2007 op-ed in the Boston *Globe*, Sudan scholar and public intellectual Eric Reeves, a contributor to this collection, suggested that while the violence may have lessened, civilians are still periodically victimized by the GOS: "Though violence in Darfur has mutated, we still receive many reports about acts enumerated in the Genocide Convention. Ethnically targeted violence, orchestrated by Khartoum, continues to be chronicled by human rights investigators, though it has certainly diminished since the height of massacres and village destruction from early 2003 through early 2005. Reports of ethnically targeted rape by Khartoum's Janjaweed militia are ongoing. The regime continues its indiscriminate aerial bombardment of African villages."[7] For example, on 25 August 2008, GOS forces attacked civilians at Kalma refugee camp, "leaving scores dead and 60 wounded."[8]

While there is clear support for UN intervention in Darfur, some prominent voices, such as Alex de Waal of Justice Africa and Mahmood Mamdani, the director of the Institute for African Studies at Columbia University, continue to advocate non-military solutions. Like Reeves, De Waal decries the lack of international involvement in the early years of the crisis, especially during what he calls the "genocidal counterinsurgency" of 2003–04.[9] He suggests, however, that the situation in Darfur looks different today than it did two or three years ago, and that the growing state of anarchy warrants peace negotiations between the GOS and Darfur rebel groups – not foreign military peacekeeping – if there is to be any hope of resolving the crisis in the long term.[10] Likewise, Mamdani asserts that a military peacekeeping intervention in Darfur could turn into a complex, drawn-out fiasco like the US invasion of Iraq:

What would happen if we thought of Darfur as we do of Iraq, as a place with a history and politics – a messy politics of insurgency and counter-insurgency? Why should an intervention in Darfur not turn out to be a trigger that escalates rather than reduces the level of violence as intervention in Iraq has done? Why might it not create the actual possibility of genocide, not just rhetorically but in reality? Morally, there is no doubt about the horrific nature of the violence against civilians in Darfur. The ambiguity lies in the politics of the violence, whose sources include both a state-connected counter-insurgency and an organised insurgency, very much like the violence in Iraq.[11]

As the international community recognizes its prior neglect of Darfur and continues to contemplate the options for future involvement in the region – including diplomacy and political pressure, sanctions and divestment, peace negotiations and military peacekeeping operations – we often hear mention of the need for significant "political will" or "public will" to support intervention. Part of the discussion about "will" necessarily includes a critical examination of the intervention tools available to the international community, and the way genocide is articulated in the 1948 UN Convention on the Prevention and Punishment of the Crime of Genocide. The convention, which defines genocide as "acts committed with intent to destroy, in whole or in part, a national, ethnical, racial or religious group," excludes groups that are targeted for their political affiliations and beliefs. Furthermore, evidence of atrocities against civilians must be accompanied by proof of the perpetrator's genocidal *intent*, and while intentionality can be difficult to prove under any circumstances, it is particularly elusive when mass killings happen under the veil of war. R2P rectifies some of these dilemmas by eliminating the Genocide Convention's burden of perpetrator intentionality and offering broader protection to civilians who are targeted for reasons other than nationality, ethnicity, race, or religion.

After the scourge of civilian carnage in the twentieth century, a "century of genocide" that occurred during an era of unprecedented scientific and technological progress,[12] the implications of the Darfur crisis extend beyond the contemporary moment in Sudan. While this volume is a contribution to the urgent public and scholarly discourse about Darfur, it also addresses issues that are intrinsic to genocide prevention and intervention *in general*, issues that are paramount to the way in which we think about our humanitarian obligations to protect civilians in a new millennium. The first section explores Darfur in the shadow of Rwanda, asking what our failure to prevent the 1994 Rwandan genocide can teach us about our political lethargy and strategic miscalculations in Darfur, and how the common characterization of Darfur as "another Rwanda" affects public support for intervention. The second section examines the ways that we characterize the violence in Darfur, including international commissions of inquiry, GOS communications and propaganda, and estimates of civilian mortality. The third and final section takes up the dilemma of genocide representation and international response by critiquing the relationship between talk and action, examining the dissemination of advocacy messages about Darfur through art exhibitions, memorials, and public human rights discourses, and evaluating the current deployment capabilities for UN peacekeepers. The eleven contributors to *The World and Darfur* come from a broad range of academic disciplines – African studies, military history, media studies, sociology, social history, literature, education, art history, and political science – and many have made significant contributions to public life and civil society in the areas of UN peacekeeping, human rights activism, community education, genocide commemoration, genocide-research projects, and atrocities-investigations teams. Despite their diverse approaches to the Darfur crisis, each contributor ultimately articulates similar concerns about the role of the international community in Darfur and the future of genocide prevention.

Background: The Crisis in Darfur

Darfur first entered the international public consciousness in 2004, just as the GOS in Khartoum and the rebels of the Sudan People's Liberation Movement/Army (SPLM/A)[13] in southern Sudan were negotiating the terms of the Comprehensive Peace Agreement (CPA) that would eventually end the Second Sudanese Civil War. Fuelled by a century of power and wealth inequities, as well as religious, cultural, and ideological differences between the mostly Muslim north and the mostly Christian and Animist south, the war lasted more than two decades, claiming the lives of over two million people and displacing at least four million more.[14] The CPA provided for the resolution of regional conflicts, the right of self-determination for the people of southern Sudan, security arrangements, and power- and wealth-sharing agreements between Khartoum and the SPLM/A.[15] The agreement generated relief and optimism in the international community, offering the hope of a lasting peace in Sudan after decades of war and carnage.[16]

Darfur, a uniformly Muslim region of approximately six million people in the western part of Sudan,[17] was largely excluded from the CPA. Although Darfurians fought for the GOS during the civil war, they remained marginalized from the centre of Sudanese power in Khartoum. Decades of oppression and neglect by the Sudanese government made Darfur ripe for rebellion, a "time bomb waiting for a fuse,"[18] and just as the GOS and the SPLM/A were moving towards a final resolution of the north-south conflict, two Darfurian rebel groups, the Sudanese Liberation Movement/Army (SLM/A) and the Justice and Equality Movement (JEM), mobilized to challenge the ruling elite in Khartoum. The rebels claimed that Sudanese President Omar al-Bashir had neglected to invest in the physical and economic infrastructure of Darfur, and that the GOS favoured the interests of regional Arabs over non-Arab peoples. The marginalization of the non-Arab Darfurians was not a new problem. Dar Fur (meaning "homeland of the Fur") was founded as an independent sultanate in 1630[19] and incorporated into the British colony of Sudan in 1917.[20] The strategy of "indirect rule" by the British colonialists produced what Gérard

Prunier calls "benign neglect"[21] in the "outlying areas" of Sudan,[22] an indifference that left Darfur isolated, underdeveloped, and politically ineffectual when Sudan achieved its independence on 1 January 1956.[23] The Darfurians remained marginalized from Khartoum in the second half of the twentieth century as the region succumbed to increasing desertification, drought, and food shortages, including a major famine from 1984 to 1985.[24]

The population of Darfur consists of a diverse mix of ethnic groups. The non-Arabs of central Darfur – including the Fur, the Tunjur, the Masalit, the Berti, and the Bergid, among other, smaller groups – are farmers, and the non-Arabs of northern Darfur – principally the Zaghawa and the Bedayat – are nomadic herders. The Arabs, who arrived in Dar Fur between the fourteenth and eighteenth centuries,[25] are usually classified into two groups: the Baggara or "cattle people" in southern Darfur, and the Aballa or "camel people" in northern Darfur.[26] Scholars and activists, including several of the contributors to this volume, sometimes characterize Darfurian ethnicity as being either "Arab" or "African." De Waal suggests that "from the viewpoint of Darfur and its 'Sudanic' orientation, 'Arab' is merely one subset of 'African,'"[27] indicating that it may be more appropriate to refer to the major ethnic divisions in Darfur as "Arab" and "non-Arab." The designation of "blackness" that often accompanies descriptions of African/non-Arab Darfurian identity is not based on discernible physical differences between Arabs and Africans/non-Arabs in the region, and, over time, activists and civil society organizations have revised their use of racial or ethnic designations in an attempt to better describe the nuances of these divisions. The Save Darfur Coalition, one of the largest Darfur advocacy groups, has issued the following official statement about the use of "ethnic terminology": "The Save Darfur Coalition avoids framing the genocide in Darfur as a conflict between 'Arabs' and 'Africans.' Using this narrative oversimplifies the calculated and horrific campaign of the Government of Sudan and its proxy militia, known as the Janjaweed, against the civilian populations and various ethnic groups of Darfur."[28] Save Darfur has adopted the terms "non-Arab black African Muslims" and "Arab black African Muslims," suggesting that both groups share a black African Muslim identity that is differentiated by distinctions between "Arabs" and "non-Arabs," not "Arabs" and "Africans."[29] Still others retain the labels "Arab" and "African" or "black African" (sometimes indicated by quotation marks) as a way of recognizing how the Sudanese characterization of Darfurian identities is heavy with the implication of a constructed racialized difference. Despite the complex integration of these ethnic and cultural groups, the regional divisions and processes of self-identification that mark the difference between Arabs and Africans/non-Arabs have dire and indelible consequences in contemporary Darfur, giving context to Darfurian rebel demands, the targeted nature of GOS and Janjaweed violence, and the United States and United Nations designations of the situation in Darfur as "genocide" or "ethnic cleansing."

In early 2003 the non-Arab SLM/A and JEM Darfurian rebels engaged in armed rebellion against the GOS and, in retaliation, the GOS launched a brutal counter-insurgency campaign against civilians who shared the same ethnicity with the rebels:[30] the Fur, the Masalit, and the Zaghawa. Attacks on villages often consisted of three phases: bombing by Antanov An-12 aircraft, machine-gun and rocket attacks by "combat helicopters and/or MIG fighter bombers,"[31] and ground attacks by the Janjaweed, who were sometimes accompanied by "regular Army units."[32] Prunier claims that the first phase of bombing was deliberately designed to target *civilians*, not rebel fighters: "[The aircraft] have no bomb bays or aiming mechanisms, and the 'bombs' they dropped were old oil drums stuffed with a mixture of explosives and metallic debris. These were rolled on the floor of the transport and dropped out of the rear ramp which was kept open during the flight. The result was primitive free-falling cluster bombs, which were completely useless from a military point of view since they could not be aimed but had a deadly efficiency against fixed civilian targets. As any combatant with a minimum of training would easily duck them, they were terror weapons aimed solely at civilians."[33] However, it was the third phase – the attacks by the Arab Janjaweed militia – that was at the core of GOS strategy in Darfur. By arming and unleashing these "devils on horseback," the GOS guaranteed that villages would be rendered uninhabitable and that many non-Arab Darfurians would be traumatized and fearful of returning home to rebuild. At the same time, the GOS remained at arm's length from the Janjaweed, claiming that they were rogue militias outside Khartoum's control.[34] Rape,[35] torture, and mass killing were frequent Janjaweed tactics, and the egregious violence and destruction initiated a mass exodus of non-Arab civilians from western Sudan, eventually producing a population of refugees and internally displaced persons (IDPs) numbering in the millions.

When he described Darfur as "one of the most forgotten and neglected humanitarian crises in the world," Jan Egeland characterized the massacres of "black Africans" by the "Arab" Janjaweed militia as "ethnic cleansing." He urged the international community to provide urgent humanitarian assistance to civilians and to support peace negotiations between the GOS and the Darfur rebel groups.[36] Darfur had, indeed, been neglected by the world. The UN began to sound the alarm about the violence in Darfur only in the latter months of 2003. By the time the media and powerful Western governments finally began to acknowledge fully the extent of the Darfur crisis in the winter and spring of 2004, the GOS and Janjaweed militia had already been committing atrocities against civilians for a year. At that point, hundreds of thousands of Darfurian survivors were living in IDP camps in Sudan or had streamed into overburdened refugee camps in neighboring Chad. The camps provided minimal services and protection. Civilians remained vulnerable to periodic Janjaweed attacks if they left the camps to collect food or firewood, and they were increasingly susceptible to disease and malnutrition in overcrowded and unsanitary living conditions. The GOS exacerbated these circumstances by actively preventing aid agencies from travelling in western Sudan and blocking shipments of necessary supplies to the region.[37]

As the Darfur story took hold in the media in the spring and summer of 2004, the two key preoccupations of the international community – what to call the violence in Darfur and how (or if) to intervene and stop it[38] – continued to resonate as several interconnected, overlapping questions. What were – and are – the moral and legal obligations of the international community, the UN, and individual Western nations to respond to the violence and to help achieve a lasting peace in western Sudan? Has the international community failed in its duty to protect innocent civilians, just as it did in Rwanda in 1994? Is a hybrid UN-AU peacekeeping force the only way to monitor ceasefires effectively, restore order, and protect civilians, or could the crisis be managed using diplomacy, political pressure, peace negotiations, sanctions, and/or economic divestment? Should the deployment of a military peacekeeping intervention in Sudan require the approval of the GOS, or is the UN permitted to violate state sovereignty under the hospices of R2P, offering protection to Sudanese civilians without the GOS's explicit consent?

The international response to Darfur between 2004 and 2008 has been, at turns, periodically encouraging and staggeringly ineffective. The UN Security Council has passed multiple resolutions on Darfur since 2004. The first major resolution – Resolution 1556 – was passed on 30 July 2004 and demanded that the GOS disarm the Janjaweed militia within thirty days or face further action.[39] The GOS did not oblige and further UN action took the form of a series of additional resolutions demanding compliance from the GOS, but without any provision for enforcement. The succession of Security Council resolutions has been possible, in part, because the killing, raping, and pillaging in Darfur has been spread out over years, not weeks as we saw during the Rwandan genocide. The relatively slow pace of mounting atrocities has allowed the UN, individual governments, and non-governmental organizations (NGOs) to study the atrocities *as they are happening*, and Darfur has been the site of multiple investigations that attempt to determine the precise content and character of the violence there. On 9 September 2004, after reviewing the findings of the United States' own such investigation by the Atrocities Documentation Team (ADT), Secretary of State Colin Powell declared the violence against civilians in Darfur to be "genocide." [40] On 18 September 2004 the UN passed Resolution 1564, which established a Commission of Inquiry to investigate the atrocities in Darfur and authorized an expanded African Union Mission in Sudan (AMIS) force to be dispatched to the region.[41] The results of the UN study of Darfur found definite evidence of crimes against humanity, including ethnic cleansing, but reserved judgment regarding genocide because the investigators could not be certain of *genocidal intent* on the part of the GOS.

On 31 August 2006 UN Security Council Resolution 1706 authorized the expansion of the existing UN Mission in Sudan (UNMIS) to include Darfur,[42] but the plan met with GOS resistance. With only 7,000 AU troops on the ground in Darfur to monitor an area the size of France, and without proper funding, logistics, training, and equipment, AMIS was unable to offer adequate protection to Darfurian civilians for the duration of its mission. While each of the UN resolutions was potentially encouraging to those who supported the strategy of UN intervention in Darfur, the United Nations made no significant efforts to follow through on many of the mandates dictated by its own resolutions. Prendergast and Thomas-Jensen write, "If there is a Guinness Book of World Records entry for most threats issued with no follow up, the international community's response to Darfur is likely setting a new standard."[43]

On 31 July 2007 the Security Council passed yet another Darfur resolution – Resolution 1769 – mandating "the deployment of a 26,000-strong joint United Nations-African Union force ... in an attempt to quell the violence in Sudan's western Darfur region."[44] While some advocates for a peacekeeping mission in Darfur, like Amnesty International, saw Resolution 1769 as a victory, others, from genocide scholars to Darfur rebel leaders, worried that the force would not have a strong enough mandate to guarantee civilian security and that it would not be deployed swiftly enough to prevent further loss of civilian life. Those opposed to military intervention worried that the deployment of additional UN-AU troops in Darfur could detract from the negotiations for a Darfur peace agreement, which they continue to see as the only real hope for a lasting peace in the region, or, even worse, that peacekeepers could inspire an increase – not a decrease – in atrocities.

A year after Resolution 1769 authorized the United Nations Mission in Darfur (UNAMID), military and police personnel levels were at 9,995, far below the UN's target of 26,000. Furthermore, NGOs and Darfur advocacy organizations claim that the international community has neglected to properly equip the UNAMID peacekeepers and that the mission is particularly in need of helicopters, trucks, engineers, and logistics support. Confounding the limitations of UNAMID, the initial hopes of the AU-brokered Darfur Peace Agreement, signed by the GOS and some of the Darfur rebels on 5 May 2006, has fallen apart, a process that began when key rebel groups refused to sign and Darfurian civilians continued to be targeted by the Janjaweed and GOS troops.[45]

Darfur in the Shadow of Rwanda

Darfur advocates, genocide scholars, and the news media often draw comparisons between the international response to the current suffering of Darfurian civilians and the abandonment of Tutsi civilians during the Rwandan genocide. A little more than a decade before the Darfur crisis, Rwandan government soldiers, Interahamwe militia, and "ordinary" Hutu civilians slaughtered 800,000 Tutsi and moderate Hutus over a period of one hundred days while the world stood by, watched, and did nothing to stop it. As the Tutsi bodies piled up in fields, churches, schools, and the Kagera River, the UN and powerful Western nations refused to call the massacres "genocide." This omission was deliberate, an attempt to avoid uttering a word that might trigger an obligation to intervene under the 1948 Genocide Convention. The wholesale abandonment of Tutsi civilians set the standard for post-Cold War international shame, compelling international leaders to endorse a resounding cry of "never again" as they made their journeys of contrition to Rwanda in the years that followed the genocide.

Can Rwanda teach us anything about the current crisis in Darfur? Is the international community failing Darfur in the same way it failed Rwanda? In "What Darfur Teaches Us about the Lessons Learned from Rwanda," Gerald Caplan questions how the international response to the Darfur crisis could be so ineffective, especially given its close chronological proximity to Rwanda and Srebrenica. Caplan suggests that there are three critical observations we can make about the international response to Rwanda and that these observations have relevance for other, subsequent cases of genocide, notably Darfur. First, the lack of response to the Rwandan genocide demonstrates that the UN Security Council – particularly the five permanent members (P5) with veto power: the United States, Britain, France, Russia, and China – has little interest in initiating meaningful forms of intervention based only upon humanitarian concerns. Without significant political or geopolitical investments in places like Rwanda or Darfur, the international community is prepared to abandon innocent civilians who are in desperate need of protection. Secondly, the disingenuous post-Rwanda public apologies by US President Bill Clinton and United Nations Secretary-General Kofi Annan, who both claimed that they did not know the full extent of Tutsi suffering during the genocide, inferred that if there was ever "another Rwanda" the Security Council could no longer claim to be ignorant about the need for immediate intervention. In spite of these apologies, the lack of interest by the P5 means that we have not pursued timely intervention in Darfur. Finally, the refusal by the international community – particularly the United States – to call the massacres in Rwanda "genocide" because it might obligate intervention suggests that if a label of "genocide" were attached to a future crisis, there would be little debate about sending in peacekeepers to protect civilians. The renewed interest in genocide prevention provided "hope that the 'next Rwanda' would not be betrayed and abandoned as the original Rwanda had been." Yet, despite the potential optimism that Caplan cultivates from our catastrophic failures to protect Tutsi civilians in 1994, he is unequivocal that the international community is failing, yet again, to stop atrocities against civilians in Darfur. Caplan laments the unwillingness of the powerful P5 nations to conceive of "a common purpose, a common humanity" that could bridge a committed international effort to fulfil the post-Holocaust, post-Rwandan genocide pledge of "never again."

Like Caplan, Brent Beardsley also offers an assessment of the lessons that the international community can learn from Rwanda, where he served as General Roméo Dallaire's staff assistant during the United Nations Assistance Mission in Rwanda (UNAMIR) from 1993 to 1994. In "Lessons Learned or Not Learned from the Rwandan Genocide," Beardsley proposes a sharp parallel between the failure of the UN to stop the genocide in Rwanda and its negligence in Darfur. Drawing upon the Canadian-commissioned Responsibility to Protect doctrine and a Clauswitzean notion of "limited war," Beardsley suggests that Darfur may be the first test case for the new R2P model. While he acknowledges that genocide prevention and intervention can involve either military or non-military strategies, he reminds us that the UN's decision to withdraw its peacekeeping troops from Rwanda in 1994 and its resistance to authorizing the use of force facilitated the massacres of hundreds of thousands of Tutsi and moderate Hutu. The atrocities in Darfur, he asserts, have not been suppressed using diplomacy and other "non-battle pole" strategies, and effective intervention in Darfur may require the use of a military peacekeeping force.

Beardsley identifies four specific lessons from Rwanda that can assist the UN in the successful implementation of a promising new R2P mandate in Sudan and in future instances of state-sponsored atrocities, genocide, or ethnic cleansing. First, he suggests, we must build international will to respond to these crimes through political leadership, media engagement, and national militaries that place "human security above national interest." Secondly, he claims that we must develop a sound methodology for humanitarian peacekeeping operations that includes adequate knowledge about the country, accurate intelligence, a fully realized R2P strategy, and an adequate UN mandate. Thirdly, we must have sufficient financial means and military resources to follow through on a peacekeeping mission that addresses the political, economic, and social roots of genocide. Finally, Beardsley demonstrates deep concern about the pace of intervention campaigns in both Rwanda and Darfur, suggesting that once diplomatic and political options are exhausted, we must move quickly and efficiently towards a "battle pole" strategy to save civilian lives. Such intervention is not a "quick fix" and indeed may require years of military involvement to help stabilize the country and support a lasting peace.

In "Media Coverage, Activism, and Creating Public Will for Intervention in Rwanda and Darfur," I also address the negligence of the international community in Rwanda, focusing, in particular, on the responsibility of the news media to inform the public about genocide, ethnic cleansing, and crimes against humanity. Using Toronto's *Globe and Mail* as a case study, I suggest that in addition to engaging in a retrospective itemization of the errors and omissions in the news coverage of Rwanda, we must critically examine the racialized language and stereotypes of "the African" that permeated the media's construction of the Rwandan genocide as "tribal warfare." I suggest that the *Globe's* depiction of Hutu and Tutsi as "primitive" tribal foes engaged in reciprocal, inevitable, retaliatory violence is a form of "blackface," a stylized depiction of African-ness that obscures the actual story of the genocide. At the same time, I suggest that the *Globe's* front-page emphasis on the plight of mostly white expatriates in Rwanda is a form of "whiteface," an exaggeration of the risk to a few hundred mostly white foreigners that replaces a concern for the grave danger facing hundreds of thousands of Tutsi civilians.

I propose that the racialized media image of Rwanda is a "floating signifier" that functions discursively and changes over time. The sign "Rwanda," which meant "tribal warfare" in 1994, is now synonymous with the failure of the international community to intervene in a preventable genocide. Indeed, as the story about Darfur broke in 2004, activists, NGOs, and news commentators immediately referred to Darfur as "another Rwanda," using our past failures as a warning about a current crisis. Increasingly savvy in new communication technologies that were largely unavailable in 2004, Darfur advocates have used the example of Rwanda to produce a groundswell of public support for intervention in Darfur. Ironically, these campaigns sometimes engage in a modified "whiteface" strategy as a way to motivate international intervention, exploiting Western narcissism and shame rather than focusing on the complex details of the Darfur crisis.

Mapping a Complex Crisis

Calling Darfur "another Rwanda" evokes the spectre of international abandonment and emphasizes the urgent need to prevent further civilian bloodshed. However, unlike Rwanda, the killing in Darfur has stretched over years, not months, giving the international community a unique opportunity to study the violence while it is in progress. Designations like "genocide," "ethnic cleansing," and "crimes against humanity" are critical for determining the way(s) that the international community should respond to Darfur, and yet scholars, NGOs, the UN, and individual governments remain divided about how to characterize GOS and Janjaweed atrocities.

In "Three Empirical Investigations of Alleged Genocide in Darfur," Eric Markusen examines assessments of the violence in Darfur by the US government, the UN, and Physicians for Human Rights (PHR). In the US government study, a twenty-four-member Atrocities Documentation Team – including Markusen himself and another *The World and Darfur* contributor, Samuel Totten – conducted 1,136 random interviews with Darfurians living as refugees in Chad in 2004. The results, which were presented to Congress and the American public, detailed Janjaweed and GOS attacks on civilians, mass killings, rapes, bombings by government aircraft, forced displacement, and survivor trauma and bereavement. It was on the basis of the ADT report that Colin Powell alleged genocide in Darfur in 2004. Following Powell's assertion of genocide, the UN Security Council revealed the results of its own study, the International Commission of Inquiry on Darfur (COI), which consisted of interviews with internally displaced people in Darfur, Darfurian refugees in Chad, leaders of rebel groups, and key members of the political and military GOS infrastructure. Markusen emphasizes that the COI confirmed the scale of the attacks on civilians and concluded that both the GOS and the Janjaweed were responsible for atrocities. Despite findings similar to those of the ADT, the COI did not name the atrocities in Darfur "genocide" because it could not prove genocidal intent on the part of the GOS. Markusen explains why the COI stopped short of invoking the Genocide Convention, and examines critiques and refutations of this decision. In February 2005, a month after the release of the COI report, Physicians for Human Rights released a report that detailed the destruction of livelihoods and means of survival for civilians in Darfur. PHR, like the ADT, determined that there was genocidal intent in Darfur.

Markusen concludes by suggesting that Darfur is unique because it is one of the few cases where alleged genocide has been studied by multiple agents and organizations while the violence is still occurring, and because it is the only one in which the UN Security Council set up a commission to investigate crimes against humanity. While these developments are relatively encouraging, particularly compared to historical instances of genocide like Rwanda, Markusen is concerned that the UN remains stuck on the issue of GOS intentionality. With or without the proof of genocidal intent, he claims, only a "robust international military intervention" will stop the GOS and the Janjaweed from committing further atrocities against civilians in Darfur.

In another reflection on GOS intentionality, Frank Chalk and Danielle Kelton analyse the broadcast content of GOS radio and television news transmissions using Arabic-to-English translations from the BBC Monitoring Service from May 2004 to August 2008. Drawing on Alexander George's theory that studying the news propaganda of an authoritarian regime provides a glimpse into their future plans, their chapter, "Mass-Atrocity Crimes in Darfur and the Response of Government of Sudan Media to International Pressure," summarizes GOS propaganda and attempts to predict the government's plans with respect to international calls for disarming the Janjaweed in Darfur, sharing oil revenues with Darfur and Southern Sudan, and implementing the Comprehensive Peace Agreement with Southern Sudan, as well as its response to the International Criminal Court (ICC) indictment of Sudan's president, Omar al-Bashir. In Chalk and and Kelton's view, the GOS distorted reports about Darfur in Sudanese domestic media in response to international criticism, claiming that charges of genocide and threats of a UN peacekeeping force are not based on humanitarian concerns but on Western, Zionist, anti-Islamic propaganda that poses an unwarranted neo-colonial threat to Sudanese sovereignty. They conclude that the GOS has no intention of honouring peace agreements that provide for the sharing of wealth and power with Southern Sudan or Darfur, and, furthermore, that non-Arab Sudanese civilians remain vulnerable to GOS and Janjaweed attacks.

Since the beginning of the Darfur crisis in 2003, this vulnerability has been particularly difficult to quantify. Although there is no mandated threshold for the number of deaths that constitute genocide under the 1948 convention, estimates of civilian mortality are critical for determining an appropriate course of action in Darfur. Eric Reeves, one of the foremost North American experts on Sudan, has written prolifically about the situation in Darfur, publishing up-to-date reports on his website (SudanReeves.org) and contributing frequent op-ed articles to national newspapers.[46] Part of Reeves's research includes critical analyses of Darfur mortality assessments, along with strong stances on genocidal violence, GOS obstructionism, UN resolutions, and international complicity. As the crisis continues to unfold, Reeves's weekly – sometimes daily – Darfur updates are required reading for English-speaking genocide scholars and concerned individuals across the globe.

In "Death in Darfur: Total Mortality from Violence, Malnutrition, and Disease: April/May 2006," a summary report of his mortality assessments in Darfur, Reeves estimates that in excess of 450,000 Darfurian civilians died of violence, disease, and malnutrition between 2003 and 2006. By focusing on the diminishment of food aid in Darfurian IDP and refugee camps, Reeves explains how the GOS has deliberately raised Darfurian civilian death tolls by withholding food aid, neglecting to secure safe conditions for aid workers in the country, and, at times, blocking aid organizations from entering the country altogether. Furthermore, he outlines several concerns about the investigative methodology behind estimated mortality rates, including ambiguities about the definition of "family member" and family size in the region. Reeves concludes with a postscript that reflects on the mortality predictions of the 2006 study, explaining how GOS interference and dangerous conditions in Darfur have prevented additional mortality studies over the last two years. He also expresses frustration about the lack of effective intervention in Darfur and the lagging timeline for the full implementation of UN resolutions to address the violence.

International Response, Intervention, and Representation

Like Reeves, the other contributors to this volume decry the political, bureaucratic, and informational barriers that have prevented the international community from staging effective action to quell the crimes against humanity in Darfur. Initially, the challenge was simply raising awareness and concern about the atrocities. Later, the problems ranged from conflicts of interest on the UN Security Council to sustaining public interest in Darfur as the crisis wore on year after year. The international community's reluctance to move from talk to action, as well as the ways we articulate human rights concerns and the intervention tools we have to address them, are paramount to understanding Darfur in the context of past and future instances of genocide, ethnic cleansing, and mass-atrocity crimes.

Samuel Totten, a pioneer of comparative genocide studies and one of the investigators on the 2004 US Atrocities Documentation Team, condemns the anemic international response to Darfur, calling it both shameful and unconscionable. In "Saving Lives in Darfur, 2003–06? Lots of Talk, Little to No Action" Totten asserts that, between 2003 and 2006, "action" consisted exclusively of passive discussions without progressing towards a resolution of the crisis (through peace negotiations) or an effective peacekeeping mission to stop the rape and massacre of civilians (through UN resolutions and interventions). To illustrate the endless succession of talking-without-acting, Totten provides an overview of three years of debates, meetings, diplomatic negotiations, and resolutions by the UN, the GOS, and Darfur rebels, the United States, and the African Union. Like many other genocide scholars and Darfur advocates, Totten claims that the options for talking were exhausted long ago, that successive rounds of debates and negotiations result only in more dead civilians, and that the only way to stop the atrocities is to support the full implementation of a UN-AU peacekeeping force with a strong Chapter VII mandate.

One of the challenges to mounting such an intervention is generating significant and sustained public and political will for involvement in the region. Broad knowledge about the atrocities in Darfur has come less from traditional news sources than from the dozens of multimedia campaigns that are designed mobilize concern about Darfurian suffering. In "Visual Advocates: Depicting Darfur," Carla Rose Shapiro examines the processes of information dissemination and advocacy in two exhibitions about Darfur: *The Smallest Witnesses: The Conflict in Darfur through Children's Eyes* and *Darfur/Darfur*. By situating her analysis of these installations in the context of a wider dialogue about the representation and memorialization of the Holocaust and the Rwandan genocide, Shapiro marks a recent museological turn towards social justice and human rights. She investigates the benefits and limits of the Darfur exhibitions through a close analysis of the exhibitions themselves and asks how artistic treatment of genocide might move the viewing public towards more effective social engagement.

Like Shapiro, Daniel Listoe suggests that effective intervention in mass atrocities and genocide relies not only upon the representation of such crimes but also upon their public reception. In "Rhetoric, Rights, and the Boundaries of Recognition: Making Darfur Public," Listoe begins by citing George Moose's statement that the Clinton administration was "psychologically and imaginatively unprepared" to confront the Rwandan genocide in 1994. He traces the delivery of facts about the Darfur massacres through the complex task of imagining and recognizing the human rights of others, suggesting that our rhetorical language and representations of "rights" are tied to interventionist impulses and denials, and that, in the face of genocide, "politics becomes a limited object rather than a process to tend to real objects, real things, real concerns, real people dying." Listoe claims that Darfur has encountered a definitional firewall; facts and impassioned pleas for international intervention have not succeeded in ending the violence there. What we need, he suggests, is *something more*, a way of making Darfur public that is also part of a process of fully imagining genocide and bringing the meaning(s) of human rights discourse into language.

The final contributor to this volume, Peter Langille, claims that the problem of intervention is rooted in the UN's inability to prevent armed conflict and human rights violations, to protect civilians, to deploy peacekeepers in a timely and efficient fashion, and to secure the delivery of humanitarian aid. In "Preventing Genocide and Crimes against Humanity: One Innovation and New Global Initiative," Langille reviews the existing options for such operations, including the African Union Standby Brigades, the United Nations, the multinational Standby High-Readiness Brigade, the European Union battlegroups, and the North Atlantic Treaty Organization. He suggests that the deficiencies of each of these options warrants support for a new initiative, a United Nations Emergency Peace Service (UNEPS), which would expand the toolbox for effective intervention in cases where civilians are at risk of genocide or ethnic cleansing. Unlike the empty UN resolutions on Darfur and the slow deployment capacity of the existing options for intervention, a dedicated UNEPS could be deployed with much greater efficiency. Not only would such a service effectively stop violence against civilians in Darfur, it would also deter future perpetrators and assist the international community in eradicating genocide in the twenty-first century.

As this volume goes to press, there have been two key developments in the Western response to the crisis. First, Darfur spent much of the summer of 2008 in the Western news media. Dubbing the Beijing Olympics the "genocide Olympics," activists mounted several high-profile campaigns designed to bring global awareness to genocide in Darfur and to pressure China on its continued diplomatic and financial support of the GOS, which is tied, primarily, to Chinese oil interests in Sudan.[47] Secondly, at the height of these protests and media campaigns, on 14 July, the prosecutor of the International Criminal Court, Luis Moreno-Ocampo, indicted Sudan's president, Omar Hassan al-Bashir, for genocide, crimes against humanity, and war crimes in Darfur.[48] The timing of the charges – a direct result of the UN Security Council's decision to refer Darfur to the ICC for investigation under Resolution 1593 in 2005 – makes some Darfur advocates and UN officials fearful of violent reprisals against UNAMID peacekeepers and aid workers, while others predict that it will erode the unity of Bashir's coalition. In either case, it will have an impact on future peace negotiations.

It remains to be seen if the UN Security Council will suspend the ICC indictment for a year, which it is permitted to do under Article 16 of the Rome Statute.[49] It also remains to be seen which countries will offer additional troops, equipment, and resources for UNAMID, and when the UN-AU force will reach adequate personnel levels and provide reliable protection of civilians and aid workers.[50] Likewise, there are important questions about how the international community can support a renewed peace process between the GOS and Darfur rebel groups, and how the UN and NGOs can continue to provide humanitarian aid amid growing instability in the region.[51]

As the crisis continues, the international community must also come to terms with its errors, omissions, and miscalculations in Darfur over the last five years. If we are to make progress in our efforts at global genocide prevention, we must support a dialogue about the international community's newly mandated responsibility to protect civilians, the complexities of representing and responding to genocide, ethnic cleansing, and crimes against humanity, and the creation of effective mechanisms for the prevention of similar atrocities against civilians in the future.

Notes

1 Warren Hoge, "U.N. Aid Says Sudan Is Tolerating Ethnic Cleansing," New York *Times*, 3 April 2004.
2 For a detailed discussion of mortality in Darfur, see Eric Reeves's chapter in this volume.
3 United Nations General Assembly, "World Summit Outcome," 20 September 2005.
4 Nsongurua J. Udombana. "An Escape from Reason: Genocide and the International Commission of Inquiry on Darfur," *International Lawyer*, vol. 40, no. 1 (2006): 42.
5 Chapter VII of the UN Charter – "Action with Respect to Threats to the Peace, Breaches of Peace, and Acts of Aggression" – authorizes the Security Council to use "air, sea, or land forces as may be necessary to maintain or restore international peace and security" (http://www.un.org/aboutun/charter/chapter7.htm.).

6 John Prendergast and Colin Thomas-Jensen, "A Plan B with Teeth for Darfur," Enough: The Project to Abolish Genocide and Mass Atrocities, May 2007, http://www.justiceafrica.org/wp-content/uploads/2007/05/Prendergast_Darfur_USHM.pdf.

7 Eric Reeves, "Op-ed: Holding Khartoum Accountable in Darfur," Boston *Globe*, 6 September 2007, http://www.boston.com/news/globe/editorial_opinion/oped/articles/2007/09/06/holding_khartoum_accountable_in_darfur/.

8 Mia Farrow and Eric Reeves, "Now Sudan Is Attacking Refguee Camps," *Wall Street Journal* online, 6 September 2008, http://online.wsj.com/article/SB122065894281205691.html?mod=googlenews_wsj.

9 In the Preface to their 2005 book, *Darfur: A Short History of a Long War*, Flint and de Waal write, "The international response to the crimes that have been committed in Darfur – and that are still being committed, by forces that still enjoy impunity – has been too little, too late." Julie Flint and Alex de Waal, *Darfur: A Short History of a Long War* (New York: Zed Books 2005), xiv.

10 Alex de Waal and Julie Flint, "In Darfur: From Genocide to Anarchy," Washington *Post* online, 28 August 2007, http://www.washingtonpost.com/wp-dyn/content/article/2007/08/27/AR2007082701339.html. The majority of other genocide scholars, such as Eric Reeves, who is a contributor to this volume, promote a Chapter VII peacekeeping mission as the only viable way to stop the killing and ethnic cleansing in Darfur and cease the spread of suffering into eastern Chad.

11 Mahmood Mamdani, "The Politics of Naming: Genocide, Civil War, Insurgency," *London Review of Books*, vol. 29, no. 5 (8 March 2007), http://www.lrb.co.uk/v29/n05/mamd01_.html.

12 Rudy Rummel estimates that 262 million civilians have been killed by democide (death by government) in the twentieth century. His estimates include victims of genocide, "politicide," and mass murder, including colonialism. Rudy Rummel, "20th Century Democides," http://www.hawaii.edu/powerkills/20TH.HTM.

13 For the SPLM/A, the Movement is the political wing of the Army. The same is true of the Sudanese Liberation Movement/Army (SLM/A), discussed below.

14 United Nations Mission in the Sudan, "Comprehensive Peace Agreement," 31 December 2004, http://www.unmis.org/english/documents/cpa-en.pdf.

15 A referendum is to be held in 2011 to determine whether Southern Sudan will obtain autonomy; in the interval, Southern Sudan has the right to govern its own affairs and participate in the national government.

In this book, we will upper case "Southern Sudan" when it refers to the region that acquired the right to self-determination under the Comprehensive Peace Agreement of 2005. For references prior to 2005, "southern" is lower cased, and, for all periods, "south," "south Sudan," and "southerners" are lower cased as well.

16 Ibid.

17 In 1994 Darfur was divided into three administrative states: North Darfur, West Darfur, and South Darfur. Julie Flint and Alex de Waal write that most Darfur Muslims "are followers either of the *Tijaniyya Sufi* sect, which originates in Morocco, or the *Ansar* followers of the Mahdi, or both." Flint and de Waal, *Darfur*, 10.

18 Gérard Prunier, *Darfur: The Ambiguous Genocide* (Ithaca, N.Y.: Cornell University Press 2005), 86.

19 Flint and de Waal, *Darfur*, 3 and 135; Prunier. *Darfur*, 8–15.

20 Flint and de Waal, *Darfur*, 12.

21 Prunier, *Darfur*, 25.

22 Ibid., 26.

23 Ibid., 36.

24 See Alex de Waal, *Famine That Kills: Darfur, Sudan*, rev. ed. (Oxford: Oxford University Press 2004).

25 Flint and de Waal, *Darfur*, 9.

26 Ibid., 5.

27 Alex de Waal, "Who Are the Darfurians? Arab and African Identities, Violence and External Engagement," Social Science Research Council, 14 December 2004, http://conconflicts.ssrc.org/hornofafrica/dewaal/.

28 Save Darfur Coalition, "Notes on Ethnic Terminology," http://www.savedarfur.org/pages/notes_on_ethnic_terminology.

29 Save Darfur Coalition, "Briefing Paper: The Genocide in Darfur," http://www.savedarfur.org/newsroom/policypapers/briefing_paper_the_genocide_in_darfur/.

30 On 18 February 2004 Amnesty International directly implicated the GOS in the attacks, saying that "it had information that government-backed militias attacked five villages in southern Darfur on Feb. 11, killing between 68 and 80 civilians ... [and] government aircraft also bombed 11 towns in west Darfur, while pro-government militia killed people fleeing." (*Globe and Mail*, "Sudanese Attacked, Rights Group Reports," 19 February 2004, A17.) Likewise, Human Rights Watch released two reports – *Darfur in Flames* in April 2004 and *Darfur Destroyed* in May 2004 – that described the raids and massacres by Janjaweed militia and government forces.

31 Prunier, *Darfur*, 100.

32 Ibid.

33 Ibid.

34 In *Darfur Destroyed*, Human Rights Watch claims that the GOS is working "hand in glove" with the Janjaweed militia. Human Rights Watch, *Darfur Destroyed*, May 2004, http://hrw.org/reports/2004/sudan0504/index.htm.

35 Notably, Janjaweed violence against civilians also includes mass rape of Darfurian women and girls by Janjaweed militia, a tactic also used by the génocidaires in Rwanda and Bosnia. Human Rights Watch describes the prevalence of rape in its 2004 report, *Darfur in Flames*: "A medical student who had been in North Darfur until late February 2004 told Human Rights Watch that he had treated more than fifty women and girls who had been raped by janjaweed and soldiers around Karnoi. In a particularly brutal incident with clear racial overtones, an eighteen-year-old woman was assaulted by janjaweed who inserted a knife in her vagina, saying, 'You get this because you are black.'" (Human Rights Watch, *Darfur in Flames: Atrocities in Western Sudan*, vol. 16, no. 5 [2 April 2004], http://hrw.org/reports/2004/sudan0404/index.htm.) Three years later, Human Right Watch released a statement that specifically addresses the role that UN-AU peacekeepers must play in protecting Darfurian women from the threat of rape: "'The mounting evidence of widespread rape in Darfur underscores why the newly approved UN-AU mission will need to be prepared to protect civilians,' said Peter Takirambudde, Africa director at Human Rights Watch. 'Peacekeepers in Darfur need the capacity to respond rapidly to threats against civilians.' Women in Darfur are also at risk of sexual violence outside the context of large attacks. Women risk being raped if they leave their camp for internally displaced people to search for firewood. In some areas, the current African Union Mission in Sudan (AMIS) has provided 'firewood patrols' to accompany groups of women once or twice a week as they gather firewood. But these patrols have often been ineffective due to poor organization, lack of resources, and lack of communication with the people who benefit from the patrols." Human Rights Watch, "Darfur: Urgent Measures Needed to Address Sexual Violence," 22 August 2007, http://hrw.org/english/docs/2007/08/22/darfur16719.htm.

36 Flint and de Waal, *Darfur*, 9.

37 Prunier, *Darfur*, 130–1.

38 Some scholars, concerned that "genocide" is not the appropriate term, have developed new language for the massacres in Darfur. Frank Chalk, a contributor to this volume, refers to the violence against Darfurian civilians as "mass-atrocity crimes." Alex de Waal calls the 2003–04 attacks on Darfurian civilians "genocidal counterinsurgency."

39 United Nations Security Council, "Resolution 1556 (2004)," http://daccessdds.un.org/doc/UNDOC/GEN/N04/446/02/PDF/ N0444602.pdf?OpenElement.

40 BBC News, "Powell Declares Genocide in Sudan," 9 September 2004, http://news.bbc.co.uk/2/hi/africa/3641820.stm.

41 United Nations Security Council, "Press Release: Security Council Declares Intention to Consider Sanctions to Obtain Sudan's Full Compliance with Security, Disarmament Obligations on Darfur," 18 September 2004, http://www.un.org/news/Press/docs/2004/ sc8191.doc.htm.

42 United Nations Security Council, "Resolution 1706 (2006)," 31 August 2006, http://daccessdds.un.org/doc/UNDOC/GEN/N06/484/64/PDF/ N0648464.pdf?OpenElement.

43 Prendergast and Thomas-Jensen, "A Plan B with Teeth for Darfur," 1.

44 United Nations Security Council, "Security Council Authorizes Deployment of United Nations-African Union 'Hybrid' Peace Operation in Bid to Resolve Darfur Conflict" (New York: Department of Public Information, 31 July 2007), http://www.un.org/News/Press/docs/2007/ sc9089.doc.htm.

45 United Nations Mission in Sudan, "Darfur Peace Agreement," http://www.unmis.org/english/dpa.htm.

46 See http://www.sudanreeves.org.

47 See Dream for Darfur, http://www.dreamfordarfur.org/; and Thomas Katie, "China Defends Right to Deny Activists' Visas," New York Times, 7 August 2008.

48 The ICC charge of "genocide" supplements the United Nations' determination of crimes against humanity and "ethnic cleansing," a claim based on the UN's inability to prove genocidal "intent" on the part of the GOS.

49 Elissa Gootman, "UN Debates Court Efforts to Prosecute Sudan Chief," New York Times, 26 July 2008.

50 The New York Times reported on 2 August 2008, in an article headlined "Sudan: Aid Group Pulls Workers from Darfur," that Doctors without Borders "pull[ed] staff members from two areas in the war-torn Darfur region because of attacks against them."

51 See Nicholas Kristof, "Prosecuting Genocide," New York Times, 17 July 2008; and Jeffrey Gettleman, "Darfur Withers as Sudan Sells Food," New York Times, 10 August 2008.

PART ONE

From Rwanda to Darfur

CHAPTER ONE

What Darfur Teaches Us about the Lessons Learned from Rwanda

GERALD CAPLAN

As the crisis in Darfur moves into its fifth year, the situation continues to deteriorate. All observers agree that violence, chaos, and bloodshed are increasing with every passing week. Nor is this an ephemeral phenomenon, bound to improve any time soon. If anything, the situation has become more complicated and the obstacles to a solution more intractable. The Darfur rebel movements have split and the rebels have become more intransigent. The Sudanese government continues to laugh in the face of those who demand that it rein in the militias, whose very existence it sometimes flatly dismisses as fiction. A growing military conflict on the Sudan-Chad border is further endangering hundreds of thousands of refugees living in camps there. The modest African Union (AU) peacekeeping force can make only a modest difference. The initial Western "strategy" to depend entirely on the AU to pacify the region – a prayer, really, rather than a reasoned position – has proved as bankrupt as was widely predicted. As this is being written, it appears that a hybrid UN-AU force will replace and incorporate the AU mission. UN agencies and international non-governmental organizations (NGOs) attempting to feed and care for the more than three million homeless Darfurians are threatened by assorted gangs of thugs, rapists, and killers, many of them operating under Khartoum's umbrella, and UN staff are being withdrawn for their own safety. With as many as 450,000 Darfurians already dead, it seems certain that the death toll, from further killings compounded by disease and hunger, will reach staggering new totals. We are now in the fourteenth year since the Rwandan genocide, and almost four years since all branches of the American government explicitly declared the crisis in Darfur to constitute a genocide. How is this possible? What are rational folk to make of it?

Background

Even before the 1994 Rwandan genocide ended, some began wondering when "the next Rwanda" would be. Not "if," but when. This marked a significant change. Despite Indonesia in 1965, Burundi in 1972, and Cambodia from 1975 to 1978, genocide had receded in the public consciousness. From the late 1960s, it is true, memory of the Holocaust was in full bloom. But the Holocaust was treated as almost a self-contained phenomenon separate from "ordinary" genocide. The earlier Armenian genocide was mainly the crusade of Armenians, and the Hereros' extermination in present-day Namibia in the opening years of the twentieth century was unknown beyond a few experts. As for the post-Holocaust massacres of half-a-million Chinese and Communists in Indonesia, the slaughter by the Tutsi army of perhaps 200,000 Hutu in Burundi, including all those with secondary education, and the deaths by beating, starving, or torture by the Khmer Rouge of a million and a half Cambodians, none quite seemed to meet the standards set down in the 1948 Convention on the Prevention and Punishment of the Crime of Genocide (UNCG).

Rwanda was different. Rwanda was a classic UNCG genocide, fulfilling all the conditions, and it reminded everyone that a half-century after the world first vowed "never again," genocide had not disappeared. What Primo Levi had said of the Holocaust was now said about Rwanda: it happened, so it will happen again. For some, it happened soon enough. For them, Srebrenica in 1995 seemed "another Rwanda," and indeed the International Criminal Tribunal for the Former Yugoslavia eventually decided that the murder of 8,000 Muslim Bosnian males by Bosnian Serb militias was indeed genocide. But this has been a controversial issue. Cold-bloodedly murdering 8,000 Muslim Bosnians was beyond question an egregious war crime, even a crime against humanity, but, some wondered, how could it belong in the same category as killing one or six million Jews?

Rwanda, however, left no room for ambiguity. Ironically, the seeming absence of genocide since 1945 had made most observers refuse to take seriously in advance that an actual genocidal conspiracy was being hatched in Rwanda before 1994. Once it was over, it seemed all but inevitable that others could, *would*, follow. For many, early in the new millennium, Darfur seemed well on its way to becoming "the next Rwanda." The urgent question then emerged: Had Rwanda taught the world any lessons that might help prevent Darfur from following in its place?

Insights Gained from Rwanda

Assuming, of course, that there really are any lessons at all that the past can teach the future, it is possible to isolate three from the unmitigated catastrophe of Rwanda in 1994. Of these, the first and most obvious is profoundly disheartening to all those who favour intervention in crises where no interests beyond the humanitarian are at stake. The second and third are apparently, or potentially, encouraging. To seek a ray of hope out of a genocide borders on the desperate, but in the curious universe of those who study genocides in order to prevent them, what else is there to hold on to?

The horror of Rwandan genocide extends beyond its intrinsic bestiality. What is also notable is, first, how swiftly it became evident that this was a perfect storm of a genocide and, second, how easily it could have been prevented. (Before addressing the betrayal of Rwanda by the "international community," genocide-prevention activists must not forget that it could have been prevented most successfully if the Hutu conspirators who plotted to "cleanse" Rwanda of its Tutsi citizens had simply called off their plot.) Yet the genocide was not formally named as such by the vast majority of governments and institutions, including the United Nations and the Organization of African Unity, until the one hundred days of slaughter had virtually come to an end. Moreover, not only was the genocide not prevented, it was not even marginally mitigated. From the first day to the last, not a single reinforcement arrived in Rwanda to bolster the puny UN force of four hundred that was trying desperately to save the relatively few Tutsi that it could.

Thus, the first lesson from Rwanda: the harsh unwelcome reminder – as if the world needed another – that the global powers-that-be are capable of almost infinite callousness and indifference to human suffering if geopolitical or political interests are not at stake. Calls for forceful intervention based strictly on humanitarian grounds, as we have learned the hard way once again in Darfur, are simply irrelevant to those with the means to intervene.

Here I refer essentially to the UN Security Council, and within that body to the remarkably powerful five permanent members (P5) who alone hold a veto over all its resolutions. Since only the UN Security Council can authorize missions, and since any one of the P5 can veto any resolution, the leverage of the United States, Britain, France, Russia, and China can hardly be exaggerated. Those who have begged for a more assertive response in both Rwanda and Darfur understand the immutability of this phenomenon. Often, middle powers are looked to as a means to exert pressure on the inner sanctum of the P5. Canada, northern Europe, and the Scandinavian countries are all seen, sometimes naively, as being less in the thrall of self-interest and more open to humanitarian projects. In trying to leverage action for Darfur, activists placed considerable hope on these countries.

The role of Belgium in 1994 shows both the leverage that a middle power can play and the perverse use it can make of that leverage. For 110 years prior to the Rwandan genocide, no external power played a more deplorable role in Africa than Belgium, a tiny country responsible for giant crimes against humanity. Belgium's historical impact on the Congo, Rwanda, and Burundi was catastrophic. The turbulent history of the entire Great Lakes region in the twentieth century would have been profoundly different if it had not been for Belgian colonial rule. Now, just as the genocide was exploding across Rwanda, the Belgian government sought to bring pressure on the Security Council to withdraw in its entirety its six-month-old UN Assistance Mission in Rwanda (UNAMIR). Rwandan government soldiers had murdered ten of Belgium's UN troops less than a day after the shooting down of the Rwandan president's plane triggered the genocide. The Belgian government decided that it was politically impossible for its troops to remain in Rwanda, and their subsequent withdrawal very substantially undermined UNAMIR's capacity. The lethal consequences of this decision are not merely theoretical, since the withdrawal immediately and directly led to the death of some 2,500 Rwandans being protected by Belgian troops at the École Technique Officielle compound in the capital, Kigali. At least the Belgian government had the good sense to feel humiliated by the decision to abandon Rwanda at its moment of greatest need, and sought to cover its guilt by convincing the entire world to share its culpability.

To the everlasting sorrow of Rwanda, the Belgians found the administration of US President Bill Clinton ready and willing. Largely for their own entirely short-term partisan reasons, with pathological UN-hating Republicans breathing down their necks, the Clintonites were unprepared to have anything whatsoever to do with sending a new UN mission to a tiny African country which, as is invariably said, almost no American could even find on a map. Among the P5, France was the only country genuinely concerned about Rwanda for its own reasons of francophone solidarity, and it was stealthily seeking a way to intervene on behalf of the Hutu extremist génocidaire government. It was left to the US ambassador to the UN, Madeleine Albright, to lead a vigorous movement in the Security Council to decimate UNAMIR's 2,500-odd force. Britain, for reasons British journalist-historian Linda Melvern is still trying to unravel,[1] fell in solidly behind the Americans. Russia and China were largely uninterested, a situation that would change significantly in the case of Darfur. At the end of the genocide's second week, with an estimated 100,000 or more Tutsi and almost all prominent moderate Hutu already dead, and the genocide gaining daily momentum, the Security Council voted to reduce the UNAMIR mission to a derisory 250 men. Force Commander Roméo Dallaire, furious and sick at heart, disobeyed this explicit instruction and managed to retain 400 men for the duration of the genocide.

Even now, it is impossible to recapitulate these events without feeling they cannot possibly be true. But as virtually all authorities on the subject agree, and as the Security Council's reaction to Darfur a decade later makes entirely plausible, they were only too true, and their lesson was clear. There seemed barely any depths to which the "international community" would not sink if it deemed them necessary to its own national interests, even if that interest was nothing more nor less than, in Belgium's case, covering up a cowardly abandonment of a people at ultimate risk, or, for the United States, winning an impending election. Political expediency was all, and human need seemed completely irrelevant.

However, two other lessons of the international reaction, distressing as they were at the time, seemed to offer a certain hope for intervention in future crises like Darfur. First, there were the lies told by both American President Bill Clinton and UN Secretary General Kofi Annan in later apologizing for their inaction during the one hundred days. Both claimed that they were insufficiently aware of the situation at the time. These claims, on the part of both men, have been repudiated beyond a shadow of a doubt. They knew everything, or at least everything they wanted to know. Nevertheless, their very disingenuousness permitted the inference that the next time "another Rwanda" loomed, if it could attain a sufficiently high public profile, the Security Council would have lost the excuse of ignorance and have little alternative but to intervene. This apparent truth initially gave heart to the movement to intervene in Darfur.

Secondly, as already noted, almost no one in an official position at the time agreed to characterize Rwanda as a genocide and in fact, led again by the Clinton administration, everyone actually denied that a genocide was in progress. This refusal to affirm the obvious was again tied directly to the Clintonites' electoral fears. Government lawyers studying the 1948 Genocide Convention appear to have decided that accepting the genocide label would trigger a major obligation on the administration to intervene actively. That such an interpretation was highly debatable is neither here nor there. It was perfectly possible to argue that a mere Security Council resolution satisfied the wording of the UNCG. But Clinton's advisers chose not to adopt this reading. Their judgment powerfully affected Clinton's public stance.

Television captured a moment of true self-debasement when a US State Department spokesperson, a certain Christine Shelly, tried to explain to reporters that Rwanda was the scene of "acts of genocide" but not of genocide. When pushed to indicate how many "acts of genocide" constitute one full genocide, Ms. Shelly, obviously humiliated beyond words, explained that she wasn't authorized to deal with that question. (To her everlasting chagrin, several documentaries on the Rwandan genocide include footage of her disastrous performance, unforgivingly immortalizing her forever.) The difference between this pathetic moment and subsequent American reactions to Darfur under President George W. Bush could hardly have been more glaring.

And, indeed, Clinton's position that there was no full-blown genocide in Rwanda unwittingly provided the glimmer of hope out of an act of unsurpassed political opportunism. If Rwanda was "not quite" a genocide, and therefore intervention was not obligatory, it surely followed logically that if a genocide were declared in the future, would it not mean that intervention was mandatory, inescapable? That logic, combined with the prospect that if a disaster was well-enough publicized, the world would have little choice but to move in, offered some real hope that the "next Rwanda" would not be betrayed and abandoned as the original Rwanda had been.

The Next Rwanda

Then came Darfur. Less than a decade after Hutu Power was defeated, the world had found its "next Rwanda." It is irrelevant to my argument that serious genocide authorities disagree about whether the conflict is a genocide or not. All agree that Darfur has many of the dimensions of a genocide, that it is an appalling catastrophe, and that robust intervention is demanded. As we know, no such intervention has ever occurred, while the situation has deteriorated substantially and become even more complex – the almost inevitable consequence of the world's meagre response. From the point of view of the hopes raised by two of the optimistic lessons from Rwanda, the response of the "international community" to the crisis in Darfur must be considered a giant, tragic setback. It is not too much to say that Darfur shows that only the first despairing lesson – the bottomless cynicism and self-interest of the major powers – remains valid, while the hopes have been largely destroyed.

After all, by the middle of 2004, at the very latest, everyone who counts knew that an overwhelming political and humanitarian man-made disaster had befallen western Sudan. On 7 April, when he rightly should have been in Kigali for the commemoration of the tenth anniversary of the Rwandan genocide, Kofi Annan was instead in Geneva unveiling a new five-point plan for genocide prevention and announcing that the world must not permit Darfur to become "another Rwanda." Everyone who counts soon either visited Khartoum to plead with the Government of Sudan that was orchestrating the crisis, or popped in at a displaced persons or refugee camp in Darfur or across the border in Chad. When Annan and Colin Powell make a stop somewhere, you know that it's already a major story. It may not have competed with the Michael Jackson trial, but, even in the mainstream media, Darfur stories, features, and opinion pieces were remarkably common for a crisis so remote and complex.

The crisis in Darfur, in other words, was fairly big news. This was unlike Rwanda. Clinton and Annan knew all about Rwanda, but media coverage for many weeks was both minimal and distorted ("tribal savagery") so the public remained largely uninformed. Yet, despite Darfur's profile, the conflicting interests of the veto-casting P5 effectively paralysed the Security Council. This time China, thirsty for Sudan's oil, and Russia, anxious to sell arms to a genocidal government, also played spoiler roles. The French, cynical to the last drop, care only about protecting their client government in neighboring Chad; as in Rwanda, the petty politics of *francophonie* trump all else for the French political establishment, including genocide or its approximation. The Security Council accordingly passed a series of powder-puff resolutions each threatening the killers in Khartoum that, if they did not rein in their Janjaweed forces, they would be forcefully confronted with – yet another resolution. Perhaps not since a representative of Rwanda's génocidaire government retained his position on the Security Council through the entire 1994 genocide has the Security Council appeared to be more of a joke than over Darfur.

The Role of the United States

Yet there was another reason for hope. Pushed by an unlikely coalition of domestic pressure groups, the US Congress and executive publicly declared in 2004 that Darfur constituted a genuine genocide under the 1948 convention. Such a radical and dramatic step was unprecedented in American history. Both chambers of Congress hastily and unanimously passed their own resolutions declaring Darfur to be a genocide with barely an explanation, let alone debate, and President Bush and Secretary of State Colin Powell each eventually followed with their own concurring declarations. To the genocide-prevention community, this seemed the moment they had so long dreamed of and planned for. What would be the point of making this declaration unless significant action was being contemplated? It was true that the Bush government, and others, were modestly generous in providing humanitarian aid to the displaced and the refugees as well as funding for the Africa Union mission to Darfur. But now, surely, with these declarations, the long-awaited moment of qualitative escalation had arrived. Now we would see the kind of forceful intervention denied Rwanda and that was crucial if the travesty in Sudan was to be ended.

In fact, all that was needed was to pay heed to the second part of Colin Powell's statement before the US Senate Foreign Relations Committee. Yes, the United States had decided, upon looking at evidence it had specifically commissioned – the exact opposite of Rwanda – that a genocide was taking place before the eyes of the world. Powell had no doubt what the world expected next, and said so explicitly: "Mr. Chairman, some seem to have been waiting for this determination of genocide to take action. In fact, however, no new action is dictated by this determination. We have been doing everything we can to get the Sudanese government to act responsibly. So let us not be preoccupied with this designation of genocide. These people are in desperate need and we must help them. Call it a civil war. Call it ethnic cleansing.

Call it genocide. Call it 'none of the above.' The reality is the same: there are people in Darfur who desperately need our help."[2] How was this possible? Had the historic declaration of genocide been nothing more than an opportunistic political ploy by the Bush administration to assuage domestic pressure groups? Could even the Bush neocons be so cynical as to play politics with genocide? If not, how could this wholly unanticipated development be explained? How could the esteemed Colin Powell participate in this destructive exercise that has done so much to debase the currency of the Genocide Convention?

Within mere months of the American government's determination of genocide in Darfur, a new Bush administration betrayal of Darfur was exposed. First came the revelation that the Central Intelligence Agency (CIA) had sent a plane to Khartoum to ferry the head of Sudanese intelligence, General Salah Abdallah Gosh, to Washington for discussions with his American peers on the "war on terror." Sudan, it appears, had become "a crucial intelligence asset to the CIA."[3] Never mind that General Gosh's name was widely assumed to be among the fifty-one leading Sudanese officials considered by the UN-appointed International Commission of Inquiry on Darfur to be most responsible for the conflict. The "war on terrorism" obviously trumps genocide.

Later we learned just how close this tie really was. In October 2005 *Guardian* reporter Jonathan Steele reported the following:

> Question: When do Bush administration officials cuddle up to leaders of states that the US describes as sponsors of international terrorism? Answer: When they are in Khartoum. I know because I saw it the other day ... We were attending the closing dinner of a 2-day conference of African counter-terrorism officials, to which the US and UK were invited as observers. The western spooks were less than happy to have the western press on hand, especially as their names were called out. But loss of anonymity was a small price for the excellent cooperation both agencies believe Sudan is giving to keep tabs on Somali, Saudi and other Arab fundamentalists who pass through its territory ...
>
> [The dinner] was in the garden of the headquarters of Sudan's intelligence service, not far from the Nile. Up stepped a senior CIA agent. In full view of the assembled company, he gave Gen-

eral Salah Abdallah Gosh, Sudan's intelligence chief, a bear hug. The general responded by handing over a goody-bag, wrapped in shiny green paper. Next up was the [British] MI6 official, with the same effusive routine.[4]

Note that the sources here are not exactly obscure bloggers or esoteric genocide preventionists. Yet what is almost as remarkable as the alliance between accused génocidaires and their American accusers is how little this alliance is recognized by experts, officials, commentators, or media discussing Sudan and Darfur. In 2006, in a fourth anniversary overview of the deteriorating situation in Darfur and the failure of attempts to convince the Khartoum government to stop the attacks, Joel Brinkley of the New York *Times* detailed the role of the American government in attempting to formulate new strategies without ever alluding to its entente with Khartoum.[5] Can it conceivably be so inconsequential? Only days later, a *Times* opinion piece by Kenneth Bacon, president of Refugees International, called on the United States to give leadership at the Security Council on Darfur; "opposition from Khartoum's allies, Russia and China," he wrote, "which can veto any Security Council action, may need to be overcome."[6] It seems inconceivable that Bacon wasn't aware that the United States is Sudan's ally as well; but then how can we account for his position? Nicholas Kristof, continuing his indispensable one-man crusade to keep Darfur alive in the mainstream American media, doesn't miss an opportunity to embarrass the Bush administration for its indifference to Darfur – "the White house couldn't be bothered with Darfur," "the US had provided band-aids."[7] Yet, in a lengthy article in the *New York Review of Books* in February 2006, Kristof never even alludes to the Bush administration's embrace of the Sudanese government.[8]

There are still Darfur activists who believe that, despite close working relationships between the Bush administration and precisely those Sudanese leaders against whom the International Criminal Court intends to issue warrants, the United States can still be relied on as an ally in pressuring Khartoum to end its war against the Fur and other Africans. Perhaps they weren't paying attention during the US congressional confirmation hearings when President Bush nominated John Bolton as US ambassador to the UN. Given all the post facto Clinton breast-beating for allowing almost a million defenceless people to die as well as the heated debates about interventions against sovereign states, one senator, Russ Feingold, asked Bolton what he thought about the United Nations' inaction during the Rwandan genocide. Specifically, Feingold asked, what would you have done had you then been the ambassador and knew everything that we know now? Bolton replied, "We don't know if, logistically, it would have been possible to do anything differently at the time." Feingold was taken aback by this insouciant response. He said only, "Your answer is amazingly passive," then went on to another issue.[9]

Look at the present situation coldly. The Khartoum government is as canny as it is treacherous, and blithely uses its leverage to continue getting away with murder in Darfur. It now has trump cards with the Americans, the Chinese, and the Russians. Those of us who urge intervention on strictly humanitarian grounds have no comparable influence whatever. The result is virtually preordained: the death and rape and suffering in western Sudan will continue, perhaps even escalate.

Are there now lessons from Darfur, given that the only lesson from Rwanda that proved relevant was the most despairing one? Is it wrong to conclude that the "Responsibility to Protect" concept that Canada so assiduously pushes at the United Nations is largely irrelevant when it comes to the decision-making processes of the world's powers? The only responsibility that the P5 nations recognize is to pursue their own national self-interests in any and all circumstances. Any conception of a common purpose, a common humanity – the very essence of the United Nations, at least in innocent theory – is the furthest thing from any powerful nation's mind. In a website dedicated to the appointment of John Bolton to the position of UN ambassador, there is a recording of Bolton discussing the role of the United States at the United Nations with neither ambiguity nor embarrassment: "The only question for the US is what's our national interest," he states matter-of-factly, "and if you don't like that, I'm sorry but that's the fact."[10] How many more calamities will it take to hammer this point home? Is it remotely realistic to expect anything different from the Obama administration?

It is hard to exaggerate the fraught nature of the present moment for the people of Darfur. It is even harder not to be disheartened both by the world's failure in Darfur and by what it portends for the next crises, whichever ones they prove to be. Fourteen years after Rwanda, five years after Darfur exploded, the "next Rwanda" is indeed proving to be the next Rwanda. And "never again" continues to be the most violated pledge of our time.

Notes

1 Linda Melvern, *A People Betrayed: The Role of the West in Rwanda's Genocide* (London: Zed Books 2000); Linda Melvern, *Conspiracy to Murder: The Rwandan Genocide* (London: Verso 2004).

2 US Department of State, "The Crisis In Darfur," Written Remarks before the Senate Foreign Relations Committee (Washington, D.C., 9 September 2004).

3 Suzanne Goldenberg, "Ostracized Sudan Emerges as Key American Ally in 'War on Terror,'" *Guardian Weekly*, 6–12 May 2005.

4 Jonathan Steele, "Darfur Wasn't Genocide and Sudan Is Not a Terrorist," *Guardian*, 7 October 2005.

5 Joel Brinkley, "Plan to End Darfur Violence Is Failing, Officials Say," New York *Times*, 28 December 2006, www.nytimes.com/2006/01/28/politics/28darfur.html?emc=etal.

6 Kenneth Bacon, "28 Days to Save Darfur," New York *Times*, 31 January 2006, www.nytimes.com/2006/01/31/opinion/31bacon.html.

7 Nicholas D. Kristof, "Genocide in Slow Motion" *New York Review of Books*, 9 February 2006, 16.

8 Ibid.

9 Fred Kaplan, "It's Time to Write a Dear John Letter" (11 April 2005), http://slate.msn.com/id/2116567.

10 www.moveamericaforward.org/index.php/SpecialProjects/SupportBolton.

CHAPTER TWO

Lessons Learned or Not Learned from the Rwandan Genocide

BRENT BEARDSLEY

From April to July 1994, in a period of about one hundred days, up to 800,000 human beings were murdered in the Rwandan genocide.[1] The "international community" failed to prevent or suppress that humanitarian catastrophe, remaining bystanders while hundreds of thousands died in one of the fastest and deadliest genocides in history. In 2004, while the world commemorated the Rwandan genocide and lamented the failure to prevent it, yet again genocide was exposed in Darfur, Sudan. To date, the Darfur genocide has claimed up to 450,000 lives. In addition, millions of people have been forced into inhuman physical conditions in refugee and displaced persons camps, which are claiming lives at a rate of up to 10,000 a month.[2] Will the international community, including Canada, also fail to prevent or suppress the genocide in Sudan? With a view to assisting in the development of our response to Darfur, I will identify the major lessons that can be learned from the Rwandan genocide. I will begin by placing the response to Darfur within the context of the Canadian-initiated policy known as the Responsibility to Protect (R2P) and a Clauswitzean-based conceptual model of conflict resolution or limited war.

Partially in response to the failure to prevent or suppress the Rwandan genocide, and in direct response to the challenge to the international community issued by United Nations Secretary General Kofi Annan in September 2000 in his millennium report *We, the Peoples*,[3] the Government of Canada commissioned the International Commission on Intervention and State Sovereignty to conduct a comprehensive examination of the relationship between humanitarian intervention and state sovereignty.[4] The commission completed its work in 2001 and its report, entitled *The Responsibility to Protect*, was presented to the secretary general and the United Nations on 18 December 2001. This document and the policy it articulates have been adopted as a key component of Canada's 2005 *International Policy Statement*.[5] In September 2005 Kofi Annan addressed world leaders at the UN summit convened to review progress since the Millennium Declaration. Annan's report, *In Larger Freedom: Towards Development, Security and Human Rights for All*, urged heads of state and governments to "embrace the responsibility to protect as a basis for collective actions against genocide, ethnic cleansing and crimes against humanity."[6] In October 2005, while scholars, activists, and students gathered at the "Crisis in Darfur" conference in London, Ontario, the General Assembly of the United Nations endorsed Annan's recommendation. At present, the Government of Canada, the United Nations, and other like-minded states and organizations are wrestling with a way to advance the objectives of the Responsibility to Protect by turning concepts and theories into action. Darfur may very well be the first test case.

The central theme of the Responsibility to Protect "is the idea that sovereign states have a responsibility to protect their own citizens from avoidable catastrophe, but that when they are unwilling or unable to do so, that responsibility must be borne by the broader community of states."[7] This policy encourages and justifies the use of non-battle (non-use-of-force) means like diplomacy; development, and humanitarian aid; international condemnation; restrictions like embargoes, travel bans, freezing assets, sanctions, and so on; commissions of inquiry; and traditional Chapter VI peacekeeping operations under the United Nations Charter.[8] If non-battle (or non-use-of-force) means are not effective in preventing or suppressing the humanitarian catastrophe, then the report recommends moving to battle or use-of-force means as a tool of last resort to prevent and suppress these crimes against humanity, genocide, and/or ethnic cleansing within several clear criteria. The report is unambiguous in its assessment that Chapter VII would need to be invoked to provide the mandate for the intervention, and a combat capable force with robust rules of engagement must be employed to suppress the genocide by fighting if necessary.[9]

In his masterpiece *On War*, Carl von Clausewitz provides a conceptual model of battle based on two types of wars.[10] The first type is an unlimited or "total war" policy in which political objectives are achieved through a strategy of annihilation, campaigns at the operational level of war of manoeuvre and/or attrition, and battles at the tactical level using fire and movement to win the decisive battle of annihilation and achieve victory. The second type of war is "limited war" – or, as we could label it today, a policy of "conflict and conflict resolution" – where the political objectives are achieved using a bipolar strategy of a non-battle pole and/or a battle pole. In the non-battle pole, the state seeks to use diplomacy, development and humanitarian aid, economic assistance, information operations, observer or peacekeeping missions, and the like as ways to achieve its policy objectives without resorting to the offensive use of force. The other pole in the bipolar strategy is the battle pole, which can be used to wage a campaign of manoeuvre or attrition, either separately or in conjunction with non-battle means, to achieve the desired political objectives. At the tactical level, the use of fire and movement remains the tool to achieve battlefield successes in support of the overall campaign plan and ultimately to achieve policy objectives.[11]

Since the end of the Cold War, the international community in general and Canada in particular have clearly confined themselves to the limited-war side of the paradigm by using a bipolar strategy to deal with threats to international peace and security. The preference of Canada and most other states, including many of our traditional allies, is first to use and exhaust all elements of a non-battle-pole strategy. Only when those means have clearly failed have Canada and other middle powers turned to the use of the battle pole, and they have done so only when their policy objectives merit the use of force as a last resort. In some cases, such as the First Gulf War, Kosovo, Timor, and Afghanistan, the Government of Canada and a substantial number of its traditional allies have demonstrated the resolve to use force in a battle-pole strategy to achieve their policy objectives. In other cases, such as Rwanda, Canada, its traditional allies, and the wider international community as represented by the United Nations did not use the battle pole but confined their response to genocide to a non-battle strategy. The use of this non-battle-pole strategy in Rwanda did not prevent or suppress the genocide, which was allowed to run its course and claimed the lives of approximately 800,000 people.[12]

The current catastrophe in Darfur has been labelled "genocide" by the Bush administration, some members of the media, scholars, human rights groups, and non-governmental organizations (NGOs) like Genocide Watch.[13] To date, efforts to confront the genocide have been limited to a non-battle-pole strategy employing tools like quiet and public diplomacy, media exposure and condemnation, commissions of investigation and inquiry, humanitarian assistance, deployment of an observer mission with a small traditional Chapter VI-type peacekeeping mission, and the threat of sanctions. Since these actions were taken, there has not been any change in the behaviour of the Government of Sudan according to many governmental, non-governmental, and media sources.[14] The Government of Sudan is either unwilling or unable to prevent or suppress the genocide, ethnic cleansing, and crimes against humanity taking place in Darfur, and as a consequence, in accordance with the United Nations' Genocide Convention and the Responsibility to Protect policy, the international community, including Canada, must now consider whether and when it will assume their legal obligation and responsibility to protect the victims in Darfur by suppressing the genocide. If non-battle-pole actions continue to have no effect, at some point in the near future, policy and strategic decision makers must confront the question of whether they will have to move to the battle pole and conduct a humanitarian intervention by using military force to stop the genocide in Darfur, or whether they will continue to follow a failed non-battle-pole strategy. However, before such a decision is taken, it would be useful to examine the failure of the non-battle-pole strategy of the international community to prevent or suppress the Rwandan genocide in 1994. Lessons can be learned from that failure, lessons that can assist us in determining how best to proceed with a bipolar strategy in Darfur.

First, must it be confirmed if in fact genocide is taking place in Darfur? According to President George W. Bush, former US Secretary of State Colin Powell, Genocide Watch, and numerous others, what is happening in Darfur is indeed a genocide. The United Nations, the Government of Canada, and other governmental and non-governmental organizations disagree and argue that, at worst, only gross violations of human rights and crimes against humanity (including ethnic cleansing) are occurring. For them, the greater challenge in Darfur is the growing humanitarian catastrophe, which has enveloped the region and placed millions at risk of death by thirst, starvation, disease, and despair. The UN decision to avoid calling Darfur a genocide produced a sigh of relief in capitals around the world and created an excuse for apathy and inaction. The debate over the use of the "G" word is very reminiscent of a similar debate we had a generation ago while watching the merciless slaughter of Rwandans. At times, such a debate provides a dose of Machiavellian humour, as if gross violations of human rights, crimes against humanity, ethnic cleansing, and catastrophic loss of innocent lives are somehow less serious than "genocide."

Early in 2004, before any serious Western attention, coverage, or discussion about "genocide" commenced, the death toll in Darfur had reached 30,000 dead and 1 million displaced. As the endless debate and ineffective responses have continued, and while non-battle-pole measures have been employed and exhausted, that death toll has risen steadily to as many as 450,000 dead and millions displaced. Under the 1948 Genocide Convention, we have an ethical, moral, and legal obligation to be precise and accurate in our use of the word "genocide," especially as a justification to violate state sovereignty and use force up to and including deadly force. R2P calls for a response of equal application for atrocities on a gross scale, regardless of whether we call these atrocities "genocide," "crimes against humanity," or "ethnic cleansing." Thus, whether we label Darfur "genocide" or not, we must have an effective response to the avoidable human catastrophe in Sudan.

The evaluation of the available evidence has led this author to conclude that genocide is, in fact, taking place in Darfur. The 1948 Genocide Convention states that genocide is "the intention to destroy in whole or in part members of a national, ethnic, racial or religious group as such." The people of Darfur are black Africans with distinct tribal and ethnic affiliations that constitute them as members of ethnic and racial groups. The Genocide Convention also states that genocide is committed by "killing, causing serious bodily or mental harm, deliberately inflicting on the group conditions of life calculated to bring about its physical destruction in whole or in part, imposing measures intended to prevent births within the group and or forcibly transferring children of the group to another group." The Janjaweed militia has killed tens of thousands of human beings in Darfur. The perpetrators have executed men, gang-raped and branded women, and abducted and enslaved children. In addition to these physical assaults, the Janjaweed has destroyed homes, wells, farms, and crops to drive the population into camps inside and outside Sudan. These refugee and internally displaced persons (IDP) camps are located in extreme desert areas, without access to water, food, shelter, or medical support. All of these well-documented abuses committed by the Janjaweed meet the requirement for defining the situation in Darfur as genocide.[15]

Under the Genocide Convention, the contracting parties, including Canada, are obliged "to take such action under the UN Charter as they consider appropriate to prevent and suppress these acts of genocide." If genocide is taking place in Darfur, the international community, including Canada, has a legal and a moral obligation to intervene.[16] Even if the designation of genocide is not unequivocally agreed upon, there can be no denial that crimes against humanity, ethnic cleansing, and an avoidable humanitarian catastrophe are taking place in Darfur. These crimes are no less heinous, resulting in hundreds of thousands of innocent lives lost. Under the policy of R2P, the international community remains obliged to stop the preventable humanitarian catastrophe in Darfur, whether we call it genocide or not.

If humanitarian intervention is considered, what type of strategy should be employed? Canada and its allies have pursued a bipolar strategy confined to the non-battle or non-use-of-force pole, and these efforts have done nothing to restrain the Government of Sudan and the Janjaweed militia. Nor are crimes against humanity something new for Sudan. For forty years, the regimes in Khartoum have employed genocide as a tool in their ethnic, racial, and religious consolidation of power, particularly in the south of Sudan, where the Dinka people were targeted in the 1980s. In the 1990s the people of the Nuba mountains were nearly obliterated in yet another genocide. As these events illustrate, governments of Sudan, with virtual immunity, have repeatedly resorted to genocide as a matter of domestic policy that has claimed the lives of up to two million of their citizens.[17] It is unlikely that the Government of Sudan will change its behaviour until it believes that the international community is serious about intervention and that it has more to lose than to gain by continuing a policy of genocide in Darfur. What the end of genocide in Sudan may require is a shift to the battle pole and the successful execution of a humanitarian intervention that uses military force to suppress the genocide.

Before such a shift from the non-battle to the battle pole is considered or conducted, it is essential to examine some lessons from the 1994 Rwandan genocide to ensure that such a shift is realistic and can be effective. Much can be learned from the failure of the international community to prevent or stop the genocide in Rwanda, lessons that can be assembled into four groups: will, way, means, and use of time.[18]

Will

We can attribute the first major group of lessons from Rwanda to a lack of will by individual nations, militaries, publics, and the media. The failure to prevent or suppress the 1994 Rwandan genocide has often been blamed on the unwillingness of the international community to risk casualties in a conflict in which it had no vital national-security interests. Will is the sustained and determined effort to achieve an objective. Where the will to act is absent, the means will seldom be found. Nowhere is this more evident than in situations where a nation considers intervening in another sovereign state to stop a genocide. The failure to respond to the Rwandan genocide – especially in May and June 1994, when sufficient evidence confirmed that the extremist Hutu government and their Interahamwe militia were committing genocide against the Tutsi population – demonstrates the inability of the international community to summon up the will to intervene in such cases. In order to respond effectively to the genocide in Darfur, then, we must marshal, one nation at a time, the international will to respond to Sudan with diplomacy, sanctions, and, if necessary, force. If we do not do so, we condemn ourselves to the status of bystanders while hundreds of thousands more people die in Darfur.

In addition to a lack of international will for intervention in Rwanda, there was also an absence of national leadership. It was easier for the political leaders of many Western nations to make pontificating speeches about providing aid while simultaneously abstaining from a material commitment to the means needed to conduct an intervention. It was easier to lay the blame on the United Nations, on the UN Assistance Mission in Rwanda (UNAMIR), and on the United States than it was to assume the risks of intervention. In many cases, the refusal to provide the means for intervention was tied directly to the lack of public will in individual nations for the intervention itself. Few people in the world had ever heard of Rwanda and they certainly did not identify it as something that was vital to their security and prosperity. Public opinion could have been mobilized only by effective political leadership, which was sorely lacking in 1994. The lesson is therefore clear that, if we are going to stop the crime of genocide, political leadership must be prepared to expend political capital for significant intervention by mobilizing public support.

The mobilization of national and public will is also enmeshed in a symbiotic relationship with the media. In order to build public will for intervention, the media must provide consistent and factual coverage of what is taking place in a genocide zone like Rwanda or Darfur. During the Rwandan genocide, the media coverage was extremely inconsistent, and Rwanda competed with the Tanya Harding trial, the O.J. Simpson trial, and the elections in South Africa in the daily news. When coverage is not sustained and consistent, we risk developing an attitude of "out of sight, out of mind"; in these circumstances, politicians have the breathing space to abdicate their leadership responsibilities and the public falsely concludes that the catastrophe has been rectified. In order to mobilize national and public will, the media must be consistently engaged.

Finally, there was a lack of military will at the Pentagon and other national military headquarters, with an overwhelming majority of US and allied military officers opposing military involvement in Rwanda in 1994. In their Cold War view, a national military exists to fight and win the nation's wars and must train, equip, and prepare for such conflicts against definable enemies in support of vital national interests. They believe that a national military should not be squandered on sideshows like peacekeeping and intervention in "someone else's conflict" in an "unimportant" area of the world. This attitude was prevalent in most major militaries in 1994 and persists in some quarters to this day. However, under enlightened political and military leadership, Canada is blazing new ground in placing human security above national interest and in transforming the Canadian Forces so as to make them better able to respond effectively and rapidly in failed and failing states to save other human beings and help them rebuild their lives in a climate of security and safety.

Other like-minded nations are moving in the same direction and even the United States has recognized that the failing and failed states of today will become the terrorist bases of tomorrow and that nation building, humanitarian intervention, human rights, and human security are essential missions for each national military within a coalition of allies in the twenty-first century. The failure to marshal international, national, public, media, and military will to intervene in Rwanda to suppress the genocide directly contributed to the success of the genocide. If we do not mobilize the will of the international community, of individual nations, of national public, of the international and national media, and of national militaries to respond to the genocide in Darfur, we will once again condemn ourselves to failing in our ethical, moral, and legal obligations to act.

The Way

The second major group of lessons of the 1994 Rwandan genocide can be examined under the rubric of a *way* or a methodology for conducting humanitarian interventions. The first lesson emerges from the lack of knowledge about Rwanda by international policy makers and their agents on the ground in Rwanda in 1994. The international community knew little about Rwandan history and culture; about the political, economic, and social root causes of the Rwandan civil war and ethnic strife; or about the false "Hamitic myth" of Tutsi and Hutu as two tribes in perpetual conflict. This lack of knowledge directly contributed to the Western failure to understand Rwandan discord and the genocide that followed. The ignorance about Rwanda by virtually every non-Rwandan decision maker during this crisis could hardly provide the foundation upon which to build a solution to the problems there. Decision makers cannot expect to be part of the solution if they do not understand the problem.

In order for a decision maker to make timely, accurate, and relevant decisions for effective action, s/he requires timely, accurate, and relevant information, commonly referred to as intelligence. Our failure to gather and analyse effectively even the most basic pieces of intelligence put UNAMIR and international decision makers in a position where we could never seize the initiative. Instead, we were always caught in an information decision cycle that was *reacting* to the extremist perpetrators of the genocide. Knowledge of the present and near future is essential to any decision maker and the failure to acquire that knowledge in Rwanda directly contributed to the genocide.

In Rwanda, we also failed to understand our ethical, moral, and legal responsibilities and obligations in the face of the crime of genocide. Genocide shocks the moral conscience of humanity while demanding that we do something to stop it. The Genocide Convention not only legalizes a response to genocide, it imposes an accepted obligation on the contracting nations to prevent, suppress, and punish the crime. In Rwanda, these ethical, moral, and legal obligations were ignored, resulting in a genocide that was wholly preventable.

But how far can we go? The simple answer is that we cannot become the perpetrator in order to stop the perpetrator. As a community of nations, as a coalition of allies, as an intervention force, we must conduct ourselves within the limits imposed by international humanitarian law or the Law of Armed Conflict. This law provides an ethical, moral, and legal compass to guide our actions, while the old Christian principles of a "just war," as stated in R2P, are as applicable today as they were when St Augustine crafted them almost two millennia ago. We must have a just cause and the right intent. We must use force as a last resort, use force proportionally, and be confident that we will be successful while not causing greater conflict or costs. We must be sanctioned in our actions by a legitimate authority. The failure to meet our obligations in Rwanda permitted a genocide to be conducted with impunity.

We need a policy to guide us in genocide prevention, and we need to develop and employ an effective strategy to direct our response to instances of genocide. R2P provides a foundation for our foreign policy, and the popularity and adoption of R2P by other nations bodes well for future effective responses to crimes against humanity. The development and effective employment of a bipolar strategy – first using non-battle or non-use-of-force means and, if that fails to prevent or stop the genocide, being prepared to use a battle or use-of-force means – to achieve those objectives is also growing in popularity and acceptance. R2P and an effective bipolar strategy are currently facing the test in Darfur. Will we rise to the challenge of effective and efficient intervention? Or is R2P simply UN rhetoric that is debated among academics and advisers, words that mislead the public into thinking that there is effective prevention of genocide while, in fact, we are abdicating our international responsibilities? The jury is out.

The final lesson from Rwanda under the subheading of "way" is the requirement for a mandate. The UN Charter is the highest law in the world in regard to international peace and security. Force may be used only in self-defence (when a nation is attacked) or when the UN Security Council authorizes its use, by any and all means, to defeat a specific threat to this international peace and security. The resolution authorizing the use of force becomes the legal mandate of the mission, its international sanction. There is no other organization in the world that provides a more legitimate, legal, credible, or transparent mandate than the United Nations, and every effort must be made to obtain a UN mandate for any response to a genocide. Such a mandate was acquired for the interventions in Bosnia in support of the Dayton Accords and in East Timor.

However, such a mandate will not always be possible to obtain. During the Rwandan genocide, the United States, the United Kingdom, Russia, China, and occasionally France all threatened to veto any UN Security Council resolution authorizing an intervention into Rwanda to stop the genocide until its final days. The result was inaction and a failure to prevent or stop the massacre of Tutsi. If we cannot obtain a United Nations mandate, does that mean that the international community cannot respond and stop a potential or actual genocide? The legal answer is yes but the moral and precedent answer is no. Regional organizations like the African Union (AU) or security organizations like NATO or even coalitions of the willing have intervened when they consider the situation to warrant intervention in the face of deadlock at the Security Council. The AU mission in Darfur, the NATO intervention in Kosovo, and the coalition interventions into Sierra Leone and Ivory Coast are examples in our recent history.

However, are such non-UN-sanctioned interventions legal? Do legitimate humanitarian requirements, like stopping a genocide to save countless human lives, provide us with the authority to override the law? This debate continues for lawyers and academics, but the reality is that the decision will be left to the leaders of the international community who are charged with confronting such a situation. Regardless, a mandate authorizing the intervention must be obtained so that multilateral (never unilateral) action can be conducted. If we cannot obtain a Security Council or AU mandate for an armed intervention to stop the genocide in Darfur, then leaders will need to determine if a security organization or coalition can authorize such a necessary action. Without some sort of intervention in Darfur, we will be condemned to act as bystanders to yet another genocide, just as we did in Rwanda when we provided too little too late.

We must develop a method to guide our response to the crime of genocide, a method that includes: knowledge of the root causes of the genocide both past and present; an ethical, moral, and legal compass to guide our actions; a clear policy; an effective bipolar strategy; and a legitimate, credible, and transparent mandate. All of these components were lacking in Rwanda and the result was an unchecked genocide. Any effective response to the genocide in Darfur will require that these five lessons be recognized and satisfied if we are to be successful in stopping this latest genocide.

The Means

The third group of lessons can be assembled under the heading of *means*. Even if political will can be marshalled and we can develop a consensus on a way ahead, the response to a genocide will be possible only if the means to intervene are available.

First, we must have a campaign plan. Too often in the 1990s, and especially in Rwanda, the "peacekeeping" band-aid became an omnibus panacea applied to any and all conflicts whether or not the conditions were appropriate. You can keep the peace only if there is a peace to keep, and the failure of so many missions in the 1990s was due to the inability to use the right tool for the job. In too many cases, simple military peacekeeping has been an attempt to treat an "infected ulcer" with a band-aid. While a dressing can cover up the infection and give it the appearance of normality, the infection will resurface again and again if antibiotics do not cure it.

Haiti is a classic example of the failure to address the underlying economic, political, and social causes of violence; there was yet another intervention there in 2004, even after the operations of the 1990s had supposedly cured the "disease." Rather than simply suppressing individual acts of genocide, then, we must address the root causes that produce genocide by developing an integrated, comprehensive, long-term, political, economic, social, humanitarian, and human rights plan that incorporates and subordinates a military/security component to solve the root causes of the conflict. The failure to bring experts and knowledge together to create and implement such a plan results in a superficial, short-term solution that guarantees the risk of a resumption of genocidal conflict in the future. The current massacres and wars in the Great Lakes region of Africa, which have claimed the lives of at least four million people since 1996 (with no end in sight), are rooted in the failure to address the fundamental causes of the Rwandan genocide in 1994. The AU observer mission and peacekeeping force in Darfur also represents half-hearted and failed attempts to stop genocide. An intervention into Sudan must have an integrated and comprehensive campaign plan that will, over time, solve the root causes of the disputes, conflicts, and hostilities that led to the atrocities in Darfur.

Non-battle-pole means like diplomacy, aid, and peacekeeping cost money. Intervention costs more money. Rebuilding after a genocide costs even more money. Strategies for addressing violent conflicts like Darfur cannot be done on the cheap without risking mission success and the lives of the rescuers and the victims. There are no cheap solutions to suppressing a genocide. The cost of UNAMIR, the failed peacekeeping force tasked with implementing the Arusha Peace Agreement in Rwanda, was budgeted at US$200 million for a thirty-month mission, and only $65 million was provided before the genocide. During the one-hundred-day genocide, nations cringed at the possible costs of an intervention and avoided their financial responsibility to support such an action. However, between the beginning of the genocide (April 1994) and the end of 1994, the international community expended over US$2 billion on humanitarian aid. This money was not aid for development, nation building, security, and so on but for basic sustenance to keep millions of human beings just barely alive and in a miserable state of existence. The international community has a clear choice: we can pay a lot today or pay a lot more tomorrow. It will never be cheaper, easier, or quicker than to start today. During a genocide, every day of killing will only add to the end costs, the difficulty of the task, and the complexity of finding lasting solutions. For any effective intervention into Darfur, necessary financial requirements must be provided.

The third means that was lacking in Rwanda was the reluctance to use force to prevent or stop the Rwandan genocide. From UNAMIR I to UNAMIR II, the international community did not want to use force to prevent or stop the genocide. Just the demonstration that the international community was prepared to use military force to stop the genocide may have deterred the génocidaires and halted the killing. However, in a worst-case scenario, the use of force may have actually been required to stop the killers, disarm militias, open humanitarian routes, and defend victims against attacks, which in each case would have involved the spilling of blood. The reluctance to approve the use of force bound the arms of UNAMIR and turned it into a "toothless tiger" that could not even bluff the killers. The lesson from Rwanda for Darfur is that humanitarian intervention to suppress genocide will require the will and the means to use force, up to and including the use of overwhelming deadly force as a last resort and proportionally against the perpetrators who refuse to stop killing or who are a threat to human security. The use of force must not only be authorized, but its use, within the law and rules of engagement, must be *expected* if the intervention force is to be effective and credible. The failure to provide this authority and capability to the AU peacekeeping force in Darfur has resulted in a continuation of the genocide. Additionally, the so-called peacekeepers themselves are being targeted in Darfur, a strategy on the part of the killers to inflict casualties on the AU force to break its will to continue the mission and to deter other would-be interveners who would enter Darfur to stop the genocide. We cannot shy away from the use of force as a last resort, as we did in Rwanda, if we hope to be effective in Darfur.

The fourth lesson of necessary means concerns the actual military force needed to conduct a humanitarian intervention. Three requirements became apparent in Rwanda: the force would need to be able to "plug and play" within any coalition; it had to be able to deploy rapidly and operate effectively in a complex, dangerous, and combat environment with protection, mobility, and firepower; and it would have to be sustained indefinitely. With the exception of the United States, and to a lesser degree a few other major powers, no other nations possessed such a capability in 1994. Their "heavy" or conscript forces could not be mobilized with the speed required to deploy in days or weeks, they were not trained to roll right into a combat environment in the middle of Africa, and they could not be logistically sustained indefinitely at this end of the earth. The reluctance of the United States to intervene, and its withholding of the means like equipment, training, and transport from poorer but willing nations, prevented the shift to a timely and effective humanitarian intervention. In 2005 such forces are now more widely available and growing with each year of force development.

The final means that was denied to UNAMIR was the willingness to take casualties in a humanitarian intervention. The death of eighteen US soldiers in Mogadishu in Somalia in October 1993 created a "Somali syndrome" that hung over UNAMIR and undermined its effectiveness.[19] Force protection – not taking risks that could endanger the lives of soldiers – was a message constantly pressed on Canadian General Roméo Dallaire. The withdrawal of the Belgians after losing ten soldiers, the withdrawal of other national contingents in fear for their lives, and the reluctance of the international community (especially the northern developed nations) to risk casualties doomed the option of moving to the battle pole.[20] If we are prepared to use force and *spill* blood for a mission, we may also be required to *shed* blood, and the international community, individual nations, their publics, and the soldiers on the ground must understand this risk. In the case of Rwanda, the international community was more comfortable with words and warnings than with shedding blood to stop a genocide. Most national leaders, with the notable exception of African leaders, were terrified of the thought of justifying casualties to their citizens and possibly facing a domestic backlash. Casualties must never be taken lightly. The loss of life of young Canadian men and women is abhorrent to us all, but the preventable deaths of hundreds of thousands of Rwandans and Darfurians should be just as abhorrent. If, as a nation, Canada is not prepared to accept the risk to the lives of its soldiers and refuse to accept the potential for unavoidable casualties, then what other nation should expect any less? With such an attitude, the entire international community will be impotent to prevent or stop genocides and millions will be condemned to death. Casualties are the price we may have to pay to save the lives of hundreds of thousands of Darfurians and it is a price that we should be prepared to pay as a nation to live in a secure, peaceful, and just world.

The Use of Time

In business, it is often stated that time is money. In genocide, time is lives. The killing in Rwanda at its peak in late April and early May 1994 reached the level of eight to ten thousand murdered each day.[21] By April 2004, 30,000 Darfurians were dead. Today, after two years of diplomacy, commissions, endless debate, consultations, discussion, deployment of an ineffective observer and peacekeeping force, and other tools of a non-battle-pole-strategy, as many as 450,000 Darfurians have died.

The first lesson from the Rwandan genocide is that, when we have recognized that the use of non-battle or non-use-of-force means has failed to stop the genocide, we are required to switch to a battle or use-of-force pole and mount an international humanitarian intervention. When do we reach that point? Is it assessed in terms of the number of lives lost? If so, how many lives must be lost before we admit failure and switch our strategy? In Rwanda, 800,000 died and we never came to a point that authorized the use of force. In Darfur, we have seen hundreds of thousands dead and we have still not come to that point. Or should it be measured in terms of time? Do we give perpetrators a month, six months, or a year to stop the genocide? In Rwanda, the genocide was over in four months. In Darfur, we have seen death and displacement spread out over years, and yet the international community has not significantly changed its strategy.

The final three lessons are the effective use of time in the near, mid- and long term. Every day of delay in a genocide costs the lives of human beings. When the decision point is reached where a humanitarian intervention is ordered, deployment of the intervention force and its launch into operations on the ground must be measured in days and weeks, not months in the near term. In Rwanda, UNAMIR II was promised to be effectively on the ground within five weeks of the approval of the mandate. Not a single contingent arrived in less than eight weeks and then only after the genocide was over. Five months later, the last rag-tag elements arrived in Rwanda. In the case of Darfur, deployment of an intervention force, if ordered, must be conducted in days and weeks and not months if thousands are to be saved.

In the mid-term, stabilizing and commencing reconstruction after a genocide will take years, not the usual three- or six-month mandates normally envisioned. UNAMIR II lasted for two years in Rwanda before it was withdrawn and never even came close to fulfilling its mid-term mission.[22] We must recognize that real security – the protected movement of displaced persons back to their homes, and the restitution of anything resembling a normal and decent life in a post-genocide environment – must be expected to take *years*. There will be no quick in-and-out missions, unless there is a desire to repeat the operation every couple of years.

Finally, in the long term, in order to solve the underlying root causes of genocide, it will take *decades*, not years, to reconstruct a viable and humane society. The failure in the 1960s to implement a long-term reconstruction plan after the early outbreaks of genocide in Rwanda, Burundi, Uganda, and Congo has sentenced the Great Lakes region of Africa to semi-annual genocides that have claimed millions of lives and will continue to claim lives until the root causes of genocide in this region are addressed.[23]

In summary, Rwanda provides numerous lessons on how not to conduct an effective anti-genocide campaign. In order to reverse this trend, the lessons of Rwanda need to be understood and addressed. If we are to have any hope of effectively responding to the genocide in Darfur, we must marshal the international, national, public, media, and military *will* to conduct a humanitarian intervention. We must develop and implement a *way* or method to intervene effectively to stop genocide that includes acquiring the knowledge of the causes of the genocide; ensuring we have an ethical, moral, and legal compass to guide our actions; establishing a clear policy governing humanitarian intervention; developing and implementing an effective bipolar strategy; and obtaining a legitimate, credible, and transparent mandate. We must acquire and commit the *means* to accomplish the mission, including the development of a multidisciplinary, integrated, and comprehensive campaign plan; obtaining the financial resources; ensuring the clear understanding that the use of force will be required; providing the military personnel capable of using force; and ensuring the acknowledgment of all stakeholders that, despite all efforts, "friendly" casualties are inevitable. We must also appreciate the effective use of *time*. When a genocide is threatened or in progress, how long should we take to use non-use-of-force methods to stop the genocide and at what point must we consider shifting our strategy if these means do not work? If we are to stop a genocide effectively and ensure that the phrase *never again* actually means something instead of the current *yet again* and *again and again*, we must clearly understand that, in the near term, we need to react in days and weeks not months; in the mid-term we will be committed for years; and in the long term we will be involved for decades.

In conclusion, this chapter has argued that the crime of genocide is occurring in Darfur and that, under the Genocide Convention and the Canadian policy of the Responsibility to Protect, Canada and a coalition of like-minded nations have a responsibility to prevent and suppress that genocide. In accordance with prudence, escalation, and the policy of R2P, our response to date has been to use non-battle-pole efforts to prevent and suppress the genocide. These best-intentioned efforts for Darfur have clearly failed, and at some point the decision must be taken to move to the battle pole and to conduct a humanitarian intervention to stop the genocide by any means necessary. Before such a decision is taken, the major lessons from the Rwandan genocide presented in this chapter must be considered and addressed if we hope to conduct an effective humanitarian intervention which will stop the genocide in Darfur. Such an intervention must establish the conditions within that society that will guarantee that genocide will never again be viewed as a tool of conflict resolution by the Government of Sudan. This approach must be presented so that a coalition of the willing, Canada, the Canadian public, and, most important, the men and women in uniform who are called upon to put their lives on the line to suppress this genocide are fully aware of exactly what is involved to conduct a successful humanitarian intervention.

Canada has a moral and a legal obligation to act. However, our actions should not be taken out of naive idealism but must be well grounded in reality and experience. The Canadians who could die or be injured in this mission and, even more, the hundreds of thousands of our fellow human beings whom we will save, deserve nothing less.

Notes

1 Gerard Prunier, *The Rwanda Crisis: History of a Genocide* (New York: Colombia University Press 1995), 261–5. Prunier, the first scholar to investigate the numbers killed in the Rwandan genocide, concluded that the total was between 800,000 and 850,000. See also Human Rights Watch, *Leave None to Tell the Story: Genocide in Rwanda* (New York: Human Rights Watch, 1999), 1. Human Rights Watch later commissioned a more extensive investigation that concluded that no less than

500,000 were killed in the genocide. There is considerable debate among scholars and bureaucrats on the exact number of people killed, and the conclusion of most is that we will never know for sure. The report of the International Panel of Eminent Personalities to Investigate the 1994 Genocide in Rwanda, *Rwanda: The Preventable Genocide* (Addis: Organization of African Unity Press 2000), 80, supports this conclusion and sets the number at no less than 500,000 and more likely up to 800,000. At this point, 800,000 has become the most generally agreed-upon number of the victims of the Rwandan genocide.

2 Gregory Stanton, "Genocide Emergency: Darfur, Sudan," *Genocide Watch* (2 April 2004), 1–3, http://www.genocidewatch.org/Never%20Again.htm. Genocide Watch, the most independent and credible genocide-monitoring organization in the world, concluded in April 2004 in this paper that genocide was taking place in Darfur. On 15 June 2005 Genocide Watch updated the death toll to 250,000 and the displaced/refugee population to 2.5 million. More recently, Eric Reeves has placed the death toll from violence, disease, and starvation at more than 450,000.

3 Foreign Affairs Canada, *The Responsibility to Protect* (18 October 2004), http://www.dfait-maeci.gc.ca/iciss-ciise/menu-en.asp.

4 International Commission on Intervention and State Sovereignty (ICISS), *The Responsibility to Protect* (Ottawa: International Development Research Centre 2001), vii.

5 Government of Canada, *Canada's International Policy Statement: A Role of Pride and Influence in the World: Diplomacy* (Ottawa: Government of Canada 2005), 9–14. The Canadian government unofficially embraced the Responsibility to Protect as part of its evolving Human Security Agenda from 2001 but officially adopted the policy as a cornerstone of Canadian foreign policy in this document.

6 United Nations, *In Larger Freedom: Towards Development, Security and Human Rights for All* (New York: UN Press 2005), chapter 4, para.135.

7 ICISS, *The Responsibility to Protect*, viii.

8 Ibid., 19–30. The R2P report presents a number of non-force options that it recommends should be employed prior to using force, under the headings of commitment to prevention, early warning and analysis, root-cause prevention efforts, direct-prevention efforts, and measures short of military action. The authors clearly conclude that non-battle means should first be attempted and exhausted before resorting to the use of force.

9 Ibid., 31–5, 57–66. The R2P report presents a series of sections on the decision to intervene, the threshold criteria of just cause, and other precautionary criteria. It also examines preventive operations, planning for military intervention, carrying out military intervention, and following

up military intervention, as well as offering a doctrine for human-protection operations.

10 Carl von Clausewitz, *On War*, ed. and trans. Michael Howard and Peter Paret (Princeton, N.J.: Princeton University Press 1976), 75–99. Clausewitz described two types of war: total or unlimited war and limited war.

11 Bernd Horn, ed., *Contemporary Issues in Officership: A Canadian Perspective* (Toronto: Canadian Institute of Strategic Studies 2000), 145–79.

12 Howard Adelman and Astri Suhrke, eds., *The Path of a Genocide: The Rwanda Crisis from Uganda to Zaire* (New Brunswick, N.J.: Transaction Publishers 2000), 185–208. In this work, Adelman provides an excellent essay on the history of Canadian policy towards Rwanda before, during, and after the genocide.

13 Stanton, *Genocide Emergency: Darfur, Sudan*, 1–3.

14 United Nations, *Security Council Resolution 1564 dated 18 September 2004* (New York: United Nations Press 2004), 1–4. This Security Council resolution passed 11–0 with 4 abstentions and under Chapter VII of the charter accused the Government of Sudan of continuing its campaign against civilians, ordered an investigation into allegations of genocide, and supported the expansion of the African Union monitoring force into a peacekeeping mission.

15 Gregory Stanton, "Genocide Emergency: Darfur, Sudan," provides the report of Genocide Watch and its conclusion that genocide is taking place in Darfur.

16 William Schabas, *Genocide in International Law* (Cambridge: Cambridge University Press 2000), 553–8. Schabas dedicates the first two chapters of his book to the efforts to develop the Genocide Convention and, in the pages noted above, provides the first two drafts of the convention and the final product, which was adopted into international law. Article VIII of the convention calls upon "the competent organs of the United Nations to take such action under the Charter of the United Nations as they consider appropriate for the prevention and suppression of acts of genocide." See Samantha Power, *A Problem from Hell: America and the Age of Genocide* (New York: Basic Books 2002), 17–170. Power includes three chapters on the struggle to develop the Genocide Convention and then the struggle to get it ratified by nations like the United States. Also see Frank Chalk and Kurt Jonassohn, *The History and Sociology of Genocide: Analyses and Case Studies* (New Haven, Conn.: Yale University Press 1990), 48–50. Canada ratified the Genocide Convention on 28 November 1949 and entered it into the Criminal Code of Canada in bills C34 and C35 under section 281.1 (1), (2), (3), (4).

17 Alex de Waal, *Who Fights? Who Cares? War and Humanitarian Action in Africa* (Trenton, N.J.: Africa World Press 2000), 37–9, 42, 45–6, 49–50, 54, 56, 60, 69, 73. The author describes the genocides in the Sudan in conjunction with a wider examination of the phenomenon of genocide in Africa.

18 Roméo Dallaire with Brent Beardsley, *Shake Hands with the Devil: The Failure of Humanity in Rwanda* (Toronto: Random House 2003). This book provides the background and a deeper explanation of the lessons of the Rwandan genocide under the four groups of *will, way, means,* and *time* examined in this chapter.

CHAPTER THREE

Media Coverage, Activism, and Creating Public Will for Intervention in Rwanda and Darfur

AMANDA F. GRZYB

On 23 April 1994 the Toronto *Globe and Mail* ran a thirteen-paragraph Reuters article entitled "UN Leaving Thousands to Die, Rwandan Pullout Critics Claim," which detailed concerns by the Organization of African Unity, the Red Cross, and Oxfam about the UN Security Council's decision to withdraw the majority of its peacekeeping troops from the United Nations Assistance Mission in Rwanda (UNAMIR). A little more than two weeks prior to the publication of the story, on 6 April, Rwandan President Juvénal Habyarimana had been killed after a missile hit his presidential plane. In the wake of Habyarimana's assassination, the extremist wing of the Hutu government – aided by a militia called the Interahamwe and "ordinary" Hutu civilians – launched a meticulously planned, systematic slaughter of approximately 800,000 Tutsi and moderate Hutu over a period of one hundred days. "UN Leaving Thousands to Die" is significant, in part, because it marks a pivotal point in the timeline of the genocide: the moment when the UN and the international community clearly demonstrated that they would not intervene to stop the massacres, the moment when Rwanda was wholly abandoned by the rest of the world.[1]

However, the article is not simply a passive record of the world's failure in Rwanda; like most Western media accounts at the time, it contributed *directly* to that failure. Buried in the back of the paper, the article originally appeared in the bottom, left-hand corner of page A15, and it includes many of the typical errors and oversights that were epidemic during the first month of coverage of the genocide.[2] Most significantly, it never clearly articulates the systematic, state-sponsored, one-sided nature of the massacres, nor does it identify the victims as

"Tutsi" and the perpetrators as "extremist Hutu," the "Rwandan government," or the "Interahamwe militia." Instead, the article suggests that the violence is spontaneous, chaotic, and reciprocal, describing the victims variably as "civilians," "people," and "refugees," and referring to the genocide as "tribal slaughter" in a "chaotic Central African state." By the fifth paragraph, the massacres are inappropriately conflated with the long-term hostilities between the Hutu-dominated government and the mostly Tutsi rebels of the Rwandan Patriotic Front (RPF): "The Red Cross said tens and perhaps hundreds of thousands of people have been killed in a bloodbath between majority Hutus and minority Tutsis that began two weeks ago after the presidents of Rwanda and neighboring Burundi, both Hutus, were killed in a rocket attack on their plane. Secretary-General Boutros Boutros-Ghali said he concluded there was no prospect of a ceasefire agreement soon between the government and the rebel Rwanda Patriotic Front."[3] By repeatedly using the word "between" – describing the massacre of Tutsi civilians as violence *between* Hutu and Tutsi, and connecting that violence to a ceasefire *between* the government and the RPF – the genocide is reduced to a "conflict" involving two equal parties who are supposedly killing each other.

Since "UN Leaving Thousands to Die" was originally a Reuter newswire, other versions of this article were printed in newspapers across the world. What makes the *Globe and Mail*'s version of the Reuter article an exceptionally fascinating post-genocide artifact is not simply its content (which is, of course, identical to the content of many news sources), but its *context*. On the very same page of the paper, adjacent to the article about Rwanda, the *Globe* ran an advertisement for an appearance by Thomas Keneally at Pantages Theatre in Toronto that reads "Meet the Man Who Kept Oskar Schindler Alive."[4] In April 1994 – a few weeks after Steven Spielberg dominated the Academy Awards with *Schindler's List* (1993), an adaptation of Keneally's historical novel, *Schindler's Ark* (1982)[5] – Keneally was coasting on the unprecedented popularity of a film that makes genocide palatable, teachable, even entertaining. On a single page of the *Globe and Mail*, readers are invited to participate in a public performance of Holocaust-related memory, in a celebration of the Holocaust rescuer, in a collective cry of "never again," while, at the same time, they are passive bystanders in a case of "again and again" as the international community abandons Rwanda in its hour of greatest need.

How can we explain such an unfortunate (and most certainly unintentional) juxtaposition? Can it function as a useful trope for understanding the politics of representing genocide in the West? Part of the answer lies in our comfortable relationship with a culture that has trained us to tolerate these sorts of disturbing contrasts without challenging the system that produces them. There is certainly nothing new about critiquing the intersection between news media, humanitarian concerns, and the social order. Indeed, John Berger cites an example that is similar to the Rwanda/Schindler juxtaposition in his 1972 BBC series *Ways of Seeing*, a critical investigation of the proliferation of promotional images in Western society. Flipping through an issue of *Sunday Times Magazine*, Berger contrasts photographs of starving refugees in Pakistan with a series of typical magazine advertisements. As the camera registers abrupt shifts from a wailing child to a cola ad, from a group of smiling, well-fed Westerners to emaciated families suffering in a refugee camp, Berger illustrates the schizophrenic (but symbiotic) cycle of news information and product promotion. Describing the *Sunday Times* sequence in a textual account of the original *Ways of Seeing* television series, Berger writes: "The shock of such contrasts is considerable: not only because of the coexistence of the two worlds shown, but also because of the cynicism of the culture which shows them one above the other. It can be argued that the juxtaposition of images was not planned. Nevertheless the text, the photographs taken in Pakistan, the photographs taken for the advertisements, the editing of the magazine, the layout of the publicity, the printing of both, the fact that advertiser's pages and news pages cannot be co-ordinated – all these are produced by the same culture."[6] Ultimately, Berger claims, our Western culture of consumption and commodification clashes with our humanitarian interests and obligations; we are easily seduced away from a full acknowledgment of the suffering refugees with a turn of the page. And, more often than not, we translate our distress at seeing images of such abject, visceral human pain into our own narcissistic feelings of guilt or shame, feelings that actually have nothing whatsoever to do with the suffering itself.

The *Globe*'s juxtaposition of the Keneally advertisement and the unspecified torment of abandoned Rwandan civilians is, using Berger's model, the product of a repressive ideology that reverberates with non-sequiturs and oppositional representations, creating what Berger calls a system of "madness." This madness presumably includes paying money to participate in the cultural phenomenon of the much-lauded *Schindler's List* Holocaust docudrama, but remaining distant from (or even indifferent to) the realities of another genocidal nightmare unfolding in Rwanda. Whether our motivations are pedagogical, cathartic, or even voyeuristic, we, in the West, have an established pattern of seeking intimacy with past tragedies while simultaneously distancing ourselves from present ones. *Schindler's List* is particularly accessible to a mass audience because it does not consist of the unbearably raw, vulnerable testimonies of Claude Lanzmann's nine-and-a-half-hour existentialist documentary film, *Shoah* (1985), where long gaps and silences gesture to the unrepresentable, deep, traumatic memory of the Holocaust. Nor does *Schindler's List* directly address the profoundly unsettling philosophical questions about responsibility that resonate so clearly in Alain Resnais's groundbreaking Holocaust documentary "meditation," *Night and Fog* (1955). Instead, Spielberg gives the Western audience what it craves: a Holocaust where the Jews are ultimately saved; where victims and bystanders rarely occupy a moral grey zone; where perpetrators are clearly distinct from ourselves, inhuman monsters rather than "ordinary men"; where sometimes showers are just showers, tools for cinematic suspense; and where Schindler, a classic Hollywood cinema hero, can help us shape incomprehensible horror into narrative resolution.[7]

Most notably for the purposes of this chapter, *Schindler's List* presents a model for genocide intervention – the singular rescuer – that does not require public will, group responsibility, or international consensus. Shot in silhouettes and low angles that are reminiscent of *Citizen Kane*, Spielberg's Schindler towers above the Jewish workers with grandiose masculinity. He is most certainly a hero, but he is also a womanizer, a charmer, and a self-made man who is able to rescue "his Jews" through a simple cash transaction with Amon Goeth, the commandant of Plaszow labour camp. It is this Western ethos of economic power, entrepreneurial innovation, and individualism that appeals to the film's North American audience, eschewing simplistic explanations about our collective "compassion fatigue," at least in the realm of highly narrativized images of atrocity.[8] Never mind the fact that the international community also abandoned six million European Jews during the Holocaust, or that, as Laurel Leff demonstrates, the elite "agenda setting" newspapers like the New York *Times* buried stories about gas chambers, mass shootings, torture, and starvation in the back pages of the paper.[9] We have Spielberg's Oskar Schindler.[10]

Given our vexed and conditional relationship with genocide narratives and our apparent preference for solutions to political and humanitarian crises that do not involve negotiating a collective effort, I would like to identify a critical set of questions that begins to emerge from page A15 of the 23 April 1994 edition of the *Globe and Mail*. What drives us to embrace the rescue story in *Schindler's List* in the spring of 1994 while we turn our backs on Rwanda at the same time? What brings us out to the theatres to see *Hotel Rwanda* – another gripping post-genocide story of singular heroism – while hundreds of thousands of civilians are massacred, raped, and displaced in Darfur? Is it simply a question of entertainment, of palatability, of cinematic distance, of the passage of time? Or do we actually seek a "silver lining" in genocidal violence? Why are we (as individuals, as Westerners, as an international community) unable or unwilling to assume our moral responsibility as witnesses and bystanders in an age of genocide, while we simultaneously look to genocide-rescue narratives to define ethical behaviour? As viscerally and intuitively appealing as I find the reductive nature of Berger's claim about the "madness" of a culture that produces these kinds of juxtapositions *(of course*, it is mad!), there is actually tremendous complexity to the ways in which our popular images of genocide flow through our ideas about moral responsibility, humanitarian obligation, and political action. I want to identify a discernible logic at work in the *Globe*'s Rwanda/Schindler, abandonment/rescuer combination, a logic that demonstrates how our Western constructions of "victim" and "rescuer," of "blackness," and of "African-ness" and "Western-ness" create discursive meanings about a bystander-self and a victim-other that can both hinder and *potentially help* public and political will for genocide prevention and intervention.

In the following pages, I will use the *Globe and Mail* as a qualitative case study of the first month of coverage of the Rwandan genocide, highlighting some of the common errors that characterized most Western media reports at the time. While these general charges have been levied against the media in the past, most recently in Allan Thompson's comprehensive 2007 anthology, *The Media and the Rwandan Genocide*, I will pay particular attention to word choices, underlying cultural narratives, and the way that media-generated meanings reflect and influence our ideas about crimes against humanity. I suggest that the *Globe*'s depiction of the 1994 Rwandan genocide as "tribal warfare" paints Africans (in general) and Rwandans, Hutu, and Tutsi (in particular) with perilously broad strokes. At the same time, the

Globe exaggerates the threat to foreign expatriates in Rwanda, misrepresenting the evacuation of Westerners as the central story coming out of Rwanda in first week of the genocide.

Situated in the context of colonial/postcolonial, Western/African, and pre-genocide/post-genocide oppositional lenses, the shifting conceptions of "Rwandan," "Hutu," and "Tutsi" help to explain Western complicity during the 1994 Rwandan genocide, but they also cast a large shadow over the current crisis in Darfur, Sudan, where a political and humanitarian catastrophe continues to unfold under the veil of long-term civil strife. A little over a decade after the Rwandan genocide, the sign "Rwanda" assumes a new semiotic distinction. The word that once meant "tribal warfare" is now synonymous with the Western failure to intervene in genocide, a legacy that directly influences the Western representation of Darfur. By describing Darfur as "another Rwanda," journalists, politicians, activists, and non-governmental organizations (NGOs) are not referring to "tribal warfare"; instead, they use the Rwandan genocide as a reference point for translating the suffering of Darfurian civilians into a now-familiar narrative of Western intervention versus abandonment. Similarly, activists have found inventive (and sometimes controversial) ways to engage Westerners in the plight of Darfurian civilians not by focusing specifically on the Janjaweed and Khartoum as perpetrators but by referencing the complicity of the West in past genocides, particularly in Rwanda. Increasingly savvy in mass communication, they disseminate information about Darfur using new media technologies that were largely unavailable in 1994. They have subsequently succeeded in creating a relatively significant – albeit late – groundswell of public and political interest in the crimes against humanity in Darfur, and in widening support for a United Nations or hybrid United Nations-African Union (AU) peacekeeping force in western Sudan.

On the one hand, the situation in Darfur appears to be strikingly simple: civilians are being systematically raped, massacred, and forcibly driven from their homes by their own government, and the world has a moral (and, some say, legal) responsibility to intervene and stop these atrocities. On the other hand, as Darfur scholars Julie Flint, Alex de Waal, and Gérard Prunier have demonstrated,[11] we have an extremely poor track record of effective political and/or military intervention and the crimes against humanity in Darfur are rooted in a long and complex web of conflict, war, insurgency, and counter-insurgency in Sudan. Indeed, by focusing so much on Western bystanders or on the inconsistent nature of Western media coverage of Darfur, some campaigns strategically employ the same overdetermined emphasis on "the Westerner" that plagued early media coverage of Rwanda in April 1994. For good and for bad, advocates of this Western focus often exploit the dual discourses of Western narcissism and Western shame in an effort to build a case for intervention in Darfur, and, as such campaigns continue, there has been an active transition from mobilizing to organizing, transforming the "save Darfur" cause into a global anti-genocide movement.

Globe and Mail Coverage of the 1994 Rwandan Genocide

In his introduction to *The Media and the Rwanda Genocide*, Allan Thompson is unequivocal in his indictment of the international media during the Rwandan genocide:

> Journalists could have had an impact in Rwanda – a sort of Heisenberg effect – had there been a significant enough media presence to influence events. The Heisenberg effect, named for German physicist Werner Heisenberg, describes how the act of observing a particle actually changes the behaviour of that particle, its velocity or direction. Arguably, more comprehensive and accurate reporting about the Rwanda genocide could have changed the behaviour of the perpetrators, mitigating the slaughter. Instead, the lack of international media attention contributed to what I would call a sort of inverse Heisenberg effect. Through their absence and a failure to adequately observe and record events, journalists contributed to the behaviour of the perpetrators of the genocide – who were encouraged by the world's apathy and acted with impunity.[12]

Alan Kuperman also singles out the Western media for its poor coverage of the genocide in a 2000 *Foreign Press Institute Report* on Rwanda: "Western media blame the international community for not intervening quickly, but the media must share blame for not immediately recognizing the extent of the carnage and mobilizing the world attention to it. They failed to report that a nationwide killing campaign was under way in Rwanda until almost three weeks into the violence. By that time, some 250,000 Tutsi had already been massacred."[13] Kuperman identifies four fundamental factual inaccuracies that were widely reported by the international media during the first three weeks of the Rwandan genocide:[14] 1) the media conflated genocide with civil war;[15] 2) the massacres were reported to be diminishing when they were, in fact, increasing;[16] 3) Tutsi death tolls were seriously underestimated;[17] and 4) media coverage focused on the capital city of Kigali and failed to report the massacres that were spreading into the countryside.[18] Although Kuperman acknowledges that many journalists fled Rwanda when foreign nationals were evacuated,[19] he does not emphasize the media's preoccupation with the danger to foreigners in Rwanda, nor does he focus on the representational significance of the proliferation of racially inflected media fabrications about reciprocal "ethnic violence" and "centuries-old tribal warfare." If we are to understand fully how the Rwandan genocide was ignored by the international community, we must expand Kuperman's analysis to include an examination of how the media's images of "Hutu" and "Tutsi" fit within the confines of Western ideas about racial and cultural difference, "the African," and the supposed "inevitability" of African suffering.

The poor coverage of the Rwandan genocide was certainly not an isolated event and it fits within a broader discourse about the way Africa is portrayed in the West. Charles Quist-Adade suggests that, in general, Western media coverage of Africa remains entrenched in the language and ideologies of colonialism, which used stereotypes to justify the widespread abuse, exploitation, and enslavement of African peoples:

Today the most primitive forms of the stereotypes of the "darkest" and "unknown" Africa are broken in the minds of Westerners, thanks to Africa's entrance into the world political arena after African countries gained independence from colonial powers. However, Africa is still interpreted through the color-sensitive eyes of Western reporters. Although they have revised and refined the old image of savagery and heathenism to some extent, they have maintained the original "African story" as told by the early explorers, colonial masters and missionaries. According to this story, the African, like the grown infant or perpetual child, has always needed European salvation and tutelage. The purpose of the original story was to prepare the minds of European citizens at home and to pave the way for the slave trade, colonization, partition and repartition of Africa. For how could the ruling elite in Europe explain the evil trilogy of their activities in Africa – enslavement, proselytizing, and the undemocratic practice of foreign domination – to their subjects at home, except to dehumanize and present Africans less than humans, heathenish, and unfit to rule themselves?

The current preoccupation of the Western media with negative occurrences, which excludes news of African achievements, suggests the media are in line with the old story line. Like the old missionaries and colonialist, the Western media consciously and unconsciously, covertly and overtly emphasize the message that Africans cannot govern themselves; that the continent "is still stuck in its primitive, bloodthirsty past"; that nations have wasted the "golden opportunity" to build civilized statehood after attaining political independence.[20]

Initially, the muted calls for international intervention during the Rwandan genocide may appear to fit Quist-Adade's criteria of an African crisis that requires European "salvation." However, Quist-Adade refers to a specific kind of interference/intervention that promotes *Western* – not African – ideological and economic interests. In the spring of 1994, Rwanda did not offer such incentives to the West, particularly because the Rwandan crisis began only months after eighteen US peacekeeping troops in Mogadishu, Somalia, were killed and some of their bodies dragged through the streets. The dominant Western media image of "the African" as "primitive" or "savage" ultimately superseded the (potentially self-serving) Western-helping impulse, and a premeditated genocide was reduced to an inevitable massacre as an extension of a "bloodthirsty past." In her "Introduction" to *Africa's Media Image*, Beverly G. Hawk also identifies the "primitive archetype" as the primary American media metaphor for African conflict.[21] She writes: "The message for the reader or viewer is that African events require a different vocabulary than those in Northern Ireland or Yugoslavia. Implicit in this vocabulary is that African events do not follow any pattern recognizable to Western reason. It is 'tribal' conflict. No one calls the violence in Northern Ireland white-on-white violence, or tribal bloodshed ... There is ... a special language employed when describing African stories."[22]

While media images of "the African" frequently fall into the parameters described by Quist-Adade and Hawk, I do not want to claim that this sort of stereotyping is a simplistic process. Rather, I subscribe to the view of post-colonial theorist Homi Bhabha, who suggests that "stereotyping is not the setting up of a false image which becomes the scapegoat of discriminatory practices. It is a much more ambivalent text of projection and introjection, metaphoric strategies, displacement, overdetermination, guilt, [and] aggressivity."[23] The Western media's tendency to depict "the African" as a racially inscribed other suggests that African-ness acts as a foil for Western subjectivity ("savage" or "tribal" Africa versus the "civilized" and "civilizing" West). This representational logic creates layers of meaning that can sometimes be quite contradictory. For example, during the Rwandan genocide, Hutu and Tutsi people were often constructed as inhabiting a single, interchangeable racialized identity: "warring" Africans whose violence was fuelled by mysterious "ancient tribal hatreds," "savages" who butchered one another indiscriminately and threatened the safety of Western expatriates. At the same time, the media image of "Rwanda" functioned as a symbol of undifferentiated, mass African suffering, of Western excess and Western guilt. These two levels of representation – and the stock metaphors and stereotypes that were used to communicate them – reveal, as Stuart Hall suggests, how the construction of "race" functions discursively as a "floating signifier."[24] Racial difference is not biologically determined or categorically prescribed; rather, shifting power relations create meaning by classifying and organizing difference through thought and language. During the genocide and post-genocide media coverage of Rwanda, the resonances of "Hutu" and "Tutsi," of "blackness" and "whiteness," of "Westerner" and "African," of "genocide" and "tribal warfare" extended beyond simple, rigid, one-dimensional stereotypes and ultimately reflected much more about Western preoccupations than they did about African experiences or self-identification.

The early reports about the Rwandan genocide in the *Globe and Mail* perpetuated the four factual errors that Kuperman identifies. Like other Western news sources, the *Globe* also established a racialized narrative of "the African" (and, by extension, "Rwandan," "Hutu," and "Tutsi") that alienated the Western reader and detracted from the *Globe*'s ability to meet its obligations to provide basic, factual information to its readership. In some cases, the *Globe*'s errors were even more egregious than those made by other national newspapers, such as the New York *Times*, in part because the *Globe* did not have its own journalists on the ground in Rwanda until early May,[25] relying, instead, on newswire services from Associated Press, Reuter, and Canadian Press. For example, on the same day that the *Globe* published the 23 April

"UN Leaving Thousands to Die" article adjacent to the Keneally advertisement, the New York *Times* ran an editorial about the UN withdrawal from Rwanda in which it referred to the massacres as "genocide," a word first used by Human Rights Watch on 19 April. The *Times* editorial read: "What looks very much like genocide has been taking place in Rwanda. People are pulled from cars and buses, ordered to show their identity papers and then killed on the spot if they belong to the wrong ethnic group."[26] The *Globe*, on the other hand, did not print the word "genocide" in association with a story about Rwanda until 29 April, when its reporter Jeff Sallot referenced Pope John Paul II's appeal for international intervention: "On Wednesday, the Pope appealed for an end to what he called genocide in Rwanda and the Vatican called for a peace conference."[27]

Failing to use the word "genocide" early on to describe the massacres was only one of numerous omissions in the *Globe*'s coverage of Rwanda, omissions that arguably extended back long before the killing commenced. There were several possible "angles" that would have allowed the *Globe* to address the volatile situation in Rwanda in the year prior to the genocide: 1) Three major studies – one by the UN and two by NGOs – were released months before the genocide, all identifying the imminent risk of Tutsi massacres; 2) the Rwandan radio station, RTLM, broadcast radical hate speech about Tutsi and moderate Hutu on a daily basis for six months prior to the genocide; and 3) a *Canadian* general, Roméo Dallaire, was put in charge of UNAMIR, which would surely have interested Canadian readers. Despite these compelling causes for concern, there were no substantial stories about Rwanda in the *Globe* during the year leading up to Habyarimana's assassination. Instead, there were a few lines in three "World in Brief" columns in July and August 1993,[28] a three-paragraph news brief about the UN's approval of a peacekeeping force in Rwanda in October 1993,[29] and passing mention of Rwanda in conjunction with the military coup in Burundi in October and November 1993.[30] Each of these articles/briefs depicted Rwanda as a place of distant, inconsequential civil strife. Notably, the most significant story about Rwanda between 6 April 1993 and 6 April 1994 appeared in the *Globe*'s Travel Section on 26 March 1994. Published less than two weeks before the genocide began, "Visits to Mountain Gorillas to Resume with African Peace" reports that a US travel company, Natural Habitat Adventures, is "once again offering a primate watch in Rwanda, the first since government and rebel forces signed a treaty in August, last year."[31] The report continues: "The gorillas actually seem to have benefitted from the war" because "the conflict caused great upheaval and disruption to illegal commerce in gorillas."[32] That the longest Rwanda story ran in the *travel section* of the paper suggests that the country's primary significance to the *Globe* in March 1994 is as an exoticized tourist destination where gorillas matter more than the untold human toll of a horrific civil war, a war that is mentioned only in conjunction with the preservation of the gorilla population.[33]

After the genocide began, the *Globe* gave Rwanda fairly steady coverage. However, muddled reports about the massacres were often buried in the back pages of the paper, and a secondary story about the evacuation of Canadian expatriates from Rwanda quickly moved from the periphery to centre stage. The coverage began on 7 April 1994, with a brief, front-page story about the plane crash that took the lives of President Habyarimana and the Burundi president, Cyprian Ntayamira, the previous day.[34] On 8 April, the *Globe's* front-page article, "Rwandan Troops Kill Prime Minister," focuses on the assassination of the moderate Hutu prime minister, Agathe Uwilingiyimana,[35] but it also provides the first descriptions of the massacres: "gangs of youths wielding machetes and clubs ... settling tribal scores by hacking and clubbing people at random."[36] The same day, a companion Reuter article published on A13, "Hutu, Tutsi Bitter Enemies," aims to provide the Western reader with "key facts about Rwanda and Burundi."[37] The article's "history" of Rwanda begins in 1990, making no mention of the multifaceted roots of the Hutu/Tutsi conflict or the legacy of Belgian colonial rule, which established Hutu, Tutsi, and Twa racial-identity cards as a way to control the indigenous population.

By the third day of the *Globe's* coverage, on 9 April, the plight of foreign nationals in Rwanda was the leading story. Written by Jeff Sallot, "Ottawa Readies Rwandan Evacuation" focuses on the approximately two hundred Canadians who need to leave Rwanda in the wake of the violence. Sallot relegates the massacres of Tutsi and moderate Hutu to the background of the story, suggesting that African deaths are less significant than phantom fears of violence against Western expatriates. In doing so, Sallot further reinforces the interpretation of genocidal violence as "tribal warfare": "[Kigali] ... had been turned into a killing ground by rampaging gangs and security forces from the rival Hutu and Tutsi tribes."[38] Similarly, on 11 April, the A1 Rwanda headline was "Foreigners Flee Rwanda,"[39] while a second story about the massacres, "Butchered Bodies Fill Morgue," was buried deeper on

A7.[40] "Butchered Bodies" is particularly visually misleading because, directly above the headline, there is a photograph of RPF rebels with guns accompanied by the following caption: "RPF rebels guard a road north of the capital, Kigali. Thousands have died in the latest outbreak of fighting between the Hutu and Tutsi tribal groups."[41] The juxtaposition of the photograph of armed RPF soldiers and the adjacent text about the "latest outbreak" of violence suggests that the RPF (not the Interahamwe) is responsible for the butchered bodies and that mass killing is part of a "normal" Rwandan cosmology. By the time "Butchered Bodies" was published, Globe readers had been given every cue to fear for the safety of Canadian expatriates, while, at the same time, they remained mystified about the threat of annihilation that was bearing down on hundreds of thousands of Rwandan Tutsi.

Almost every report about massacred civilians in the month of April was organized within a rubric of civil war and tribalism, encouraging Globe readers to interpret the violence as an indiscriminate and inevitable force. Day after day, the Globe published newswire stories that portrayed the genocide of Tutsi civilians as "savage chaos,"[42] "ethnic violence,"[43] "tribal war,"[44] and "tribal bloodletting."[45] The motivation for the massacres was usually articulated in the form of a paradox: the victims were killed "at random," but as a function of "settling scores" in a media fabrication that explained mass killing as simultaneously anarchic *and* methodical, arbitrary *and* purposeful. One particularly troubling version of this paradox appeared in "A History of Hate in Central Africa" on 13 April, the Globe's first editorial on the massacres. The editorial interrogates – but ultimately perpetuates – the myth of the "inevitable" and "reciprocal" nature of the massacres by asking, "Are the Hutu and the Tutsi fated to go on killing each other generation upon generation?"[46] In its primary account of Rwanda's history, it refers to "chaos and slaughter" and "savage violence between the area's two main groups, the Hutus and the Tutsis," but it also succeeds in undermining this description by suggesting that "the Hutu-dominated army used the death of the president as an excuse to settle scores."[47] While the notion of "settling scores" makes the regrettable assertion that the murder of civilians is a kind of revenge killing (implying that the victims must have *done something* to be massacred), it also suggests – contrary to the tone in the rest of the editorial – that the violence is premeditated and state-sponsored, *not* chaotic.

Reflecting on the early media descriptions of "chaos" in Rwanda, BBC reporter Mark Doyle writes: "I have to admit that during the first few days, I, like others, got the story terribly wrong. Down on the ground, up-close – if you could get close enough, safely enough – it did look at first like chaos. I said so. I used the word chaos. What I could see clearly in the first few days was the shooting war between the Rwandan Patriotic Front (RPF) and the government, and the dead bodies. It was not clear who had killed whom, not at first, and the shooting war appeared chaotic with shifting front lines, a lot of noise and a lot of red hot lead flying around."[48] Doyle was able to alter and correct his initial descriptions of "chaos" about a week after his first report because he remained on the ground in Rwanda, rather than reporting from Nairobi or relying on stringers to pass along second-hand (and potentially politically tainted) information. He used first-hand observations and verified information where he could, and his coverage evolved to be more accurate as he gained a greater under-standing of the extent of the violence and the identity of the victims and perpetrators. Without its own reporter in the field throughout the month of April, the *Globe* had no such consistency and instead con-tinued to run a mix of newswire stories that propagated the paradox of random/targeted massacres, relying upon a standing stereotype of "primitive" Africans engaged in "tribal bloodletting."[49] Like most large corporate news companies, the *Globe*'s choice not to engage its own international journalists in Rwanda had both economic and ideologi-cal motivations. African news was expensive to produce, especially for a subject the *Globe* deemed inconsequential to the average Westerner.

The first fully accurate description of the victims and perpetrators was buried as an A12 story, "Rwandan Rebels Vow to Fight until Army Halts Killing," on 27 April.[50] However, this moment of precision was undermined by subsequent lapses in what was clearly a cycle of prog-ress and regress in the *Globe*'s Rwanda reportage. On 30 April, after publishing a few relatively accurate stories, the *Globe* reiterated its stock descriptions of "tribal warfare" and "an orgy of ethnic murder" in an introductory blurb to an otherwise very affective testimonial article, "Rwanda: It Was Terrible. It Was beyond Imagination."[51] Writ-ten by an anonymous Hutu witness to the genocide, "Rwanda: It Was Terrible" provides details about the ethnic-identity cards, the road-blocks, the killing campaigns that extended beyond Kigali, and the identity of the primary victims ("If you are Tutsi, you are killed"[52]), but these details are undermined by the framing references to reciprocal, chaotic, tribal slaughter. Even a month into the genocide, on 6 May, when other news sources were clearly calling the massacres in Rwanda "genocide," the *Globe* published an editorial, "Stanching Rwanda's Wounds," that supported the initial withdrawal of UN troops and their later return. The editorial perpetuates the notion that the genocide is civil warfare by warning that the "UN should not try to insert itself between the two warring sides or favour one side over the other."[53] The words "Hutu," "Tutsi," and "genocide" are not even mentioned in passing. It appears that the *Globe* – and the newswire services it relied upon for information about Rwanda – could not resist the seduction of the "primitive," "tribal" African stereotype, even as it occasionally printed accurate stories that stated the contrary: an intricate and premeditated genocide, a long campaign of centralized anti-Tutsi propaganda, a well-trained militia of genocidal killers equipped with tens of thousands of machetes, and clear evidence that the mass killing of Tutsi civilians was state-sponsored and one-sided.

From "Blackface" to "Whiteface"

I have shown that, throughout the early weeks of the genocide, the *Globe* consistently relied upon newswires, without any continuity of reportage, to construct reductive, racialized descriptions of warring Hutu and Tutsi as a kind of shorthand for the "Rwanda story." If race, racial difference, and African-ness operate as floating signifiers in these articles, then the label of "tribal warfare" is both constitutive and expressive, signifying that massacres are a "normal" and "inevitable" feature of life in Central Africa. I want to suggest that the *Globe*'s dominant image of Rwanda in 1994 is expressed through the inscription of a kind of *blackface,* a term originally used to describe the racist portrayal of African Americans by white actors adorned in black face paint in the United States during the nineteenth and early twentieth centuries. Just as American blackface minstrelsy involved the theatrical, comic performance of "blackness" against the backdrop of American racism, so the stylized, exoticized performance of "savage" African caricatures in the *Globe* obscures the reality of the Rwandan genocide, the legacy of colonialism, and the complexity of diverse African subjectivities.

Once the *Globe* paints the Rwanda story "black" by retreating to stereotypes that bury the most crucial information about the genocide, it proceeds to transpose narcissistic Western interests onto the then decentralized story of Tutsi massacres. The *Globe* reader's initial, confusing concern about Rwandan civilians is quickly replaced by the persistent message that mostly white Westerners are engulfed by "savage chaos" in Rwanda, and that the rescue of these Westerners (as opposed to the Tutsi civilians whose risk of death eclipses any dangers to expatriates) is a moral necessity. In other words, the blackface narrative is inverted, relegated to the background through the promotion of a kind of *whiteface narrative* that places the evacuation of a few hundred mostly white Western expatriates above the plight of hundreds of thousands of Rwandan genocide victims. On 12 April, for example, the paper ran three Rwanda articles: "Shaken Canadians Arrive in Nairobi" on A1, "Foreigners Flee Rwandan Bloodbath" on A12, and "Rare Mountain Gorillas in Rwanda Put at Risk by Bloody Tribal Conflict" on A12.[54] In each of these articles, the true centre of the Rwanda story – the genocide of Tutsi civilians – is transformed into a murky but monolithic blackface that is thrust into the background and replaced by a whiteface narrative that is preoccupied with the safety of Westerners and the fate of Rwandan mountain gorillas (recall the gorilla's habitat as a coveted Western tourist destination in the March 1994 travel article).

Nowhere is this whiteface more clearly exemplified than on 14 April, when the *Globe* published a photograph (without a story attached) above the fold on the front page. The photograph shows a hysterical white woman being escorted by two white Belgian soldiers. Another soldier stands behind them, and about twenty Rwandan civilians – mostly men – provide a striking visual backdrop for the woman's dramatic rescue. The caption reads: "TERRIFYING ESCAPE: Belgian paratroopers lead a frightened woman from a crowd in Kigali yesterday. Rebels and government troops continued to battle in the Rwandan capital." Initially, the caption seems to describe the photo accurately enough; the woman does look frightened, and she is indeed surrounded by a "crowd." But there are really *two* narratives at work here, one that is overtly constructed by the photo's frame and caption and one that is concealed. The overt narrative is, of course, the rescue of the expatriate woman, which dominates the visual frame and relies upon the caption-constructed performance of blackface by the anonymous Rwandans behind her. The second repressed, obscured, ignored narrative is the horror faced by those same Rwandans, a truth that is lost in the transposition of a white Western body (and Western interests) onto Tutsi civilian suffering. The combination of the image and the caption suggests to us that the Rwandans are a menacing bunch – rebel or government troops (or both) who are the perpetrators of the chaotic, reciprocal violence of "tribal warfare" – and that the white woman is being rescued from the impending threat of this "crowd" in the nick of time. Like the stream of A1 stories about the evacuation of Westerners from Rwanda in the first week of the genocide, the photo narrates a form of privileged, unselfconscious Western-ness that is not overtly recognized at the time, let alone challenged. In 1994 the photo and its caption participate in a blackface/whiteface duality in which African bodies are merely part of a mass, undifferentiated crowd. The crowd threatens the life of a single white expatriate woman, who is clearly the primary recipient of empathy and identification from the Western reader.

What the caption fails to communicate is that the Western woman in the foreground obscures the most important story that this picture holds. The Rwandan civilians who fill out the background of the photograph are, in fact, would-be Tutsi massacre victims who have taken refuge in Kigali psychiatric hospital. Video footage of the same scene, rebroadcast in the 2004 PBS Frontline documentary, *Ghosts of Rwanda*, provides a context that is entirely missing from the *Globe* photo and caption. The footage reveals that, for several days, the desperate Tutsi refugees in the photo have been hiding from the Interahamwe at the hospital, where they appear to have some protection as long as the trapped Western staff members remain there with them. Appealing to the soldiers who have come to the rescue of the Western hospital staff, and then to the journalists who have accompanied the soldiers in order to cover the Western evacuations, the Tutsi "crowd" begs for protection from the Interahamwe, who have surrounded the hospital and already killed some members of their group. The soldiers, the journalists, and the Western hospital staff do not come to the aid of the Tutsi refugees, choosing, instead, to flee without them. One Belgian journalist later reported hearing Interahamwe gunfire "the moment [they] left."[55] Most – if not all – of the Rwandans whose images adorn the background of the photograph were massacred the same day – quite possibly the *same hour* – that the white Western woman was swept from the hospital to safety. The *Globe's* blackface/whiteface version of a "terrifying escape" is, in actuality, a terrifying abandonment.

Darfur: "Another Rwanda"

It is the precisely the issue of this *abandonment* that weighs so heavily on Western nations after the Rwandan genocide, and that has surfaced, yet again, during the last five years of state-sponsored atrocities in Darfur, where rapes, massacres, and forced displacement have been variably called genocide, ethnic cleansing, and crimes against humanity. Journalists, activists, and politicians often construct Darfur as "another Rwanda," using our lack of intervention in the 1994 genocide of the Tutsi people as an icon for Western selfishness and UN ineptitude.

Although all state-sponsored killing campaigns have at least some features in common,[56] the designation of Darfur as "another Rwanda" refers less to a conflation of the Janjaweed and the Interahamwe, or to a direct comparison between the Darfurians and the Tutsi, than it does to the troubling international response to large-scale massacres. When "Rwanda" is uttered in conjunction with Darfur, the word that once signified "primitive," "chaotic," "tribal" warfare now signifies the worst Eurocentric tendencies towards selfish complicity, sluggish bureaucracy, and ineffective political intervention. We are not simply classifying the violence in Darfur as "genocide" or "crimes against humanity," we are referencing our own guilt and shame about the collective failure of the international community to prevent genocide in Rwanda in 1994.

Although there are some basic similarities between Darfur and Rwanda in terms of the nature and classification of the violence, there are also important differences.[57] Most significantly, the Rwandan genocide took place during a period of one hundred days, while the Darfur atrocities are being committed slowly and sporadically over a period of years. The slower pace in Darfur has had four immediate and contradictory effects on media coverage. First, the initial Janjaweed attacks on villages appeared spontaneous and isolated at first. Subsequently, the media was primarily alerted to the systematic nature of the atrocities by NGOs like Justice Africa, the International Crisis Group, Amnesty International, and Human Rights Watch – not by government sources or their own investigative journalism – and coverage came far too late, almost a year after the violence against civilians commenced. Secondly, once the news media started to cover Darfur in the second year of the crisis, the extended timeline of the violence gave them time to obtain fairly accurate information. Several major newspapers provided comprehensive coverage, including outstanding reports by Nicholas Kristof at the New York *Times*, Emily Wax at the Washington *Post*, and Stephanie Nolen at the *Globe and Mail*. This coverage also included far more editorial responses than were printed during the Rwandan genocide, as print-media outlets assumed a greater sense of responsibility for alerting the public to urgent humanitarian crises. Television coverage was not nearly as consistent, with entertainment stories often eclipsing international news about Sudan.[58] Thirdly, as the killing in Darfur has worn on month after month for more than four years, newspaper coverage has ebbed and flowed. Interest in Darfur has peaked at certain points in 2004 and 2006 and virtually dropped off the media radar at other points. The coverage has been decidedly inconsistent, with clusters of Darfur stories often followed by weeks of silence. For the general public, the uneven treatment gives the inaccurate impression that the atrocity crimes in Darfur must have abated, or even ceased altogether. Finally, while we can confidently refer to the *Globe* as "mainstream media" in 1994, the media landscape looks radically different today. The relatively slow progress of the genocidal campaign in Darfur has given scholars, activists, NGOs, and bloggers the time to develop extensive websites with up-to-date information and commentary about Darfur, and many North Americans are more likely to get news about Darfur online than from traditional or formerly mainstream media sources like newspapers and television.

It was NGOs, not the UN or the media, who made the first observations about the escalating crisis in Darfur. In March 2003, after the Darfur rebels launched their first attacks on Government of Sudan (GOS) military installations, the British-based NGO Justice Africa offered early predictions about a counter-insurgency campaign by the GOS: "The crisis in Darfur underscores the need for a fully representative political process in Sudan as an integral part of the peace settlement ... The mountainous terrain controlled by the Darfur opposition group makes it exceptionally difficult for the GoS to mount a military operation using ground forces. Some military response is likely, however, perhaps using aircraft. Serious humanitarian concerns arise in the context of such military actions."[59] In May 2003 Justice Africa reiterated its humanitarian concerns about Darfur, particularly the potential for violence against Darfurian civilians: "The Sudan army is not prepared to deal with such tactics and has only two possible military responses. One is the use of air power ... the other is the familiar 'divide and rule' approach of arming local militia ... The latter has been canvassed. If followed, it would run the risk of creating a vicious internecine war targeting civilians."[60] In July 2003 Amnesty International released a statement identifying a "humanitarian crisis looming in Darfur."[61] It called for "an International Commission of Inquiry to examine the factors behind the deteriorating situation in Darfur, investigate abuses and suggest mechanisms to bring to justice the perpetrators of human rights violations"; for "Darfur to be urgently included in the human rights monitoring set up under the IGAD [Intergovernmental Authority on Development] peace process"; and for "the Sudan government to protect the people of Darfur."[62] By January and February 2004, Justice Africa deemed Darfur a "humanitarian and human rights disaster" and insisted that it was "critically important that heavyweight international mediation and humanitarian intervention be brought to bear on this crisis."[63] Likewise, the United States Holocaust Memorial Museum and the International Crisis Group launched urgent appeals for international intervention the same year and also encouraged public activism. These NGO campaigns provided foundational sources for some of the first media reports about Darfur, and they deserve credit for bringing the atrocities to the attention of the world.

Unlike its universally poor coverage of the Rwandan genocide, the *Globe and Mail* has, at times, provided some first-rate reporting about Darfur and taken strong editorial stances favouring UN and Canadian intervention there. However, the *Globe* – like most other news sources – was very slow to pick up the Darfur story at the beginning. For the entire year 2003, the print edition of the *Globe* carried only one story about the violence in the Darfur region, "Government Troops Slain, Sudanese Rebels Say," and that story did not run until December.[64] As the GOS continued its campaign of air attacks and Janjaweed massacres of Darfurian civilians through the fall of 2003, it also began to block humanitarian aid from reaching Darfur, adding a new and ominous bureaucratic element to the killing process. In *Darfur: The Ambiguous Genocide*, Gérard Prunier writes:

> The GoS then took measures which introduced genocidal proportions into the conflict by going deeper than the massacres themselves and targeting the very livelihood of the civilians who had survived the violence. It blocked the US Chargé d'Affaires and a USAID delegation from travelling to Nyala under the pretext that "they had not complied with the administrative regulations," and on 15 November it blocked a first shipment of food aid for Darfur arriving at Port Sudan from the United States on the pretext that the wheat and sorghum cargo "was genetically modified." A few days later Ibrahim Mahmood Hamid, Minister

of Humanitarian Affairs, declared that there was no food emergency in Darfur. Death had moved to the administrative level.[65]

Even though the GOS's obstruction of aid to Darfurian massacre survivors followed months of killing, raping, and forced displacement, Darfur still did not merit attention from the international media. The New York *Times*, which eventually provided excellent coverage of Darfur, did not run its first story addressing the crisis until 17 January 2004.[66] Likewise, the *Globe*'s news about Sudan in 2003 focused exclusively on the north-south civil-war peace negotiations, with Darfur coverage beginning only in early February 2004. On 2 February the *Globe* ran its second newswire brief about civilian deaths in Darfur, "Sudanese Forces Accused of Killing 175 Civilians," which reported: "Sudanese forces and pro-government militiamen have burned several villages and killed more than 175 civilians in western Sudan during a recent government offensive."[67] A 2 February editorial also briefly mentioned new GOS attacks on "unrelated rebel groups in the western part of the country" in an otherwise positive editorial praising the end of Sudan's north-south civil war as the sort of "good news" that the Western media often overlooks. Prunier claims that the Darfur story did not really take off until the media had a workable "angle," which didn't arrive until March 2004:

> [What] actually "blew the ratings" was the interview given by the UN Human Rights Coordinator for Sudan, Mukesh Kapila, to the UN's own IRIN network in March. Kapila declared that Darfur was "the world's greatest humanitarian crisis" and that "the only difference between Rwanda and Darfur is now the numbers involved." He quoted a tentative figure of 10,000 casualties – having worked in Rwanda at the time of the genocide there he knew what he was talking about. And although Rwanda itself had been neglected in its hour of need ten years before, it had by then become the baseline reference for absolute evil and the need to care. Newspapers went wild, and the *New York Times* started to write about "genocide." The "angle had been found: Darfur was a genocide and the Arabs were killing the Blacks. The journalists did not seem unduly concerned by the fact that the Arabs were often black, or that the "genocide" was strangely timed given Khartoum's diplomatic goals in Naivasha. Few

people had ever heard of Darfur before; its history was a mystery nobody particularly wanted to plumb, but now there was a good story: the first genocide of the twenty-first century.[68]

Between February and May 2004, the *Globe* ran between one and five Darfur stories a month. In June, the number jumped to about ten, and from July to September there were between twenty-five and thirty Darfur news stories, commentaries, and editorials a month (excluding letters to the editor, which accounted for even more commentary). From October to December, the number of articles dropped off to between seven and ten a month, which was less but still a relatively significant number for a distant crisis. Although the coverage came late and ebbed and flowed throughout the year, the *Globe* provided its readers with consistent information and commentary about Darfur in 2004. Not only did the paper avoid many of the mistakes evident in its 1994 coverage of Rwanda, it carried quotes and commentaries that called Darfur "another Rwanda," referencing, albeit indirectly, its own culpability in the meagre international response there.

Prunier suggests that the Asian tsunami disaster on 26 December 2004 replaced Darfur as the humanitarian story of the moment: "Darfur instantly vanished from the TV screens and the pages of newspapers. The media could only handle one emotion-laden story at a time, not two, and the tsunami was much more politically correct than Darfur; it was unpolitical, only emotional."[69] In the case of the *Globe*'s coverage, Darfur did not "instantly vanish" after the tsunami, but it did not return to the fever pitch that revolved around the "genocide debate" in the summer of 2004 until two years later, in the summer of 2006. In 2005, the second year of GOS-sponsored atrocities against Darfurian civilians, there were six stories in January, three to five a month from February to April, ten in May, and less than four a month from June to December. During two months, August and December 2005, there were no stories that directly addressed the situation in Darfur, although multiple stories about the death of Sudan's vice-president, John Garang, did make peripheral reference to the continuing violence in Darfur. As the crisis continued, year after year, it was often the NGOs, aid agencies, and Darfur activists who succeeded in bringing Darfur back into the public consciousness, a fact that produced an increasing number of stories that focused on humanitarian aid to the region. Without the efforts and advocacy of these organizations, media coverage would surely have continued to wane.

Darfur: Activism and Advocacy

While the media has played a role in keeping Darfur in the public discourse, it is the NGOs and Darfur activist organizations that have truly kept up the pressure for international intervention. These groups include broad-based coalitions like Save Darfur; large scale NGOs, including Amnesty International, Human Rights Watch, and OXFAM; student groups, such as STAND and STAND Canada; genocide-monitoring organizations like the United States Holocaust Memorial Museum Committee on Conscience, Genocide Watch, Enough: the project to abolish genocide + mass atrocities, and the Genocide Intervention Network; religious groups, particularly Christian groups in the United States and Jewish groups across the globe; and small, community-based grass-roots organizations such as Canadians against Slavery and Torture in Sudan (CASTS), which disseminates frequent updates to group members by e-mail and speaks to local groups about human rights in Sudan. Individual advocates have also made an impact, including journalists like Nicholas Kristof at the New York *Times* and public intellectuals like Alex de Waal and Eric Reeves.

Many of these Darfur campaigns and advocates are faced with difficult choices about how to promote their Darfur messages and motivate public support without overwhelming their target audiences. While some large NGOs and individual scholars like de Waal and Reeves can reach a limited, elite audience through a combination of newspaper op-eds, scholarly publications, and detailed online analysis (websites, online papers, and blogs), other organizations choose to target a broader audience through more mainstream discourses. For the latter groups, the media coverage of the Rwandan genocide reveals an additional, unexpected lesson: when the Western public is faced with reports of atrocity and genocide, it is often motivated to act based not on altruism but on its own narcissism and shame. Indeed, some Darfur advocacy campaigns deliberately exploit this Western self-interest by strategically and self-consciously translating Darfur into the same sort of whiteface that inadvertently dominated the early coverage of the Rwandan genocide in newspapers like the *Globe and Mail*. Rather than fighting against Western narcissism, they take advantage of it.

One of the most fascinating examples of this brand of self-interested public consciousness about genocide is the way that the news media itself became a core target of Darfur advocates in 2005. In a 26

July 2005 op-ed column in the New York *Times*, Nicholas Kristof rails against network TV coverage of Darfur:

> Serious newspapers have done the best job of covering Darfur, and I take my hat off to Emily Wax of *The Washington Post* and to several colleagues at *The Times* for their reporting. *Time* magazine gets credit for putting Darfur on its cover – but the newsweeklies should be embarrassed that better magazine coverage of Darfur has often been in *Christianity Today*.
>
> The real failure has been television's. According to monitoring by the Tyndall Report, ABC News had a total of 18 minutes of the Darfur genocide in its nightly newscasts all last year – and that turns out to be a credit to Peter Jennings. NBC had only 5 minutes of coverage all last year, and CBS only 3 minutes – about a minute of coverage for every 100,000 deaths. In contrast, Martha Stewart received 130 minutes of coverage by the three networks.
>
> Incredibly, more than two years into the genocide, NBC, aside from covering official trips, has still not bothered to send one of its own correspondents into Darfur for independent reporting.[70]

Kristof publicly denounces his fellow journalists and condemns their inconsistent coverage of Darfur, but some advocacy groups go even further by using the poor news coverage itself as an "angle" to engage the public. In this sense, Darfur is constructed strategically, yet again, as "another Rwanda," an idea that the 2005 awareness and advocacy campaign "Be a Witness," organized by the Genocide Intervention Network and the Centre for American Progress, capitalizes on.[71] The campaign consists of a television advertisement and a companion website revealing the lack of Darfur coverage on network TV news, and comparing this omission to the proliferation of entertainment stories and celebrity gossip. The advertisement – which was initially meant to play on network affiliates in the Washington, D.C., area – juxtaposes news images of Michael Jackson, the Runaway Bride, and the Katie Holmes–Tom Cruise romance with images of starving Darfurian children and bombed-out villages. It ends with a voiceover: "You can't stop a genocide if you don't know about it. Tell the media to be a witness." While the ad suggests that we should know more about Darfur, it doesn't offer up such information itself. Nor does it give the atrocities context by mentioning the GOS or the Janjaweed. In fact, the word "Darfur" is never uttered in the ad; instead, it appears on a map as a background image. This campaign is about Western responsibility and media complicity, and it is the West that lies at the heart of the "Be a Witness" Darfur genocide narrative. The fragmented bodies of Darfur victims are secondary to a complaint about the lack of "serious news" and the prevalence of celebrity spectacle in the media.

Likewise, a series of television advertisements by the Save Darfur Coalition launched in 2006 are also deliberately designed to "mobilize shame" in the West. One of the ads, "How Will History Judge Us," reframes Darfur as a story about Western culpability. A series of slides showing Darfurian victims is accompanied by a voiceover, in which Allison Janney asks, "How will history judge us if they're killed? If he's starved? If she's raped ... again? Genocide is ravaging Darfur. 400,000 Dead. 2.5 million displaced. Saving Darfur will take immediate action by a strong UN peacekeeping force, and that will take leadership from President Bush. President Bush, stop the genocide, now." Like the "Be a Witness" campaign, Save Darfur's campaign strategically avoids any mention of the GOS or Janjaweed perpetrators; there is no actor in the sentence "genocide is ravaging Darfur." In fact, the closest thing to a named perpetrator in the ad is George Bush, who is admonished to "stop the genocide." A second controversial advertisement in the Save Darfur campaign goes a step further. "Voices from Darfur" consists of a series of mostly white Westerners reading from heartrending scripts of Darfurian survivor testimony. In this case, it is not just the perpetrators who are missing but the victims themselves, who are now physically displaced, replaced with Westerners who, presumably, "speak" for those who cannot speak themselves. Rather than making space for the real voices of the oppressed Darfurians, Save Darfur participates in what we might call a strategic recolonization of the African image. It is in this sense that Darfur is represented in the public discourse as "another Rwanda." Our deepest concern is about the indictment of the Western media ("tell the media to be a witness"), the culpability of the international community ("how will history judge us?"), and the strategic translation/appropriation of Darfurian testimony by Western voices (an odd appropriation in that it functions to disembody a group of people who are being killed BECAUSE of the way in which their bodies have meaning for the perpetrators).[72]

While not all Darfur campaigns have been as deliberately provocative as the ads from "Be a Witness" and Save Darfur, virtually all of the groups rallying for an end to the violence in Darfur try to engage a

Western audience and many have taken advantage of communications technologies that were not widely available in 1994. Some of the savvier media campaigns include mtvU's online video game, "Darfur Is Dying," in which the user chooses a Darfurian victim identity and navigates life in a refugee camp;[73] Amnesty International's 2007 "Instant Karma: The Campaign to Save Darfur," which includes a petition and a double CD with covers of John Lennon songs that functions as a joint awareness/fundraising mechanism;[74] and the 2007 USHMM's Crisis in Darfur / Google Earth Mapping Initiative, which uses online satellite images of Darfur to allow the public to "witness the destruction for [itself]."[75] Celebrity activists have also emerged in full force, including Angelina Jolie's online diary detailing her tour of Darfurian refugee camps on the USHMM website; George Clooney's highly publicized visit to Chad in 2006; and a 2007 Darfur activist guide, *Not on Our Watch*, co-authored by actor Don Cheadle and John Prendergast of the International Crisis Group.[76] Larger Darfur advocacy groups, like Save Darfur, have also made use of promotional products like hats, T-shirts, and green bracelets to promote an interventionist message.

If these high-profile campaigns are to be truly successful, if they are to move from simple awareness to tangible efforts for change in Darfur, they must continue to work in tandem with the direct activism campaigns of grass-roots and campus organizations like STAND and CASTS. Traditional outlets of activism – rallies, petitions, teach-ins, and group pressure on government officials to support intervention – help the public make a transition from knowledge to action. In the end, the success of genocide-prevention activism will rely on sustaining a broad-based social movement, a transition from *mobilizing* the public around the issue of Darfur to *organizing* a comprehensive social concern about the prevention of all present and future instances of genocide, ethnic cleansing, and crimes against humanity across the globe. Building political and public will for genocide prevention means moving from memory to pedagogy, from Schindler to the UN, from the classroom to the campus, and, ultimately, from a discourse of shame and narcissism to a discourse of responsibility.

Notes

1 For general information about the failures of the international community during the Rwandan genocide, see Linda Melvern, *A People Betrayed: The Role of the West in Rwanda's Genocide* (London: Zed Books 2000); Samantha Power, *A Problem from Hell: America and the Age of Genocide* (New York: Perennial 2002), 329–89; Roméo Dallaire with Brent Beardsley, *Shake Hands with the Devil: The Failure of Humanity in Rwanda* (Toronto: Random House Canada 2003).

2 For an overview of the role of the media in the Rwandan genocide – including extremist Hutu propaganda, Western and African media coverage of the genocide, and the media trial at the International Criminal Tribunal for Rwanda – see Allan Thompson, *The Media and the Rwanda Genocide* (Ann Arbor, Mich.: Pluto Press 2007).

3 "UN Leaving Thousands to Die, Rwanda Pullout Critics Claim," *Globe and Mail*, 23 April 1994, A15.

4 "Meet the Man Who Kept Oskar Schindler Alive [advertisement]," ibid.

5 Thomas Keneally, *Schindler's Ark* (London: Hodder and Stoughton 1982).

6 John Berger, *Ways of Seeing* (London: British Broadcasting Corporation and Penguin Books 1972), 152.

7 For a range of scholarly responses to *Schindler's List*, see Yosefa Loshitzky, ed., *Spielberg's Holocaust: Critical Perspectives on Schindler's List* (Bloomington: Indiana University Press 1997).

8 For more information about the theories of "compassion fatigue," see Susan D. Moeller, *Compassion Fatigue: How the Media Sell Disease, Famine, War and Death* (New York: Routledge 1999).

9 For more information about the failures of the media in coverage of the Holocaust, see Laurel Leff, *Buried by the Times: The Holocaust and America's Most Important Newspaper* (New York: Cambridge University Press 2005).

10 Notably, *Hotel Rwanda*, the first film about the Rwandan genocide to break into the North American market, is also built around a palatable rescue narrative.

11 See Julie Flint and Alex de Waal, *Darfur: A Short History of a Long War* (London: Zed Books 2005), and Gérard Prunier, *Darfur: The Ambiguous Genocide* (Ithaca, N.Y.: Cornell University Press 2005).

12 Allan Thompson, "Introduction," *The Media and the Rwandan Genocide*, 3.

13 Kuperman's original *International Press Institute Report* article is reprinted in Alan J. Kuperman, "How the Media Missed the Rwandan Genocide," in Thompson, ed., *The Media and the Rwandan Genocide*, 256–60.

14 Some correspondents who reported on the Rwandan genocide, such
    as Mark Doyle (British Broadcasting Corporation) and Anne Chaon
    (Agence France-Presse), emphasize a distinction between individual
    journalists who worked on the ground in Rwanda and "the media" as a
    business, institution, or corporation. See Ann Choan, "Who Failed in
    Rwanda, Media or Journalists?" in Thompson, ed., *The Media and the
    Rwanda Genocide*, 160–6, and Mark Doyle, "Reporting the Genocide,"
    in ibid., 145–59.

15 Kuperman, "How the Media Missed the Rwanda Genocide," 256.

16 Ibid., 256–7.

17 Ibid., 257.

18 Ibid.

19 Kuperman writes, "The evacuation of foreign nationals left few report-
    ers in the countryside after the first few days or in the capital after the
    first week." Ibid., 258.

20 Charles Quist-Adade, *In the Shadows of the Kremlin and the White
    House: Africa's Media Image from Communism to Post-Communism*
    (Lanham, Md.: University Press of America 2001), 97–8.

21 Beverly G. Hawk. "Introduction: Metaphors of African Coverage,"
    Africa's Media Image (New York: Praeger Publishers 1992), 7.

22 Ibid., 7–8.

23 Homi K. Bhabha, "The Other Question: The Stereotype and Colonial
    Discourse," in Jessica Evans and Stuart Hall, eds., *Visual Culture: The
    Reader* (London: Sage 1999), 377.

24 *Race, the Floating Signifier: Featuring Stuart Hall*, prod. Sut Jhally, dir.
    Sut Jhally, 85 min. (Northampton, Mass.: Media Education Foundation
    1996), DVD.

25 *Globe and Mail* journalist Jeff Sallot filed a report from Nairobi, "13
    Killed in Attack on Kigali Refuge," on 2 May, followed by a report from
    Kigali, "Rwandan Orphans, Helpers Slain," on 4 May. Prior to these
    articles, all coverage about the situation on the ground in Rwanda
    came from newswire services (presumably, some newswire services
    had reporters in Rwanda, some had reporters in Nairobi, and some got
    reports from stringers inside Rwanda).

26 "Cold Choices in Rwanda," New York *Times*, 23 April 1994, A24.

27 Jeff Sallot, "Why Rwanda Is Not Bosnia," *Globe and Mail*, 29 April 1994,
    A13.

28 Three brief mentions appeared in the *Globe*'s "World in Brief" section:
    "Rwanda Observer" (CP), 5 July 1993, A4, reports the appointment of
    Canadian General Roméo Dallaire to oversee the Rwandan peace pro-
    cess; "Rwandan Foes Agree" (AP), 5 August 1993, A9, reports the tenta-
    tive peace agreement between the RPF and the Rwandan government;
    and "Food Shipments Stop" (AP), 16 August 1993, A5, reports that "Red

Cross has suspended shipments of food to up to 200,000 people driven from their homes by three years of civil war in Rwanda."

29 "UN Votes to Send Force to Rwanda" (New York Times Service), 6 October 1993, A2.

30 One report about Burundi briefly mentions a similar risk in Rwanda: "[Burundi] remains on the brink of a civil war that could seep into neighboring Rwanda, which has a similar mix of ethnic groups, relief officials and Western diplomats say." Donatella Lorch, "Bloodbath Just Latest Chapter in Ethnic Hatred" (New York Times Service), *Globe and Mail*, 24 November 1993, A17.

31 "Visits to Mountain Gorillas to Resume with African Peace," *Globe and Mail*, 26 March 1994, F10.

32 Ibid.

33 Indeed, the sole photograph attached to a Rwanda report between 6 April 1993 and 6 April 1994 is the image of a mountain gorilla adjacent to the travel story.

34 "Two Presidents Die in Crash" (AP), *Globe and Mail*, 7 April 1994, A1.

35 "Rwandan Troops Kill Prime Minister" (AP, CP, Reuter, and Staff), *Globe and Mail*, 8 April 1994, A1.

36 Ibid.

37 "Hutu, Tutsi Bitter Enemies" (Reuter), *Globe and Mail*, 8 April 1994, A13.

38 "Ottawa Readies Rwandan Evacuation" (Sallot, with staff, Reuter, AP), *Globe and Mail*, 9 April 1994, A1.

39 "Foreigners Flee Rwanda" (AP, Reuter, CP), *Globe and Mail*, 11 April 1994, A1.

40 "Butchered Bodies Fill Morgue" (AP), *Globe and Mail*, 11 April 1994, A7.

41 Ibid.

42 *Globe and Mail*, "Foreigners Flee Rwanda."

43 Ibid.

44 "Rare Mountain Gorillas in Rwanda Put at Risk by Bloody Tribal Conflict" (Reuter), *Globe and Mail*, 12 April 1994, A12.

45 "Foreigners Flee Rwandan Bloodbath" (Reuter and CP), *Globe and Mail*, 12 April 1994, A12.

46 "A History of Hate in Central Africa," *Globe and Mail*, 13 April 1994, A22.

47 Ibid.

48 Mark Doyle, "Reporting the Genocide," 145.

49 A few examples, among many others: "Ottawa Readies Rwandan Evacuation"; "Butchered Bodies Fill Morgue"; and "Rwandan Butchery Continues Unabated" (AP and CP), 18 April 1994, A1.

50 "Rwandan Rebels Vow to Fight until Army Halts Killings" (AP), *Globe and Mail*, 27 April 1994, A12.

51 "Rwanda: It was Terrible. It Was beyond Imagination" (AP), *Globe and Mail*, 30 April 1994, D5.

52 Ibid.

53 "Stanching Rwanda's Wounds," *Globe and Mail*, 6 May 1994, A26. ·

54 *Globe and Mail*, "Rare Mountain Gorillas."

55 *Ghosts of Rwanda*. dir. Greg Barker, 85 min. (PBS Frontline: WGBH Education Foundation, 2004), DVD.

56 There are several prominent theories regarding the roots of genocide. For a typology of genocide, see Frank Chalk and Kurt Jonassohn, *The History and Sociology of Genocide* (New Haven, Conn.: Yale University Press 1990). For a theory about the relationship between genocide and non-democratic states, see Rudy Rummel, *Death by Government: Genocide and Mass Murder in the Twentieth Century* (New Brunswick, N.J.: Transaction Publishers 1994). For a theory about the recognizable stages of genocide, see Gregory Stanton, "The 8 Stages of Genocide," http://www.genocidewatch.org/8stages.htm.

57 See Scott Straus "Rwanda and Darfur: A Comparative Analysis," *Genocide Studies and Prevention*, vol. 1, no. 1 (2006): 41–56.

58 For a case study of television coverage of Darfur in 2005, see the "Be a Witness" campaign: http://www.beawitness.com.

59 Justice Africa. "Prospects for Peace in Sudan: March 2003," http://www.justiceafrica.org/blog/2003/03/14/prospects-for-peace-in-sudan-march-2003/.

60 Justice Africa, "Prospects for Peace in Sudan: May 2003," http://www.justiceafrica.org/blog/2003/05/27/prospects-for-peace-in-sudan-may-2003/.

61 Amnesty International, "Sudan: Looming Crisis in Darfur," 1 July 2003, http://web.amnesty.org/library/Index/ENGAFR540412003?open&of=ENG-SDN.

62 Ibid.

63 Justice Africa, "Prospects for Peace in Sudan: January 2004," http://www.justiceafrica.org/blog/2004/01/31/prospects-for-peace-in-sudan-january-2004/. In a February 2004 briefing report, Justice Africa also stated clearly, "As well as humanitarian assistance, the Darfur war needs immediate political attention by the international community." Estanislao Oziewicz, "Humanitarian Crisis Looms in Sudan," *Globe and Mail*, 13 February 2004, A17.

64 "Government Troops Slain, Sudanese Rebels Say," *Globe and Mail*, 8 December 2003, A14. Another AP newswire brief, "Clashes in West Sudan Kill 30 Rebels," appeared five months earlier, but only in the online edition of the paper (*Globe and Mail online*, "Clashes in West Sudan Kill 30 Rebels," 13 July 2003, http://www.globeandmail.com).

65 Prunier, *Darfur: The Ambiguous Genocide*, 108.

66 Ibid., 127. Prunier cites the first US article about Darfur as "War in Western Sudan Overshadows Peace in the South," New York *Times*, 17 January 2004, A3.

67 "Sudanese Forces Accused of Killing 175 Civilians," *Globe and Mail*, 2 February 2004, A10

68 Prunier, *Darfur: The Ambiguous Genocide*, 127.

69 Ibid., 128.

70 Nicholas Kristof, "All Ears for Tom Cruise, All Eyes on Brad Pitt," New York *Times*, 26 July 2004, http://www.nytimes.com/2005/07/26/opinion/26kristof.html.

71 http://www.beawitness.org.

72 The Save Darfur ads are in good company. In 2006 Keep a Child Alive launched the "I am African" campaign, which included an image of Gwenyth Paltrow in stylized tribal face paint. Likewise, a September 2006 cover of *The Independent*'s Produce RED "Africa issue" included an image of Kate Moss in blackface.

73 mtvU, "Darfur Is Dying," http://www.darfurisdying.com/.

74 Amnesty International, "Instant Karma: The Campaign to Save Darfur," http://www.amnesty.ca/instantkarma/.

75 USHMM Crisis in Darfur / Google Earth Mapping Initiative, http://www.ushmm.org/googleearth/projects/darfur/.

76 Don Cheadle and John Prendergast. *Not on Our Watch: The Mission to End Genocide in Darfur and Beyond* (New York: Hyperion 2007).

PART TWO

The Crisis in Darfur

CHAPTER FOUR

Three Empirical Investigations of Alleged Genocide in Darfur*

ERIC MARKUSEN

This chapter concerns what is widely regarded as the first genocide of the twenty-first century: the deliberate slaughter – as well as slower death through displacement, starvation, thirst, and disease – of more than 450,000 people from three tribes (the Fur, Zaghawa, and Masalit) in the Darfur region of Sudan.[1] The principal perpetrators of this carnage are the Government of Sudan (GOS) and Arab militia (known as Janjaweed) who have been hired, equipped, and trained by the GOS to attack farms, villages, and towns inhabited by their designated victims. This genocide began in early 2003 as a counter-insurgency war against armed rebel groups consisting of members of the Fur, Zaghawa, and Masalit tribes, but the campaign against the rebels escalated into crimes against humanity and genocide against the innocent civilians in those groups who were not involved in the insurgency. (While members of rebel groups have also been accused of attacks against civilians, the attacks committed by the government and the Arab militia have been far greater in their scale and extent.)

In the spring and summer of 2004, as people around the world observed the tenth anniversary of the Rwandan genocide of 1994, the violence in Darfur continued to escalate, and United Nations officials and human rights groups issued strident warnings of a growing death toll. That may have helped create an incentive to try and do more for the Darfurian victims than was done for the Rwandan victims a decade earlier. In Washington, D.C., the US Congress passed unanimous resolutions calling the conflict "genocide" and demanding a more robust response by the United States and the United Nations.[2] US Secretary of State Colin Powell visited Sudan, as did UN Secretary General Kofi Annan, and both called attention to the crisis. Human rights organizations like Amnesty International and Human Rights Watch issued reports of murder, rape, and deaths from hunger and thirst. The UN Security Council passed several resolutions condemning the violence and calling on the Government of Sudan to disarm the Janjaweed militia. The United States and other nations donated millions of dollars for humanitarian assistance to the displaced Darfurians. The African Union (AU) launched a peace-monitoring mission consisting of about 7,300 troops on the ground, and later the UN authorized a hybrid UN-AU mission that was launched in 2008.

In addition to these yet unsuccessful attempts to halt the killing and dying and mitigate the suffering, several empirical investigations into the nature of the violence have been conducted. This chapter examines three of them: one by the United States government, one by the United Nations, and one by a non-governmental organization (NGO), Physicians for Human Rights.[3] A peace agreement signed in early May 2006 between the Government of Sudan and the largest rebel group, while a hopeful sign, is no guarantee that the situation will improve in the near future. Indeed, Sudan expert Eric Reeves warned in late April 2006 that many internally displaced persons (IDPs) and refugees are in danger of dying each month as a result of direct violence, deprivation, and inadequacy of humanitarian assistance.[4]

The US Atrocities Documentation Team

In the summer of 2004, the US Department of State and the US Agency for International Development (USAID) hired an NGO, the Coalition for International Justice, to undertake a field investigation to determine the validity of allegations that genocide was being committed in Darfur.[5] Twenty-four investigators from eight nations (including the author) were hired to interview refugees from Darfur who had survived the initial attacks on their homes and villages and managed to make their way to the relative safety of refugee camps and settlements on the Chad side of the border with Sudan. Each investigator was paired with an interpreter who could speak English, Arabic (the lingua franca of Sudan), and at least one of the dialects spoken by the refugees. After a short training period in Abeche, a Chadian city near the border with Sudan, the members of the Atrocities Documentation Team (ADT) were deployed in small groups to more than a dozen camps and settlements along the border.

Investigators randomly selected tents or other occupied spaces in the camps and then randomly chose individuals within them to interview. Interviews were based on an eight-page *Darfur Refugees Questionnaire*, designed by the US State Department, the Coalition for International Justice, and the American Bar Association.[6] Investigators, through their interpreters, asked basic demographic information (name, age, tribe, occupation, etc.) and then queried respondents about the details of their experiences during and after the attacks on their homes and villages, and also during their flight from Darfur to Chad.

The overall goal was to conduct a total of 1,200 interviews, which was deemed to be a statistically significant sample of the approximately 200,000 Darfurians thought to be eking out an existence as refugees in Chad. Although this goal was thwarted by local contingencies including bad weather during the rainy season, vehicle breakdown, and security concerns, a total of 1,136 random interviews were conducted and statistically analysed by the US State Department.

Findings of the ADT

Findings from the Atrocities Documentation Team were presented to Congress and the American public in September 2004 in an eight-page report, *Documenting Atrocities in Darfur.*[7] The report states that "a US Government project to conduct systematic interviews of Sudanese refugees in Chad reveals a consistent and widespread pattern of atrocities in the Darfur region of western Sudan."[8] It goes on to state that "the non-Arab population of Darfur continues to suffer from crimes against humanity."[9] The analysis of 1,136 interviews suggests "close coordination between GOS (Government of Sudan) forces and Arab militia elements, commonly known as the Jingaweit [Janjaweed]."[10] The report also notes that the vast majority of respondents reported that there had been no rebel activity in the vicinity of their villages prior to the attacks.

The data revealed a typical pattern of attack. In 67 per cent of the cases, Sudanese military aircraft bombed and/or strafed the village, often just before dawn. After the aerial attacks, GOS military forces and Janjaweed militia surrounded the village; then they moved in, killing and raping many of those who had survived the bombing. The attackers then systematically plundered the villages, taking household goods, seeds, farm tools, and livestock. After looting everything of value, the houses and other buildings were burned and, often, wells poisoned by dumping dead humans and animals into them. According to the report, "four-fifths [of the respondents] said that they had witnessed the complete destruction of their villages."[11]

The report notes that 61 per cent of the refugees interviewed reported witnessing the killing of at least one member of their nuclear or extended family.[12] Many stated that multiple family members had been killed: spouses, children, parents, siblings, cousins, and so on. Moreover, 28 per cent reported that members of their families or people from their villages who had survived the initial attacks had died on the flight from Darfur to Chad.[13]

Sixteen per cent of the respondents witnessed or experienced rape. The report suggests that the rapes probably "are under-reported because of the social stigma attached to acknowledging such violations of female members of the family."[14] Another reason for the under-reporting of rape is that children were not interviewed. During the interview process it became clear that children as young as seven years old were targeted for rape. It is probable, too, that under-reporting took place because half of the interviewers, and all of the interpreters, were men, a fact that likely made it even more difficult for women to admit to being raped and for men to admit that their wives or daughters had been raped.

A fifth of the respondents reported either being beaten themselves or seeing others beaten; 44 per cent reported either being shot or witnessing others being shot.[15] Many respondents still bore scars from bullets, knives, and shrapnel from anti-personnel bombs dropped by government aircraft during attacks. Many of those who survived the initial attacks died from untreated injuries on the several-day (or longer) trek to relative safety in Chad.

Mental harm was even more pervasive. As noted above, two-thirds of the respondents said that at least one family member had been killed, and many of those lost multiple family members. It was not uncommon to interview a woman who had lost her husband and one or more children as well as other relatives (including a mother and/or father or one or more brothers and/or sisters). In addition to agonizing bereavement, the refugees had experienced the loss of homes and property and were currently living in extremely difficult conditions with utter uncertainty about the future.

The US Determination of Genocide

On the basis of data collected by the ADT, as well as other evidence including satellite imagery, on 9 September 2004 Secretary of State

Colin Powell, in testimony before the Senate Foreign Relations Committee, officially accused the Government of Sudan and the Janjaweed of genocide. Powell stated: "When we reviewed the evidence compiled by our team and then put it beside other information available to the State Department and widely known throughout the international community, widely reported by the media and by others, we concluded – I concluded – that genocide has been committed in Darfur, and that the government of Sudan and the Janjawid [sic] bear responsibility, and that genocide may still be occurring."[16] Powell went on to state that "we believe the evidence corroborates the specific intent of the perpetrators to destroy a group 'in whole or in part' – the words of the [genocide] convention. This intent may be inferred from their deliberate conduct."[17] Factors that led Powell to infer genocidal intent were identified by one of the key individuals with whom Powell consulted at the time, then-US ambassador-at-large for war crimes, Pierre-Richard Prosper, a former prosecutor for the International Criminal Tribunal for Rwanda. In a telephone interview, Prosper told this author and Stephen Kostas about a telephone conversation he had had with Powell concerning the crucial matter of inferring genocidal intent. Kostas, in an article based in part on this telephone interview, reported: "Powell and Prosper had a long conversation about the actions of the government in Khartoum: [quoting Prosper] 'How they created these militias; they had the ability to rein them in and then did not; they acted in concert with the *Janjaweed* ... in attacking these villages ... the aerial bombardment and then *Janjaweed* would come in; and then the fact that the Government of Sudan would block humanitarian assistance to people in need.' It was enough, Prosper says, 'to form the intent.'"[18]

In the very same testimony, however, Secretary of State Powell asserted that the finding of genocide required no change in US policy towards Sudan, which at that stage involved mainly diplomatic pressure to disarm the Janjaweed, as well as donation of money for humanitarian assistance and some logistical support for the African Union force in Darfur. Powell stated, "Mr. Chairman, some seem to be waiting for this determination of genocide to take action. In fact, however, no new action is dictated by this determination."[19]

The US government did undertake another unprecedented initiative at the international level when it utilized Article 8 of the UN Convention on the Prevention and Punishment of the Crime of Genocide (UNCG) to request the UN Security Council to take actions "appropriate for the prevention and suppression of acts of genocide" in Darfur and to launch an official UN investigation of alleged genocide and other crimes in Darfur.[20]

The International Commission of Inquiry on Darfur

On 18 September 2004, after several days of debate, the UN Security Council passed Resolution 1564, which called for the establishment of an international commission of inquiry on Darfur, whose mandate included four tasks: investigating allegations of violations of international law by all parties to the conflict, determining if acts of genocide had occurred, identifying the perpetrators, and suggesting means of holding those responsible accountable.[21] The five-member commission, headed by Antonio Cassese, former president of the International Criminal Tribunal for the Former Yugoslavia, quickly hired thirteen experts for the investigative team – fewer than it would have liked, owing to budget constraints. The commission made two visits to Sudan: from 7–21 November and from 9–16 January. Smaller teams of commissioners and members of the investigative team also made short visits to Eritrea (to meet with rebel leaders), Addis Ababa (to meet with African Union officials), and Chad (to collect additional evidence, including interviews with refugees from Darfur).

While the ADT had focused almost exclusively on interviews with victims, the International Commission of Inquiry on Darfur (COI) had a much broader purview and used a variety of collection methods. In addition to interviews with internally displaced persons in Darfur and refugees in Chad, the COI was able to interview many key members of the Sudanese political and military leadership, leaders of the rebel groups, and others. In addition to conducting interviews, the COI made observations of destroyed villages from the air and on the ground, examined mass graves, and reviewed prior reports from UN, NGO, and other sources (including the data and findings from the ADT).

Findings of the Commission of Inquiry

The 177-paged report of the commission of inquiry was given to UN Secretary General Kofi Annan on 25 January 2005 and released to the public at the same time. Empirical findings of the COI are consistent with those of the ADT as well as other investigations by human rights organizations. In its discussion of findings, the COI emphasized "two irrefutable facts about the situation in Darfur ... Firstly, there were more than one million internally displaced persons (IDPs) inside Darfur ... and more than 200,0000 refugees from Darfur in neighboring Chad ... Secondly, there were several hundred destroyed and burned villages and hamlets throughout the three states of Darfur."[22] The COI later noted that as many as 2,000 villages may have been destroyed at the time of its investigation.[23]

Referring to attacks against civilians, the COI found that "the vast majority of attacks on civilians in villages have been carried out by the Government of Sudan armed forces and Janjaweed."[24] As did the ADT, the COI noted that attacks against villages often involved government aircraft.[25] Referring to the killing of civilians in the attacked villages, the COI concluded that "the Government of Sudan and the Janjaweed bear responsibility for an overwhelming majority of the murders of civilians committed during the conflict in Darfur."[26] They also asserted that "the mass killing of civilians in Darfur is likely to amount to a crime against humanity."[27]

The COI found that the Government of Sudan and the Janjaweed have been responsible for the great majority of destroyed villages and displacement of the population. Referring to the "large-scale destruction of villages in all the three states of Darfur," the COI found that this destruction was a "joint venture by the Janjaweed and the Government forces."[28] It concluded: "The destruction of property in Darfur was clearly part of a systematic and widespread attack on the civilian population; it clearly had a detrimental effect on the liberty and livelihood of those people, being deprived of all necessities of life in the villages ... and the fact that the vast majority of villages destroyed belonged to African tribes would also indicate that it is carried out 'discriminatorily ...' [and] may well amount to the crime of persecution, as a crime against humanity."[29] In the same vein, the COI found that "looting was mainly carried out against African tribes and usually targeted property necessary for the survival and livelihood of these tribes."[30] Allegations that attacks by government forces and the Janjaweed against African villages were in response to rebel presence and/or armed activities in or near the villages were also investigated. Like the ADT, however, the COI found that this rationale was not valid. According to the COI report, "the Commission did not find any evidence of military activity by the rebels in the major areas of destruction that could in any way justify the attacks on military grounds."[31]

The COI paid particular attention to allegations of rape. Consistent with the other reports, it found at least three patterns of rape: rape during attacks on villages, rape of women abducted during attacks and held for periods of time, and rape of women and girls when they left IDP camps to obtain firewood or water.[32] After presenting several detailed case studies based on interviews with rape victims, the COI found that rape appeared to "have been used by the Janjaweed and Government soldiers (or at least with their complicity) as a deliberate strategy with a view to achieve certain objectives, including terrorizing the population, ensuring control over the movement of the IDP population and ensuring its displacement."[33] In addition, the COI found that the widespread rape and sexual assault against the three "African" tribes may amount to a crime against humanity.[34]

The COI also found evidence of violations of international law committed by members of rebel groups, though on a far smaller scale than those committed by the Government of Sudan and the Janjaweed. In paragraph 268, the report notes, "From the Commission's findings it is clear that the rebels are responsible for attacks on civilians, which constitute war crimes. In general, the Commission has found no evidence that attacks by rebels on civilians have been widespread, or that rebel attacks have systematically targeted the civilian population." However, it should be noted that more recent accounts indicate that certain factions of the rebel movement may have escalated attacks against civilians in the nearly eighteen months since the COI report was released. For example, on 19 May 2006, a New York *Times* correspondent wrote that "the tactics of the rebels have grown so similar to those of their enemies [Government of Sudan forces and Janjaweed] that an attack on this dusty village [Tina] bore all the marks of the brutal assault that first forced its people to flee their homes three years ago. Soldiers in uniform, backed by men toting machine guns on camels, flooded the village, burning huts, shooting, looting and raping."[35]

The Question of Genocide for the UN

Despite the similarity of empirical findings by the ADT and the COI, the UN commission, unlike the US State Department, did not conclude that the crimes committed by the GOS and the Janjaweed amounted to genocide. Indeed, in its executive summary, the report stated that "the Commission concluded that the Government of Sudan has not pursued a policy of genocide."[36]

The COI noted in its report that a finding of genocide requires the presence of three elements: evidence that acts prohibited by the Genocide Convention were committed; evidence that these acts were committed against members of a group protected under the UNCG; and evidence of specific genocidal intent. The commission found abundant evidence of the first element, prohibited acts, committed by the GOS and the Janjaweed; they included "systematic killing of civilians belonging to particular tribes ... large scale causing of serious bodily or mental harm to members of the population belonging to certain tribes, and ... massive and deliberate infliction on those tribes of conditions of life bringing about their physical destruction in whole or part."[37] The commission emphasized the latter point in paragraph 638, where it asserted that "the pillaging and destruction of villages, being conducted on a systematic as well as widespread basis in a discriminatory fashion, appears to have been directed to bring about the destruction of the livelihoods and means of survival of these populations."[38] Regarding the second necessary element, the commission concluded that, despite the fact that primary victims shared a number of key cultural features, including language and religion, with the chief perpetrators, "it may be concluded that the tribes who were victims of attacks and killings subjectively make up a protected group [under the terms of the Genocide Convention]."[39]

However, the commission found the third essential element for a determination of genocide – genocidal intent – lacking, and therefore it concluded that the crimes committed by the GOS and the Janjaweed did not amount to genocide. It did acknowledge that "the scale of the atrocities and the systematic nature of the attacks, killing, displacement and rape, as well as racially motivated statements by perpetrators ... could be indicative of genocidal intent." But the commission cited "other *more indicative* elements that show the lack of genocidal intent."[40] Thus, in a number of cases, the attackers did not kill as many of the victims as they could have;[41] many persons forced from their homes were collected in camps, rather than killed outright;[42] villages of mixed Arab-African populations were not attacked;[43] and some victims were beaten but not killed when their property was plundered.[44]

This reasoning is open to criticism. Eric Reeves has pointed out that the language of the Genocide Convention refers to the intent to destroy a protected group in whole or in part and that significant and substantial parts of the attacked groups in Darfur were in fact killed during the attacks, with many more dying in the aftermath. Reeves also notes that the conditions in the IDP camps have resulted in many thousands of deaths as the result of hunger, dehydration, and disease – all aggravated by the deliberate obstruction of the delivery of humanitarian aid by GOS and Janjaweed forces. On the basis of these and other considerations, Reeves suggests that "indeed, so egregiously poor are the legal and factual arguments about the issue of 'genocidal intent' that we must conclude this Commission did not feel politically free to make a determination of genocide."[45] Reeves's suggestion is given weight by the fact that, even before the COI investigators went into the field to collect evidence of crimes, they were told by the president of the commission that he did not expect a finding of genocide. In an article on the investigations of genocide in Darfur, genocide scholar Samuel Totten, who was one of the twenty-four investigators on the US Atrocities Documentation Team, quotes one of the COI investigators, who was discussing the pre-deployment meeting of the COI in Geneva: "'Commissioner Antonio Cassese, who had traveled to Khartoum and some parts of Darfur for a few days and had conducted some interviews, stated that he felt that we would find that there were two elements of genocide missing: (1) target groups (victims are from mixed tribes) and (b) *mens rea* (intent). He talked for a while and my personal opinion was that he was telling us that the outcome of the investigation should [be] that it was not genocide that was occurring ... I felt it was very inappropriate for him to plant this opinion in the investigators' minds prior to starting the investigation and other investigators felt uncomfortable about it as well.'"[46]

Another critique of the reasoning behind the commission's negative finding on the question of genocide has been made by Jerry Fowler, who has questioned whether the elements cited above by the commission as being "indicative" that the GOS and the Janjaweed did not have genocidal intent are actually weightier than such other elements as the widespread and systematic killing, raping, looting, and plundering. Fowler also suggests that the COI, by assuming that genocidal intent must be shown "beyond reasonable doubt," employed too demanding a standard for the purpose of the investigation, that is, to determine whether acts of genocide had been committed. "This standard," Fowler states, "is clearly wrong under the circumstances. The commission was not a court of law, nor was it adjudicating the fate of individual defendants. Quite to the contrary, the commission was called upon only to make a threshold finding on the basis of which the UN Security Council would decide whether to take additional action."[47]

Yet another critique of the COI's finding that genocide had not been committed has been made by attorney Andrew Loewenstein, who had been one of the investigators on the US Atrocities Documentation

Team. Like Reeves, Loewenstein questions the commission's reasoning that elements indicative of genocidal intent were outweighed by elements supposedly "more indicative" that there was not genocidal intent. But Loewenstein also notes that the Government of Sudan obstructed the ability of the COI to collect evidence in the field and suggests that the COI could have "stated that it couldn't yet make a determination [on the question of genocide] because of the government's obstruction."[48]

Notwithstanding these criticisms, it should be noted that the commission did not rule out the possibility that in the Darfur conflict *"single individuals,* including Government officials, may entertain a genocidal intent."[49] The commission went on to state, "Should the competent court decide that in some instances certain individuals pursued genocidal intent, the question would arise of establishing any possible criminal responsibility of senior officials either for complicity in genocide or for failure to investigate, or repress and punish such possible acts of genocide."[50]

The COI also emphasized the seriousness of the crimes committed in Darfur. In paragraph 522, it states: "The above conclusion that no genocidal policy has been pursued and implemented in Darfur by the Government authorities, directly or through the militias under their control, should not be taken in any way as detracting from, or belittling, the gravity of crimes perpetrated in that region. As stated above genocide is not necessarily the most serious international crime. Depending upon the circumstances, *such international offences as crimes against humanity or large scale war crimes may be no less serious and heinous than genocide.* This is exactly what happened in Darfur, where massive atrocities were perpetrated on a very large scale, and have so far gone unpunished."[51]

Aftermath of the Commission of Inquiry

After reviewing and debating the COI report, on 31 March 2005, the Security Council passed Resolution 1593, in which, concurring with the commission, it decided to refer the situation in Darfur to the International Criminal Court (ICC). The vote was eleven for the resolution, none against, and four abstentions (Algeria, Brazil, China, United States). The United States, despite its strong opposition to the ICC, chose not to veto the resolution; nor did China, despite its dependency on Sudan for oil.

Less than a week later, UN Secretary General Kofi Annan handed over to the ICC a sealed list of fifty-one names of people suspected by the COI of grave crimes under international law on the basis of evidence it collected. In addition to the list of possible people to be indicted, the ICC prosecutor was also given nine boxes containing more than 2,500 items, including photos, video footage, interview transcripts, documents, and other evidence collected by the COI.

On 29 June 2005 ICC Prosecutor Luis Moreno-Ocampo presented a report – based on review of the COI evidence, as well as more than 3,000 other documents and other sources – to the UN Security Council. In his address to the council, Ocampo stated: "There is a significant amount of credible information disclosing the commission of grave crimes within the jurisdiction of the Court having taken place in Darfur. These crimes include the killing of thousands of civilians, the widespread destruction and looting of villages, leading to the displacement of approximately 1.9 million civilians. The conditions of life resulting from these crimes have led to the deaths of tens of thousands from disease and starvation, particularly affecting vulnerable groups such as children, the sick and the elderly. Information also highlights a pervasive pattern of rape and sexual violence."[52]

The Physicians for Human Rights Report

In February 2005 Physicians for Human Rights (PHR), an international NGO, released its report, *Darfur: Assault on Survival*.[53] Intended to complement other investigations like the ADT and the COI, which focused on killing, rape, and other forms of direct violence against persons, PHR concentrated on the destruction of livelihoods, that is, the means of survival. In three trips to the region (May 2004, January 2005, and July 2005), PHR conducted in-depth interviews with refugees living in Chad who came from three specific villages in Darfur (one Fur, one Masalit, and one Zaghawa) that had been attacked and destroyed by the GOS and/or the Janjaweed. At the beginning of its report, PHR stressed the inherently difficult survival in Darfur, even without GOS and Janjaweed attacks: "It is also important to understand that outside of village life, Darfur is an extremely difficult place to survive. At the foot of the expanding Sahara desert, it is known for its searing heat, recurrent drought and minimal infrastructure. While Darfurians have developed complex coping mechanisms enabling them to thrive within their villages, when people are herded from their homes and chased into a land that offers little shelter from the forbidding sun and penetrating winds, no potable water and no animals for food, milk and transport, they succumb to starvation, dehydration and disease."[54]

PHR notes in its report that, as of early 2006, "nearly two million people have been uprooted and displaced, and an estimated 90% of non-Arab villages in the region have been attacked, looted, or razed to the ground."[55] An estimated 2.5 million people are living within Darfur in camps for internally displaced persons, with another 200,000 struggling to survive in refugee camps in Chad.[56] On the basis of its interviews, PHR concluded that the Darfuris' means of survival were being systematically eliminated in a least three ways: first, the destruction of homes and looting of property and livestock; second, forcible displacement into extremely inhospitable environments; and, third, deliberate efforts by the GOS and the Janjaweed to impede the delivery of humanitarian assistance to desperate and vulnerable internally displaced persons.

Like the ADT and the COI, PHR found evidence of widespread and systematic mass killing as well as death from deprivation. A high percentage of their respondents witnessed the death of a family member. Among the many examples quoted in the report is a thirty-five-year-old man, who reported: "'I witnessed the execution of six cousins, who were all shot as I was fleeing. I saw a woman carrying her child, who was being chased by the *Janjaweed*, and she was attacked, raped and then they threw her child into the fire.'"[57] Further evidence of the scale of killing is contained in the report's discussion of family size before and after the attacks. In one of the villages, the pre-attack family size was on average 12.5 persons; after the attack it was 5.2 (based on respondents' statements about family members known dead or else missing and presumed dead).[58]

PHR concluded that, in addition to committing direct killing and causing serious physical and mental harm to non-Arab civilians in Darfur – both of which are prohibited acts under the UN Genocide Convention – the GOS and the Janjaweed were intentionally and systematically violating Article IIc of the convention, which prohibits creating "conditions of life calculated to bring about ... physical destruction in whole or part" of a group protected by the convention. The report notes that "in most attacks on the non-Arab villages of Darfur since the start of the conflict in 2003, the GOS and Janjaweed forces have burned dwellings, looted personal possessions, stolen livestock, poisoned or destroyed wells and irrigation systems, uprooted or burned fruit trees and destroyed crops, food and seed supplies. The attackers also burned and looted schools and other civic buildings in larger towns. Many villages have been entirely razed."[59]

Thus, PHR confirmed the conclusion reached by the US government that the GOS and the Janjaweed are committing genocide against non-Arab groups in Darfur. Unlike the COI, PHR found both direct and indirect, circumstantial evidence of genocidal intent. With respect to direct evidence of genocidal intent, the report notes that "survivors interviewed by PHR reported that their attackers shouted such things as 'Exterminate the Nuba!' ... These types of statements are classic admissions as to a perpetrator's mental state, in this case, evincing the intent to 'exterminate' the 'Nuba,' i.e. the non-Arab group being attacked."[60] The report continues:

> PHR's investigations reveal overwhelming evidence from which genocidal intent may be inferred: only non-Arab populations were targeted in the utter eradication of villagers and village life; the atrocities have been committed on a massive scale; the GOS/Janjaweed exhibit the same pattern of atrocities across time and against different non-Arab ethnic groups, including, critically, systematically destroying anything that can sustain life; victims are targeted because of their membership in particular groups; the GOS refused access to the area ... These and other findings, individually and collectively, suggest the mental state of the perpetrators, namely an intent to destroy certain ethnic groups 'in whole or in part.'[61]

Conclusion

Never before has an alleged case of genocide been studied so thoroughly while under way. Never before has a government conducted an official investigation into allegations of ongoing genocide, and then accused another government of genocide, and then utilized Article 8 of the Genocide Convention to urge the United Nations to take action. Never before has the UN Security Council established a commission to assess whether or not genocide was occurring and then been able to refer the situation to an international court for further investigation and prosecution of perpetrators. Compared with the relative inaction and avoidance of the international community during the 1994

Rwanda genocide and the 1995 Srebrenica massacre (in which Bosnia Serb forces slaughtered as many as 8,000 unarmed Bosniak men and boys), the Darfur investigations, the willingness of the US government to call the killings "genocide," and the subsequent referral to the ICC are all, arguably, steps forward in the struggle to establish the rule of law over the rule of force and the struggle against impunity for perpetrators of atrocities.

However, as noted at the beginning of this chapter, such steps, while necessary and potentially significant for future deterrence of similar crimes, are woefully inadequate. Although they may have some future value for potential victims of mass violence, they do little or nothing to stop the killing and dying. Only a robust international military intervention will suffice to force the GOS and the Janjaweed, as well as leaders of rebel groups, to stop attacks on innocent civilians and enforce security in the region. The genocide in Darfur needs no more study: it must be stopped.

Notes

* This chapter is based in part on a shorter and earlier publication, "Genocide in Darfur: Studied, but Not Stopped," that appeared in *African Renaissance*, vol. 3, no. 3 (2006): 43–51. It is based also on lectures given at the Nordic Africa Institute in Uppsala, Sweden, in April 2006, and at the Galilee Colloquium on Humanitarian Intervention at Kfar Blum, Israel, in June 2006.

1 Eric Reeves, "Quantifying Genocide in Darfur (Part 1): Current Data for Total Mortality from Violence, Malnutrition, and Disease," Sudan Research, Analysis and Advocacy, 28 April 2006, http://www.sudanreeves.org/index.php?name=News&file= article&sid=102 (accessed 2 July 2006).

2 Scott Straus, "Darfur and the Genocide Debate," *Foreign Affairs*, vol. 81, no. 1 (2005): 123–33.

3 For more information about the methodology and findings of these investigations, see Samuel Totten and Eric Markusen, eds., *Genocide in Darfur: Investigating the Atrocities in the Sudan* (New York: Routledge 2006).

4 Reeves, "Quantifying Genocide in Darfur (Part 1)."

5 Totten and Markusen, eds., *Genocide in Darfur*.

6 Jonathan Howard, "Survey Methodology and the Darfur Genocide," in Totten and Markusen, eds., *Genocide in Darfur*, 59–74.

7 US State Department, *Documenting Atrocities in Darfur*, State Publication 11182 (9 September 2004), http://www.state.gov/g/drl/rls/36028.htm (accessed 11 May 2006).

8 Ibid., 1.

9 Ibid., 2.

10 Ibid.

11 Ibid., 4.

12 Ibid., 1.

13 Ibid.

14 Ibid., 7.

15 Ibid., 1.

16 Colin Powell, "The Crisis in Darfur" (Oral Testimony before the Senate Foreign Relations Committee, 9 September 2004).

17 Ibid.

18 Stephen Kostas, "Making the Determination of Genocide in Darfur," in Totten and Markusen, eds., *Genocide in Darfur*, 111–26.

19 Ibid.

20 Ibid.

21 United Nations Security Council, *Security Council Resolution 1564* (18 September 2004), http://www.state.gov/documents/organization/36436.pdf (accessed 2 July 2006).

22 United Nations, *Report of the International Commission of Inquiry on Darfur to the United Nations Secretary-General: Pursuant to Security Council Resolution 1564 of 18 September 2004* (25 January 2005), http://www.un.org/News/dh/sudan/com_inq_darfur.pdf (accessed 11 May 2006), para. 206.

23 Ibid., para. 236.

24 Ibid., para. 240.

25 Ibid., para. 243.

26 Ibid., para. 271.

27 Ibid., para. 293.

28 Ibid., para. 315.

29 Ibid., para. 321.

30 Ibid., para. 389.

31 Ibid., para. 313.

32 Ibid., para. 334.

33 Ibid., para. 353.

34 Ibid., para. 360.

35 Lydia Polgreen, "Violent Rebel Rift Adds Layer to Darfur's Misery," New York *Times*, 19 May 2006.

36 United Nations, *Report of the International Commission of Inquiry on Darfur*, s. II, para. 1.

37 Ibid., para. 507.

38 Ibid., para. 638.

39 Ibid., para. 512.

40 Ibid., para. 513; emphasis added.

41 Ibid.

42 Ibid., para. 515.

43 Ibid., para. 516.

44 Ibid., para. 517.

45 Eric Reeves, "Report of the International Commission of Inquiry on Darfur: A Critical Analysis (Part 1)," Sudan Research, Analysis and Advocacy (2 February 2005), http://www.sudanreeves.org/modules.php?op=modload&name=Sections&file=index&req=viewarticle&artid=489&page=1 (accessed 6 June 2006).

46 Samuel Totten, "The U.S. Investigation into the Darfur Crisis and Its Determination of Genocide," *Genocide Studies and Prevention*, vol. 1, no. 1 (2006): 57–78.

47 Jerry Fowler, "A New Chapter of Irony: The Legal Implications of the Darfur Genocide Determination," *Genocide Studies and Prevention*, vol. 1, no. 1 (2006): 29–40.

48 Andrew Loewenstein, "Genocide Deniers: Words Fail," *New Republic Online*, 5 May 2006, https://ssl.tnr.com/p/docsub.mhtml?i=20060515&s=loewenstein051506 (accessed 6 June 2006).

49 United Nations, *Report of the International Commission of Inquiry on Darfur*, s. II, para. 520; emphasis in original.

50 Ibid.

51 Ibid., para. 522; emphasis in original.

52 Luis Moreno Ocampo, "Statement of the Prosecutor of the International Criminal Court Mr. Luis Moreno Ocampo to the Security Council on 29 June 2005 Pursuant to UNSCR 1593," *International Criminal Court* (2005), http://www.icc-cpi.int/library/cases/LMO_UNSC_On_DARFUR-EN.pdf (accessed 6 June 2006).

53 Physicians for Human Rights, *Darfur: Assault on Survival, A Call for Security, Justice, and Restitution* (2005), http://www.soros.org/resources/articles_publications/publications/assault_20060201/phrreport_20060201.pdf (accessed 6 June 2006).

54 Ibid., 2.

55 Ibid.

56 Ibid., 13.

57 Ibid., 22.

58 Ibid., 27.

59 Ibid., 29.

60 Ibid., 42.

61 Ibid., 43.

CHAPTER FIVE

Mass-Atrocity Crimes in Darfur and the Response of Government of Sudan Media to International Pressure*

FRANK CHALK AND DANIELLE KELTON

This chapter examines Government of Sudan (GOS) domestic radio and television news broadcasts as indicators of the Sudanese government's intentions in Darfur and Southern Sudan. It addresses a number of important questions. Does the GOS genuinely intend to share authority over Darfur's and Southern Sudan's oil and other natural resources and grant their citizens fair portions of the revenues accruing from their sale? Will the government in Khartoum call off and disarm the Janjaweed militia, ending its harassment, rape, and murder of civilians in Darfur? Is the GOS serious about implementing the Comprehensive Peace Agreement (CPA) for the south?

It was Alexander George, political scientist, RAND corporation researcher, and strategist, who distilled the observation from Second World War propaganda research that one of the surest indicators of an authoritarian government's intentions and future plans was the carefully crafted information it fed to its people in their own language.[1] Refining studies of the broadcasts of German radio during the war, George found that Joseph Goebbels and his aides had prepared the German public for important changes in policy through anticipatory news releases and commentaries. He diagramed the relationships as follows:[2]

Situational Factor ← Elite Estimate ← Elite Expectation
← Elite Intention ← Propaganda Strategy ← Content or Policy

Directives and guidelines issued weekly and sometimes daily by Goebbels's Ministry of Propaganda preceded new directions in Nazi policies and explicitly suggested stories designed to shape how the public would respond to them.[3] By these means, George argued, the Nazi elite minimized the probability of sparking a backlash before making policy changes and signalled the response it wanted to evoke among its own citizens when a prepared action was implemented. Reinforcing Alexander George's analysis, intellectual and cultural historian Jeffrey Herf's recent research in the transcripts of domestic German radio broadcasts and wall posters has shown that they provided one of the earliest and most sustained warning indicators of Hitler's intention to annihilate the Jews of Europe.[4]

The Government of Sudan's crimes against humanity and the potential for genocide in the Darfur region of western Sudan loom large in current debates over the responsibility of other nations to protect vulnerable populations from their own governments.[5] One purpose of this chapter is to assess just how seriously observers should take the frequent declarations of the GOS in international forums reiterating its desire for peace and reconciliation with the armed guerillas of Darfur and the south. This is an issue with important current policy implications for the Security Council of the United Nations, other states, non-government organizations (NGOs), and student organizations seeking to halt mass-atrocity crimes in Darfur.

The Republic of Sudan is a nation of some 41.2 million persons occupying the largest land area in Africa. With a literacy rate of 61.1 per cent (71.8 per cent for men and 50.5 per cent for women),[6] radio broadcasting is by far the most important medium for communicating news within the country. This chapter is based on extensive research in translations of transcripts from Arabic to English covering the major government-owned broadcasters and websites in Sudan accessed through a subscription to the BBC Monitoring Service. Those broadcasters monitored by the BBC include Republic of Sudan Radio (Arabic/Omdurman), Sudan TV (Arabic and, rarely, English/Omdurman), the Sudanese Media Centre website (Arabic/Khartoum), and the Sudan News Agency (SUNA) website (Arabic and English/Khartoum).

Although there were only 250,000 television sets in Sudan in 2002, the GOS has frequently initiated policy changes by first preparing the attitudes of the members of the educated elite, who are numerous among Sudanese with access to TVs and the Internet.[7] Access to the web is growing in Sudan but was limited to 1.14 million users in 2005.[8]

Intimidation of Editors and Reporters in Sudan

Named "one of the world's most repressive regimes for the independent media" in 2005 by Freedom House, the domestic media in Sudan
operate in one of the most tightly controlled and restricted environments in Africa.[9] "The Government [of Sudan] directly controlled
radio and television and required that they reflect government policies," and "television has a permanent military censor to ensure that
the news reflected official views," reported the US Department of
State in 2005.[10] Amnesty International confirms that the clampdown
on freedom of expression is especially severe for Sudanese journalists
reporting on the Darfur crisis. Intimidation, harassment, and impris-
onment of journalists, Amnesty concludes, have "prevented the majority of Sudanese from understanding what is happening in Darfur or
debating solutions which might bring peace to the province."[11]

The GOS seeks to control all news about Sudan. Sudan's police and
intelligence agencies, both civilian and military, regulate the movements of journalists, domestic and foreign. Government interference
spans a broad spectrum of responses including lengthy interviews
by the police, detention in cells, beatings and torture of journalists,
and the suspension and closing of media outlets.[12] Some issues are
more sensitive than others. The media are almost certain to be cen-
sored when they report on the army and its activities.[13] Article 25 of
the Press Law of Sudan forbids the publication of any news about the
armed forces without their prior authorization.[14] The National Press
Council banned discussion of the peace process in the south of Sudan
until the government decided to negotiate the Comprehensive Peace
Agreement.[15] Articles on slavery in Sudan are banned, as is any criticism of the government and its policies.[16] Interviews with opposition
politicians and news about their parties are similarly banned.[17]

Foreign media and NGOs face stringent restrictions as well. Al-
Jazeera's office in Khartoum was raided by police, and its broadcast
equipment seized, because the Qatar-based TV station interviewed
members of opposition groups in December 2003.[18] Al-Jazeera was
accused of "transmitting numerous programmes 'stuffed with false
information and poor biased analyses.'"[19] In January 2004 the GOS
permanently closed Al-Jazeera's office, accusing it of promoting false
reports about Sudan.[20] The Khartoum bureau chief of Al-Jazeera was
sentenced to one month in prison for reporting false information and
obstructing customs officers in their duties in April 2004.[21] Ameri-

can freelance photographer Brad Clift was detained and placed under house arrest in April 2005 for taking photos and interviewing refugees in Darfur.[22] And in May 2005 two Médecins sans Frontières representatives were arrested and charged with "spying" and publishing false information when they reported the details of five hundred rape cases in West Darfur.[23]

The Government of Sudan accomplishes the suppression of news within a framework of bureaucratic regulations and "exhausting security restrictions" designed to furnish opportunities for intimidating reporters and representatives of NGOs.[24] According to Amnesty International, a Sudanese cannot travel in Darfur "without authorization from the national security and intelligence, the military intelligence, or the police." In May 2004 the GOS promised visas within forty-eight hours to all humanitarian personnel, but strenuous restrictions continued to be applied to the movement of staff and the use of radios. Humanitarian workers in refugee camps, Amnesty International reports, "still have to send a 'notification' ... to travel elsewhere in Darfur." If their travel is delayed for any reason, they have to submit another request. Foreign journalists are almost always required to take along with them a GOS minder assigned by the Ministry of Information when they visit Darfur.[25]

The Distorted Versions of the Darfur Situation in Sudan's Domestic Media

Official government broadcasters in Sudan distort the news of international reactions to the Darfur situation. Here are three important examples.

1   Secretary of State Powell's Statement Accusing Sudan of Genocide in Darfur, September 2004

On 9 September 2004, testifying before the Senate Foreign Relations Committee, United States Secretary of State Colin Powell applied the word "genocide" to the Government of Sudan's policies and actions in Darfur.[26] The government-sponsored broadcasting media of Sudan treated his statement as a non-event. They simply did not report it.[27] Nor had the broadcast media covered an earlier UN Security Council resolution, number 1556, which demanded that the GOS fulfil its commitments to disarm the Janjaweed and bring them to justice.[28]

Similarly, the broadcast media failed to inform the Sudanese radio audience that, just days after Powell's testimony, the Security Council had adopted Resolution 1564 threatening sanctions against Sudan if it did not seek to end the violence and negotiate a comprehensive peace agreement with rebels in Sudan's southern regions.[29]

The first Sudanese broadcast to mention Powell's assertion appeared one week following his Senate Committee testimony, when Islamic cleric Sheik Abdeljalil al-Nazir al-Karuri, the imam of the Al-Shahid (The Martyr) Mosque in Khartoum, ended his weekly Friday night sermon on Sudan Radio by charging that Powell's allegation of genocide in Darfur was just another American lie designed to help the Zionist cause, a lie he placed in the same vein as the American claim that Iraq had possessed weapons of mass destruction before the US invasion.[30] Al-Karuri, who on 20 August had delivered a splendid non sequitur asserting that Sudan could not be committing genocide in Darfur because it did not possess any nuclear weapons, is one of the few non-government commentators trusted by Sudan Radio to rebut live on-air foreign officials critical of Sudan's policies in Darfur.[31] But Powell's charge of genocide, a word rarely heard in Sudanese broadcasts, quickly disappeared from Radio Sudan following al-Karuri's sermon.

Sudan's broadcast blackout of Powell's allegation is one indication that Sudanese government officials do not trust the average Sudanese to confront the damage done to Sudan's international reputation by Khartoum's support for the Janjaweed. Literate Sudanese, perceived in Khartoum as potential troublemakers by virtue of their reading skills, could peruse more reasoned statements in Sudan's Arabic-language press from Minister of Foreign Affairs Mustafa Osman Isma'il and the Sudan News Agency attributing Powell's remark to pre-election American campaign politics and the Bush administration's search for votes in November.[32]

2 Kofi Annan's Visit to Sudan, May 2005

Kofi Annan, the United Nations secretary general, visited Sudan in May 2005, two months after the UN Security Council passed a resolution referring the atrocity crimes in Darfur to the new International Criminal Court (ICC) at The Hague and only days before the ICC launched an investigation of persons suspected of authorizing or committing such crimes.[33] Delivering his monthly report to the Security

Council following his visit, Annan observed that the level of violence in Darfur was lower than a year earlier but had mounted in May.[34] While he noted some improvements in the situation, Annan characterized Janjaweed militia activity in the area as a serious threat to civilians.[35]

The Sudanese government media twisted and distorted Annan's statements to polish the government's image. In its version, in his meeting with Foreign Minister Isma'il, Annan had focused on *rebel* atrocities in Darfur, emphasized his appreciation of Sudan's cooperation with the UN, and underscored the government's positive role in accomplishing the Southern Sudan peace agreement.[36] The government media in Sudan omitted completely from its reports Annan's criticisms of the government. Rather, the Sudan News Agency reported on 31 May that Annan was overwhelmed by the positive developments in Darfur and had complimented the government of Sudan for respecting the Darfur ceasefire.[37] Annan's visit to Sudan also provided an occasion to represent the GOS as the injured party in the Darfur dispute. Viewers of Sudan TV were informed on 27 May that the Sudanese Women's Union and other civil society organizations had presented Annan on his arrival with a letter protesting unjust UN resolutions against Sudan; they accused the UN of spreading chaos, threatening social security, and arousing conflicts in Darfur.[38]

3   Secretary Rice's Visit to Sudan, July 2005

US Secretary of State Condoleezza Rice flew into Khartoum on 21 July 2005. She delivered a strong message to President al-Bashir, declaring that his government had "a credibility problem" and that she wanted to see "actions not words" by his government to quell the violence in West Darfur.[39] Sudan's violations of human rights in Darfur stood directly in the way of improved relations between Sudan and the United States, Rice stated.[40] She concluded her meeting with al-Bashir by insisting that the violence in Darfur, especially against women, was a major obstacle to normalizing relations with the United States. [41]

Sudan's government media presented the story of her visit rather differently. According to Republic of Sudan Radio on 21 July, Rice had lauded the efforts made by the government to resolve the crisis and held out the possibility of upgrading relations between Sudan and the United States.[42] President al-Bashir had thanked Rice for the efforts made by the United States to bring peace in Sudan, according to Sudan

Radio.[43] US journalists travelling with Rice were manhandled by Sudanese security personnel and barred from the meeting between Rice and al-Bashir.[44] No official Sudanese government media mentioned this event, although Rice released a statement declaring that she was outraged and demanded an official apology.[45] Rice and al-Bashir had spent ten minutes seated in silence because al-Bashir's guards refused to admit her translator to the meeting.[46] Six days prior to Rice's arrival, Sudan TV had beamed a message to the American secretary of state from Sheik al-Karuri, the Muslim cleric who regularly chanted Friday night prayers live from the Al-Shahid Mosque in Khartoum: end American government partiality for Israel, he demanded, "de-link [US] policies from the Jewish lobby groups," and disassociate your country from "the Jewish issue" since the Jews "want to destroy even the USA itself."[47]

Triggers Prompting Government of Sudan Misinformation

Foreign criticism and international sanctions against the Government of Sudan provide the major triggers for its disinformation campaigns in the official domestic media. Distortion and highly selective fact picking characterize these government campaigns. On 7 May 2004 a major UN human rights report prepared by the UN Commission on Human Rights accused Sudanese troops and militia in Darfur of committing war crimes and crimes against humanity.[48] The carefully worded UN report provoked what appears to be the Sudanese government media's first public admission to its own people that the world suspected Sudan of genocide in Darfur. Throughout the summer and fall of 2004, the Sudanese domestic media vigorously responded to the mention of the word "genocide." Radio Sudan declared that any suggestion of genocide was simply Western propaganda reflecting Zionist influence and Western jealousy of Sudan's great wealth and rich culture.[49] The media enthusiastically quoted statements from officials of the African Union (AU) and the World Health Organization who said they saw no evidence of genocide in Darfur.[50] Sheik al-Karuri alleged on Sudan TV after Friday night prayers that US government sympathy for the Darfur rebels arose from American lust to gain control of Sudan's oil reserves in the region.[51]

On 30 July 2004 the UN Security Council waded into the fray, demanding in Resolution 1556 that the Government of Sudan honour its commitments to disarm the Janjaweed militia and bring its members to justice.[52] The Security Council put some teeth into its resolution by endorsing the deployment of international monitors in Darfur.[53] The GOS responded domestically by condemning any notion of foreign involvement in Darfur. Prominent government figures spoke out on radio and television to denounce the "Zionist attack" on Sudan.[54] Any foreign intervention in Darfur, they claimed, would be tantamount to the recolonization of the country.[55] On TV, a Muslim cleric blamed the usual suspect, Israel, insisting that the United States called the tune for the UN and acted only because it wished to advance the interests of the "Zionist entity."[56] Sudan's foreign affairs minister found the thirty-day implementation deadline for the disarmament of the Janjaweed difficult and illogical.[57]

The UN Security Council's demand on 18 September 2004 that Sudan fulfil its commitment to end the violence in Darfur and reach a comprehensive peace agreement with the groups seeking autonomy from Khartoum, embodied in Resolution 1564,[58] evoked a by now familiar hostile response from Sudanese government leaders. This time Sheik al-Karuri set the tone on Sudan TV by accusing those behind the resolution of committing genocide by enlisting in the "Zionist project" and harming all Muslim nations as a result.[59] Al-Karuri further accused the United States of trumping up the charge of genocide just so it could intervene.[60] President al-Bashir declared that he had detected a conspiracy between Zionists and Freemasons to stage a coup and undermine the security of the Sudanese people.[61] Sudan Radio news analysts reported charges in the National Assembly that Zionists supporting the Darfur rebels had deliberately stalled peace talks and were arming Darfur groups seeking autonomy.[62] The editors of the Sudan TV website floated the claim that Israel had agreed to transport American weapons and ammunition to set up a separate US-Israeli state in western Sudan.[63]

On 31 March 2005 the frustrated members of the UN Security Council referred to the Office of the Prosecutor of the new International Criminal Court at The Hague a sealed list of persons suspected of committing serious war crimes in Darfur.[64] Sudan TV immediately labelled the referral unjust. Radio Sudan reported that the minister of information, Abd-al-Basit Sabdarat, had declared that by virtue of the referral the Security Council was "killing the Rome Charter."[65] Speaking on Sudan Radio, President al-Bashir termed the referral invalid and intended to serve Western and Zionist interests.[66] The National Congress Party[67] pledged never to cooperate with the ICC and to block any attempt at Western intervention.[68] Following these declarations, Sudan Radio sought support for mass demonstrations backing the government leaders' position and condemning the UN Security Council. The secretary general of the Organization for the Defence of Faith and the Country slammed the referral as an attempt to discredit the sovereignty of Sudan.[69] The minister of foreign affairs claimed on the website of the Sudan Media Centre that the call of the Israeli delegation for an investigation of slavery in Sudan at the meeting of the UN Commission on Human Rights confirmed Israel's hidden role in aggravating the Darfur crisis and conspiring against Sudan.[70]

The ICC launched its Darfur investigation on 6 June 2005, but Sudan refused a visa to Luis Moreno-Ocampo, the ICC's chief prosecutor, when he sought to visit Darfur to draw up a list of war criminals for indictment.[71] Sudanese government officials scrambled to mount their own war-crimes process, attempting to prove that they could handle the situation without international intervention. Rather than "inappropriately" hand its accused nationals over to the ICC, the Government of Sudan declared on its website a few days later, it would try them before local courts. On 11 June, Sudan TV reported the formation of a special Sudanese criminal court to deal with Darfur war crimes.[72] One hundred and sixty low-level suspects were accused of minor crimes before the court.[73] Sudan's justice minister, Ali Muhammad Uthman Yasin, quickly declared that he considered the Sudanese court a substitute for the ICC's investigation, which should now be aborted.[74] All references to the ICC disappeared from Sudanese radio and television following the justice minister's declaration.

From August 2005 until February 2006, negotiations between representatives of the Government of Sudan and the rebels were frequently delayed and constantly on the verge of stalling. The independent media outside Sudan widely reported that the talks were in imminent danger of collapse.[75] Nevertheless, the domestic government media in Sudan portrayed the talks for their home audience as progressing nicely, simultaneously disseminating exaggerated stories of rebel attacks on AU peacekeepers and Darfur civilians.[76] After many months of stalling by Sudanese representatives, the UN Security Council met to consider targeted sanctions against specific government officials. The government media moved into high gear, echoing old themes and introducing new ones into its domestic broadcasts. Sudan Radio reported street demonstrations in Al-Fashir, with demonstrators rejecting all forms of intervention.[77] Government of Sudan officials speaking on Sudan Radio and TV blasted any move towards the deployment of UN troops to Darfur, stressing that African Union troops had the situation in Darfur under control.[78] Sudanese officials characterized the stationing of UN troops in the region as "unacceptable,"[79] a violation of Sudan's national sovereignty,[80] and a step down the road to Sudan's recolonization.[81] Sudanese TV played interviews with militant demonstrators proclaiming that they were ready to defend their country against UN troops regardless of the cost.[82]

In April 2006 the UN Security Council imposed targeted sanctions on four Sudanese nationals including two individuals with positions in the Sudanese government and two affiliated with Darfur rebel groups.[83] Calling the sanctions "regrettable," Sudan Radio accused the Security Council of impeding the Darfur peace process.[84] It emphasized the capacity of Sudan's judiciary and police to punish the malefactors already charged before the Sudanese tribunal without informing listeners of the specific charges against them. Sheik Karuri, Sudan TV's Friday evening cleric, reacted to the sanctions by repeating his familiar litany of conspiracies against Sudan and charging that those who welcomed the US initiative at the Security Council were the same people who welcomed recolonization and US policies which benefited only "the Zionist entity."[85]

Key Themes in Government of Sudan Domestic Broadcasts and Web Media

The Government of Sudan has insisted that it will do everything possible to prevent the deployment of a UN peacekeeping force in Darfur, with President al-Bashir totally rejecting UN forces and declaring that "he would prefer to be a leader for the resistance in Darfur rather than being a President of an occupied country."[86] For al-Bashir, acceptance of UN forces would lead Sudan into "a tunnel of international hegemony, imposition of guardianship on it, violation of its national sovereignty and regional position, and confiscation of its national political will."[87] The narrative under development by President al-Bashir prophesies the destruction of Sudan as a state resulting from a Zionist-inspired, Western-backed conspiracy unless all Sudanese steadfastly unite to oppose the presence of UN troops in Darfur. His explanation for Sudan's problems in Darfur is simple: the Zionist, Western, anti-Islamic conspiracy is at work. Seven connected themes converge clearly in Sudan's government-sponsored and coordinated broadcast and web media.

1 Sudan Is a Sovereign Nation and UN Involvement Constitutes Meddling in Sudan's Internal Affairs, Eroding Sudan's Sovereignty.

Taking the position that the Darfur crisis is purely an internal matter, on 29 September 2004 the Government of Sudan refuted the right of any international organization – for example, the UN Office of the High Commissioner for Refugees – to talk about greater autonomy for Darfur.[88] The Sudanese government regularly arranges carefully staged, "angry" street demonstrations, denunciations by civil society organizations, and pronouncements by Sufi leaders to demonize United Nations attention to the plight of Darfur's residents.[89]

2 The Government of Sudan Has the Darfur Situation under Control and Does Not Need Foreign Help. It Is Dedicated to the Peace Process and Progress Is Being Made towards Economic and Social Development in Darfur.

The Government of Sudan emphasizes any evidence it can create that its policies in Darfur are humanitarian, successful, and have the situation under control. Under pressure to accept UN troops, Sudan launched an anti-measles campaign, triumphantly trumpeted on Sudan TV as if the belated immunization of children driven into refugee camps with their families, suffering from dehydration and malnutrition and threatened with rape if they search the countryside for firewood, will somehow compensate for the deaths of some 270,000 Darfurians, most of them children and elderly persons.[90] Sudanese TV news frequently reports plans for new development projects in Darfur and the voluntary return of some internally displaced persons (IDPs) to their homes,[91] ignoring the destruction by the government-sponsored Janjaweed and Sudanese military aircraft of 75 per cent of the villages in Darfur and the creation of many more IDPs.[92]

President al-Bashir predicted the prosecution of war criminals by the Sudanese courts in fair and public trials in stories posted on the Sudan News Agency website in Arabic and English, but to date no senior Sudanese official connected to the Janjaweed assault on innocent civilians has been brought before the bar of justice in those courts.[93] Rather, Mawlana Mahmud Abkam, the chairman of the special criminal court for the Darfur states, has announced, contrary to the testimony of hundreds of rape victims, that in Al-Fashir and Nyala "there were no testimonies which indicated that rape was the result of a planned and systematic group act."[94] He complains, according to the Sudan News Agency, that none of the rape victims interviewed by the Western media "had filed a suit with any legal authority so that it could make a judgment or carry out the necessary investigations," as if he expected the women to trust courts created by the same government that unleashed the Janjaweed's campaign of terror and ethnic cleansing in the first place.[95] Typifying the minimalist approach of the Sudanese government to prosecuting war criminals for their actions in Darfur was the conviction and sentencing to death by the special court of two hapless Sudanese regular soldiers on 16 November 2005 for beating to death a man whom they mistook as a member of a rebel group.[96]

Controlling and coordinating the domestic media as tightly as it does, the Government of Sudan can dissemble at home with impunity. It boasted of progress in providing security and badly needed provisions for the Darfur refugee camps in June 2006 after refusing Norwegian UN Humanitarian Coordinator Jan Egeland entry to the Darfur region only two months earlier.[97] The government justified its action on the preposterous basis that it feared for his safety because of the publication in the Danish press of cartoons offensive to many Muslims, as if Darfurians followed the world media over coffee and croissants every morning and waxed indignant over Egeland's heinous Scandinavianness.[98]

3 Foreign Pressure on Sudan Amounts to a Hostile Attack on the Nation and a New Form of Recolonization.

Sudanese government leaders constantly reiterate the theme that UN intervention in Darfur with the stationing of UN troops in the western provinces would constitute a new form of colonization. Claiming that Sudan welcomes the presence of a small African Union force to monitor developments in Darfur, Sudan rejects the stationing of UN troops despite the clear insufficiency of the present AU force.[99] Sudanese Muslim cleric Al-Karuri had even accused former South African president Thabo Mbeki, a veteran fighter against apartheid, of advocating the fresh colonization of Sudan for asking Sudan to permit the stationing of UN troops in Darfur.[100] Pursuing this theme, President al-Bashir projects himself onto the wider screen of History, declaring that Sudan will not be the first nation to be recolonized.[101]

A bizarre facet of the Government of Sudan's campaign to mobilize public opinion against introducing a UN force to Darfur and its insistence that such a force would mean the "recolonization" of Sudan is that in March 2005 the government accepted the UN plan to station 10,000 UN troops in Southern Sudan to monitor compliance with the Comprehensive Peace Agreement.[102] Even stranger is the fact that Sudan Radio has never broadcast a word recognizing the existence of this UN military force, while Sudanese TV regularly refers to the UN troops in the south without any apparent malice.[103] Such dual channelling of vital information is a perfect illustration of the government's practice of entrusting information to the domestic elite audience with access to Sudan TV and government websites, while keeping radio listeners, the majority of Sudanese, in the dark.

4   United Nations Interest in the Darfur Crisis Serves a Western-Zionist Agenda, Is Part of Foreign Conspiracies Directed against Sudan, and Is Not Motivated by Genuine Humanitarian Concerns.

Sudanese officials perceive the international campaign over Darfur as a Zionist assault on Sudan. Mirroring the anti-Israeli views of many of Sudan's leading personalities, today's official Sudanese media blames Israel, the West, and the Freemasons for provoking foreign protests against the fate of civilians in Darfur.[104] The official Sudanese media identify Israel and the American "Jewish lobby" as Sudan's special nemeses. Typical were the claims of the governor of North Darfur in July 2004 that Zionists were leading an extensive campaign against Sudan regarding the Darfur issue and the statement by Sudan's interior minister that the Zionist lobby was behind a misinformation campaign against Sudan.[105] When peace talks between Sudanese government representatives and Darfur rebel groups stalled in September 2004, Radio Sudan reported the allegation of the speaker of the National Assembly that Zionist and American pressure was responsible.[106] In November 2004 Sudan TV reported on its website that the United States and Israel planned to establish a separate state in western Sudan called Zaghawa.[107] It further reported that this area contained a stockpile of US ammunition and weapons transported by Israeli aircraft and personnel.[108]

The long and complex history of Sudan's animus towards Israel sheds light on the ebbs and flows of Islamist fundamentalism as an influential factor in the politics of Sudan. Sudan's declaration of war on Israel during the Arab-Israel war of June 1967 encouraged Israel to supply arms to southern Sudanese rebels via Ethiopia and Uganda starting in 1969.[109] Although Sudan had no diplomatic relations with Israel in the 1980s, in 1984, responding to American pressure, the Sudanese government of President Gaafar al-Nimeiri secretly cooperated with Israel in the airlifting of some 10,000 Ethiopian Jews from Sudan to Israel in Operation Moses.[110] Nimeiri was overthrown the following year, and in June 1989 the National Islamic Front seized power in a coup spearheaded by General Omar Hassan al-Bashir, who had served in the Egyptian army in the October 1973 Middle East war.[111] One way that al-Bashir's new government signalled its Islamist identity was to offer "residency to any Arab or Muslim."[112] Among those attracted by this offer to reside in Sudan were both the man believed to have masterminded the 1983 bombing of the US Marine barracks in Beirut and none other than "Carlos the Jackal."[113] In 1991, after his expulsion from Saudi Arabia, Osama bin Laden also established his main base in Khartoum. There he forged close links with Hassan al-Turabi, then the speaker of Sudan's House of Representatives and the head of the National Islamic Front.[114] An enthusiastic Islamist, President al-Bashir sympathized strongly with the Palestinian cause.[115] But he still coveted good relations with Washington.

In 1996 President al-Bashir expelled bin Laden from Sudan after terrorist death threats against American diplomatic personnel led the United States to close its embassy in Khartoum.[116] Two years later, on 7 August 1998, al-Qaeda operatives blew up the US embassies in Nairobi and Dar es Salaam and US-Sudan relations hit their nadir.[117] The Clinton administration retaliated for these attacks on 21 August, firing cruise missiles against a factory in Khartoum alleged to be manufacturing nerve-gas components for use by bin Laden.[118] When the United States invaded Afghanistan after bin Laden's teams destroyed the World Trade Center in 2001, demonstrators in Khartoum rallied to claim that this invasion served Zionist interests[119] and Sudanese Islamic leaders like Hassan al-Turabi proclaimed the innocence of bin Laden.[120]

5   *The People of Sudan Are Opposed to UN Intervention in Their
Region and the Solution to Its problems Lies in the Hands of Darfur's
People, Who Oppose Foreign Interference. Sudan Will Resist by Force
if Necessary Any Efforts to Station UN Troops in Darfur.*

In August 2004, as widely reported in the Sudanese domestic media,
President al-Bashir and his allies mobilized backing from political, civil
society and Islamic organizations, governors of states, distinguished
Sufi leaders, and youth and student unions across Sudan to stage a
show of strength in opposition to the idea of stationing UN troops in
Darfur.[121] The Government of Sudan mobilized tens of thousands of
demonstrators in Khartoum's Martyrs Square on 4 August 2004 to
denounce the UN resolution on Darfur and condemn "all manner of
interference in the country's affairs." Demonstrators were brought out
by announcements of the government-backed rally on Sudan TV and
Sudan Radio the day before which featured Sudanese leaders calling
on all Sudanese to join the protests and interviews with politicians
and community leaders who charged that the West was trying to harm
Sudan. "In a spirit and power of faith, the masses of Khartoum state
... raised their voices high in rejecting the US-British threats against
Sudan," Radio Sudan's Khartoum correspondent exulted.[122]

In September 2004, with international pressure mounting for Sudan
to accept the stationing of foreign monitors in Darfur, the domestic
government media shifted their line to emphasize that the Darfurians
themselves rejected UN forces. On 18 September, Ahmad Ibrahim al-
Tahir, the speaker of the National Assembly, declared that the solution to the Darfur problem lay in the hands of the people of Darfur.[123]
President al-Bashir reiterated this point on 13 November 2005.[124] Early
in 2006, Sudanese government leaders launched a campaign to build
support for al-Bashir's theme.[125]

In March 2006 Sudanese leaders ratcheted up the intensity of their
campaign against the use of UN troops, bringing their message to
English speakers in Southern Sudan and to TV viewers. An English-
language story in the Juba *Post* on 2 March reported Minister of
Defence al-Rahim Muhammad Hasayn's boast that the army was willing to fight UN intervention and to "sacrifice our souls for the nation"
to ensure that Sudan did not become another Iraq.[126] And on 8 March,
Sudan TV featured a demonstration mounted by the Organization for
the Defence of Faith and the Country and the demonstrators' message
that they were ready to defend the nation whatever the cost.[127]

6   The African Union Is Fully Capable of Fulfilling Its Responsibilities in the Darfur Region without UN Reinforcements and Those Who Belittle the African Union's Abilities Do So from Anti-African motives.

After emphasizing for many years that it was fully capable of handling the Darfur situation and protecting its people, Sudan came under increasing pressure from the UN Security Council to accept an African Union monitoring force in Darfur. At the outset, Sudan's government danced frenetically around the role that an AU force might play in Darfur. In April 2004 it agreed in a signed ceasefire agreement with rebel groups in Darfur to allow AU military observers to monitor and report on the implementation of the ceasefire, and in June President al-Bashir stated on Sudan TV that the AU had a place in the Darfur process.[128] Near the end of July, after nothing had changed on the ground, the European Union threatened to take "appropriate further steps" if Sudan did not act to end the fighting, precipitating a declaration from Foreign Affairs Minister Mustafa Osman Isma'il that Sudan would fight foreign troops if they invaded Sudan.[129] Finally, at the beginning of August, the Sudanese News Agency reported in English, but not in Arabic, that the secretary general of the ruling National Congress Party recognized the important role that the AU might play in resolving outstanding issues in Darfur.[130] The Government of Sudan, according to BBC News, agreed to cooperate with the AU even though there was no formal agreement on a peacekeeping force.[131] None of these assurances that Sudan recognized a role for the AU were announced on Sudan Radio but limited instead to Sudan TV and one English-language press release from the Sudan News Agency.

Understanding that it would take a large force to monitor the ceasefire in Darfur, the AU prepared to deploy a startup brigade of 2,000 troops, but Foreign Affairs Minister Isma'il swiftly denounced this move. "The security of Darfur," he asserted, "is the responsibility of Darfur alone."[132] Isma'il would permit only 300 AU troops whose mission would be limited solely to protecting the ceasefire monitors, he said on 9 August 2004.[133] Sudanese listeners to Radio Sudan heard Sudanese Ambassador Uthman al-Sayyid insist that there was no agreement among the Government of Sudan, the African Union, and the United Nations to transform the AU troops into peacekeepers, that maintaining security remained the responsibility of the GOS, and that the AU would be allowed to deploy only 300 troops, rather than the 2,000 the AU expected.[134]

Just a week before the 30 August 2004 deadline set by the UN Security Council for the Sudanese government to face sanctions unless it started protecting civilians and disarmed its forces, Sudanese official and chief negotiator Majzoub al-Khalifa had rejected Nigerian President and African Union Chairman Olusegun Obasanjo's call for 2,000 AU troops to enter Darfur. Al-Khalifa insisted that the government would itself carry out the disarmament of its Janjaweed militia and the rebel groups: "The security role is the role of the government of Sudan and its security forces," he declared, concluding: "If there's a need, it will be discussed."[135] The Sudanese chief negotiator's statement provoked Abubakar Hamid Nour, coordinator for the rebel Justice and Equality Movement (JEM), to explode: "There is no way we can let our enemies disarm us. They are still killing us and bombing us."[136] On 26 October 2004 Sudan Radio finally reported that the National Assembly had approved expanding the number of AU troops in Darfur to 3,200.[137] Foreign Affairs Minister Isma'il declared that the African Union would be in charge of observing a ceasefire, identifying violations, building trust between the conflicting parties, monitoring the flow of humanitarian aid to the affected people, creating a suitable atmosphere for cessation of hostilities, and opening up opportunities for development.[138] He insisted that the government and the AU rejected the participation of any special foreign police force in Darfur.[139] The government also refused offers of US and Australian aircraft, except through the African Union.[140] He reiterated that only the GOS was capable of bringing peace and stability to Darfur.[141]

The attitude of the Government of Sudan towards its African Union shield has been ambivalent from the start. As early as October 2004, Sudanese government leaders had begun to insinuate that stationing more AU troops in Darfur could lead to a major AIDS epidemic in Sudan. Some members of Sudan's Parliament expressed the fear that "such large troops [sic] could affect the behaviour of inhabitants living in small villages, consequently spreading diseases."[142] On 7 September 2005 Minister of Health Ahmed Bilal Osman seized on the deaths from AIDS of two AU peacekeepers to announce that his government would refuse residence permits to any resident foreigner, including members of the AU forces, who tested positive for AIDS.[143] That same day, the health minister proclaimed that all AU and UN troops must undergo further tests for AIDS, with deportation following for those who tested positive.[144] As late as January 2006, the Government of Sudan charged AU troops with smuggling into Darfur "bombs, ammunition and explosives" and alleged that they were "spreading AIDS."[145]

Confronted by mounting pressure from the Security Council to accept the stationing of a robust and well-equipped UN force in Darfur, the Government of Sudan has ultimately grown to appreciate the political value of welcoming under-equipped and understaffed AU soldiers. It gradually converted the African Union's observer mission into a thick shield with which to fend off proposals that the UN dispatch troops to Darfur and to defend itself against United States charges of genocide in Darfur.[146] Only the African Union could make an objective determination of whether or not genocide was taking place, the Foreign Ministry declared in Arabic on the SUNA website in February 2006.[147] The Sudanese cabinet swiftly affirmed its confidence in the African Union's ability to maintain peace and stability in Darfur.[148] Praising the AU's ability to handle the Darfur situation in March, President al-Bashir declared on Sudan TV that the AU was capable and had the necessary experience to do the job.[149] In June, Radio Sudan reported to its wider audience the Ministry of Foreign Affairs claim that proposals to transfer the AU mission to the UN belittled the AU's capability and the ability of Africans to resolve their own problems.[150]

In August 2006, however, Sudanese officials seemed ready to abandon their cosy relationship with the African Union if it acted without regard for Sudan's wishes. In June, when AU leaders endorsed Security Council calls for the stationing of UN reinforcements in Darfur, Sudan's Foreign Ministry lashed out, charging via Sudan Radio that the AU had no right to invite UN troops to join AU forces in Sudan.[151] If the AU was unable to do the job, the Foreign Ministry affirmed, the Government of Sudan could look elsewhere and exercise its exclusive right to invite another regional or international power to assist in Darfur.[152] Paying heed to this threat, Sudan TV broadcast a rare statement in English by the African Union commission chairman on 21 June 2006 offering his opinion that his mission could not be converted into a UN mission without the permission of the GOS.[153]

But in June 2007 the threat of sanctions and overwhelming pressure from the African Union, as well as the governments of China and the United Kingdom, forced the Government of Sudan to accept in principle the creation of the United Nations-African Union Mission in Darfur (UNAMID), a hybrid multilateral force.[154] In two broadcasts on 1 August 2007, Sudan's foreign affairs minister, D. Lam Akol, and Khartoum's permanent representative to the UN, Adb al-Mahmud Abd al-Halim, laid down tropes that anticipated the obstructionist policies Sudan would deploy over the next twelve months. First, they emphasized, "the resolution said the troops will be an African one" (sic), and second, the "resolution did not contain sanctions, unlike the first and second copies of the [draft] resolutions."[155] Granting Sudan a veto over the nationalities of troops recruited for UNAMID and withdrawing the threat of sanctions if it did not facilitate the deployment of UNAMID to sustainable bases crippled the mission from the start.

7   International Attention to the Darfur Crisis Strengthens the Bargaining Position of the Rebel Groups and Makes Unlikely a Lasting Peace in the Region.

Finally, Sudanese officials consistently argued in the first half of 2006 that the introduction of sanctions and the insertion of a UN peacekeeping force would only invigorate the Darfur rebels and encourage more groups of Sudanese armed dissidents to take a hostile stance in the future. Imposing sanctions, Sudan's foreign minister declared on 29 January 2006, would obstruct the implementation of the CPA for Southern Sudan and send the wrong message to negotiators at the ongoing Darfur peace talks in Nigeria's federal capital, Abuja.[156] On 20 February 2006 Sudan Radio reiterated Sudanese objections to a UN peacekeeping force.[157] It reported Sudanese civil society organizations telling members of a visiting US congressional delegation that foreign intervention would only make matters worse.[158] After the US Congress disregarded this advice and passed a resolution condemning Sudan's Darfur policies, a representative of Sudan's foreign ministry warned on 7 April 2006 that further sanctions against the perpetrators of crime in Darfur would hinder efforts to achieve a political solution in the Abuja negotiations.[159] In the months that followed, the Government of Sudan did everything possible to fulfil its prophecies, splitting the Darfur resistance by buying off its leaders and reviving disputes over land and water rights.

How the Media Prepares the Population for Changes in Policy

The premise of this chapter is that the nature and tone of Sudan's government radio and TV coverage – that which is broadcast and that which is not – provide a reliable advance indicator of the Government of Sudan's intentions for wealth sharing, political power sharing, and security arrangements in Darfur. But do we know that Sudan's government conforms to Alexander George's theories and utilizes its media to prepare Sudan's population for changes in government policy? For a preliminary answer to that question, we can employ two events as controls – the preliminary wealth-sharing agreement of 31 December 2003 and the Comprehensive Peace Agreement for Southern Sudan of 9 January 2005 – and examine their treatment by the GOS's media before, during, and after these agreements were negotiated.

The Government of Sudan media were apparently given very little notice before the signing of the first agreement. The negotiations prior to December 2003 were characterized by the South African Institute for Security Studies as "secretive, elite driven, [and] narrowly focused."[160] Government broadcast media virtually ignored the peace talks with the rebel Sudan People's Liberation Movement/Army (SPLM/A) until December 2003, just before the signing of the first wealth-sharing agreement in January. On 11 and 17 December 2003, Sudan Radio for the first time announced that the southern rebels and the GOS soon were expected to sign a partial agreement on sharing wealth derived from national resources and that progress was being made on power sharing.[161] Evidently, the government was unsure of itself and could not agree on what direction to spin the news of the negotiations. Serious internal divisions over tactics, strategy, and factional power struggles within the National Islamic Front certainly contributed to that uncertainty.[162]

Without a clear consensus on wealth or power sharing among its members, Sudan's ruling political elite dropped stories about those key topics from government-owned broadcast outlets from 5 January 2004 until 17 December 2004, when Sudan Radio announced that a high-level government delegation was discussing the transfer of oil revenues and the setting up of branches of the central bank in the south.[163] The policy logjam had been broken.

Four days later, on 21 December 2004, Sudan Radio trumpeted the signing of an agreement on power sharing between SPLM/A President John Garang and Sudanese Vice-President Ali Osman Taha. Announcing generalities while stressing the value of avoiding "the devil" of details became an important mantra the government used in its statements about the negotiation of agreements with the rebel group.[164] Thus, Sudan Radio and TV referred frequently to wealth sharing but never announced that the wealth-sharing protocol provided for a 50–50 split of oil revenues between north and south.[165] In January 2005 President al-Bashir set out on a tour of Southern Sudan, proclaiming that the war was over and development of the south would soon follow, but key details of the wealth-sharing agreement remained unsettled and many vital facets of the CPA remain contested between the government and the SPLM/A.[166]

The Government of Sudan turned the accepted principle of conflict-resolution negotiation, which favours first seeking agreement on broad principles, into a defensive strategy calculated to subvert meaningful results. Beneath the government's ambivalence towards broadcasting the details of wealth sharing lay a multitude of motives. Although "an unwritten understanding that the SPLM [Sudan People's Liberation Movement] would receive either the finance or energy ministry" underlay the CPA, the SPLM/A was denied both ministries, forcing it to depend on the government for data on the value of Sudan's annual oil revenues and permitting government officials to understate those revenues at will.[167] Senior SPLM/A official Salva Kiir is the source of the assertion that President al-Bashir is convinced that the southerners will eventually vote for separation in the referendum scheduled to be held in 2011, six years after the signing of the CPA, regardless of who controls the finance and energy ministries.[168] In the meantime, Sudan continues to fund its growing domestic arms industry with revenues from its oil exports, which constituted 42 per cent of total government revenue in 2002 and amounted to 70 per cent of Sudan's total export revenues in 2005.[169]

Salva Kiir, the controversial southern politician named first vice-president of Sudan following the death of John Garang in a helicopter crash, expected the SPLM/A's appointees to the National Petroleum Commission to provide him with data on the quantity of oil being produced in the south, but events unfolded contrary to his expectations.[170] Interviewed by the Khartoum *Monitor*, Riek Machar, vice-president of Southern Sudan, declared that the Khartoum government had failed to transfer $500 million in oil revenue to his region, that the SPLM/A had no idea of the correct figures for oil revenues, and that only SPLM/A control of the energy ministry would provide a transparent means for dealing with this problem.[171]

Salva Kiir later came to recognize his mistake in not fighting harder to secure the finance or energy portfolio for the SPLM. In July 2006 he admitted that the National Petroleum Commission was dysfunctional, alleging that the National Congress Party of President al-Bashir refused to accept the mechanism that would ensure a 50–50 split of the oil revenues.[172] As of early August 2006, the National Petroleum Commission was meeting infrequently and the Government of Sudan and the SPLM/A were debating whether the commission should be an advisory or a decision-making body.[173] The National Congress Party's avoidance of the "devil" of details now seems to have been part of a strategy to gain international acceptance by signing a comprehensive peace agreement but rendering the agreement meaningless by bogging down its implementation in a welter of disputes over the meaning of its vague generalities. Death by a thousand cuts looms as the fate awaiting the Comprehensive Peace Agreement. By not broadcasting the details of wealth sharing and keeping fuzzy the specifics of the CPA, the Government of Sudan has given itself every opportunity to evade the intent of its two most important signed undertakings with the south. Sudan's broadcast strategy provides a valuable window on its true intention, which is looking more and more as if it is to retain exclusive control over the distribution of the oil revenues.

Sudanese government-owned broadcasters treated news of the negotiation of the Darfur Peace Agreement (DPA) with the same vagueness and lack of details with which they portrayed the Comprehensive Peace Agreement for the south. On 16 September 2005, Sudan Radio announced the start of the first phase of talks on power sharing, wealth sharing, and security arrangements.[174] As in the case of the CPA, after talks teetered on the verge of collapse throughout October and November,[175] President al-Bashir was quoted on Sudan Radio at the end of November declaring that the atmosphere at the talks was "suitable" for success.[176]

On 11 April 2006 the UN Security Council endorsed the deadline of 30 April 2006 set by the African Union for a comprehensive agreement between Sudan and the Darfur rebels.[177] All through February and March 2006, Sudan Radio and TV announced progress at the talks, but independent newspapers such as *al-Mashahir* emphasized that power- and wealth-sharing issues remained unresolved.[178] On 26 April, only four days before the deadline of 30 April and one day after the UN Security Council sanctioned four alleged war criminals in the Darfur conflict, did the Sudanese government and the rebels arrive at a preliminary understanding.[179] In a typically vague report, bereft of any specific details, Sudan Radio announced on 21 May that the minister for foreign affairs had explained the clauses on wealth sharing, power sharing, and security arrangements in Darfur to the ambassadors present at the Abuja peace negotiations.[180]

Ignored in reports emanating from Sudan Radio was the rejection of the peace accord by many of the Darfur rebels and the Sudanese government's armed attacks on groups in Darfur that refused to sign.[181]

On 2 July, Jan Pronk, UN special representative of the secretary general in Sudan, announced that the Darfur Peace Agreement was on the verge of collapse because it did not resonate with the people of Darfur. "So far," declared Pronk on his personal blog (www.janpronk.nl), "nothing has been done. None of the deadlines agreed in the text of the agreement have been met."[182] Violence in Darfur has escalated since the DPA was signed and violations of the accord have been ignored, Pronk reported on 6 July.[183]

Conclusion

The massive international campaign to end the Government of Sudan's support for Janjaweed attacks on unarmed civilians in Darfur has given birth to Khartoum's current strategy. Threatened with severe sanctions by the UN Security Council, the government pursued the appearance of compromising and granting greater autonomy and wealth sharing to rebellious regions. After dragging out negotiations for as long as possible, Khartoum agreed to sign nebulous peace agreements with the south and the west that led to years of disputation and negotiation over the meaning of their ambiguous terms. Prior to the signing of these peace agreements, Sudanese government broadcasters transmitted optimistic messages reporting steady progress and a positive atmosphere at the talks even in periods when the talks had collapsed and the Darfur rebels had rejected the terms of proposed peace agreements.[184]

We have learned from our analysis of Sudanese government broadcasts that there are different patterns for the government's use of Sudan Radio, Sudan TV, and the Internet. The Government of Sudan uses Sudan TV and the websites of the Sudanese News Agency to anticipate policy changes and shape the reactions to them among Sudan's educated elite. The government acts as if it fears and respects the potential for political activism among educated Sudanese. Radio Sudan, on the other hand, addresses poor workers and farmers with little time for politics and anti-government activities. Radio Sudan rarely anticipates policy changes. Rather, it is largely a valuable tool for mobilizing participation in government-organized mass demonstrations by the poor in Sudan's largest cities, strengthening the government's claims that any attempt to insert UN troops for the enforcement of peace in Darfur would meet with massive resistance from the majority of Sudanese. Yet, without UN troops, the African Union forces stationed in

Sudan are ill-equipped to protect civilians from Khartoum's twin policies of "divide and displace."[185]

Current indications from Sudan's broadcasts are that the National
Congress Party-dominated government in Khartoum will drag out the
process of implementing its signed agreements for as long as possible,
banking on its armed opponents in the south and in Darfur to sell
out or continue fighting among themselves, and relying on the tendency of the international community to lose patience and focus its
attention elsewhere. John Prendergast, one-time senior adviser to the
International Crisis Group, summarized the prospects for Darfur and
the south in a telling op-ed piece in the Boston *Globe* on 16 July 2006.
He wrote: "The regime in Khartoum has taken the measure of the
international community and believes it will face no consequence for
continuing to support the *Janjaweed* and blocking a UN peacekeeping
mission. As one high-ranking Sudanese government official brazenly
told me this week, 'The United Nations Security Council has threatened us so many times we no longer take it seriously.' That state of
impunity and arrogance is dangerous to the international system and
deadly to the people of Darfur."[186]

Unprepared by Sudan's government controlled media for the loss
of revenue that would accompany any seriously implemented sharing of oil revenues with the south and the west, and schooled by the
government media to regard southerners and Darfurians as fractious,
disorganized, and backward interlopers in the serious work of governing Sudan, Arab northerners are unready for accommodation with
the southern and western regions of the country which contribute the
bulk of its revenues. This is the surest indication that the Government
of Sudan has no intention of living with signed agreements pledging
greater autonomy, revenue sharing, and an integrated defence force
to the leaders of dissident movements in the south and the west. The
international community will ignore this evidence at its peril. The
struggle of the people in southern and western Sudan for greater
autonomy, a fair share of oil revenues, and security from attack has
only just begun.

Notes

* Frank Chalk would like to acknowledge the vital help he received at the start of his study of radio broadcasting from sociologist Kurt Jonassohn, his colleague and then co-director of the Montreal Institute for Genocide and Human Rights Studies (MIGS) at Concordia University, as well as the valuable research assistance provided for this paper and his current work on radio broadcasting and mass-atrocity crimes by MIGS graduate student-fellow Erin Jesse and MIGS interns Maha El-Kadi, Chiara Fish, Inken Heldt, Tara Tavender, and Scarlett Trazo. The outstanding research contributions of Danielle Kelton fully justify her listing as the co-author of this work. Helen Scadding Sproul of the BBC Monitoring Service (Caversham Park, U.K.), fulfilled every request for data with the enthusiasm and professional elan one expects from the BBC. Any errors of fact or interpretation are Frank Chalk's alone. Portions of this chapter were originally presented at the University of Western Ontario Conference on the Crisis in Darfur, 30 October 2005, London, Ontario.

1 Alexander George, "Prediction of Political Action by Means of Propaganda Analysis," *Public Opinion Quarterly*, vol. 20, no. 1, Special Issue in Political Communication (1956): 334–45; and *Propaganda Analysis: A Study of Inferences Made from Nazi Propaganda in World War II* (Evanston, Ill.: Row, Peterson 1959).
2 George, *Propaganda Analysis*, 47.
3 Ibid., especially chapter 2, "A General Action Schema for Propaganda Analysis," and chapter 11, "Prediction of an Elite's Major Actions."
4 Jeffrey Herf, "The 'Jewish War': Goebbels and the Antisemitic Campaigns of the Nazi Propaganda Ministry," *Holocaust and Genocide Studies*, vol. 19, no. 1 (2005): 51–80. Herf's research revises the conventional wisdom in the field, shaped by Hannah Arendt and others, which held that little in the German media substantially revealed the ferocity or the timing of the Nazis' actual implementation of their genocidal intentions towards the Jews of Europe. For a discussion of Arendt's early insights and change of position, see ibid., 54–5.
5 On the Responsibility to Protect, sometimes abbreviated as R2P, see Report of the International Commission on Intervention and State Sovereignty, *The Responsibility to Protect* (Ottawa: International Development Research Centre 2001).
6 "Key Facts: Sudan," UN Food and Agriculture Organization, http://www.fao.org/reliefoperations/app_sudan_intro_en.asp (accessed 30 June 2006); CIA, *The World Factbook*, "Sudan, Literacy,"

http://www.cia.gov/cia/publications/factbook/geos/su.html (accessed 30 June 2006).

7 Estimate from the Country Profile: Sudan, December 2004, "Telecommunications," Library of Congress: Federal Research Division, http://lcweb2.loc.gov/frd/cs/profiles/sudan.pdf (accessed 30 June 2006).

8 CIA, *The World Factbook*, "Sudan, Communications 2006," http://www.cia.gov/cia/publications/factbook/geos/su.html (accessed 30 June 2006).

9 International Press Institute, "World Press Freedom Review – 2005 – Sudan," http://www.freemedia.at/cms/ipi/freedom_detail.html?country=/KW0001/KW0004/KW0104/ (accessed 4 August 2006).

10 US Department of State, *Country Report on Human Rights Practices, 2005*, "Sudan, Section 2, Respect for Civil Liberties, including: a. Freedom of Speech and Press," http://www.state.gov/g/drl/rls/hrrpt/2005/61594.htm (accessed 4 August 2006).

11 Amnesty International Report, "Sudan – Intimidation and Denial – Attacks on Freedom of Expression in Darfur" (August 2004), http://web.amnesty.org/library/print/ENGAFR541012004 (accessed 7 July 2006).

12 US Department of State, *Country Report on Human Rights Practices, 2005*, "Sudan, Section 2, Respect for Civil Liberties, including: a. Freedom of Speech and Press," http://www.state.gov/g/drl/rls/hrrpt/2005/61594.htm (accessed 4 August 2006); "Sudan Suspends S Southern Paper," Reuters, 25 June 2005, http://www.sudantribune.com/article_impr.php3?id_article=10366 (accessed 30 May 2006); "Columnist Spends Weekend in Prison for Criticizing President," Reporters without Borders, 3 January 2006, http://www.sudantribune.com/article_impr.php3?id_article=13369 (accessed 30 May 2006).

13 "Sudanese Newspaper Suspended for Report on Defense Forces," AFP, 30 September 2003, http://www.sudantribune.com/article_impr.php3?id_article=427 (accessed 30 May 2006); "Sudanese Army Takes Newspaper to Court for 'Demeaning' Article," Associated Press, 14 July 2005, http://www.sudantribune.com/article_impr.php3?id_article=10645 (accessed 30 May 2006).

14 Amnesty International, "Sudan – Intimidation."

15 "New Crackdown on the Press in Sudan," Human Rights Watch News, 1 August 2003, http://www.hrw.org/press/2003/08/sudan080103.html (accessed 30 May 2006).

16 Ibid.; "Persecuted Sudanese Journalist Flees Country," Human Rights Watch News, 12 November 2003, http://www.sudantribune.com/

article_impr.php3?id_article=859 (accessed 30 May 2006); "Sudan Suspends Newspaper despite Promise to Stop Media Censorship," Associated Press, 10 November 2003, http://www.sudantribune.com/article_impr.php3?id_article=935 (accessed 30 May 2006).

17 "Sudan Arrests Editor, Cracks down on Press," UPI, 12 September 2004, http://www.sudantribune.com/article_impr.php3?id_article=5392 (accessed 30 May 2006); "Sudanese Government Lifts a 2 ½-year Ban on Pro-opposition Newspaper," Associated Press, 12 May 2005, http://www.sudantribune.com/article_impr.php3?id_article=9512 (accessed 30 May 2006).

18 "Al Jazeera TV Says Police Raid Its Khartoum Office," Reuters, 17 December 2003, http://www.sudantribune.com/article_impr.php3?id_article=1179 (accessed 30 May 2006).

19 Amnesty International report, "Sudan – Intimidation."

20 "Khartoum Shuts down Jazeera Office for Good," QNA, 1 January 2004, http://www.sudantribune.com/article_impr.php3?id_article=1341 (accessed 30 May 2006).

21 "Sudanese Court Jails Al-Jazeera Journalist for One Month," Associate Press, 10 April 2004, http://www.sudantribune.com/article_impr.php3?id_article=2438 (accessed 30 May 2006).

22 "Freelance Photographer Detained in Sudan," Associate Press, 27 April 2005, http://www.sudantribune.com/article_impr.php3?id_article= 9296 (accessed 30 May 2006).

23 "World Press Freedom Review – 2005: Sudan," International Press Institute, http://service.cms.apa.at/cms/ipi/freedom_detail-new.html?country=/KW001/KW004/KW0104 (accessed 30 May 2006).

24 Amnesty International report, "Sudan – Intimidation."

25 Ibid.

26 Glenn Kessler and Colum Lynch, "U.S. Calls Killings in Sudan Genocide," Washington Post, 10 September 2004, http://www.washingtonpost.com/wp-dyn/articles/A8364-2004Sep9.html (accessed 22 July 2006).

27 "Sudanese TV, Radio Coverage of Darfur on 9–16," BBC Monitoring Service, Source: BBC Monitoring Research in English, 16 September 2004.

28 United Nations Security Council (UNSC) Resolution 1556, adopted 30 July 2004.

29 UNSC Resolution 1564, adopted 18 September 2004.

30 "Sudanese Friday Preacher Says 'There Is No Genocide in Darfur,'" BBC Monitoring Service, Source: Sudan TV, Omdurman, in Arabic, 1030 Greenwich Mean Time (gmt), 17 September 2004.

31 "Sudan: Friday Preacher Says USA Making Inroads into Darfur to Enjoy Its Oil," BBC Monitoring Service, Source: Sudan TV, Omdurman, in Arabic, 20 August 2004.

32 "Sudan Criticizes Powell 'Dangerous' Remarks on Darfur," BBC Monitoring Service, Source: SUNA, in Arabic, 13 September 2004.

33 "Secretary General Visits Sudan (27–29 May 2005)," http://www.un.org/av/photo/sgtrips/sgsudanmay05.htm (accessed 25 July 2006).

34 "UN and Sudanese Team Goes to Darfur, Annan Reports Security Slightly Better," UN News Service, 16 June 2005, http://allafrica.com/ stories/printable/200506160003.html (accessed 22 July 2005).

35 Ibid.

36 "Kofi Annan Arrives in Sudan to Discuss Darfur, Peace Agreement," BBC Monitoring Service, Source: Sudan TV, Omdurman, in Arabic, 1000gmt, 27 May 2005; "UN's Annan in Talks with Sudanese Foreign Minister; to Visit Darfur 28 May," BBC Monitoring Service, Source: Republic of Sudan Radio, Omdurman, in Arabic, 0400gmt, 28 May 2005.

37 "Annan 'Overwhelmed' by Developments in Darfur, Says UN Envoy to Sudan," BBC Monitoring Service, Source: SUNA, in Arabic, 31 May 2005.

38 "Sudanese Women Protest to Visiting Annan over UN Resolutions," BBC Monitoring Service, Source: Sudan TV, Omdurman, in Arabic, 1000gmt, 27 May 2005.

39 "Rice Says Sudan Has Credibility Problem on Darfur," Reuters, 21 July 2005, http://www.sudantribune.com/ article_impr.php3?id_article=1074.s. (accessed 25 June 2006).

40 Ibid.

41 Ibid.

42 "Rice Visits Sudan's Troubled Darfur Region," BBC Monitoring Service, Source: Republic of Sudan Radio, Omdurman, in Arabic, 1300gmt, 21 July 2005.

43 "Sudan Thanks USA for Supporting Peace Process," BBC Monitoring Service, Source: Sudan TV, Omdurman, in Arabic, 1000gmt, 21 July 2005.

44 Joel Brinkley, "Sudanese Guard Roughs up US Aides and Reporter as Rice Visits," New York Times, 22 July 2005.

45 Ibid.

46 Ibid.

47 "Sudan: Friday Sermon Urges USA to De-link Its Policies from Jewish Lobby," BBC Monitoring Service, Source: Sudan TV, Omdurman, in Arabic, 1035gmt, 15 July 2005.

48 "Violations in Darfur, Sudan May Constitute War Crimes, Crimes against Humanity, UN Human Rights Office Report Says," UN Press Release AFR/921 HR/4744, 7 May 2004. For the complete report, see UN Commission for Human Rights, "Report of the High Commissioner for Human Rights: Situation of Human Rights in the

Darfur Region of the Sudan," 7 May 2004, 61st session, E/CN.4/2005/3, http://www.unhchr.ch/pdf/chr60/ECN420053.doc (accessed 6 August 2006).

49 "Sudanese Official Says Western Quarters Targeting Sudan because of Its Wealth," BBC Monitoring Service, Source: Republic of Sudan Radio, Omdurman, in Arabic, 1600gmt, 24 July 2004.

50 "Sudanese, Chadian Leaders Meet in Ethiopia over Darfur," BBC Monitoring Service, Source: Republic of Sudan Radio, Omdurman, in Arabic, 0400gmt, 8 July 2004; "WHO Regional Boss Denies Occurrence of 'Genocide' in Darfur," BBC Monitoring Service, Source: Republic of Sudan Radio, Omdurman, in Arabic 1600gmt, 20 August 2004.

51 "Sudan: Friday Preacher Says USA Making Inroads into Darfur to Enjoy Its Oil."

52 UNSC Resolution 1556, adopted 30 July 2004.

53 Ibid.

54 "Sudanese TV and Radio Coverage of Darfur 1–2 August," BBC Monitoring Service, Source: BBC Monitoring Research, 2 August 2004; "Darfur Urges Mobilization against 'US-Zionist Conspiracy,'" BBC Monitoring Service, Source: Sudan TV, Omdurman, in Arabic, 1900gmt, 3 August 2004.

55 "Sudan: Vice-President Taha Says Foreign Intervention over Darfur 'Dreams,'" BBC Monitoring Service, Source: Sudan TV, Omdurman, in Arabic, 1900gmt, 9 August 2004.

56 "Sudanese Friday Preacher Calls for a United Front to Defend Nation," BBC Monitoring Service, Source: Sudan TV, Omdurman, in Arabic, 1030gmt, 30 July 2004.

57 "Sudan Rejects UN Resolution on Darfur," BBC Monitoring Service, Source: Sudan TV, Omdurman, in Arabic, 1900gmt, 1 August 2004.

58 UNSC Resolution 1564, adopted 18 September 2004.

59 "Sudanese Friday Preacher Says 'There Is No Genocide in Darfur.'"

60 Ibid.

61 "Sudanese President Says 'Zionism, Free Masons' behind Coup Plot," BBC Monitoring Service, Source: Sudan TV, Omdurman, in Arabic, 0700gmt, 26 September 2004.

62 "Sudanese Delegation Says Western, Zionist Influence Clear at Darfur Talks," BBC Monitoring Service, Source: Republic of Sudan Radio, Omdurman, in Arabic, 1600gmt, 18 September 2004.

63 "US-Zionist Plan to Set up a Zaghawa State," BBC Monitoring Service, Source: Sudan TV website, Omdurman, in Arabic, 0001gmt, 10 November 2004.

64 UNSC Resolution 1593, adopted 31 March 2005.

65 "Sudan Calls for General Mobilization against UN Resolution in Darfur," BBC Monitoring Service, Source: Republic of Sudan Radio, Omdurman, in Arabic, 0400gmt, 2 April 2005.

66 "Sudanese Leader Vows Not to Respect UN Resolution on Darfur Crimes," BBC Monitoring Service, Source: Republic of Sudan Radio, Omdurman, in Arabic, 1323gmt, 2 April 2005.

67 The National Islamic Front (NIF) staged the 1989 coup; later it created the National Congress Party as a front. Both still exist, with the NIF constituting the inner core of the pro-Islamist forces within the GOS. See Alex de Waal, ed., *War in Darfur and the Search for Peace* (Cambridge, Mass.: Harvard University Press, 2007), 13–14; and http://www.nationmaster.com/encyclopedia/National-Islamic-Front.

68 "Sudan Calls for General Mobilization."

69 "Sudan: 'Angry' Anti-UN Demonstrations to be Staged in Capital," BBC Monitoring Service, Source: Republic of Sudan Radio, Omdurman, in Arabic, 0400gmt, 5 April 2005.

70 "Sudanese Minister Says Darfur Rebels 'Benefiting from the Jewish Campaign,'" BBC Monitoring Service, Source: Sudanese Media Center website, Khartoum, in Arabic, 27 March 2005.

71 Chris Stephen, "Sudan Stalling over War Crimes Inquiry, United Nations Told," *The Scotsman*, 30 June 2005, http://news.scotsman.com/international/cfm?id=718442005 (accessed 2 August 2006). By 2006, the ICC had set up an office in Chad, just across the border from Darfur, to collect evidence from survivors of Janjaweed and Sudanese government attacks. See Fritz Roy A. Sterling, "Sudan: ICC Reports Evidence of Large-Scale Massacres," International Press Service News Agency, 15 June 2006, http://www.ipsnews.net/news.asp?idnews=33635 (accessed 1 August 2006).

72 "Programme Summary of Sudanese TV News," BBC Monitoring Service, Source: Sudan TV, Omdurman, in Arabic, 1900gmt, 11 June 2005.

73 "Sudan's Darfur Crimes Courts to Hold First Hearing 18 June," BBC Monitoring Service, Source, AFP News Agency, Paris, in English, 16 June 2005.

74 "Sudanese War Crimes Court Reportedly Questions Its Legal Status – UN Report," BBC Monitoring Service, Source: UN Integrated Informational Network, Nairobi, in English, 24 June 2005.

75 "Darfur: Talks Stalled by Violence," Reuters, 14 October 2005; "Darfur Talks Marred by Fighting," BBC, 1 February 2006, http://news.bbc.co.uk/2/hi/africa/4671422.stm (accessed 6 August 2006); Joel Brinkley, "U.S. Presses Sudan and Rebels to Reach Darfur Peace Pact," New York *Times*, 4 May 2006.

76 "Darfur Rebels Reportedly Vandalize Schools, Health Centres," BBC
    Monitoring Service, Source: Sudanese Media Centre website, in
    Arabic, 8 November 2005; "Sudan Optimistic about the Next Round
    of Darfur Peace Talks," BBC Monitoring Service, Source: *Al-Mashahir*
    website, in Arabic, 9 November 2005; "Five AU Soldiers Wounded in
    Sudan's Darfur Region," BBC Monitoring Service, Source: *Al-Mashahir*
    website, in Arabic, 2 December 2005; "Sudanese Government, Darfur
    Rebels Discuss Wealth Sharing," BBC Monitoring Service, Source:
    Sudan TV, Omdurman, in Arabic, 13 December 2005; "Sudan: Seven
    Killed, Twenty Injured in Rebel Ambush in Western Darfur State," BBC
    Monitoring Service, Source: Republic of Sudan Radio, Omdurman, in
    Arabic, 1700gmt, 25 December 2005; "Sudan – UN Agency Says Darfur
    Rebels Attacked Food Convoy," *Al-Mashahir* website, in Arabic, 9
    February 2006.
77 "Sudan: Darfur Residents Protest against Calls for UN Peacekeeping
    Troops," BBC Monitoring Service, Source: Republic of Sudan Radio,
    Omdurman, in Arabic, 1300gmt, 17 January 2006.
78 "Sudan Leader Stresses Need for AU Intervention in Darfur," BBC
    Monitoring Service, Source: Republic of Sudan Radio, Omdurman, in
    Arabic, 1300gmt, 15 January 2006; "Programme Summary of Sudanese
    TV news," BBC Monitoring Service, Source: Sudan TV, Omdurman, in
    Arabic, 1900gmt, 4 March 2006; "Sudanese President Says AU Troops
    'Capable of Handling Darfur Issue,'" BBC Monitoring Service, Source:
    Sudan TV, Omdurman, in Arabic, 0855gmt, 28 March 2006.
79 "Sudan: Intervention by UN Forces in Darfur 'Unacceptable' –
    Governor," BBC Monitoring Service, Source: Republic of Sudan Radio,
    Omdurman, in Arabic, 1300gmt, 25 February 2006
80 "Sudanese Political Organizations Reject Foreign Intervention," BBC
    Monitoring Service, Source: Republic of Sudan Radio, Omdurman, in
    Arabic, 1300gmt, 4 March 2006; "Sudanese President Praises 'Open-
    hearted Dialogue' at Summit," BBC Monitoring Service, Source: Sudan
    TV, Omdurman, in Arabic, 0800gmt, 29 March 2006; "Sudan Opposed
    to Foreign 'Interference' over Darfur Crisis, Says VP," BBC Monitoring
    Service, Source: Republic of Sudan Radio, Omdurman, in Arabic,
    25 May 2006.
81 "Sudanese Political Organizations Reject Foreign Intervention";
    "President al-Bashir Says Sudan Will Not Be 'Recolonized,'" BBC
    Monitoring Service, Source: Sudan TV, Omdurman, in English,
    20 June 2006.
82 Programme Summary of Sudanese TV News," BBC Monitoring
    Service, Source: Sudan TV, Omdurman, in Arabic, 1900gmt, 6 March
    2006; "Programme Summary of Sudanese TV News," BBC Monitoring

Service, Source: Sudan TV, Omdurman, in Arabic, 1900gmt, 8 March 2006.

83 The UN placed restrictions on the assets and international travel of Major-General Gaffar Mohamed Elhassan, the commander of the Western Military Region for the Sudanese air force; Adam Yacub Shant, the commander of the Sudanese Liberation Army (a rebel group); Gabril Abdul Kareem Badri, the field commander of the National Movement for Reform (another rebel group); and Sheikh Musa Hilal, the paramount chief of the Jalul tribe in North Darfur (a top Janjaweed commander). See "Darfur: UN Council Imposes Sanctions on Four Individuals, Urges Peace Accord," UN News Center, 25 April 2006, http://www.un.org/apps/news/story.asp?NewsID=18247&Cr=Sudan&Cr1 (accessed 18 July 2006).

84 "Sudan Says UN Resolutions on Sanctions 'Regrettable,'" BBC Monitoring Service, Source: Republic of Sudan Radio, Omdurman, in Arabic, 1300gmt, 26 April 2006.

85 "Sudanese Cleric against UN Troops in Darfur; Predicts Fall of USA over Iraq War," BBC Monitoring Service, Source: Sudan TV, Omdurman, in Arabic, 1030gmt, 26 May 2006.

86 "President al-Bashir Affirms Rejection of UN Forces in Darfur," 29 June 2006, Sudan News Agency dispatch, http://www.SUNA-sd.net/DetialsE.asp?id=301621 (accessed 30 June 2006).

87 Ibid.

88 "UNHCR Chief Has No Authority to Talk about Darfur Autonomy – Sudanese Official," BBC Monitoring Service, Source: SUNA website, in Arabic, 29 September 2004.

89 "Sudan: 'Angry' anti-UN Demonstrations to be Staged in Capital"; "Sudanese Political Organizations Reject Foreign Intervention"; "Programme Summary of Sudanese TV News," BBC Monitoring Service, Source: Sudan TV, Omdurman, in Arabic, 16 March 2006.

90 "Programme Summary of Sudan TV News," BBC Monitoring Service, Source: Sudan TV, Omdurman, in Arabic, 24 June 2006; Eric Reeves, "Quantifying Genocide in Darfur: May 13, 2006 (Part 2)," http://www.sudanreeves.org/index.php?name=News&file=article&sid=104 (accessed 7 August 2006).

91 "Programme Summary of Sudan TV News," BBC Monitoring Service, Source: Sudan TV, Omdurman, in Arabic, 11 June 2006; "Programme Summary of Sudan TV News," BBC Monitoring Service, Source: Sudan TV, Omdurman, in Arabic, 13 June 2006.

92 "Approximately 75 percent of all villages in Darfur were burned by February 2005, leaving precious little remaining to destroy; many experts believe this is the reason that large-scale violence subsided

in early summer 2005 and not from any change in policy or sudden government beneficence or, in fact, AU intervention." See William G. O'Neill and Violette Cassis, "Protecting Two Million Internally Displaced: The Successes and Shortcomings of the African Union in Darfur," *Occasional Paper*, Brookings Institution-University of Bern Project on Internal Displacement, November 2005, 18, http://www.brookings.edu/fp/projects/idp/200511_au_darfur.pdf (accessed 7 August 2006).

93 "Al-Bashir Says No Citizen Will Be Tried outside Sudan," BBC Monitoring Service, Source: SUNA website, in English, 3 April 2005; "Sudanese President Reiterates 'Solemn Pledge' Not to Hand over Darfur Suspects," BBC Monitoring, Service, Source: SUNA website, in Arabic, 27 April 2005. The International Commission of Inquiry on Darfur recommended to the United Nations that the Sudanese Special Courts for Darfur should be closed down, declaring: "The fact that the Specialised Courts apply principally to the Darfurs and Korduvan, rather than to the whole of the Sudan, calls into question the credibility and reliability of these Courts. The purpose of the courts is too glaring to miss. The Government would do a great service to its judicial system if it took steps to repeal the decree that established the Courts. The Commission recommends that the Government ensure the closure of the Courts." See International Commission of Inquiry on Darfur, "Report of the International Commission of Inquiry on Darfur to the United Nations Secretary-General," 25 January 2005, Geneva, 110–15.

94 "Sudan: Darfur Rapes Not 'Planned, Systematic,' Judge Says," 24 October 2005, BBC Monitoring Service, SUNA website, Khartoum, in Arabic.

95 Ibid.

96 "Sudanese Court Sentences Two Soldiers to Death for Darfur War Crime," BBC Monitoring Service, *Al-Mashahir* (Almshaheer) website, Khartoum, in Arabic, 17 November 2005.

97 "Programme Summary of Sudan TV News," BBC Monitoring Service, Source: Sudan TV, Omdurman, in Arabic, 13 June 2006; "Programme Summary of Sudan TV News," BBC Monitoring Service, Source: Sudan TV, Omdurman, in Arabic, 25 June 2006; "Sudan 'Blocks' UN Trip to Darfur," BBC News, 3 April 2006 http://news.bbc.co.uk/go/pr/fr/-/2/hi/africa/4870954.stm (accessed 19 July 2006).

98 Marc Lacey, "Sudan Blocks Visit of U.N. Official to Darfur," New York *Times*, 3 April 2006, http://www.sudan.net/news/posted/12726.html (accessed 7 August 2006).

99 "Sudan Condemns UN's 'Insistence' to Deploy Military Mission in Darfur," BBC Monitoring Service, Source: Republic of Sudan Radio, Omdurman, in Arabic, 15 June 2006.

100 "Sudanese Cleric Hails Somali Islamic Courts' Victory in Mogadishu," BBC Monitoring Service, Source: Sudan TV, Omdurman, in Arabic, 16 June 2006.

101 "President al-Bashir Says Sudan Will Not Be 'Recolonized.'"

102 As of 30 April 2006, the UN Mission in south Sudan (UNMIS) force contained 9,265 uniformed personnel, including 8,034 troops, 635 military observers, and 596 police supported by 671 international civilian personnel, 1,242 local civilians, and 99 United Nations volunteers. "Sudan – UNMIS – Facts and Figures," United Nations, Department of Peacekeeping Operations, http://www.un.org/Depts/dpko/missions/unmis/facts.html (accessed 4 August 2006).

103 UNMIS was created on 24 March 2005 by Security Council Resolution 1590. Sudan TV reported on 28 March that the Sudanese defence minister had briefed the cabinet on the UN resolution. On 21 April 2005 the Sudanese News Agency website announced the formation of a government body to coordinate with the UN mission in the south.

104 "Sudan: Official Claims War in Darfur 'US-Zionist' Plot to Fan Conflict," BBC Monitoring Service, Source: Al-Ra'y al-Amm website, 29 April 2003; "Sudanese President Says 'Zionism, Free Masons' behind Coup Plot."

105 "Programme Summary of Sudanese TV News," BBC Monitoring Service, Source: Sudan TV, Omdurman, in Arabic, 1900gmt, 1 July 2004; "Sudanese Interior Minister Accuses Eritrea of Being behind Darfur Crisis," BBC Monitoring Service, Source: Sudanese TV, Omdurman, in Arabic, 19 July 2004.

106 "Sudanese Delegation Says Western, Zionist Influence Clear at Darfur Talks."

107 "US-Zionist Plan to Set up a Zaghawa State."

108 Ibid.

109 "Sudan People's Liberation Army," Federation of American Scientists Intelligence Resource Program, http://www.fas.org/irp/world/para/spla.htm (accessed 16 June 2006).

110 In June 1985, after Nimeiri was overthrown in a coup, Sudan's first vice-president, Omar Mohammed el-Tayeb, was placed on trial by the makers of the coup for his alleged role in this airlift and charged with accepting $2 million from the CIA, a sum purportedly received from Jewish organizations. In 1986 el-Tayeb was sentenced to two consecutive thirty-year jail terms for his role in the operation. See Sheila Rule, "Ex-Sudan Aide Gets 2 Jail Terms for Role in Ethiopian Airlift," New York Times, 6 April 1986.

111 Frontline, "Hunting Bin Laden," PBS, http://www.pbs.org/wgbh/pages/frontline/shows/binladen/who/alqaeda.html (accessed 19 July 2006); "Omar al-Bashir," New Internationalist, October 2001,

http://www.thirdworldtraveler.com/Zeroes/Omar_al-Bashir.html
(accessed 19 July 2006).

112 Emily Wax, "Sudan's Unbowed, Unbroken Inner Circle: Tight Web of
Savvy Leaders Withstands International Criticism," Washington *Post*,
3 May 2005, http://www.washingtonpost.com/wp-dyn/content/
article/2005/05/02/AR2005050201451_pf.html (accessed 25 July 2006).

113 Ibid.

114 David Blair, "Man Who Harbored Bin Laden Is Lodestar for
Terrorists," *The Telegraph*, 30 January 2006, http://telegraph.co.uk/
news/main.jhtml?xml=/news/2006/01/30/wturab30.xml&sSheet=/
news/2006/01/30/ixworld.html (accessed 1 August 2006).

115 "Mubarak, Bashir Discuss Significant Issues," *Arabic News*,
14 May 2001, http://www.arabicnews.com/ansub/Daily/
Day/010514/2001051446.html (accessed 3 August 2006).

116 Wax, "Sudan's Unbowed, Unbroken Inner Circle."

117 James Risen, "Sudan, Angry at U.S. Attack, Freed Bomb Suspects,
Officials Say," New York *Times*, 30 July 1999,
http://www.library.cornell.edu/colldev/mideast/sudsus.htm (accessed
25 July 2006); Michael Grunwald and Vernon Loeb, "Charges Filed
against Bin Laden," Washington *Post*, 5 November 1998, A17.

118 Ibid.

119 "Sudan: Anti-American Demo Staged in Khartoum," BBC Monitoring
Service, Source: SUNA website, in English, 8 October 2001.

120 For Turabi's view that bin Laden "is a friend who has not transgressed
against anyone in the first place, neither by making a statement nor by
a leaflet ... it was the Western media that built a monument for him as
the person who struggled against the West and against imperialistic
hegemony and was followed by some people who had emotion," see
Sudan Tribune, 4 November 2005, http://www.sudantribune.com/
article.php3?id_article=12393 (accessed 25 July 2006).

121 "'Massive' Demo Plan on August 4 to Support Sudan's Darfur Stand,"
BBC Monitoring Service, Source: Sudan TV, Omdurman, in Arabic,
1900gmt, 3 August 2004.

122 BBC News, "Sudanese Media Rally Public," 5 August 2005.

123 "Sudanese Delegation Says Western, Zionist Influence Clear at Darfur
Talks."

124 "Certain Foreign Circles Fanning War in Darfur – Sudanese
President," BBC Monitoring Service, Source: SUNA website, in
English, 13 November 2005.

125 "Sudanese Political Organizations Reject Foreign Intervention";
"Programme Summary of Sudanese TV News," BBC Monitoring
Service, Source: Sudan TV, Omdurman, in Arabic, 1900gmt, 6 March

2006; "Programme Summary of Sudanese TV News," BBC Monitoring Service, Source: Sudan TV, Omdurman, in Arabic, 14 March 2006; "Programme Summary of Sudanese TV News," BBC Monitoring Service, Source: Sudan TV, Omdurman, in Arabic, 16 March 2006; "Programme Summary of Sudanese TV News," BBC Monitoring Service, Source: Sudan TV, Omdurman, in Arabic, 1900gmt, 7 April 2006; "Programme Summary of Sudanese TV News," BBC Monitoring Service, Source: Sudan TV, Omdurman, in Arabic, 4 July 2006.

126 "Sudan Ready to Fight UN Intervention, Minister Says," BBC Monitoring Service, Source: Juba *Post*, in English, 2 March 2006.

127 "Sudanese Civil Society Groups Organize Anti-UN Demos in Khartoum," BBC Monitoring Service, Source: Sudan TV, Omdurman, in English, 1500gmt, 8 March 2006.

128 "Empty Promises? Continuing Abuses in Darfur, Sudan," Human Rights Watch Briefing Report, 11 August 2004, http://hrw.org/ backgrounder/africa/sudan/2004/sudan0804.pdf (accessed 24 July 2006).

129 "Sudan 'Will Fight Foreign Troops,'" CNN, 27 July 2004, http://edition. cnn.com/2004/WORLD/africa/07/27/sudan.main/ (accessed 24 July 2006).

130 "Sudanese Official Says African Union Capable of Solving Darfur Conflict," BBC Monitoring Service, Source: SUNA website, in English, 2 August 2004.

131 "UN Says Sudan Agrees to Darfur Steps," BBC, 5 August 2004, http://news.bbc.co.uk/2/hi/africa/3540366.stm (accessed 24 July 2006).

132 "Sudan Rejects AU Peace Force," BBC, 9 August 2004, http://news.bbc.co.uk/2/hi/africa/3549208.stm (accessed 24 July 2006).

133 Ibid.

134 "Sudan Radio Reports State Rejection of Deployment African Peacekeepers in Darfur," BBC Monitoring Service, Source: Republic of Sudan Radio, Omdurman, in Arabic, 0420gmt, 9 August 2004.

135 "Sudan Rejects Peacekeepers during Darfur Talks," PBS Online Newshour, 23 August 2004, http://www.pbs.org/newshour/updates/ sudan_08-23-04.html (accessed 26 July 2006).

136 Ibid.

137 "Sudanese Parliament Approves Expansion of AU Troops in Darfur," BBC Monitoring Service, Source: Republic of Sudan Radio, Omdurman, in Arabic, 1500gmt, 16 October 2004.

138 Ibid.

139 Ibid.

140 Ibid.

141 Ibid.

142 "Sudanese MPs Say More AU Forces in Darfur 'Could Spread Diseases to Villages,'" BBC Monitoring Service, Source: *Al-Khartoum*, Khartoum, in Arabic, 2 October 2004.

143 "Sudan Orders Fresh AIDS Tests for Peacekeepers, Issues 'Behavioral Code,'" *Sudan Tribune*, 7 September 2005, http://www.sudantribune.com/article_impr.php3?id_article=11527 (accessed 24 July 2006).

144 Ibid.; "Sudan to Detect HIV/AIDS among Resident Foreigners," *Sudan Tribune*, 7 September 2005, http://www.sudantribune.com/article_impr.php3?id_article=11523 (accessed 24 July 2006); "Sudan: In the Driving Seat," *Africa Confidential*, vol. 46, no. 20 (7 October 2005): 2.

145 Ibid.; "Sudan Seizes UN Containers Containing 'Bombs, Ammunition," BBC Monitoring Service, Source: *Al-Khartoum*, Khartoum, 17 January 2006.

146 The African Union soldiers also lacked "money, aircraft and signals technology." See "Sudan: 'Beyond That Now,'" *Africa Confidential*, vol. 47, no. 2 (20 January 2006): 5.

147 "Sudan Terms 'Totally Untrue' US Claims of Genocide in Darfur," BBC Monitoring Service, Source, SUNA website, in Arabic, 18 February 2006.

148 "Sudanese Cabinet Rejects Foreign Intervention in Troubled Darfur Region," BBC Monitoring Service, Source: SUNA website, in Arabic, 26 February 2006.

149 "Sudanese President Says AU Troops 'Capable' of Handling Darfur Issue."

150 "Sudan Condemns UN's 'Insistence' to Deploy Military Mission in Darfur."

151 Ibid.

152 Ibid.

153 "AU Chief Says Mandate in Darfur Remains Unchanged," BBC Monitoring Service, Source: Sudan TV, Omdurman, in English, 21 June 2006.

154 For details regarding the formation and mandate of UNAMID, see http://www.un.org/Depts/dpko/missions/unamid/mandate.html.

155 "Sudan UN Envoy Says Darfur Resolution Considered Khartoum 'Concerns,'" BBC Monitoring Service, Source: Republic of Sudan Radio, Omdurman, in Arabic, 1 August 2007; and BBC Monitoring Service, Source: "Programme Summary of Sudan Radio News," 0400 gmt, Omdurman, in Arabic, 1 August 2007.

156 "Sudanese Foreign Minister Warns Sanctions to Threaten Peace Agreement," BBC Monitoring Service, Source: *Al-Khartoum*, in Arabic, 29 January 2006.

157 "Sudan Reiterates Objection to UN Peacekeeping Force," BBC Monitoring Service, Source: Republic of Sudan Radio, Omdurman, in Arabic, 20 February 2006.

158 Ibid.

159 "Sudan Slams US Congress Resolution on Darfur," BBC Monitoring Service, Source: *Al-Watan*, in Arabic, 7 April 2006.

160 Institute for Security Studies (Pretoria, South Africa), "The Sudan IGAD Process: Signposts for the Way Forward," *African Security Analysis Programme*, Occasional Paper, 13 February 2004, 7, http://www.sudantribune.com/IMG/pdf/IGAD_peace_ process20040213.pdf (accessed 29 July 2006). Published as ISS Paper no. 86 (March 2004) without pagination at: http://www.issafrica.org/ pubs/papers/86/Paper86.htm.

161 "Sudanese Radio Reports Progress at Peace Talks in Kenya," BBC Monitoring Service, Source: Republic of Sudan Radio, Omdurman, in Arabic, 0400gmt, 11 December 2003; "Sudanese Government, Rebels Expect to Sign Partial Accord on Resources," BBC Monitoring Service, Source: Republic of Sudan Radio, Omdurman, in Arabic, 1600gmt, 17 December 2003.

162 Eric Reeves, "Hopes Fading in Naivasha (Kenya) for Sudan Peace," http://www.blue-nile.org/September-2003.htm (accessed 29 July 2006).

163 "Sudanese Government Delegation in Kenya Discusses Wealth Sharing," BBC Monitoring Service, Source: Republic of Sudan Radio, Omdurman, in Arabic, 1600gmt, 17 December 2004.

164 See, for example, the comments on the "devil" of details of Sayyid al-Khatib, the official spokesperson of the Sudanese government negotiating team at Naivasha in his interview with the London-based Arabic newspaper *Al-Sharq al-Awsat*, translated by the BBC Monitoring Service and reproduced in "Sudan Govt., SPLM Agree to Transform Bilateral Peace Deal to a National One," *Sudan Tribune*, 1 June 2004, http://www.sudantribune.com/article_impr.php3?id_article=3205 (accessed 1 August 2006).

165 The Sudan Radio Service, funded by the US Agency for International Development and broadcasting in English from Kenya, announced the oil revenue protocol and the 50–50 split on 12 November 2004. We have found no reference to the 50–50 split of oil revenues in any broadcast originating with Sudan Radio and TV.

166 "Sudanese President Addresses Biggest Town in South," BBC Monitoring Service, Source: Republic of Sudan Radio, Omdurman, in Arabic, 10 January 2005.

167 Human Rights Watch, "The Impact of the Comprehensive Peace Agreement and the New Government of National Unity on Southern

Sudan," no. 1 (March 2006): 7, http://hrw.org/backgrounder/africa/sudan0306/sudan0306.pdf (accessed 2 August 2006).

168 Ibid., 8.

169 Human Rights Watch, *Sudan, Oil and Human Rights* (New York: Human Rights Watch, 2003), 59. Available at: http://www.hrw.org/reports/2003/sudan1103/. See also US Energy Information Administration, "Sudan: Background," http://www.eia.doe.gov/emeu/cabs/Sudan/Background.html (accessed 3 August 2006).

170 Ibid., citing Salva Kiir's speech at American University, Washington, D.C., 6 November 2005.

171 "South Sudan Vice-President Interviewed on Oil Revenue, Refugees, Other Issues," BBC Monitoring Service, Source: Khartoum *Monitor* website, 27 January 2006.

172 James Morgan, "Sudan's Kiir Says There Is Slow Progress in Peace Implementation," *Sudan Tribune*, 20 July 2006, www.sudantribune.com/article_impr.php3?id_article=16729 (accessed 2 August 2006).

173 UNSC, "Report of the Secretary-General on the Sudan," s/2006/426, 23 June 2006.

174 "Sudan's Abuja Peace Negotiators to Conduct Workshops to Consolidate Opinions," BBC Monitoring Service, Source: Republic of Sudan Radio, Omdurman, in Arabic, 1600gmt, 16 September 2005.

175 "Sudan's Darfur Cease-fire Agreement 'on Brink of Collapse,'" BBC Monitoring Service, Source: *Al-Mashahir* website, 15 October 2005; "Sudanese Peace Talks Adjourned, Progress 'Negligible,'" BBC Monitoring Service, Source: *Al-Ra'y al-Amm* website, 21 October 2005.

176 "Sudan's Al-Bashir Says Atmosphere 'Suitable' for Success of Abuja Talks," BBC Monitoring Service, Source: Republic of Sudan Radio, Omdurman, in Arabic, 28 November 2005.

177 "UN Security Council Says Darfur Peace Deal Must Occur by April 30th," *Sudan Tribune*, 11 April 2006; UNSC Presidential Statement, 11 April 2006, S/PRST/2006/16.

178 "Sudan: Power, Wealth-sharing Committees Continue Meetings in Abuja," BBC Monitoring Service, Source: Republic of Sudan Radio, Omdurman, in Arabic, 7 February 2006; "Sudan, Darfur Rebels Fail to Agree on Power Sharing in Abuja," BBC Monitoring Service, Source: *Al-Mashahir* website, 13 February 2006.

179 UNSC Resolution 1672, adopted 25 April 2005; "Programme summary of Sudanese TV News," BBC Monitoring Service, Source: Sudan TV, Omdurman, in Arabic, 15 March 2006.

180 "Sudan: State Minister Briefs Ambassadors on Abuja Peace Accord," BBC Monitoring Service, Source: Republic of Sudan Radio, Omdurman, in Arabic, 1500gmt, 21 May 2006.

181 Xan Rice and Ewen MacAskill, "Darfur Peace Hopes Collapse as Rebels Reject Proposed Deal," *Guardian*, 1 May 2006.

182 "'Darfur Peace Deal on Brink of Collapse,' UN's Pronk," Associated Press, 2 July 2006, http://www.janpronk. nl/index.php?article16480 (accessed 6 August 2006).

183 "Darfur Violence Worse since Peace Deal – UN Pronk," Reuters, 6 July 2006, http://www.sudantribune.com/article.php3?id_article=16552 (accessed 6 August 2006).

184 "Sudanese Government, Rebels Close to Deal – Vice President," BBC Monitoring Service, Source: *Al-Ra'y al-Amm* website, in Arabic, 15 May 2004; "Sudan's Darfur Cease-fire Agreement on Brink of Collapse"; "Sudan Optimistic about the Next Round of Darfur Peace Talks"; "Sudan, Darfur Rebels Fail to Agree on Power Sharing in Abuja"; "Sudanese Vice-President Meets Darfur Rebel Leader," BBC Monitoring Service, Source: SUNA website, in Arabic, 10 April 2006; "No Breakthrough in Talks between Sudanese Government, Darfur Rebels," BBC Monitoring Service, Source: UN Integrated Regional Information Network, in English, 11 April 2006.

185 Human Rights Watch, *Sudan, Oil and Human Rights*, 50–9.

186 John Prendergast, "A Dying Deal in Darfur," Boston *Globe*, 16 July 2006, http://www.crisisgroup.org/home/index.cfm?id=4265&l= (accessed 3 August 2006).

CHAPTER SIX

Death in Darfur: Total Mortality from Violence, Malnutrition, and Disease: April/May 2006

ERIC REEVES

This chapter is a verbatim transcription, with minor editorial modifica-tions, of a text originally produced in April/May 2006 and posted on my website, www.sudanreeves.org. A new Postscript has been added to bring the analysis up to the present (October 2008). The appendix, fol-lowing the Postscript, was also part of the original 2006 text.

The analysis presents a statistical assessment of human destruction in Darfur to April/May 2006. Attempting to survey all the most significant extant mortality data from Darfur and eastern Chad, it builds on fifteen previous systematic attempts, also found at my website, to chronicle the scale of the Darfur genocide, analysing both violent mortality and mor-tality from violence-related disease and malnutrition. Largely because of obstruction and intimidation by the Khartoum regime, and a persis-tent climate of extreme insecurity, no further collections of data bearing on excess mortality have been systematically undertaken in Darfur. Nor has there been any comprehensive effort on the ground to collect data bearing specifically on violent mortality since 2005.

Currently extant data, in aggregate, strongly suggest that total excess mortality in Darfur, over the course of more than three years of deadly conflict, exceeded 450,000 in mid-2006. As Rwanda marks a grim twelfth anniversary, we must accept that while vast human destruc-tion in Darfur has unfolded plainly before us, we have again done little more than watch, offering only unprotected humanitarian assistance while some 450,000 people have perished as a result of violence, as well as consequent malnutrition and disease. Human destruction to date, however, certainly does not mark the conclusion of the world's moral failure in responding to genocide in Darfur; on the contrary, this massive previous destruction may be our best measure of what is impending.

For, terrifyingly, all current evidence suggests that hundreds of thousands of human beings will die in the coming months from these same causes. A rapidly accelerating contraction of humanitarian reach and capacity has left three-quarters of a million civilians without any assistance whatsoever in Darfur and eastern Chad; many hundreds of thousands of other innocent human beings have only exceedingly tenuous access to aid. Further, the UN World Food Program announced in April 2006 that it was halving food rations for Darfur and eastern Sudan: "Millions of vulnerable people in the western Sudanese region of Darfur and eastern Sudan will receive half-rations of food beginning on Monday, due to a significant shortfall in funding, the United Nations World Food Programme said … Aid agencies are particularly concerned about the effect of reduced rations in Darfur, where rampant insecurity and continued displacement cause enormous suffering. 'Food must come first. We cannot put families who have lost their homes and loved ones to violence on a 1,000-calorie-a-day diet.'"[1] But such a diet is precisely what confronted the people of Darfur in April 2006, when children under five were already dying in large numbers likely owing to rising malnutrition rates.[2] Almost four million people in the greater humanitarian theatre are classified as "conflict-affected" by the UN. They are in need of humanitarian assistance, primarily food aid that has now been cut to half of what human beings require to live.

The pre-positioning of food in anticipation of the coming rainy season is no longer a realistic goal, since the massive shortfall in April 2006 food deliveries to Darfur suggests that there is simply far too little available: "Between 1 and 24 April [2006], the UN World Food Program transported a total of 10,597 tons of food in the three Darfur states, realizing only 29% of the April [2006] plan due to a serious shortage of food available in Port Sudan and in the hubs of El Obeid and Khartoum."[3] The immense human needs in Darfur persist even as international aid capacity is diminishing because of funding shortfalls and dramatically increasing insecurity on the ground. In the same month that rations were cut, the New York *Times* filed the following report from Khartoum: "'The situation for humanitarian workers and the UN has never been as bad as it is now,' said one senior aid official here who requested anonymity because aid agencies that have spoken out have been targeted for harassment and expulsion. 'The space for us to work is just getting smaller and smaller.' ... 'You start wondering, "what will it take?"' the official said. 'How bad does it have to get before the international community acts?'"[4] These are good questions. How many people must die? How much suffering must we witness? The answers already offered by the world community represent a failure beyond shame.

Khartoum's Genocidal Logic

Khartoum's decision to launch a large-scale, coordinated military offensive in South Darfur just prior to the diminishment of rations appeared designed to assure the failure of the Abuja (Nigeria) peace process. Human Rights Watch reported:

> The Sudanese government has launched a new military offensive in South Darfur that is placing civilians at grave risk. An April 24 [2006] attack on a village in rebel-controlled territory used Antonov aircraft and helicopter gunships indiscriminately in violation of the laws of war, and displaced thousands of civilians who had sought safety there ... The April 24 attack on Joghana village appears to be part of a broader government offensive in South Darfur ... According to eyewitness reports, government forces and militias began attacking Joghana at 7am on April 24. Civilians who fled the town said that an Antonov plane and two helicopter gunships were used and that the Antonov dropped bombs that killed civilians, although the numbers of dead and injured could not be verified. Thousands of displaced persons were living in Joghana, controlled by the rebel Sudan Liberation Army (SLA), after fleeing earlier attacks on their villages.[5]

Likewise, both Reuters and the UN's IRIN (Integrated Regional Information Networks) outlet in Abjuba reported comments by several leaders of the Sudanese Liberation Movement Army (SLM/A) – the larger of the two Darfur rebel movements active in 2006 – that suggest strong disapproval of the "final" draft peace agreement proposed by the African Union (AU). Nor is there any evidence that Khartoum would abide by any signed agreement, even one with very weak guarantees and guarantors. It is critical to remember that the National Islamic Front (NIF) regime has never abided by a single agreement with any Sudanese party. Not one, not ever. Impending failure in Abuja (or in the implementation of an Abuja agreement), along with Khartoum's highly provocative large-scale military offensive, augurs a resumption of extremely fierce fighting throughout Darfur.

As a direct result, wholesale humanitarian evacuations from even larger, inaccessible areas (many thousands of square kilometres in Darfur, especially West Darfur and the Jebel Marra region) continue to occur. On 28 April 2006 the UN announced that insecurity and attacks on aid workers and operations in North Darfur, primarily by the rebel movements, may force the suspension of humanitarian activities in this area: "Unless rebel attacks against UN and other relief operations in a northern sector of Sudan's strife-torn Darfur region stop immediately, the world organization will be forced to suspend all assistance to 450,000 vulnerable people living in the area until safety can be assured, a top UN official warned today."[6] Huge areas in eastern Chad are also inaccessible because of Khartoum's success in exporting genocidal destruction by means of its regular forces, its Janjaweed militia proxies, and the Chadian rebel groups that enjoy very substantial support from Khartoum's National Islamic Front.

Populations weakened by three years of conflict, utterly without food reserves and facing a large-scale collapse in humanitarian assistance, have already started dying in large numbers, even greater than those that prompted UN High Commissioner for Refugees Antonio Guterres to declare, following an assessment mission to Darfur in October 2005, that "people are dying and dying in large numbers."[7] In fact, available data in early 2006, including information from the UN's World Health Organization (WHO), suggest that well over 6,000 Darfurian civilians are dying every month because of war-related causes.

In a briefing to the UN Security Council on 21 April 2006, Jan Egeland, UN under-secretary general for humanitarian affairs, described the situation in stark terms: "'I think it's a matter of weeks or months that we will have a collapse in many of our operations,' Egeland told reporters after briefing the Council on the crises in Darfur, northern Uganda and Chad. 'As I told the Security Council today, I don't think the world has understood how bad it has become of late.'"[8] In March, Egeland had been equally forthright: "[Those in] unreachable areas, [Egeland] said, 'will soon get massively increased mortality because there is nothing else but international assistance.' He expected deaths to increase markedly within weeks."[9] Mortality certainly increased significantly in the intervening six weeks between Egeland's statements, although the humanitarian community has no way of accurately assessing the scale of the increase. At the beginning of April 2006, Egeland again declared that "'the only way that we can avoid a massive loss of lives – massive – is by enabling this humanitarian operation, which is on the ground, to be able to do its job.'"[10]

In the Absence of Humanitarian Intervention

All that can reverse the ebbs and flows of humanitarian access and ongoing human destruction in Darfur is urgent intervention, with all necessary military resources and an appropriately robust mandate for civilian and humanitarian protection. In the spring of 2006, there were no signs that the UN had plans for such an urgent, well-equipped, and robust mission. And the view from NATO, at its 28 April 2006 meeting in Sofia, Bulgaria, is captured in a single sentence: "'We are in the early planning stages for what we can offer next but the consensus is that the NATO footprint should be as limited as possible,' said one observer of the foreign ministers' talks in the Bulgarian capital Sofia."[11] The Reuters dispatch summarized the views of Western foreign ministers: "Alliance ministers agreed on Friday [28 April 2006] that any presence should be limited and only in support of African or UN efforts."[12] Since the African Union had agreed, in principle, to hand over the Darfur mission to the UN only at the end of September 2006, the NATO decision worked to preserve the status quo. Khartoum's obstructionist policies also reduced the possibility of rapid response by the UN. In 2006 the National Islamic Front regime denied visas to members of a UN Department of Peacekeeping Operations assessment mission, and NIF President Omar al-Bashir threatened to turn Darfur into a "graveyard" for any non-African Union forces,[13] putting him squarely on the same page with Osama bin Laden, whose January 2006 audio-tape urged al-Qaeda's "holy warriors" to attack the "crusade" in Darfur.[14]

That bin Laden's "crusade" consists of attacks on humanitarian efforts to save Muslims in Darfur, whose entire population is Muslim, is an obscene irony that seems to matter no more to al-Bashir and the NIF than it does to bin Laden, who was hosted by the NIF from 1991 to 1996 and who maintained very close ties with Khartoum for a number of years after decamping to Afghanistan. In assessing Khartoum's particular response to the humanitarian effort that bin Laden describes as a "crusade," we must bear in mind Egeland's 2006 report to the Security Council on fourteen categories of deliberate and highly consequential NIF obstruction of international relief efforts.[15] This relentless obstructionism has consequences that will ultimately be measured in the many tens of thousands of innocent lives lost because humanitarian assistance was prevented from reaching desperately needy civilians. Of the various actions by Khartoum that "deliberately inflict on the [African tribal groups of Darfur] conditions of life calculated to bring about [their] physical destruction in whole or in part" (1948 UN Genocide Convention, adapted from Article 2, clause [c]), obstruction of humanitarian aid must rank as one of the most conspicuous and "deliberate" inflictions, as well as one of the most deadly.

Retrospective Analysis of Mortality in Darfur

This analysis surveys the quantitative data relevant to an assessment of human mortality in Darfur between February 2003 and May 2006. Numerous methodological problems present themselves in any such effort, particularly given the heterogeneous sources of data, for both violent mortality and deaths from disease and malnutrition. The alternative to struggling with these difficulties, however, is acquiescing before transparent misrepresentations of human destruction in Darfur. An egregious example is the figure of "180,000 deaths," cited by the Associated Press and others as representing global mortality in Darfur. This figure does not come close to representing the true number of deaths in Darfur by 2006, as even the most cursory account of its provenance reveals.

In March 2005 the UN promulgated a figure of 180,000 as representing deaths from disease and malnutrition over the preceding eighteen months, a number based on the UN World Health Organization mortality study and update.[16] Using the WHO rate of 10,000 deaths from disease and malnutrition per month,[17] and multiplying this rate by eighteen months (going back to September 2003), the UN arrived at a figure of 180,000. However, this figure did not include in any significant way violent mortality, even though humanitarians throughout Darfur have consistently reported that violent mortality was the primary cause of death through summer 2004. Nor did the figure include mortality prior to September 2003; and, of course, it takes no account of mortality subsequent to March 2005 (again, the date of original UN promulgation). The figure also takes no account of mortality in Chad. In short, the use of "180,000" as a global mortality figure is a reporting scandal, an example of journalistic moral slovenliness that works to discount, indeed statistically elide, the lives of as many as 300,000 human beings.

To be sure, a number of particular difficulties confront any effort to quantify the number of civilians who have died violent deaths since February 2003. But there are very significant systematic data, as well as important generalized assessments and anecdotal data. A good example of the latter appears in the January 2006 study by Physicians for Human Rights (PHR), which has undertaken a number of assessment missions to Darfur and eastern Chad. In "Darfur: Assault on Survival," PHR presents (on the basis of well-constructed interviews of carefully selected individuals in three representative locations) a shocking finding: "Prior to the [military] attacks the 46 [Darfurian] men and women PHR interviewed had a total of 558 people in their households. Of these, 141 were 'confirmed dead' – their deaths were witnessed or their bodies found – while 251 were 'killed or missing' – meaning their whereabouts were unknown. The average household size [defined as 'people who eat out of the same pot'] before the attacks was 12.1; after it was 6.7."[18] This report represents violent mortality of 45 per cent for the family populations interviewed. We need not believe that the population sample in the report is statistically representative of Darfur as a whole to see that huge areas have suffered enormous violent human destruction. An epidemiological study of violence in West Darfur, published in the British medical journal *The Lancet*, found that 95 per cent of those displaced had been violently displaced.[19] Well over two million people have now been displaced, either internally within Darfur or into eastern Chad, suggesting that at least two million have been violently displaced. Even if the PHR figure of 45 per cent mortality among the population of violently displaced persons overstates by 100 per cent the violent mortality rate for Darfur as a whole, this would still imply statistically that approximately 450,000 human beings had died violent deaths.

Though the number of 450,000 is staggering, this is precisely the characterization made almost two years ago by Asma Jahangir, then UN special rapporteur on extrajudicial, summary, or arbitrary executions, who reported in late June 2004 that the "number of black Africans killed by Arab militias in the Darfur region of Sudan is 'bound to be staggering.'"[20] According to the United Nations News Centre,

"Ms. Jahangir said that during her visit, 'nearly every third or fourth family' she spoke to in the camps for internally displaced people (IDPs) within Darfur had lost a relative to the militias. 'It's very hard to say [accurately] how many people have been killed,' she said, but interviews with IDPs indicated it would be 'quite a large number. They are bound to be staggering.'"[21]

Retrospective Analysis of Violent Mortality as of September 2004

The primary source of comprehensive, statistically significant data on violent mortality in Darfur remains the September 2004 study by the Coalition for International Justice (CIJ). On the basis of 1,136 carefully randomized interviews, conducted among the Darfurian refugee population in Chad at a number of camp locations along the border, the CIJ found that "sixty-one percent [of those interviewed] reported witnessing the killing of a family member."[22] At the time of the study, the total number of refugees in Chad was approximately 200,000. If we assume that this population of persons displaced from Darfur represented the many hundreds of thousands of violently displaced persons within Darfur at the time, then the total number people represented by the CIJ study was well over 1.5 million, and might have reached to 2 million.

How do we establish the approximate contemporaneous figure for those people violently displaced, either into camps, into towns, within inaccessible rural areas in Darfur – or into Chad? In what was in 2004 the most recent "Darfur Humanitarian Profile," the UN Office for the Coordination of Humanitarian Affairs estimated that 1.45 million people had been displaced into accessible camps within Darfur.[23] The UN report also estimated that an "additional 500,000 conflict-affected persons are in need of assistance,"[24] and it is reasonable to assume that a great many of these people were also displaced. Moreover, the figure for people displaced within IDP camps was based on UN World Food Program registrations, and significantly understated the actual internally displaced population.

Thus, out of a total displaced population in Darfur of approximately 1.75 to 2 million, we require an estimate of the number of persons who experienced violent displacement of the sort that had at the time created over 200,000 refugees in Chad. Given the extremely high level of village destruction throughout Darfur, and the tenacity with which

these people have sought to cling to their land and livelihoods, displacement per se is a very likely indicator of violent displacement. Here
again lies the relevance of the epidemiological study published in *The
Lancet*, which offered clear evidence that displacement is overwhelm-
ingly related to violent attacks. In two camps, Zalingei and Murnei,
statistically rigorous assessments found that "direct attack on the village" accounted for displacement of 92.8 per cent of the Zalingei population and 97.4 per cent of the Murnei population (the combined camp
population was approximately 110,000).[25]

If we very conservatively assume that 80 per cent of the total displaced populations that remained in Darfur were driven to flee by "direct attack on villages," the number of violently displaced persons in
late 2004 was approximately 1.4 to 1.6 million – including the refugee population in Chad. The average family size in Darfur is between
five to six, suggesting that a population of 1.6 to 1.8 million represents
roughly 265,000 to 360,000 families. If randomized interviews by the
Coalition for International Justice found that "sixty-one percent [of
those interviewed] reported witnessing the killing of a family member," then this yields a mortality figure for violent deaths of 160,000
to 210,000 human beings as of early September 2004. This number
represents approximately 10,000 violent deaths per month since the
outbreak of major conflict in February 2003. While violent mortality declined significantly after the summer of 2004, it has remained
enormous.

In the absence of additional statistically significant data, we must
make assumptions about continuing levels of violent human destruction on the basis of rates from September 2004. Assuming an average
50 per cent decline in violent mortality for the remaining months of
2004, and a 75 per cent decline in violent mortality for 2005 and 2006,
this still yields an additional 60,000 violent deaths. In turn, this estimate yields a range of 220,000 to 270,000 total violent deaths since the
outbreak of major conflict.

Caveats and Other Considerations

There is some chance that, despite randomizing of interviews in Chad,
and multiple camp locations at which interviews were conducted, over-
laps existed in the "family members" identified as having been seen
killed. This is a negligible number if "family" refers to nuclear family.
Indeed, the chances of overlap even for members of extended families

are quite small, given the diversity of interview locations. More significant is the fact that those people conducting interviews for the CIJ found that interviewees often reported more than one family member had been killed, often several more than one. Yet the statistical derivation offered here presumes that only one family member had been killed among the 61 per cent who reported seeing (at least) one family member killed.

Secondly, the CIJ study could not take account of the number of families in which all members were killed, and who thus had no reporting presence in the camps where interviews took place. It does report that 28 per cent of those interviewed "directly witnessed" persons dying from the consequences of displacement before reaching Chad. These deaths must also be considered the direct consequence of violence, if not violent deaths per se, and would significantly increase violent mortality totals. Of additional statistical significance, the CIJ study indicates that 67 per cent of those interviewed "directly witnessed" the killing of a non-family member" (see appendix 1 at the end of this chapter).

The CIJ study explained the randomizing techniques within the camps: "Refugees were selected using a systematic, random sampling approach designed to meet the conditions in Chad. Interviewers randomly selected a sector within a refugee camp and then, from a fixed point within the sector, chose every 10th dwelling unit for interviewing ... One adult [from the dwelling unit] was randomly selected [for interviewing]."[26] Given these techniques and the number of camp locations (nineteen), the figure of 67 per cent of refugees "directly witnessing" the killing of a non-family member strongly suggests that assumptions made in this analysis may lead to significant underestimation of violent mortality. For clearly a very large percentage of those who witnessed the violent death of a family member (61 per cent of those interviewed) also witnessed the death of a non-family member, that is, the deaths of at least two persons.

Retrospective Analysis of Mortality from Disease and Malnutrition

If we accept as a reasonable point of statistical departure the UN estimate of 180,000 deaths from disease and malnutrition (March 2005), the calculation of additional non-violent mortality between March 2005 and April 2006 requires an appropriate Crude Mortality Rate

(CMR). A UN World Health Organization-overseen study (June 2005) provides precisely such a CMR.[27] While there was great variability in the CMR (deaths per affected 10,000 of population per day) within the three Darfur states, in some areas the mortality rate was well in excess of the "crisis level." (The "crisis level" for adults is a CMR of 1.0; for children under five it is 2.0.) In the camps for displaced persons in South Darfur, for example, the CMR for children under five was 2.6, well above the "crisis level."

It is also important to note the limitations in reach of this study of mortality rates in Darfur. In North Darfur and West Darfur, the study was able to sample populations in camps for the displaced, displaced populations outside the camps, and conflict-affected residents. But in South Darfur, where violence had been greatest during the six-month period covered by the study (November 2004–May 2005), only the camps for internally displaced persons were surveyed. In other words, this study tells us nothing about the mortality rate among displaced persons outside camps in South Darfur, or among resident conflict-affected populations.

These omissions suggest a very serious gap, especially since the previous WHO study – published in September/October 2004 – included only the mortality rate for the large Kalma camp (near Nyala, South Darfur). South Darfur is far and away the most populous of the three Darfur states, with a population of 3.1 million, almost twice that of West Darfur (1.6 million) or North Darfur (1.6 million).[28] Because the WHO-overseen study did not include the very large areas to which the UN (for security reasons) had no access, many hundreds of thousands of people are not represented. These people were largely beyond the reach of UN and non-UN humanitarian assistance (food aid to rural areas by the International Committee of the Red Cross [ICRC] is the most notable exception), and, therefore, they almost certainly experienced mortality rates significantly higher than those populations with access to humanitarian aid. Indeed, the thesis of the June 2005 UN mortality rate study was that humanitarian assistance was responsible for the decline from the very high mortality rates revealed by the September/October 2004 WHO study. Conversely, the continuing absence of humanitarian assistance strongly suggested that significantly higher mortality rates prevailed in areas not surveyed by the study.

What was the size of the contemporaneous population for which the late June 2005 study was relevant? "Darfur Humanitarian Profile" no. 16 represented conditions as of 1 July 2005 and indicated a conflict-affected population of 3.2 million people in Darfur;[29] the UN High Commission for Refugees offered at the time a figure of approximately 200,000 Darfurian refugees in eastern Chad. In his April 2006 report to the UN Security Council, UN humanitarian chief Jan Egeland estimated a conflict-affected population of 3.5 million in Darfur, while at the same time reporting a figure of 250,000 Darfurian refugees in Chad. The number of internally displaced and conflict-affected Chadians exceeded 100,000 in 2006, suggesting a total population of almost 4 million human beings affected by the Darfur genocide.

Given the limitations in access on the part of the June 2005 WHO-overseen mortality study in Darfur, it is reasonable to assume a global CMR of 0.9 (0.1 higher than the study figure of 0.8 for areas accessible to humanitarians); from this number, we must subtract a figure of 0.3 (what the United Nations International Children's Emergency Fund [UNICEF] suggests is a "normal" CMR for Darfur). Thus, monthly mortality in Darfur attributable to disease and malnutrition in June 2005 stood at over 6,000 (derived from a conflict-generated CMR of 0.6 for a population of 3.4 million x 30 days=6,100 "excess" deaths per month).

While humanitarian conditions continued to improve through July 2005, increased violence and insecurity beginning in August 2005 almost certainly marked the end of any improvement in the CMR. After September 2005, at which time the UN withdrew all non-essential humanitarian personnel from West Darfur, humanitarian access continued to contract, even as camps for displaced persons become more vulnerable. That month also saw the first direct attack by the murderous Janjaweed militia on a camp for displaced persons – Aro Sharow camp in West Darfur, home to approximately 5,000 defenceless civilians. Such attacks have subsequently increased in scale. Humanitarian evacuations and withdrawals also accelerated significantly in 2006.

It seems reasonable to assume that the CMR obtained in June 2005 did not improve by the middle of 2006, even as the number of conflict-affected persons (the "denominator" for mortality calculations) increased by over 400,000 people. Assuming a total conflict-affected population in Darfur and eastern Chad of 3.8 million, monthly mortality (using the CMR of the June 2005 WHO-overseen study) is over 6,800 per month. Assuming an average monthly mortality figure of 6,500 since the March 2005 UN promulgation of a figure of 180,000 deaths from disease and malnutrition, the total number of such deaths in April 2006 stood at 260,000. If violent mortality is in the range of 220,000 to 270,000, total mortality in April 2006 was approximately 480,000 to 530,000 human beings.

If Jan Egeland was correct in December 2004, arguing that as many as 100,000 people could die every month in the event of full-scale humanitarian withdrawal,[30] then the equivalent figure as of April 2006 must approach 150,000 deaths per month. For in December 2004 approximately 2.6 million people were affected by the conflict in Darfur and eastern Chad; by April 2006, this figure had risen to over 3.8 million, an increase of over 45 per cent. Such numbers seem incomprehensible. Yet all indicators point both to large-scale collapse in humanitarian operations and access, and consequent human mortality that will indeed exceed the moral imagination. The brutal realities on the ground in Darfur and eastern Chad are everywhere in evidence; the remorseless unfolding of Khartoum's genocidal logic is there for all to see.

In conclusion, the first part of this mortality assessment, surveying all extant data as of 28 April 2006, estimates that since the outbreak of major conflict in Darfur (February 2003), over 450,000 people have died from violence, disease, and malnutrition.[31]

Prospects for Security

There is no evidence to date that the signing of the Abuja accord will improve the security situation on the ground in either Darfur or eastern Chad.[32] On the contrary, there were numerous reports of extremely serious violence in connection with the large-scale military offensive launched by Khartoum in the Gereida area (South Darfur) just days before the deadline for the Abuja draft agreement. Reports of violence along the Chad/Darfur border were also increasingly serious in the spring of 2006, and large numbers of civilians were moved away from the border area. A Reuters report of 11 May 2006 noted the growing concern of Lousie Arbour, the then UN high commissioner for human rights:

The International Criminal Court must act more decisively to bring to trial those guilty of war crimes in Darfur because Sudanese officials have so far proved incapable of doing so, the top UN human rights official said. [Arbour], just back from a visit to Sudan, said on Thursday [11 May 2006] that despite government promises no official had been tried and punished for any of the serious human rights violations committed in the vast western region of Africa's largest state. 'Progress is invisible,' she told a news conference. 'I believe we must call on the ICC [International Criminal Court] to act more robustly, and visibly discharge the mandate ... that the UN Security Council has conferred on it.'[33]

What went unsaid by Ms. Arbour is that Khartoum adamantly refused to permit entry to any of the ICC investigators, and made abundantly clear that it would not permit the extradition of either witnesses or suspects. Certainly, among the fifty-one names referred to the ICC are a number of the most senior and powerful members of the National Islamic Front, and they will obviously not extradite themselves. Further, lead ICC prosecutor Luis Moreno-Ocampo reported to the Security Council in June 2005 that he was quite aware that his investigation posed a significant risk to witnesses in Darfur as well as to humanitarians: "The information currently available highlights the significant security risks facing civilians, local and international humanitarian personnel in Darfur. These issues will present persistent challenges for the investigation."[34] How does Arbour propose to deal with these "security risks"? How does she propose that the ICC gain access to witnesses of mass executions, crimes against humanity, and genocide in Darfur? Does she imagine that those responsible for these crimes will permit any investigation on Sudanese territory? Yet again we witness a senior UN leader posturing rather than proposing serious responses to ongoing obduracy on the part of Khartoum's génocidaires.

Arbour did highlight Khartoum's bad faith in undertaking its obligations under the Comprehensive Peace Agreement (January 2005) between the regime and the Southern Sudan People's Liberation Movement: "'We are somewhat neglecting the need to support the peace deal in southern Sudan,' [Arbour] said. Despite the accord, there was 'no visible improvement either in the physical security or the economic well-being of the people.'"[35] This critical truth tells us much about the meaning of the accord signed in Abuja. While Khartoum may, for the sake of appearances, temporarily reduce levels of military activity, there is simply no reason to believe that the various provisions for wealth sharing and power sharing, or for security arrangements, will be respected over the longer term. The génocidaires will simply wait, knowing that so long as the African Union remains the sole guarantor of the various security "guarantees," there will be no meaningful peace in Darfur, and ethnically targeted human destruction will continue.

There is unlikely to be a similarly calculated patience on the part of the Janjaweed, as New York *Times* correspondent Lydia Polgreen courageously reported on 12 May 2006 in a searing dispatch from Menawashie, South Darfur:

> It took three months for Fatouma Moussa to collect enough firewood to justify a trip to sell it in the market town of Shangil Tobayi, half a day's drive by truck from here. It took just a few moments on Thursday [11 May 2006] for janjaweed militiamen, making a mockery of the new cease-fire, to steal the $40 she had earned on the trip and rape her.
>
> Speaking barely in a whisper, Ms. Moussa, who is 18, gave a spare account of her ordeal. 'We found janjaweed at Amer Jadid,' she said, naming a village just a few miles north of her own. 'One woman was killed. I was raped.'
>
> Officially, the cease-fire in the Darfur region went into effect last Monday [8 May 2006]. But the reality was on grim display in this crossroads town, where Ms. Moussa and other villagers were attacked Thursday as they rode home in a bus from Shangil Tobayi. The Arab militiamen who attacked them killed 1 woman, wounded 6 villagers and raped 15 women, witnesses and victims said.[36]

What are the prospects for a robust international force to protect women like Fatouma Moussa? How likely is it that wealthy nations with modern armed forces will provide the troops and military resources that might serve as guarantor of the Abuja accord and bring true peace to Darfur? In fact, the odds for robust humanitarian intervention or even meaningful peacekeeping remain obscenely long.

UN or US Intervention to Halt the Killing in Darfur?

On 17 February 2006 US President George W. Bush asserted that a security force for Darfur will require "NATO stewardship, planning, facilitating, organizing, probably double the number of peacekeepers that are there now, in order to start bringing some sense of security."[37] Yet, as NATO officials in Brussels were quick to insist at the time,

"NATO stewardship" actually means deploying a few dozen advisers. In April 2006 NATO officials again suggested only a minimal alliance presence in Darfur. Those expecting that the UN will take urgent and robust action, with meaningful authority to stop the genocide in Darfur and end the killing, will wait in vain.

How Serious is the Bush Administration about Confronting Khartoum's Génocidaires?

On 13 May 2006 the *Washington Post* published a story revealing that the US State Department had decided to grant an extended personal visa to one of Khartoum's most vicious génocidaires.[38] If we want to understand why Khartoum remains emboldened in its conduct of genocide in Darfur, why a "climate of impunity" continues to reign in Darfur, why the voice of the United States is so compromised, we must see the implications of admitting to this country Ali Ahmed Karti, former head of the notoriously brutal Popular Defence Forces (PDF), a paramilitary militia organized and funded by Khartoum and recently often fighting alongside the better known Janjaweed.

Beyond its depredations in Darfur, the PDF was a key military instrument in the scorched-earth clearances in southern Sudan during the most brutal phase of the north/south conflict in the oil regions of Upper Nile Province, as well as in neighbouring Bahr el-Ghazal Province. As the *Washington Post* reported in May 2006, Human Rights Watch offered a telling vignette of Karti in 1999: "PDF coordinating director Ali Ahmad Karti read out the names of the brigades that had been sent to the field, including the 'Protectors of the Oil Brigade,' and promised that more brigades would be created."[39] These "brigades" engaged in unspeakable acts of violence and human destruction, including attacks on humanitarian workers. As this writer reported in the *International Herald Tribune* on 23 January 2001:

> The International Committee of the Red Cross – the very symbol of neutral, international humanitarian aid – was savagely attacked at its medical base in Chelkou, southern Sudan, on January 12 [2001]. The attack was carried out by militia forces allied with the radical National Islamic Front regime that rules from Khartoum. All buildings were destroyed, all expatriate workers withdrawn, villagers have been killed, and the ICRC is deeply concerned about the fate of their Sudanese workers.

This act of barbarism by the Khartoum-backed Popular Defense Forces (PDF) completely destroyed the ICRC medical facilities at an important humanitarian site in the southern province of Bahr el-Ghazal. Reuters newswire, as well as extremely reliable sources from the ground, reported the destruction.[40]

Yet the man ultimately responsible for the actions of these PDF "brigades" was officially granted an extended personal visa to visit the United States, even as he was almost certainly facing indictment by the International Criminal Court in its investigations of crimes in Darfur. The Washington *Post* reports that Karti was scheduled to meet with US Assistant Secretary of State for African Affairs Jendayi Frazer, one of several Bush administration officials to distinguish herself with disingenuousness and foolishness in speaking about Darfur:

> Frazer planned to meet Friday at the State Department with a top Sudanese official linked by human rights groups to the violence in Sudan's Darfur region that the Bush administration has labeled as genocide. But the official, deputy foreign minister Ali Ahmed Karti, did not show up for the meeting, a State Department spokesman said.
>
> David Sims, a spokesman for the Africa bureau headed by Frazer, said a meeting had been planned but Karti 'just decided he didn't want to make it.' Frazer, who last week was in Abuja, Nigeria's capital, for intensive talks that led to a tentative peace agreement on Darfur, did not have qualms about meeting with Karti, Sims said.[41]

Frazer had "no qualms" about meeting this brutal génocidaire, and Karti had "no qualms" about ignoring an appointment with a senior State Department official, which tells us a great deal about Bush administration's Darfur policy in 2006, and how it was perceived in Khartoum.

Karti's leisurely visit to the United States came just a year after the CIA flew another of Khartoum's senior génocidaires to Washington, namely, Major-General Saleh Abdalla Gosh, head of Khartoum's notorious Mukhabarat (the National Security and Intelligence Service [NSIS]). Gosh is one of the primary architects of the Darfur genocide, and his name appears on a recent (January 2006) confidential annex produced by a UN panel of experts commissioned to determine responsibility for ongoing violence and civilian destruction in Darfur.

The panel cited Gosh for "failure to take action as Director of NSIS to identify, neutralize and disarm non-state armed militia groups in Darfur [the Janjaweed]" and for "command responsibility for acts or arbitrary detention, harassment, torture, denial of right to fair trial."[42] Failure to disarm the Janjaweed, so largely under his control, puts Saleh Gosh directly at odds with the only demand of significance made of Khartoum, in the form of UN Security Council Resolution 1556.[43] But why should Gosh fear consequences from the United Nations – or the United States? After all, his central role in the Darfur genocide was not enough to prevent the CIA from flying him to Washington in April 2006 (at his request) for a briefing on terrorism intelligence.

Certainly the feeble and exceedingly short list of those sanctioned on 25 April 2006 (per Security Council Resolution 1591, March 2005) does not begin to touch any of the senior NIF génocidaires, including Gosh, Abdel Rahim Mohamed Hussein (defence minister and former minister of the interior), Elzubeir Bashir Taha (minister of the interior), and Major-General Ismat Zain al-Din (director of military operations of the Sudanese Armed Forces). Here again, the most important consequences of moral and political cowardice take the form of emboldened political calculations in Khartoum. Far from being an action that changed the regime's thinking, this painfully weak sanctions resolution signals only that there is no international political ability or diplomatic will to punish those most directly responsible for genocide in Darfur.

Humanitarian Mortality Indicators

There is no simple way to capture the extraordinary urgency conveyed by increasingly numerous dispatches from UN and non-governmental humanitarian organizations. But Kofi Annan, who has done more than his share of posturing on Darfur, offers a blunt assessment of the current funding crisis for Darfur and eastern Chad (where only 16 per cent of total funding needs have been met by 2006, even as food needs are skyrocketing because of the insecurity deriving mainly from Khartoum-backed violence): "Without massive and immediate support, the humanitarian agencies will be unable to continue their work, which means that hundreds of thousands more will die from hunger, malnutrition and disease."[44] *Hundreds of thousands more will die.* With a grim irony, given his role at the time, Annan went on to declare that "Darfur was potentially the [UN Security] council's biggest test since the 1994 genocide in Rwanda."[45] To Annan's credit, there is very little more that can be said either about prospective mortality in Darfur and eastern Chad, or about the implications of our ongoing failure to respond with a robust humanitarian intervention.

Amidst this overwhelming crisis, it is important to recall again that, in the spring of 2006, the Khartoum regime controlled a national food stockpile of 300,000 to 500,000 metric tons of grain, according to officials at the US Agency for International Development. Instead of releasing this grain for humanitarian purposes, Khartoum kept grain prices artificially high, thus making it impossible for the UN's World Food Program to buy food in-country. This burden adds enormously to the cost of food, and these increased costs ultimately diminish humanitarian capacity, translating into human death through malnutrition and related diseases.

A wholesale implosion of humanitarian operations also remains a distinct possibility, one highlighted in a May 2006 interview offered by Jan Egeland: "Everybody now discusses the optimal kind of UN mission – for next year for nine months from now. This whole thing could unravel in nine days or nine weeks because we have no money to continue lifesaving humanitarian work."[46] It was Egeland who also highlighted in a 20 April 2006 report to the Security Council fourteen categories of Khartoum's obstruction and harassment of humanitarian workers and operations – conduct that severely attenuates humanitarian efficiency and thereby also increases costs.[47] At a time of desperate financial shortfall, such obstructionism is a tool of genocide.

Jan Egeland's record is one of singular honesty among UN officials who were in senior positions in 2004, when the genocide in Darfur was so clearly before the eyes of the world. His retrospective glance in a 2006 *Wall Street Journal* op-ed gives us all too clear an image of our failure: "I first spoke to the UN Security Council on Darfur two years ago, calling it ethnic cleansing of the worst kind. Today, I could simply hit the rewind button on much of that earlier briefing. The world's largest aid effort now hangs in the balance, unsustainable under present conditions. If we are to avoid an imminent, massive loss of life, we need immediate action – from the Government of Sudan, the rebels, UN Security Council members and donor governments."[48] Such "action" is nowhere in prospect, and we must accept the terrible truth that "imminent, massive loss of life" has already begun. "The worst form of ethnic cleansing" – and here even those who cannot pronounce Darfur and the "g-word" together must find a near-synonymous phrase for "genocide" – proceeds apace.

Postscript

The Darfur genocide has a long history. It must include, for example, the Khartoum-backed Arab militia attacks on the Massaleit people of West Darfur in 1999: at the direction of the National Islamic Front regime, dozens of villages were attacked by the Janjaweed, and many hundreds of Massaleit civilians were killed. The non-Arab (or "African") Massaleit, along with the Fur and Zaghawa, have been the primary targets of Khartoum's counter-insurgency strategy of ethnic slaughter. The means of human destruction have included violence as well as what the 1948 UN Convention on the Prevention and Punishment of the Crime of Genocide refers to as "deliberately inflicting on the group conditions of life calculated to bring about its physical destruction in whole or in part" (Article 2, clause [c]).

This history of ethnic destruction certainly extends back to the military coup mounted by the National Islamic Front in June 1989, which deposed an elected government and deliberately aborted Sudan's best chance for a north/south peace agreement since independence in 1956. Many thousands of non-Arab Darfuris had died in ethnically targeted attacks orchestrated by this savage regime prior to February 2003, the date usually used as the *terminus a quo* for the Darfur genocide.

As noted at the outset of this chapter, the number of people who have died from conflict-related causes since May 2006 is unknown. What we do know, however, is that in areas to which international humanitarian organizations had access, the Crude Mortality Rate for the most part dropped to normal ranges by 2006. This is quite extraordinary and a testament to the courageous, determined, and skilful efforts of the individuals who collectively have made up the world's largest humanitarian effort. But this is also the world's most imperilled humanitarian effort. Jan Egeland's grim warning, cited in this analysis, remains all too apt for the situation in 2008: there will be cataclysmic human mortality in the event of humanitarian withdrawal. Moreover, large-scale food shortages beginning in the spring of 2008 resulted in widespread malnutrition for millions of conflict-affected civilians over the remainder of the year – a situation that quite possibly will persist into 2009.

The convulsion of ethnically targeted violence from 2003 through early 2005 has given way in the main to more chaotic fighting, although this is, as Human Rights Watch suggested in a September 2007 report, "Chaos by Design" on Khartoum's part. Current violence involves banditry, widespread attacks, and intimidation by Janjaweed militia, as well as infighting among rebel factions, which have also attacked humanitarian convoys. Whatever unity held the rebel movements together disappeared with the signing of the poorly conceived and disastrously consummated Darfur Peace Agreement in Abuja, Nigeria in May 2006.

But large-scale assaults on African tribal populations, involving coordinated military actions by Khartoum and its Janjaweed militia proxies, still occur. In February 2008, for example, many tens of thousands of people were forced to flee their homes north of el-Geneina, capital of West Darfur, as a Janjaweed militia force, accompanied by Khartoum's helicopter-gunship assaults, swept through a number of undefended villages. It is likely that hundreds more died in these assaults, though no comprehensive mortality figures were promulgated by the UN force then on the ground (this force was denied access to the region in the assaults' aftermath, as were humanitarians).

The situation is now simply too chaotic to conduct the kind of statistically significant mortality studies that would give us a clearer picture of what happened in the period 2003–06 and subsequently. And with every year that the genocide continues (it will enter its seventh year in February 2009), evidence becomes weaker, more remote, less recoverable. Memories become less reliable; families continue to break apart; death from whatever causes eliminates many of those who might provide key data; and the remains of massacres and destroyed villages become less revealing, less accessible to the kind of forensic investigation that has never taken place. Indeed, there are many reliable reports that Khartoum has devoted considerable resources to obscuring the sites of larger massacres, including using helicopters and trucks to scatter human remains over desert areas.

For all the limitations of the mortality assessment offered here, it is far from clear that we will ever have the large, randomized cluster sampling that is the preferred statistical method of epidemiologists and social scientists. Total genocidal mortality has certainly continued to increase significantly since May 2006, but we might not be able to quantify that increase in meaningful fashion. Khartoum's resolute opposition to any investigation of global mortality will continue so long as the regime controls access to Darfur.

Given its limitations, and the need to make key assumptions in the absence of adequate data or relevant context in some cases, it might be asked: Is an assessment such as the present one justified? Here it is important to remember how urgent and dire were the warnings of large-scale mortality coming from senior UN officials, such as UN coordinator for humanitarian affairs Egeland and Asma Jahangir, then UN special rapporteur on extrajudicial, summary, or arbitrary executions. It was Jahangir, for example, who reported in late June 2004 that the "number of black Africans killed by Arab militias in the Darfur region of Sudan is 'bound to be staggering.'" Do such generalizations, coming from senior UN officials, permit agnosticism about what "staggering" mortality might mean quantitatively?

The very first mortality assessment in the series leading to the present effort was a modest attempt to correct what was transparently a massively understated UN mortality figure of 3,000 dead for the entire Darfur conflict, promulgated through March 2004, more than a year into the most violent phase of ethnically targeted human destruction. Sudan Focal Point/Europe, a highly reliable but little known advocacy and research organization, had sent a team to eastern Chad in January 2004, and its estimate at the time had an upper range of 30,000. We know now that this, too, massively understated human mortality at that moment, but it was still ten times the UN estimate. Notably, there was no methodology even alluded to in the UN promulgation of a figure of 3,000, nor was any context provided. It was simply a number, without clear ownership even within the UN.

Working from this initial statistical revision, I have sought in the many succeeding analyses to attend as fully as possible to all relevant data, even if these data are heterogeneous in ways that create methodological difficulties. In the present analysis, I offered a number of generalizations that subsequently proved in need of significant qualification; a number of predictions proved, at the time, excessively dire, though they were often echoing the views of highly informed humanitarian officials. The range of governing assumptions about violent mortality appears, in retrospect, to suggest that the lower-end figures offered were more appropriate. Despite these acknowledgments, I stand firmly by the statistical analysis as well as the attendant political and military analysis.

We may never now just how "staggering" genocidal mortality has been in Darfur, or will be; but the scale of human destruction is such that, for political, legal, and moral reasons, it is incumbent that we do as much as possible with the data we have. Not to do so is to continue by other means the international betrayal of the people of Darfur, who have lost so many and suffered so much.

Appendix 1: "Family Size" in Darfur

The primary source of comprehensive, statistically significant data on violent mortality in Darfur remains the September 2004 study "Documenting Atrocities in Darfur," by the Coalition for International Justice. On the basis of 1,136 carefully randomized interviews, conducted among the Darfurian refugee population in Chad at a number of camp locations along the border, the CIJ found that "sixty-one percent [of those interviewed] reported witnessing the killing of a family member."[49]

Some have raised legitimate questions about the meaning of "family member," and, in particular, whether this refers to nuclear or extended family. Much confusion might have been avoided if the CIJ investigators had made this distinction clearly, but they did not. Even so, their data are far too important to ignore, given the scale and comprehensiveness of the study. This writer has argued that it is statistically reasonable to use "nuclear family" size (for Darfur, five to six) as the basis for calculating violent mortality through August 2004, and as establishing a base rate for subsequent violent mortality. The justifications for this assumption are complex and partially arbitrary (though, I would argue, cautious), but, together, I believe they suggest that deployment of a figure equivalent in value to "family size" (five to six) works conservatively in governing the calculation of violent mortality.

It is critical to understand first how significant the underreporting of violent mortality is when the category includes only those interviewees who "reported witnessing the killing of a family member." For excluded from consideration are all families in which mortality (from all causes) was complete, thus leaving no possibility of a reporting presence in Chad. The number of families destroyed in their entirety is not known; but it is certainly a very high number, given the large (and statistically telling) number of surviving families in which only *one* member reports being alive. This alone could push the violent mortality total much higher.

Also not included in reports of those "witnessing the killing of a family member" are deaths that followed violent attack. The CIJ study reports that 28 per cent of those interviewed "directly witnessed" persons dying from the consequences of violent displacement before reaching Chad. These deaths must be considered the direct consequence of violence, if not violent deaths per se, and would also significantly increase violent mortality totals.

As significant as these factors are in underreporting of violent mortality, they do not speak directly to the question of family size. Here we must look at the nature of the interviews conducted by CIJ, and what they reveal beyond the bare fact that "sixty-one percent [of those interviewed] reported witnessing the killing of [at least one] family member." One detailed assessment by a genocide scholar who was among those conducting the CIJ interviews is especially revealing:

> For me, [asking about the witnessing of family members killed] was the single most painful part of the whole interviewing experience, because the vast majority had indeed witnessed more than one family member being killed, and it obviously pained the respondents to recite the names, relationship, cause of death (shooting, death from the bombing, stabbing, burning, clubbing). I usually stopped writing the information down after the fifth person, both because I ran out of space on the questionnaire form and because I didn't want to prolong the ordeal for the respondent.
>
> My clear recollection is that the types of relationship mentioned by our respondents were: son or daughter, husband or wife, mother or father, grandmother or grandfather, aunt or uncle, or cousin. I don't recall cases of more distant relatives being mentioned. This may be because they started with more immediate family and then I stopped after five. I don't really know. But my impression is that most of our respondents lost multiple members of their nuclear families as well as grandparents, aunts and uncles and cousins. Bottom line: the 61% who said they had witnessed a family member killed is a gross underindication of the extent of killing.[50]

This investigator is confident, on the basis of communications with other investigators, that his experience was not anomalous.

In turn, a simple way of conceiving of the statistical significance of such reporting is the following. If, instead of construing the meaning of "sixty-one percent reported witnessing the killing of a family member" as meaning "one and only one family member," we reasonably assume that these data represent an average of two "family" members seen killed, then even if "family" represents "extended family," this "extended family" could be as large as ten to twelve and the calculations by this writer using a "nuclear family" figure (five to six) would hold true. If the average number of "family" members seen killed was as great as three, then the calculations for violent mortality would hold for an "extended family" figure of fifteen to eighteen.

Again, these calculations do not include violent mortality experienced by families that perished in their entirety – or violent mortality represented by the 28 per cent of those interviewed who "directly witnessed" persons dying from the consequences of violent displacement before reaching Chad. Statistically, the effect of any attempt to include these deaths in the figures for "families" reporting "witnessing the killing of a family member" is to increase the size of the statistical range for "extended family," and thus a figure that would continue to yield mortality in the range of 160,000 to 210,000 human beings as of early September 2004.

In the absence of additional statistically significant data, we must make assumptions about continuing levels of violent human destruction on the basis of rates from September 2004. Assuming an average 50 per cent decline in violent mortality for the remaining months of 2004, and a 75 per cent decline in violent mortality from 2005 and 2006 to date, this still yields an additional 60,000 violent deaths. This in turn yields a range of 220,000 to 270,000 total violent deaths since the outbreak of major conflict.

Notes

1 United Nations Integrated Regional Information Networks (IRIN), "Sudan: Food Rations Drastically Cut in Darfur," 28 April 2006, http://www.irinnews.org/Report.aspx?ReportId=58871.
2 UNICEF-Sudan Nutrition Office, "Darfur Nutrition Update," *UNICEF*, 3 (March-April 2006), http://www.unicef.org/infobycountry/files/ DarfurNutUpdateMarchApril06.pdf.
3 United Nations World Food Program, "Emergency Report No.17, 28 April 2006," United Nations World Food Program 28 April 2006, http://www.wfp.org/english/?ModuleID=78&Key=684.
4 Lydia Polgreen, "U.N. Agency Cuts Food Rations for Sudan Victims in Half," New York *Times*, 29 April 2006, section A.
5 Human Rights News, "Sudan: Government Offensive Threatens Darfur Civilians," Human Rights Watch, 27 April 2006, http://hrw.org/english/ docs/2006/04/26/sudan13276.htm.

6 United Nations News Centre, "UN Aid in Northern Darfur Will Be Suspended Unless Rebel Attacks Stop," United Nations News Centre 28 April 2006, http://www.un.org/apps/news/story.asp?NewsID=18287&Cr=Sudan&Cr1=Darfur&Kw1=darfur&Kw2=sudan&Kw3=#.

7 Glenn Kessler, "U.S. Prods, Makes Promises to End Violence in Sudan's Darfur Region," Washington *Post*, 4 November 2005, http://www.washingtonpost.com/wp-dyn/content/article/2005/11/03/AR2005110301989_pf.html.

8 IRIN, "Sudan: Darfur Relief operation Could Collapse, Warns Egeland," 21 April 2006, http://www.irinnews.org/report.aspx?reportid=58804.

9 Edith M. Lederer, "U.N. Official: Violence Leaves Thousands in Darfur without Food and Facing Death," Associated Press, 14 March 2006, http://web.lexis-nexis.com.proxy2.lib.uwo.ca:2048/universe/document?_m=6ec6669bd7e0b5d8fef0727efbaddc54&_docnum=1&wchp=dGLbVtb-zSkVb&_md5=0afe4373fe6efcb0a4e086df54220b0d.

10 IRIN, "Sudan; UN Envoy Criticises Obstruction by Government," United Nations Office for the Coordination of Humanitarian Affairs, 5 April 2006, http://web.lexis-nexis.com.proxy2.lib.uwo.ca:2048/universe/document?_m=f51b0f6ce805be6d5b8d75ef8ed40f4d&_docnum=1&wchp=dGLbVtb-zSkVb&_md5=f6dfbb2ae5457fac5c8e8f839db75101.

11 Reuters, "NATO Plans Limited Presence," China Daily Source: *Financial Times* Information Limited – Asia Intelligence Wire, 28 April 2006, http://web.lexis-nexis.com.proxy2.lib.uwo.ca:2048/universe/document?_m=1a2b08521b7fc211798204f63b59c762&_docnum=1&wchp=dGLbVtb-zSkVb&_md5=724747eb22ca46692583f289bc044c21.

12 Ibid.

13 Alain Navarro, "Sudan to Rally Arab Support against Foreign Troops in Darfur," Agence France Presse, 26 March 2006, http://web.lexis-nexis.com.proxy2.lib.uwo.ca:2048/universe/document?_m=28a8607481b57df811ba609071a023ff&_docnum=3&wchp=dGLbVtb-zSkVb&_md5=5fb440a50e63ab57f45e209051b5b990.

14 Newsday, "Bin Laden Threatens America, Offers Truce on His Terms: U.S. Not Safe from Attack, al-Qaeda Leader Warns in First Statement since Dec., 2004," Edmonton *Journal*, 20 January 2006, http://web.lexis-nexis.com.proxy2.lib.uwo.ca:2048/universe/document?_m=9450a17c0e606bfa12622dd60821a848&_docnum=6&wchp=dGLbVtb-zSkVb&_md5=e4adc5b6964dba2bd0c37f157292012a.

15 United Nations Office for the Coordination of Humanitarian Affairs, "Fact Sheet on Access Restrictions in Darfur and Other Areas of Sudan," United Nations Office for the Coordination of Humanitarian Affairs, 20 April 2006, http://ochaonline.un.org/News/Emergencies/ComplexEmergencies/Sudan/tabid/1255/Default.aspx.

16 "Threatened UN Staff Leave Darfur," BBC News, 16 March 2005, http://news.bbc.co.uk/go/pr/fr/-/1/hi/world/africa/4354933.stm.

17 David Nabarro, presenter, "Mortality Projections for Darfur," World Health Organization, 15 October 2004, http://www.who.int/mediacentre/news/briefings/2004/mb5/en/.

18 Physicians for Human Rights, "Darfur: Assault on Survival," January 2006, http://physiciansforhumanrights.org/library/report-sudan-2006.html.

19 Evelyn Depoortere et al., "Violence and Mortality in West Darfur, Sudan (2003–04): Epidemiological Evidence from Four Surveys," *The Lancet*, vol. 364, no. 9442 (1 October 2004), http://image.thelancet.com/extras/04art9087web.pdf.

20 United Nations News Centre, "Sudan: UN Human Rights Expert Expects Large Number of Deaths in Darfur," 29 June 2004, http://www.un.org/apps/news/story.asp?NewsID=11191&Cr=sudan&Cr1=&Kw1=darfur&Kw2=sudan&Kw3=.

21 Ibid.

22 US State Department, *Documenting Atrocities in Darfur*, State Publication 11182 (9 September 2004), http://www.state.gov/g/drl/rls/36028.htm.

23 Office of UN Residence and Humanitarian Coordinator for the Sudan, "Darfur Humanitarian Profile," Humanitarian Information Centre, no. 6 (1 September 2004): 5.

24 Ibid., 9.

25 Depoortere, "Violence and Mortality in West Darfur, Sudan (2003–04)."

26 US State Department, *Documenting Atrocities in Darfur*.

27 United Nations World Heath Organization and Federal Ministry of Health, Sudan, "Mortality Survey among Internally Displaced Persons and Other Affected Populations in Greater Darfur, Sudan," September 2005, http://www.emro.who.int/sudan/media/pdf/CMS%20Darfur%202005%20final%20report_11%2010%2005.pdf.

28 Office of UN Deputy Special Representative of the UN Secretary-General for Sudan UN Resident and Humanitarian Coordinator, "Darfur Humanitarian Profile no. 8," United Nations Sudan Information Gateway, 1 November 2004, http://www.unsudanig.org/docs/Darfur%20Humanitarian%20Profile%20Narrative%20November%202004.pdf.

29 Office of UN Deputy Special Representative of the UN Secretary-General for Sudan UN Resident and Humanitarian Coordinator,

"Darfur Humanitarian Profile no. 16," United Nations Sudan Information Gateway, 1 July 2005, http://www.unsudanig.org/docs/Darfur%20Humanitarian%20Profile%20Narrative%20July%202005.pdf.

30 Mark Turner, "Middle East & Africa: UN Weighs up Stopping Aid Work in Darfur," *Financial Times* [U.K.], 16 December 2004, http://search.ft.com/ftArticle?startDate=16%2F12%2F2004&dsz=0&dse=true&queryText=Egeland&endDate=16%2F12%2F2004&activeTab=ftNews&aje=false&resultsToReturn=10&id=041216001002.

31 Eric Reeves, "Quantifying Genocide in Darfur: Part 1," sudanreeves.org., 28 April 2006, http://www.sudanreeves.org/index.php?name=News&file=article&sid=102.

32 Eric Reeves, "Why Abuja Won't Save Darfur," *New Republic*, 10 May 2005, http://www.sudanreeves.org/Sections-req-viewarticle-artid-565-allpages-1-theme-Printer.html.

33 Richard Waddington, "Arbour Urges ICC to Act on Darfur Crimes," Reuters, 11 May 2006, http://www.swissinfo.org/eng/international/ticker/detail/Arbour_urges_ICC_to_act_on_Darfur_crimes.html?siteSect=143&sid=6709149&cKey=1147356552000.

34 Luis Moreno-Ocampo, "Report of the Prosecutor of the International Criminal Court to the UN Security Council Pursuant to UNSCR 1593 (2005)," International Criminal Court, 29 June 2005, 8.

35 Waddington, "Arbour Urges ICC to Act on Darfur Crimes."

36 Lydia Polgreen, "Truce Is Talk, Agony Is Real in Darfur War," New York *Times*, 12 May 2006, http://web.lexis-nexis.com/universe/document?_m=4d62542f4bcb4400e78150e5a3607bfc&_docnum=1&wchp=dGLzVzz-zSkVA&_md5=92618483f95df42632149d94d8bb0119.

37 David E. Sanger, "Bush Sees Need to Expand Role of NATO in Sudan," New York *Times*, 17 February 2006, http://web.lexis-nexis.com/universe/document?_m=68eaf72e42851cbe6c7ccd539743335b&_docnum=3&wchp=dGLzVzz-zSkVA&_md5=d35cb3e680d16c49a549821183c35e18.

38 Glen Kessler, "Sudanese Official Is a No-Show at State Department," Washington *Post*, 13 May 2006, http://www.washingtonpost.com/wp-dyn/content/article/2006/05/12/AR2006051201977.html.

39 Ibid.

40 Eric Reeves, "Khartoum Blasts the Red Cross," *International Herald Tribune*, 23 January 2001, http://www.iht.com/articles/2001/01/23/ederic.t.php.

41 Kessler, "Sudanese Official Is a No-Show at State Department."

42 Guy Dinmore, Andrew England, and Mark Turner, "Sudan Ministers Named in Leaked UN Darfur List," *Financial Times* [U.K.], 22 February 2006, http://web.lexis-nexis.com/universe/document?_m=8eb66fee88c

d7e6dd8923f9c040fc4b4&_docnum=107&wchp=dGLbVtb-zSkVA&_m
d5=24e7097c2be48da6d3be887cb8efe0af.

43 United Nations Security Council, "Security Council Demands Sudan
    Disarm Militias in Darfur," Press Release SC/8160, 30 July 2004,
    http://www.un.org/News/Press/docs/2004/sc8160.doc.htm.

44 United Nations News Centre, "No Time to Lose in Setting up UN Force
    for Sudan's Darfur Region – Annan," United Nations News Centre, 9
    May 2006, http://www.un.org/apps/news/story.asp?NewsID=18412&Cr
    =Sudan&Cr1=&Kw1=darfur&Kw2=support&Kw3=.

45 Simon Tisdall, "Six Month Delay for UN Darfur Force," *The
    Guardian*, 11 May 2006, http://www.guardian.co.uk/international/
    story/0,,1772013,00.htmL.

46 Jan Egeland, interview by Rob Anderson, *New Republic*, 12 May 2006,
    http://www.tnr.com/doc.mhtml?i=w060501&s=anderson050506.

47 United Nations Office for the Coordination of Humanitarian Affairs,
    "Fact Sheet on Access Restrictions in Darfur and Other Areas of
    Sudan."

48 Jan Egeland, "Killing Fields," *Wall Street Journal*, 4 May 2006.

49 US State Department, *Documenting Atrocities in Darfur*.

50 Coalition for International Justice investigator, confidential e-mail
    message to author, 1 May 2006.

PART THREE

Representation
and Response

CHAPTER SEVEN

Saving Lives in Darfur, 2003–06?: Lots of Talk, Little to No Action

SAMUEL TOTTEN

Despite the fact that mass killing and rape of black Africans in Darfur, along with the systematic destruction of their villages, began in early 2003, no outside troops entered Darfur until August 2004. And even then, only 300 African Union (AU) troops were sent to an area roughly the size of France (first, 150 from Rwanda and then, later the same month, 150 from Nigeria). The AU's mandate, though, did not include the protection of the black African civilians (most of whom belonged to one of three tribal groups: the Fur, Massaleit, or Zaghawa); rather, the AU troops were designated, at the insistence of the Government of Sudan (GOS), to be "cease-fire monitors" whose main task was to provide protection for the outside experts monitoring human rights violations. By August 2004, the United Nations had estimated that "almost 50,000 deaths had occurred and that at least 500 black Africans were being killed or dying on a daily basis from unattended injuries, starvation or disease." One million black Africans had also already been driven from their villages into the mountains, deserts, or internally displaced persons (IDP) camps or across the border into Chad.

The fact that the killing, rape, and destruction of village after village had gone on for well over a year before any action was taken to help the black African population is unconscionable. In light of all of the promises that were made over the past two decades as a result of the international community's anaemic response to one man-made humanitarian disaster after another in such places as Iraq in the late 1980s, Rwanda in 1994, and Srebrenica in 1995, to name but three, the reaction to the Darfur crisis/genocide is nothing short of shameful.[1]

Talk, Talk, and More Talk

Throughout the latter half of 2003 and most of 2004, the vast majority of "action" taken in regard to the Darfur crisis was talk, talk, and more talk by the international community as innocent men, women, children, and babies were viciously attacked by GOS troops and Arab militia (Janjaweed, meaning men on horseback with guns or, more colloquially, devils on horseback). And, even though an ever-increasing (but always inadequate) number of AU troops began trickling into Darfur in August 2004, talk dominated throughout the rest of 2004, 2005, and well into 2006. More specifically, while the number of AU troops in Darfur numbered about 7,000 in 2006, almost all sources, including the AU, readily recognize and admit that that number cannot adequately secure the safety of the black Africans.

Undoubtedly, there is a need for "talk" (be it declarations of concern, urgent warnings issued by non-governmental organizations [NGOs], or others, and, of course, diplomatic discussions) when a crisis is on the horizon and/or has already broken out. Indeed, the warnings issued by various UN agencies and the US Holocaust Memorial Museum's Committee on Conscience, the major report cum warning by Human Rights Watch in April 2004, and even the resolution by the US Congress (22 July 2004) that declared genocide was being perpetrated in Darfur were all helpful in bringing the issue to the attention of the general public, media, and others.

But talk – and mainly talk – can go too far, and it has vis-à-vis the crisis in Darfur.[2] Indeed, when violence is about to break out and/or actually has broken out, the situation *demands* that all of the diplomatic efforts, peace talks, debates, declarations, and resolutions (including attempts at mediation and conflict resolution and the threat of sanctions) be, at the very least, complemented by a strong military mission (preferably with a Chapter VII mandate under the UN Charter) for the express purpose of stanching the killing. If that does not happen – and it hasn't in Darfur – then talk, as the adage goes, is cheap. But, while the talk is cheap, the price paid by the targeted population is not: they often "pay" with that which is most precious to them: their lives, the lives of their loved ones, their livelihoods, their land, their villages, and, of course, their homes.

What follows is an overview of some of the innumerable resolutions, talks, debates, and diplomatic efforts that the United Nations, individual nations, regional organizations, and the actors involved in the Darfur conflict (the Government of Sudan and the rebel groups) have engaged in from December 2003 through mid-February 2006, and what, if anything, resulted. To drive home the point that such talk is, paradoxically, both cheap and horrifically costly, the number of black African deaths as a result of the crisis is delineated according to the same timeline as mentioned above. December 2003 has been selected as the starting point for this discussion for that is when the UN's under-secretary general for humanitarian affairs and emergency relief coordinator, Jan Egeland, declared that Darfur was "one of the worst humanitarian crises in the world." In other words, by that point, the international community was "put on notice" that the situation in Darfur was dire.

The United Nations

Undoubtedly, the UN, in its various capacities, contributed significantly to drawing attention to the ever-increasing violence in Darfur, but it is also a fact that the UN has done little to nothing to stop the killing, rape, and devastation. From December 2003 through March 2004, various UN officials issued strong statements regarding their alarm over the situation in Darfur. By April 2004, hundreds of thousands and possibly up to one million black Africans had fled in terror from their villages. An early study of violence and mortality in Darfur conducted by Doctors without Borders conservatively estimated that about 3,000 black Africans had been killed by January 2004.[3] From late October 2003 through late February 2004, the Sudanese government "almost completely banned humanitarian agencies from Darfur,"[4] which exacerbated the situation on the ground and resulted in large numbers of deaths from starvation, disease, and unattended wounds and injuries.

Just two months later, on 19 March 2004, the United Nations humanitarian coordinator for Sudan, Mukesh Kapila, claimed that "ethnic cleansing" was being perpetrated in Darfur by GOS troops and Arab militia: "The only difference between Rwanda and Darfur now is the numbers involved ... [The slaughter in Darfur] is more than just a conflict, it is an organized attempt to do away with a group of people.'"[5] Not a month later, on 2 April 2004, in a briefing to the Security Council, Jan Egeland also described the crisis in Darfur as a case of ethnic cleansing. The result of such warnings was a "pre-approved, tepid statement to the press" by the Security Council president in "which he expressed concern at the 'humanitarian crises' in Darfur but refrained from acknowledging that the human rights situation [was] the cause of the humanitarian crisis."[6] Concerned about the reports emanating out of Darfur, the UN Office of the High Commissioner for Human Rights (OHCHR) finally sent a team to Darfur between 5 and 15 April in order to conduct an investigation into the alleged human rights violations against the black Africans. The report, which was never officially made public, "strongly condemned the Sudanese government's abuses in Darfur, which it said might constitute crimes against humanity and war crimes. The government, it asserted, was conducting a "'reign of terror' directed at the African Fur, Massalit and Zaghawa."[7] Initially, the European Union (EU) seemed ready to act on the findings, but, in a classic case of backsliding and realpolitik, it then had second thoughts:

> At the last minute the E.U., which had co-sponsored a strong resolution condemning the abuses and reestablishing the mandate for a special rapporteur for human rights, backed down. E.U. members reportedly feared insufficient support from key African and Arabic members of the UN body, who had bowed to Sudanese pressure. Instead, a weaker decision eventually passed. This decision included the appointment of an independent expert on human rights but failed to condemn the crimes against humanity and war crimes or other violations of international humanitarian law committed by the Sudanese government. Only one member voted against this watered down statement – the United States – and two members abstained, Australia and Ukraine. [Thus,] the world's preeminent human rights body failed to perform the role for which it was created, limiting itself to expression of "deep concern" – rather than condemnation – over the situation in Sudan.[8]

During this same period, at the tenth anniversary commemoration of the 1994 Rwandan genocide (7 April 2004), UN Secretary General Kofi Annan spoke about the human rights disaster in Darfur. In part, Annan said: "[The] reports [about Darfur] leave me with a deep sense of foreboding ... Whatever terms used to describe the situation, the international community cannot stand idle."[9] He continued: "It is vital that international humanitarian workers and human rights experts be given full access to the region, and to the victims, without further delay ... If that is denied, the international community must be prepared to take swift and appropriate action."[10] By "action," Annan explained, he meant military action. But military action would be a last resort and relied on in only the most "extreme" situation. Tellingly, what he meant by "extreme" was left unsaid.

By then, hundreds of thousands of people had fled Darfur, and a conservative estimate of those who had been killed was approximately 10,000.[11] That number did not take into account those who had perished from starvation, illness, or other causes as a result of the crisis. One can only surmise that hundreds of thousands of people on the move against their will and 10,000 killed did not, at least according to the secretary general's way of thinking, constitute an "extreme" situation, for the UN continued to forego a military intervention.

On 8 April 2004 the Government of Sudan and the rebel groups (the Sudan Liberation Movement/Army [SLM/A] and the Justice and Equality Movement [JEM]) signed the N'djamena Ceasefire Agreement.[12] However, shortly after the ceasefire went into effect (11 April 2004), it was broken. Human Rights Watch asserted that

> the ceasefire ... was followed almost immediately by allegations of violations, mainly continuing *Janjaweed* attacks on civilians. This was unsurprising given the government's lack of commitment to disarm and disband the groups. The ceasefire agreement referred to the government's responsibility to "neutralize" the militias, but did not define this term. Many observers are concerned that the government may simply incorporate the militias in the police and regular armed forces, an alarming possibility given the gravity of their crimes.[13]
>
> Additional flaws in the April 8 ceasefire agreement included the lack of a clear timetable and structure for international monitoring and the lack of any mechanism to monitor ongoing human rights abuses that continue to affect tens if not hundreds of thousands of Darfurians. The ceasefire also lacked measures to reverse ethnic cleansing, such as an agreement that the Sudanese government would immediately withdraw the *Janjaweed* militias from those parts of Darfur it seized from 2003 to the present ... By late April, the ceasefire monitors had not yet deployed. Reports of ceasefire violations and the consistent lack of protection for civilians continued to grow.[14]

Just over a month and a half later, on 25 May 2004, another UN presidential statement, issued under the auspices of the Security Council, "reiterate[d] its grave concern at the ongoing humanitarian crisis and widespread human rights violations, including continued attacks on civilians that are placing the lives of hundreds of thousands at risk."[15] The presidential statement then voiced deep concern over the "continuing reports of large-scale violations of ... international humanitarian law in Darfur, including indiscriminate attacks on civilians, sexual violence, forced displacement and acts of violence, especially those with an ethnic dimension," and demanded that those responsible be held accountable.[16] Yet again, more talk, no action. No action that is by the international community, despite the fact the GOS troops and Janjaweed continued to carry out its murderous actions against the black Africans.

At the end of May 2004, the GOS finally agreed to allow the AU to deploy a force in Sudan to monitor the implementation of the April 2004 ceasefire that had been signed by the government and the rebel groups. While this was a start in the right direction, it was also largely cosmetic in light of the fact that Sudan insisted that the AU troops be deemed "ceasefire monitors" versus troops with the mandate to halt the violence. Concomitantly, and as mentioned at the outset of this chapter, the number of troops allowed in by the GOS could do little more than serve as a presence – and even then, in only a fraction of the tremendous land mass that makes up Darfur.

At that time, the UN reported that up to a half a million children were suffering from hunger and disease as a result of being violently forced with their families from their villages into under-equipped IDP camps. It also reported that refugee children were dying every night in Darfur from starvation. In response, Carol Bellamy, director of the United Nations International Children's Emergency Fund (UNICEF), warned: "During my visit to Darfur, it was clear that people are continuing to flee their villages ... Many [women] said their husbands were killed ... It [is] now a race against time to provide children and their families with basic life-saving services such as clean water, sanitation, nutrition, shelter and health care."[17] Addressing the same circumstances, Annan described the crisis in Darfur as a "humanitarian emergency of catastrophic proportions." Be that as it may, the talk continued bereft of any real action to stanch the killing and dying.

On 3 July 2004 the GOS and Secretary General Annan issued a joint communiqué in which the GOS promised "to immediately start disarming the *Janjaweed* and other armed outlaws groups," "allow the deployment of human rights monitors," and "ensure that all individuals and groups accused of human rights violations are brought to justice without delay."[18] Still, the GOS and the Janjaweed kept up their attacks in Darfur.

In mid-July and in response to the continued attacks, US Secretary of State Colin Powell began circulating a draft resolution that threatened the GOS with sanctions if it continued to fail to implement the agreements delineated in the July 3rd communiqué. On 30 July 2004 the UN Security Council adopted Resolution 1556, a severely watered-down version of Powell's draft. Strikingly, the resolution no longer even contained the word "sanctions." Instead, it stated that the Security Council would consider "further actions" against Sudan, under Article 41 of the UN Charter, if the GOS did not rein in the Janjaweed within thirty days, commit to negotiating a political settlement, and prosecute the militia leaders who were responsible for perpetrating the killings, rapes, and destruction of villages. According to Article 41, "the Security Council may decide *what measures not involving the use of armed force* are to be employed to give effect to its decisions, including complete or partial interruption of economic relations and of rail, sea, air, postal, telegraphic, radio and other means of communication and the severance of diplomatic relations."[19] Making use of Article 41, however, underscored the international community's lack of intention to commit itself to quelling the actions of the GOS and the Janjaweed, actions that were widely recognized as constituting, at the least, crimes against humanity. And that was the message that the Sudanese government obviously picked up, for it continued to disregard the latest "threat" and to do little to nothing to halt the ongoing large-scale human rights violations.

Despite the watering down of the resolution and the fact that, in the words of John Danforth, US ambassador to the United Nations, "it had been nearly four weeks since the GOS had signed a joint communiqué with the Secretary-General on its commitment to take specific action to address the situation in Darfur and had kept none of those promises," the US ambassador took an equivocal stance: "The last thing we wanted to do was *lay the ground work for sanctions*, but the Government of Sudan has left us no choice ... So the resolution adopted is our necessary response if we are to help save the people."[20] Such a weak response to such a weak resolution suggests that either someone high up in the US government was not truly adamant about applying swift, tough sanctions on Sudan in order to press it to halt the genocidal actions in Darfur or some official (possibly Danforth) saw absolutely no point in lodging a complaint. Possibly it would not have done any good to issue a complaint, but then again it may have drawn valuable attention to the crisis as well as the Security Council's inadequate and ineffective response to it.

Gunter Pleuger, Germany's ambassador to the United Nations, was more forceful than Danforth, observing that "while the Council had been deliberating, the killing and suffering in the province had continued."[21] Brazil's ambassador to the UN, Ronaldo Mota Sardenberg, went even further, stating that he regretted that "the resolution did not add vigor by acting under Chapter VII, which, [in my] opinion, it had not done, for the reference to Articles 41 was a compromise."[22]

By this point (late July 2004), over one million black Africans had fled their homes and were displaced in IDP camps in Darfur and an estimated 188,000 others had fled to Chad. Conservative estimates of those who had been killed had increased to between 30,000 and 50,000.[23] Other researchers put the total number of dead as high as 100,000.

Not only did the GOS refuse to, as the UN resolution demanded, rein in the Janjaweed or bring any of the perpetrators to justice, it reportedly convinced untold numbers of Janjaweed to become Sudanese soldiers and police officers.[24] This made the situation much worse, being roughly equivalent to letting murderers, rapists, and thieves out of prison to serve as members of a "neighborhood watch" committee in a local community.

On 30 August 2004 Annan reported to the Security Council that the GOS had neither halted its attacks against civilians nor helped to protect them. But, instead of urging the Security Council to follow through on its threat to sanction the GOS, Annan simply called on the council to support the AU's offer to deploy troops to Darfur. Even if the Security Council had voted to provide the AU with more resources and/or training for its under-resourced and ill-prepared troops, the situation would have been problematic since the AU mission would still have been operating under a totally inadequate mandate. A half-month later, on 13 September 2004, the World Health Organization (WHO) issued a mortality report in which it indicated that 6,000 to 10,000 black Africans were dying *each and every month* in Darfur. It further asserted that, while many people were dying of diarrhea, the greatest cause of death was murder.

On 18 September 2004, at the urging of the United States, the Security Council adopted Resolution 1564, which, in part, established an International Commission of Inquiry on Darfur (COI) for the express purpose of "investigating reports of violations of international humanitarian law and human rights law in Darfur by all parties, to determine also whether or not acts of genocide have occurred, and to identify the perpetrators of such violations with a view to ensuring that those responsible are held accountable." The adoption of the resolution, though, was agreed upon only after "the United States agreed to water down language *that explicitly threatened sanctions against Sudanese officials and/or the country's oil industry* if Khartoum failed to comply" with the measures spelled out in the resolution.[25] The watered-down wording stated that the UN would "consider" imposing sanctions on Sudan if it failed to bring the Janjaweed under control and refused to accept a larger AU observer mission. Again, this proved to be no more than mere talk comprised of idle threats. Indeed, by this juncture, after so many idle threats, it would not have been surprising if Sudanese officials had begun to consider the Security Council as little more than a paper tiger. How could it not? Time and again, the Security Council was more bluff than action when it came to Darfur. (Another example: the Security Council's threat on 30 July that it would impose sanctions if Sudan failed to rein in the Janjaweed within thirty days was virtually dismissed by the GOS. And when the GOS made no attempt to meet the conditions of the resolution, no sanctions were forthcoming.)

The UN Security Council, though, was not about to stop issuing resolutions. Thus, on 19 November 2004, it passed Resolution 1574, which demanded, in part, that "[the Sudanese] Government and rebel forces and all other armed groups immediately cease all violence and attacks, including abduction, refrain from forcible relocation of civilians [and] ensure that their members comply with international humanitarian law."[26] No warnings, threats, or any other type of coercive action was mentioned should the parties neglect to follow through on their past agreements to cease and desist from fighting and fail to provide adequate protection for the civilians in the area.

On 25 January 2005 the findings of the UN's Commission of Inquiry on Darfur were released. The COI stated that GOS troops and the Janjaweed had clearly committed widespread and heinous international crimes, including crimes against humanity and war crimes. The finding that drew the most attention was the COI's assertion that, at least in regard to the highest GOS officials, the critical element of genocide intent was not found. That said, the COI report stated that the crimes committed "may be no less serious and heinous than genocide." Furthermore, the report noted that "a competent court on a case by case basis" could still make a determination that certain individuals, including GOS officials, possessed genocidal intent.

The COI report has been praised by some as a "dramatic example of high performance by the UN Secretariat ... competent and thorough"[27] and "both empirically and legally ... serious and thoughtful."[28] Conversely, the report has been lambasted as "badly compromised in its tendentious and poorly reasoned conclusion about the absence of evidence of 'genocide intent' on the part of Khartoum in Darfur. Indeed, so egregiously poor are the legal and factual arguments ... that we must conclude the Commission did not feel politically free to make a determination of genocide."[29] Speculation abounds as to whether the United Nations purposely avoided describing the crisis in Darfur as a case of genocide, knowing that if it did it could obligate the UN, under the UN Convention on Genocide, to take action (including, if merited, force). Only the members of the commission and upper-echelon UN officials know for sure, and thus far no one has shed light on the decision.

Laudatory or not, it is also a fact that, while COI personnel carried out their investigation in December 2004 and January 2005, many thousands of black African Darfurians continued to die. The deaths were the result not so much of brutal attacks – for, "by the time the Commission of Inquiry began its work, Sudan Government Military Intelligence and the *Janjaweed* had largely completed theirs"[30] – as of genocide by attrition.[31]

A major question is: What evidence did the COI really need to have before it could conclude that the black Africans required concrete help to stave off ongoing attacks and deaths due to starvation, dehydration, and disease? Indeed, was it really necessary to corroborate the finding of numerous investigations and reports, emanating from both the UN and other reliable organizations and agencies, that every day, week, and month that went by without action meant an ever-increasing number of deaths? By this time, *the UN itself*, among others, conservatively estimated that 70,000 black African Darfurians had already perished.[32] Indeed, just a month later, the United States Department of State's Bureau of Intelligence and Research (2005) estimated that between 98,000 and 181,000 people black Africans had died in Darfur since March 2003. Instead of another investigation, would it not have been wiser to institute an effective intervention to halt the atrocities no matter what they were called?

On 29 March 2005, by a vote of twelve to zero, with Russia, China, and Algeria abstaining, the UN Security Council passed Resolution

1591, which authorized sanctions (freezing of assets and travel restrictions) on individuals responsible for violating international law in Darfur. It also "demanded" that Sudan immediately halt air attacks against Darfurian villages and called for the banning of the movement of arms into Sudan by all non-state actors. Furthermore, it mandated that the GOS request permission from the UN panel to move any type of weapons systems and military supplies into Darfur. The resolution also charged Secretary General Kofi Annan with appointing a panel of experts (along with a committee from the council) to study and design the sanctions package. Undoubtedly, this was a real attempt at a concrete action that could have had positive results, but just over two months later, on 2 June 2005, frustrated at the lack of action vis-à-vis this latest resolution, Peter Takirambudde, executive director of the Africa division of Human Rights Watch, issued a terse statement in which he said: "U.N. sanctions on those responsible for the violence in Darfur would have some teeth if implemented. But after two months of foot-dragging, Security Council members still haven't taken steps toward appointing a panel."[33] Six months later there was still no action. This time, in almost total exasperation, Takirambudde asserted that "the Sudanese government's systematic attacks on villains in Darfur have been accompanied by a policy of impunity for all those responsible for the crimes ... [It] feigns compliance with international demands by setting up committees that produce absolutely no results ... Nine months ago the Security set up a Sanctions Committee to penalize individuals responsible for abuses in Darfur, but it has yet to act against anyone."[34] Thus, even with what seemed to be the best of intentions, the Security Council, once again, ended up spewing nothing but hot air when it floated the possibility of issuing sanctions.

On 31 March 2005, as a direct result of the COI report, the UN Security Council passed a resolution (Resolution 1593) referring the crisis in Darfur to the International Criminal Court (ICC). On 5 April 2004 the COI provided the ICC with the names of fifty-one suspects, comprised of both government officials and army officers, who had allegedly perpetrated crimes against the black Africans of Darfur. While both of these actions were positive steps to seek justice on behalf of the black Africans, it is also a fact that neither is likely, in the short run, to save the lives of imperilled Darfurians. Indeed, as time would tell, they were still at the mercy of the GOS and the Janjaweed. Besides, the actual arrests of the alleged perpetrators (if, in fact, any are arrested), along with their trials, will take years to complete. By that time, who knows how many more deaths will occur in Darfur? Thus, the refer-ral, as significant as it is in conveying the message that impunity is no longer acceptable for those who commit such atrocities, does not and cannot, at least in and of itself, take the place of a strong Chapter VII military intervention to halt the killing.

In mid-2005 there was a sharp tapering off of attacks by the GOS and the Janjaweed. However, between September and October 2005, such attacks were back at full tilt.[35] Why the attacks waned is subject to conjecture, and could have included any and/or a combination of the following: the fact that most of the black African villages in the three states of Darfur had been destroyed and few people were left to kill; a knee-jerk, but temporary, reaction by the Sudanese government to the referral to the ICC; a reaction to the sanctions imposed (as min-imal as they were) by the Security Council; a "diplomatic" ploy used during the peace talks with the rebel groups; diplomatic pressure by the United States, which now saw Sudan as a "partner" in fighting ter-rorism; diplomatic pressure by another country; or a simple regroup-ing of GOS forces and the Janjaweed.

In January 2006 the United Nations began publicly speaking about "deploying a larger force of its own peacekeeping troops to replace those of the African Union."[36] However, the GOS was adamant that it would not allow UN troops to be deployed in Darfur.

The GOS and the Main Rebel Groups

Well over a year into the Darfur crisis, representatives of the GOS, the Sudanese Liberation Movement/Army, and the Justice and Equality Movement, among others, had begun holding peace talks. Rounds of talks – the Inter-Sudanese Peace Talks – were initiated on 17 July 2004 and by February 2006 there had been seven such rounds. The talks were heated and rife with disagreements (ranging from who should attend the meetings and how they should be conducted to major issues concerning the settlement of the crisis). They were also bogged down by periodic walkouts. To a large extent, the talks resulted in just that – talk.

On 6 July 2005, at the conclusion of the fifth round of peace talks, the GOS and the two main rebel groups (the SLM/A and the JEM) adopted a "Declaration of Principles" which called for new security arrangements in Darfur and for the return of some 200,000 refugees in Chad and nearly two million internally displaced persons to their villages. The Declaration of Principles also stated that "there should be respect for different ethnic and religious groups across Sudan, as well as an equitable distribution of national wealth."[37] Reaching agreement on the declaration "took the warring sides almost four weeks of talks in the Nigerian capital, Abuja [to work out], after progress was slowed by splits within the two rebel groups and arguments over the presence of Chad and Eritrea as mediators."[38] Claire Soares, a journalist with the UN Office for the Coordination of Humanitarian Affairs, noted that while the "four previous rounds of talks in Abuja had ended in stalemate, and while this fifth round produced the declaration of principles, it failed to deal with the nitty-gritty of bringing peace to this semi-desert region."[39] Ultimately, the finalization of the accompanying peace settlement was postponed until the end of August in order to allow for all actors to attend to the "finer details." By the start of the sixth round, which began in September, the details still had not been worked out.

The sixth round opened on 15 September 2005 and crumbled on 20 October as a result of the fact that the rebels, who had fractured into new and smaller groups, could not come to a consensus as to who should take the lead in the talks or what the strategy should be. A third rebel group, the National Movement for Reform and Development (NMRD), asserted that it would not recognize the outcome of the talks if it was not included in them. Also, beginning in September and continuing through October, the killing and death toll in Darfur actually spiked. In fact, the death toll in Darfur during the latter period was at its highest since the hottest point of the crisis back in mid-2004.

Along with all of their fits, starts, and halts, the meetings also resulted in one broken promise and agreement after another. For example, two accords (in which the GOS agreed to create a no fly-zone over Darfur, to ban military flights over rebel-controlled territories, to disarm the Janjaweed, and to allow humanitarian aid workers unimpeded access to the refugees) signed on 9 November 2004, by the GOS, the SLM/A, and the JEM, were broken almost immediately. More specifically, the very next day, 10 November, GOS troops broke one of the agreements when it attacked numerous Darfurian refugee camps – an action witnessed by both AU and UN observers.

The seventh round of peace talks between the GOS and the rebel groups began in November 2005 and continued into early 2006, but for months at a time little headway was made. Indeed, the start-again, stop-again mode of the talks exemplified the nature of the efforts. On

4 January 2006 the *Sudan Tribune* reported that "talks between the warring parties of Sudan's Darfur region over power-sharing arrangements [had become] deadlocked, thus impeding the search for an overall peace deal to end three years of bloodshed."[40] On 24 January 2006, speaking out of disappointment and not a little anger, Dr Salim Ahmed Salim, the African Union special envoy for Darfur and chief mediator, noted that two months after the start of the seventh round of talks the various parties had not kept their promises and thus the results were not "commensurate with the time spent."[41] He further observed that "every passing day meant more suffering for the people of Darfur."[42]

The very next day, 23 January 2006, the peace talks came to a complete halt as rebel delegations withdrew to await the result of President Omar al-Bashir's bid to win the chairmanship of the AU. When Sudan retracted its bid, the talks resumed. Commenting on the talks, the UN's IRIN news organization reported the following: "So far, the 15 months of talks in Nigeria between the rebel groups and the Sudanese government have made little progress beyond a fragile cease-fire, frequently broken by all sides. Gunmen are still targeting unarmed civilians and the AU force of 7,000 on the ground lacks the funds and military capacity to protect civilians against attack. Humanitarian workers estimate that more than 180,000 people have been killed and nearly two million forced to flee their homes because of bloodshed. The UN special envoy for Sudan Jan Pronk has called for an international force of between 12,000 and 20,000 to protect civilians against attack and separate the warring sides."[43] Only time will tell if all of the talk results in something positive in regard to bringing an end to all of the killing and dying in Darfur.

The United States

On 24 June 2004 the United States House of Representatives submitted a resolution "declaring genocide in Darfur." This resolution, which was then referred to the House Committee on International Relations, was notable. Unlike what transpired, for example, during the 1994 Rwandan genocide, this time members of Congress actually spoke out about the occurrence of genocide in another part of the world and attempted to do something positive. That being said, what was also notable was that, by June 2004, an estimated 30,000 to 100,000 black African Darfurians had already perished as a result of the crisis. (The numbers vary depending on the source. The huge discrepancy between the two figures is due to the ongoing disagreement among the UN, individual governments, NGOs, and scholars in regard to the best way to ascertain the mortality rate in Darfur.) The question that comes to the fore is: What took members Congress so long to take such action? In other words, what were they waiting for? For the number to climb to "genocidal proportions" before speaking out? To ascertain whether the "issue" was going to "silently go away," "disappear," or "fall off the radar," so to speak? No one really knows except for the members themselves and they have not commented on the matter.

A full month before the submission of the resolution, on 20 May 2004, Doctors without Borders (Médecins sans Frontières) reported that "the whole population [of Darfur] is teetering on the verge of mass starvation."[44] It continued: "Water systems, crops and livestock were looted or destroyed during attacks on villages. People have not been able to plant and no harvest is expected this year. The whole population faces food shortages and is in danger of starvation in the very near future unless substantial food distributions can be organized. As people are weakened by hunger, they will only become more vulnerable to disease. Threats of malaria and diarrheal diseases will only increase with the onset of the rainy season, and the death and suffering could escalate to catastrophic proportions."[45]

It is also worth noting that, a month prior to the House of Representatives' submission of its resolution, a US official had asserted, off the record, that it would be miraculous if "only" 100,000 black Africans perished throughout the summer of 2004." And, in early June 2004, Andrew Natsios, the director of the US Agency for International Development (USAID), estimated that at least a third of a million refugees were "likely to perish for lack of food or basic medicines."[46]

A month later, on 22 July 2004, the US House of Representatives and the US Senate passed a concurrent resolution[47] declaring that the situation in Darfur constituted "genocide" and calling on the Bush administration to "seriously consider multilateral or even unilateral intervention to stop genocide in Darfur, Sudan, should the United Nations Security Council fail to act; and to impose targeted sanctions, including visa bans and the freezing of assets of the Sudanese National Congress and affiliated business and individuals directly responsible for the atrocities in Darfur, Sudan."

Ultimately, just as the UN failed to take any concrete action to halt the killing, so did the United States and virtually every other nation outside Africa. And thus, while Congress' call for action was extremely positive (even if late in coming), the lack of action by the United States, the UN, and the rest of the international community spoke volumes. Tellingly, and ironically, instead of sitting on the sidelines and pretending that nothing horrific was happening in Darfur – as the United States and others did during the Rwandan genocide – this time everyone seemed to know about the horrors but still did little to nothing to end the killing.[48]

In September 2004, following a US State Department-sponsored investigation (Atrocities Documentation Project or ADP) during which twenty-four investigators interviewed over 1,000 refugees from Darfur for the express purpose of systematically collecting data to enable the US government to ascertain whether genocide had been and/or was being committed in Darfur, US Secretary of State Colin Powell declared that genocide had been committed by the GOS and the Janjaweed. In his statement to the Senate Foreign Relations Committee on 9 September, Powell stated that, while "the government of Sudan and the *Janjaweed* bear responsibility, some seem to have been waiting for this determination of genocide to take action. In fact, however, no new action is dictated by this determination. We have been doing everything we can to get the Sudanese Government to act responsibly."[49] The latter half of Powell's assertion – "we have been doing everything we can to get the Sudanese Government to act responsibly" – was not, in fact, true. If anything, it was disingenuous. Granted, the US government adhered to Article 8 of the United Nations Convention on the Prevention and Punishment of Genocide (UNCG) by referring the Darfur crisis to the UN, but it hardly did all it could "to undertake to prevent the genocide."[50] Indeed, while the US government acted within the letter of the UNCG, it was far from acting within the spirit of it.

Reportedly, the United States sponsored UN Resolution (1564) in order to apply real pressure on the GOS to end the violence in Darfur. However, the give and take among the various Security Council members that preceded the council's vote virtually purged the resolution of any measures that would impose real pressure on Sudan. Instead of following through on its earlier threat of applying "further measures" if the GOS failed to comply with its obligations under Resolution 1556, the UN, again, simply issued another threat of "possible sanctions" against individual members of the government and Sudan's petroleum industry. And this was true despite Secretary General Annan's report to the Security Council on 30 August 2004 that Sudan, "despite the commitments it ha[d] made and its obligations under Resolution 1556,"[51] had once again failed both to halt its attacks against the black African civilians and to ensure their safety. As for the United States government, it hardly blinked at the watered-down resolution and certainly did not balk at the result. Ostensibly, according to its way of thinking, it had indeed done its duty and Darfur was now the United Nations' problem.

Instead of rolling over as it did, the United States, based on its finding of "genocide," could have applied real pressure on its allies and on the Security Council to implement a Chapter VII intervention in Darfur for the purpose of halting the killing, raping, and death by attrition. Likewise, it could have pushed as hard as possible for serious sanctions against Sudan that were capable of hamstringing it in various ways. It also could have pushed as strongly as possible for the immediate establishment of a no-fly zone over Darfur. On its own, and without the imprimatur of the Security Council, the United States could have promised and provided ample materiel (weapons, vehicles, and other equipment) and key resources for the AU troops being deployed to Darfur. Likewise, it could have offered to help train AU troops destined for Darfur.[52]

That said, and as previously noted, Resolution 1564 also called on Secretary General Annan to establish an International Commission of Inquiry for the purpose of investigating violations of human rights and humanitarian law and ascertaining whether the actions of the GOS and the Janjaweed in Darfur constituted genocide. In other words, the US resolution basically called for yet another study of what was taking place in Darfur, even though the United States had just completed a statistically significant study that "found genocide."

Concerning Resolution 1564, Human Rights Watch stated that

the U.N. Security Council passed a resolution on Sudan, once again holding out the threat of sanctions on the country's leaders and its oil industry if the government fails to curb ethnic violence ... In light of the massive human rights and humanitarian law violations in Darfur, Human Rights Watch believes that the Security Council should take stronger action to end the atrocities in Darfur including imposing arms and oil embargoes, stepping up the African Union's presence in Darfur ... and abandoning the plan for so-called "safe areas" to be guarded by Sudanese police and security forces. Most important, the UN must name

the government of Sudan as the party responsible for the continuing abuses in Darfur.[53]

Again, the question remains: For the targeted group on the ground,
does it really matter whether the killing and rape of many thousands
of people are deemed genocide or crimes against humanity? While
both the United States and the UN basically concurred that grave violations of humanitarian law had been and were continuing to be committed, the international community crawled along at a snail's pace in
an attempt to figure out what it could and should do (or, possibly more
accurately, what it could get away with not doing) and, as a result,
did little to nothing. Human Rights Watch's recommendations made
complete sense, but no entity, including the United Nations, acted
upon them.

On 2 March 2005, six months after Congress' concurrent resolution declared that genocide was being perpetrated in Darfur, US senators Jon S. Corzine (D-NJ) and Sam Brownback (R-KS) introduced the
Darfur Accountability Act 2005 (s. 495), a bipartisan piece of legislation which they asserted would provide the means to end the genocide
in Darfur. The bill called for immediate US and international action.
In doing so, it sought the following: a new UN Security Council resolution with sanctions ("to impose sanctions against perpetrators or
crisis against humanity in Darfur, Sudan, and for other purposes");
concerted US diplomacy to achieve an effective UN Security Council resolution; an extension of the current arms embargo to cover the
Government of Sudan; the establishment of a military no-fly zone over
Darfur; the freezing of assets and the denial of visas to those individuals responsible for genocide, crimes against humanity, and war crimes;
increased and immediate assistance to the AU; and the naming of a
presidential envoy for Sudan. Initially, human rights activists and various others jubilantly welcomed the Darfur Accountability Act. However, the White House looked askance at the new act and applied pres-
sures on its Republican allies in Congress to vote against it. Ultimately,
the vote was delayed until the act died a slow, inauspicious death, the
victim of politics at its worst.

By this time, as we have seen, the death toll of black Africans in Darfur – according to the US State Department's Bureau of Intelligence
and Research – had reached an estimated 98,000 to 181,00 people, an
appalling loss of life that was attributed to violence, disease and malnutrition as a result of the conflict.[54] In its report, "Sudan: Death Toll

in Darfur," the bureau noted and then commented on the fact that "wildly divergent death toll statistics, ranging from 70,000 to 400,000, result from applying partial data to larger, nonrepresentative populations over incompatible time periods. Violent deaths were widespread in the early stages of this conflict, but a successful, albeit delayed, humanitarian response and a moderate 2004 rainy season combined to suppress mortality rates by curtailing infectious disease outbreaks and substantial disruption of aid deliveries."[55] But Eric Reeves, who conducted his own study of mortality rates in Darfur, cited the higher number as the more accurate of the two.[56]

The Bush administration's efforts since 9 September 2004 (the date of its declaration of genocide in Darfur) have been numerous but hardly adequate, and, in some cases, not only inadequate but totally counterproductive. It has provided tens of millions of dollars of humanitarian aid for the refugees and internally displaced persons, but its assistance to the AU forces on the ground in Darfur has been minimal at best. And, par for the course, in place of a serious attempt to deal with the problems on the ground, words, words, and more vacuous words have been spoken. For example, during a speech to the UN General Assembly on 21 September 2004, President Bush mentioned Darfur but neglected to say anything about the need for immediate international action to halt the killing. On 18 October 2004 Bush promised the AU mission in Darfur a grand total of two military transport planes. On 1 November 2004 Bush extended Executive Order 13067, which was initially invoked during the Clinton administration, to maintain sanctions against Sudan, and, in doing so, commented that the policies and actions of the GOS "pose an unusual and extraordinary threat to the national security and foreign policy of the United States," and yet his administration did nothing concrete to halt the ongoing killing, rape, and destruction. On 19 November 2004 the United States sponsored UN Resolution 1574, which called on the GOS, the Janjaweed, and the rebel forces to cease and desist from their violent actions. The resolution also contained wording to the effect that it supported an increase in the number of AU observers in Darfur to 3,320. By this time, everyone in the international community clearly knew that what was needed on the ground to stop the atrocities and genocide by attrition were not "observers" or "monitors" but troops that could actually provide protection to the black African victims and stave off the attacks of the GOS and the Janjaweed. Deploying several thousand more observers in such a situation was tantamount to attempting to plug a breached levee with wads of bubble gum. On 31 March 2005 the United States abstained during a vote by the UN Security Council in regard to whether it should adopt a resolution to refer the Darfur situation to the International Criminal Court. The resolution was adopted by a vote of eleven in favour, none against, and four abstentions (Algeria, Brazil, China, and the United States). Between 20 and 22 April, Major-General Salah Abdallah Gosh, chief of Sudan's intelligence agency, was flown to the United States on a CIA executive jet for secret meetings on the issue of terrorism. Gosh had been accused by various human rights organizations and members of Congress of having planned and directed military attacks against civilians in Darfur. On 25 April 2005 media outlets reported that the White House had pressured its allies in Congress to delete the Darfur Accountability Act from the upcoming budget supplemental-appropriations bill, asserting that it could adversely affect the north-south peace process in Sudan. From May 2005 to November 2005, most of the White House's comments on Darfur repeated what it had said previously. Its primary actions included providing funding to support NATO and EU efforts to assist the AU mission.

Cognizant of the fact that the Darfur Accountability Act was moribund, congressmen Henry Hyde (R-IL), Donald Payne (D-NJ), Tom Lantos (D-CA), Ed Royce (R-CA), Tom Tancredo (R-CO), Frank Wolf (R-VA), Sheila Jackson Lee (D-TX), and Michael Capuano (D-MA) introduced, on 30 June 2005, the Darfur Peace and Accountability Act (HR 3127). It was modelled on the previous Darfur Accountability Act but did not include, this time around, the authorization of force, a no-fly zone, or petroleum-related sanctions. It did include, though, provisions to "expand the African Union Mission in Sudan and give the force a stronger mandate in order to protect civilians, humanitarian operations and deter violence in the region." It also allowed the imposition of "asset and travel sanctions against individuals deemed by the President to be perpetrators of the atrocities in Darfur."[57]

Then, on 18 October 2005, John Bolton, the US ambassador to the United Nations, curiously denied permission to Juan Mendez, special adviser on genocide to Secretary General Kofi Annan, to report on his recent trip to Darfur. In a classic case of doublespeak, Bolton said, "We need action, not talk." This led *Spiegel* to muse: "The Americans appear to have had multiple motives for the action. One is that Washington never shies away from weakening UN General Secretary Kofi Annan's position when it sees fit. But Bolton may also have been trying to prevent Mendez from creating a wave of outrage in the Security Council that could force the issue on how the crimes being committed in Darfur should be labeled. Deeply shaken by his recent visit to Darfur, where close to 200,000 civilians have been murdered, Mendez said 'we have not turned the corner on preventing genocide from either happening or happening again, depending on the perspective, in Darfur.'"[58]

In early November, US government officials acknowledged that "the international efforts to stanch the bloodshed cannot succeed" by continuing along the path they had taken for close to three years.[59] In a New York *Times* article on 6 November 2005, "Surge in Violence in Sudan Erodes Hope," Joel Brinkley wrote:

At the same time [as the aforementioned acknowledgment], more than 100 members of Congress, Republicans and Democrats, alike, are accusing the [Bush] administration of appeasing the Sudanese government, despite its complicity in the deaths of at least 200,000 people.

In Darfur, desperate refugees are now kidnapping Sudanese aid workers and holding them hostage in their teeming camps to gain attention for their grievances. International aid workers trying to feed more than two million refugees say the roads in Darfur are so crowded with bandits and killers that they have to deliver food by air, but the Sudanese government has suddenly cut off supplies of jet fuel ... Government forces are attacking and strafing civilians from aircraft again, after promising the United Nations this year that they would ground their air force in Darfur ... American officials and aid workers say the [Sudanese] government still pays some of the militiamen, known as *Janjaweed*.

Observing this, 108 members of [the US] Congress assailed the [US] government's strategy, saying it "appears conciliatory at a time when the violence in Darfur grows worse and the plight of its victims more terrible ..." Specifically, the lawmakers accused the [Bush] administration of "engaging in a policy of appeasement" toward the Sudanese government, first by granting a waiver to the sanctions in place against Sudan so its government, "whose objectives are genocidal," could hire a Washington lobbyist to promote its views ... John Prendergast, the former director of African Affairs in the National Security Council in the

Clinton Administration and who is now senior adviser for the International Crisis Group, complained that the Sudanese government was defying American, United Nations and European demands to end the violence "and yet there is no cost for Sudan, no penalty. They are out of control, but they have a complete state of immunity."[60]

On 18 November 2005 the US Senate passed the Darfur Peace and Accountability Act, but, just as the US House of Representatives was about to follow suit, the White House applied pressure to alter the measure. Purportedly, the Bush administration objected to *any inclusion of sanctions* on the Sudanese government. By the time Congress recessed in December, the House had not voted on the act, and by February 2006 there still had been no vote.

February 2006 spawned numerous responses to Darfur by the US government, including some that were strangely contradictory. During the first week of February, the month during which the United States held the presidency of the Security Council, the US ambassador to the UN, John Bolton, asked that Secretary General Annan begin planning the replacement of the AU contingent on the ground by a stronger UN force. But then, on 3 February, Assistant Secretary of State for African Affairs Jendayi Frazer, in what seemed to be a curious attempt to distance the Bush administration from its earlier declaration of genocide, told reporters that "it is not the government [GOS] directing the militia attacking civilians ... [The current] situation is very different than it was. It's not as systematic ... It is a very serious situation, [but] it's a series of small attacks and incidents."[61]

On 16 February 2006 US Senators Sam Brownback (R-KS) and Joe Biden (D-DE) introduced a resolution calling for NATO troops to help the AU halt the genocide in Darfur. The resolution also called on President Bush to advocate in favour of sending NATO troops – "including Americans if need be" – to support the AU, on the UN Security Council to approve a Chapter VII peace-enforcement mission, and on NATO to enforce a no-fly zone in Darfur. Brownback declared: "The world has known for too long of the atrocities in Darfur. We must do more than declare a genocide: we must do all we can to stop the killings, and we must do it now."[62]

On 17 February, US Secretary of State Condoleezza Rice boldly asserted that genocide was continuing in Darfur and called on the AU to allow UN peacekeepers to assist it in an effort to halt the killing and ongoing mass rape. On the same day, and reportedly as a result of strong pressure placed on him by Christian and Jewish leaders, President Bush also called on the UN and NATO to assist the AU: "I'm in the process now of working with a variety of folks to encourage there to be more troops, probably under the United Nations ... But it's going to require, I think, a NATO stewardship, planning, facilitating, organizing, probably double the number of peacekeepers that are there now."[63]

Then, on 20 February, Bolton criticized Secretary General Annan for not being more aggressive in creating a plan for the deployment of a UN force in Darfur. The UN immediately denied the accusation. John Prendergast, formerly an "African hand" with the US State Department and now a specialist on Sudan with the International Crisis Group, asserted that US criticism of the UN was "hypocritical ... The US has not been forward-leaning on this issue. It's disingenuous to claim that the United Nations is not doing all it should."[64]

The African Union

In April 2004 the African Union created the Cease-fire Commission (CFC) for the purpose of monitoring the ceasefire that had just been brokered by Chad and agreed upon by the Sudanese government and two rebel groups, the SLM/A and the JEM. As mentioned earlier, that August the AU initially sent 150 Rwandan troops to Darfur, quickly followed by 150 soldiers from Nigeria. By March 2005, the AU had approximately 2,000 troops in Darfur, most of whom were based around the state capitals. The AU's goal, however, was to have 3,500 troops on the ground by that time.

Hoping to increase its number of troops substantially, the AU stated that it planned to deploy 7,000 troops in Darfur by September 2005. It did not meet its goal, but it did deploy about 6,000 by mid-October. As of February 2006, there were 7,000 AU troops on the ground. Various experts, however, insist that, at a minimum, 15,000 to 20,000 troops are needed to police Darfur.

While the AU has roundly criticized all of the parties involved for unlawful actions and roundly condemned those guilty of human rights violations, its ability to stave off the violence has been sorely limited. In fact, the AU force's movements largely consist of three or four patrols a day, all in the relative proximity of its bases. The tendency is, if possible, to avoid contact with the GOS and the Janjaweed, and that is due to the fact that the AU troops are outmanned and "outgunned."

Significantly, the UN mission in Darfur has received only approximately half of the requested funding. In 2005, for example, the AU budget for the mission in Darfur was approximately $220 million, of which the EU provided approximately $100 million and the United States $45 million. Canada has also been generous, providing tens of millions of dollars and, in July 2005, the loan of 105 armoured vehicles with training and maintenance assistance and spare parts for a year. No one, however, including the AU, has claimed that it has enough personnel on the ground, enough well-trained troops, enough weaponry, enough transport planes, enough four-wheel vehicles, or enough badly needed equipment and resources of other kinds.

Tellingly, Roméo Dallaire, the Canadian general who was commander of the United Nations mission to Rwanda prior to, during, and following the 1994 Rwandan genocide, asserted in October 2004 that only a series of integrated solutions that include intervention will succeed. Additionally, Dallaire stated that what was needed to provide "*real* protection was between 24,000 to 44,000 well-trained and well-equipped troops, preferably a mix of AU and NATO troops or AU and Western troops."[65] Complicating the entire situation has been the AU's insistence from the outset that the Darfur crisis is an African problem that is to be solved by the Africans. As a result, the AU is strongly opposed to intervention by any forces not from Africa. That situation must change if the black Africans are to have any chance of being protected.

Conclusion

At the end of January 2006, in an article entitled "Plan to End Darfur Violence Is Failing, Officials Say," in the New York *Times*, Joel Brinkley reported the following:

> The broad strategy for ending the carnage in Darfur, Sudan ... is collapsing as the violence and chaos in the region seem to grow with every passing week, United Nations and Bush administration officials say.
>
> After three years of bloodshed that has already claimed more than 200,000 lives, officials say they are struggling to devise

an effective new strategy ... Peace talks have nearly halted after government and Darfur rebel negotiators, in the latest round, showed an unwillingness to seriously discuss anything except sharing Sudan's oil wealth ... One of the Sudanese president's latest positions, articulated in a published interview this month, is that the government-backed militias known to be behind most of the violence are actually a fictitious creation of the media and the United States Congress.

"The looming threat of complete lawlessness and anarchy draws nearer," Kofi Annan, the United Nations Secretary General, lamented earlier this month as he urged nations to do more.

... The United States and Europe have both declined to provide further financial support for the effort, and African Union leaders say money to conduct the operation will run out in March.

... The United Nations is considering deploying a larger force of its own peacekeeping troops to replace those of the African Union, but the discussions are at an early, preliminary stage ... But the Sudanese government insists it will not accept United Nations forces on its territory ... Western leaders have all but given up on a key part of their strategy, trying to persuade Sudan's president, Omar al-Bashir, to disarm the militias that are responsible for a large part of the violence.

The United States say his government continues to finance the militias, even though Sudanese officials claim to be working hard to bring peace to Darfur. A special United Nations committee said this month that the Sudanese government had "abjectly failed to fulfill its commitment to identify, neutralize and disarm militia groups."[66]

As stated at the outset of this chapter, when a major national or international crisis is imminent (or has erupted), the UN, individual nations, regional organizations, non-governmental organizations, and others must attempt, to the best of their ability, to stave off potential violence or, if such violence is already occurring, bring it to an end. Certainly, the least inflammatory way of doing so is via various diplomatic efforts, including secret and/or public discussions, the issuance of resolutions (including the threat of sanctions), and peace talks (followed by declarations and the signing of agreements). Yet, when such efforts begin to consume months and months of time, if not years, and little to no effort is made to go beyond the incessant and unproductive talk and anemic resolutions with idle threats, then such efforts are nothing short of counterproductive. That is particularly true when human beings – men, women, children, and babies – are being brutally attacked and killed each and every night and day. At some point (and preferably early on), somebody, somewhere needs to realize that something more than talk and band-aid-like approaches (for example, deploying military observers who lack the mandate, personnel, and resources to halt the killing) are needed to bring the crisis to an end. When that does not happen, the international community is guilty of nothing less than being a bystander to yet another genocide. And what that means is that you and I – that is, every single adult – are also guilty of being bystanders for we are all members of the international community.

The paradox then is this: while individuals must speak up in order to prod their governments to act in good conscience and to do so in a way that truly contributes to halting murder, rape, and death by attrition, individual nations, regional organizations, and the United Nations must not rely on talk alone but must also act to stop the atrocities. Put another way, each individual must recognize that, when a genocide is either about to break out or already has, it is imperative that those in authority at all levels be constantly reminded that during such crises not only is talk cheap, but when there is all talk and no action it can be – and often is – deadly for those on the ground.

Notes

1 This is not to infer that the international community totally neglected the plight of the black Africans, for hundreds of millions of dollars worth of medical supplies, food, tents, and even a limited amount of military equipment for use by the African Union has been supplied by the United States, Canada, Great Britain, the European Union, and the United Nations. However, what has not been provided is adequate protection against continued murder, rape, and other types of assaults and brutality. Furthermore, owing to the lack of an adequate mandate and an inadequate number of troops, tons of supplies have either not reached the people in need in time (that is, before they fell victim to malnutrition or disease) or have been stolen by the GOS and the Janjaweed.

2 It is important to note that the Naivasha talks and the peace agreement resulting from them cast a huge shadow over the entire Darfur situa-

tion. More specifically, various officials with the United Nations, the European Union, and the African Union (not to mention individual nations) were, off and on, more than a little tentative about pushing Sudan too far on the Darfur issue out of fear of (1) upsetting the progress of the Naivasha talks while they were in progress, and (2) unravelling the peace agreement that resulted from such talks. Seemingly, such officials were ready to sacrifice one group of people to certain death, rape, and the destruction of their communities in order to placate a temperamental and murderous regime and meet its unreasonable demands. Not only has such tentative behaviour resulted in too much talk, weak resolutions, and idle threats, but, as Human Rights Watch notes, "the fact that the U.S. and European policy-makers have not been unified in their approach to Darfur ... permitted the government of Sudan to play various governments against each other to its own advantage, with the Europeans implicitly criticizing the U.S. for being too aggressive and perhaps threatening the Naivasha talks" ("Too Little, Too Late: Sudanese and International Response 2004," *Human Rights Watch*, vol. 16, no. 6A [3 May 2004]: 10); http://hrw.org/reports/2004/ sudan0504/8.htm).

3 Evelyn Depoortere et al., "Scientific Survey Confirms Humanitarian Disaster in Darfur," *The Lancet*, 1 October 2004, 1, http://www.scienceblog.com/community/older/2004/5/ 20044890.shtml.

4 Human Rights Watch, "Too Little, Too Late," 1.

5 United Nations Integrated Regional Information Networks (IRIN), "Mukesh Kapila and Darfur's Realities in Early 2004," 22 March 2004, www.isg-iags.org/authors/reeves/reeves07062005.html.

6 Human Rights Watch, "Too Little, Too Late," 3. Notably, despite all the expressions of concern and "early warnings" by various actors, this was the first time that the issue of Darfur was formally discussed by the UN Security Council. Such a response reiterates what many scholars have asserted over the years, namely, that even the most sophisticated genocide-early-warning-system is of little to no use if there is not the political will by the international community to respond in a timely and effective manner.

7 Human Rights Watch, "Darfur in Flames: Atrocities in Western Sudan," *Human Rights Watch*, no. 16, 5A (15 April 2004), http://hrw.org/reports/2004/sudan0404/.

8 Ibid., 6–7.

9 William M. Reilly, "U.N. Marks Rwanda Genocide a Decade Later," United Press International, 7 April 2004, http://washingtontimes.com/ upi-breaking/20040407-045604-5685r.htm.

10 Ibid.

11 Depoortere, "Scientific Survey," 1.

12 The N'djamena Ceasefire Agreement came about only as a result of strong pressure applied by both US President George W. Bush and UN Secretary General Kofi Annan (Human Rights Watch, "Too Little, Too Late").

13 In fact, that is exactly what happened. For a discussion as to how the GOS incorporates members of the Janjaweed into the ranks of the police and the regular armed forces, see Human Rights Watch, "Empty Promises? Continuing Abuses in Darfur, Sudan," A Human Rights Watch Briefing Paper, 11 August 2004, http://hrw.org/backgrounder/africa/sudan/2004/.

14 Human Rights Watch, "Too Little, Too Late," 2.

15 United Nations Security Council, "Security Council Demands Sudan Disarm Militias, in Darfur, Adopting Resolution 1556 (2004) by Vote of 12–0–2," Press Release SC/8160, 30 July 2004, http://www.un.org/News/Press/docs/2004/sc8160.doc.htm.

16 Ibid.

17 BBC News, "UN Pleads for New Darfur Funding," 15 June 2004, http://news.bbc.co.uk/1/hi/world/africa/3810471.stm.

18 United Nations, "Joint Communiqué between the Government of Sudan and the United Nations on the Occasion of the Visit of UN SG to Sudan," 29 June-3 July 2005, http://www.un.org/news/dh/sudan/sudan_communique.pdf.

19 United Nations Security Council, "Security Council Demands Sudan Disarm Militias, in Darfur." Emphasis added.

20 Ibid. Emphasis added.

21 Ibid.

22 Ibid.

23 Depoortere, "Scientific Survey," 1.

24 Human Rights Watch, "Empty Promises?" As of February 2006, the GOS and the *Janjaweed* were still killing and raping black Africans – but not in the latter's villages because most villages had been burned to the ground; instead, the perpetrators were carrying out attacks in both IDP camps in Darfur and refugee camps in Chad.

25 Colum Lynch, "U.N. Puts Sanctions into Play," Washington *Post*, 19 September 2004, A01. Emphasis added.

26 United Nations Security Council, "Security Council Resolution 1574," 19 November 2004, 3.

27 John L. Washburn and Wasana Punyasena, "The Commission of Inquiry: A United Nations Success Story," *UNA-USA Policy Brief, No. 10* (July 2005): 1, 3.

28 The Times Literary Supplement Staff, "Deep Down in Darfur," TLS Highlights – Times Online, January 2006, 3, http://www.tls.timesonline.co.uk/article/0,25346-1886267_5,00.html.

29 Eric Reeves, "Report of the International Commission of Inquiry on Darfur: A Critical Analysis (Part 1)," www.sudanreevcs.org, 2 February 2005, http://www.sudanreeves.org/modules.php?op=modload&name= Sections&file=index&req=viewarticle&artid=489&page=1.

30 Times Literary Supplement, "Deep Down in Darfur," 3.

31 Physicians for Human Rights, *Darfur: Assault on Survival: A Call for Security, Justice and Restitution* (Cambridge, Mass., 2006), 33, 35–43.

32 Numerous scholars and human rights organizations have claimed that the estimate of 70,000 deaths is not conservative but simply inaccurate. For example, Dr Jan Coebergh , a physician with an interest in epidemiology who had worked in Darfur prior to the outbreak of violence, stated: "The figure widely quoted between October 2004 and January 2005 is 70,000. But this figure is almost certainly wrong; the true death toll is nearer 300,000. The figure of 70,000 dead derives from a misreading of a WHO study on mortality made in mid-September 2004 (50,000 dead) and updated (to 70,000) in a statement given to journalists on 14 October by Dr. Nabarro, head of World Health Organization emergency response efforts. He was, as he has subsequently explained, only estimating deaths among the displaced population in camps and did not include those still living in the countryside, living in the three state capitals, in camps inaccessible to humanitarian aid, and amongst the refugees in Chad. And he was only estimating deaths from disease and malnutrition, specifically excluding deaths from violence, wherever those deaths occurred. He was also making an estimate from 1 March 2004 to October 2004, excluding the loss of life previous to that, and of course since then. It continues to be widely quoted three months later, and as if no one has died in Darfur since October 2004, despite his estimate that 6,000–10,000 people would die per month for the next few months, giving a figure of around 90,000–100,000 dead from disease and malnutrition in the camps accessible to aid since March 2004." (Jan Coebergh, "Sudan: Genocide Has Killed More Than the Tsunami," *Sudan Tribune*, 31 January 2005, http://www.sudantribune.com/ spip.php?article7757).

33 Human Rights Watch, "UN Sanctions for Darfur Stalled in Committee," Press Release, 2 June 2005, http://hrw.org/english/docs/2005/06/02/ darfur11066.htm.

34 Human Rights Watch, "UN: Put Sudan's Top Leaders on Sanctions List," Press Release, 15 December 2005, http://www.hrw.org/english/ docs/2005/12/09/sudan12186.htm.

35 In fact, on 1 October 2005, Ambassador Baba Ganan Kingibe, special representative of the chairperson of the African Union Commission, issued a press statement on the deteriorating security situation in Darfur. Commenting on the "series of violations of ceasefire that

occurred in Darfur since the conclusion of the 5th round of the Abuja Peace talks," he stated that "the extent of collapse of the security situation in Darfur during this period is even more ironic and regrettable given the high hopes for an early resolution of the Darfur crisis generated by the adoption of the widely acclaimed Declaration of Principles on the 5 of July 2005. We all hoped the [in] intervening period between then and the resumption of the 6th Round of Talks in Abuja on 15 September, all the parties would endeavor to consolidate these positive gains, to maintain calm on the ground ... Unfortunately, this was not to be. You would recall that in the past one month we witnessed series of violation (sic) in Darfur, with widespread violence against villages, commercial and humanitarian conveys and even IDP camps ... These violations were variously attributed to unidentified armed militia, the 'Janjaweed' or even some Chadian rebels." Press Statement by Ambassador Baba Gana Kingibe, Special Representative of the Chairperson of the African Union Commission on the Deteriorating Situation in Darfur, Sudan, 1 October 2005, 1, 2–3, http://www.sudantribune.com/article_impr.php3?id_article=11871.

36 Joel Brinkley, "Plan to End Darfur Violence Is Failing, Officials Say," New York *Times*, 28 January 2006, www.nytimes.com/2006/01/28/politics/28darfur.html.

37 Claire Soares, "Nigeria-Sudan: Darfur Talks Adjourn until August after Sides Agree on Some Basics," IRIN, 6 July 2005, 1, http://www.sudaneseonline.com/enews2005/jul7-70067.shtml.

38 Ibid.

39 Ibid., 2.

40 Sudan Tribune Staff, "Darfur Talks at Stalemate over Power-Sharing Dispute," *Sudan Tribune*, 4 January 2006, 1.

41 Quoted in African Union, "7th Round of Inter-Sudanese Peace Talks on the Conflict in Darfur," Press Release no. 22, 24 January 2006, http://www.amis-sudan.org/aboujadocs/22_AU%20Special%20Envoy%20and%20Chief%20Mediator%20Convenes%20Plenary%20Session__24Jan06%5B1%5D.doc.

42 Ibid.

43 IRIN, "Sudan: Darfur Talks Halt over al-Bashir's Bid for AU Chair," UN Office of the Coordination of Humanitarian Affairs, 23 January 2006, 1.

44 Doctors without Borders/Medecins sans Frontières, "On the Brink of Mass Starvation in Darfur," Press Release, 20 May 2004, 1, http://www.doctorswithoutborders.org/pr/2004/05-20-2004.cfm.

45 Ibid.

46 Editorial, "As Genocide Unfolds," Washington *Post*, 20 June 2004, B06.

47 A concurrent resolution is "a legislative proposal that requires the approval of both houses but does not require the signature of the presi-

dent *and does not have the force of law*. These resolutions are often used to express the sentiments of both the House of Representatives and the Senate" (emphasis added) (http://www.answers.com/topic/concurrent-resolution, 4). Be that as it may, the passage of the concurrent resolutions may have applied pressure on the White House and the State Department to focus more intently on the crisis in Darfur.

48 This, though, was complicated by the African Union's insistence that it did not want non-Africans to intervene in Darfur, an issue discussed later in this chapter. By this time, the estimated death toll had risen, at least by another 6,000 and, according to many NGOs and various scholars, possibly as much as 10,000.

49 Colin Powell, "The Crisis in Darfur," Testimony before the Senate Foreign Relations Committee, 9 September 2004, http://www.state.gov/secretary/former/powell/remarks/36042.htm.

50 United Nations General Assembly, "United Nations Convention on the Prevention and Punishment of Genocide" (9 December 1948), Article 1.

51 Kofi Annan, "Report of the Secretary-General pursuant to Paragraphs 6 and 13 to 16 of Security Council Resolution 1556 (2004)," S/2004/703 United Nations Security Council, 30 August 2004, http://daccess-ods.un.org/access.nsf/Get?Open&DS=S/2004/703&Lang=E&Area=UNDOC.

52 The United States, of course, could have approached other nations (e.g., Britain and Canada) or NATO to join it in a non-UN-sanctioned intervention, but this possibility never seems to have been considered. In fact, with the United States already engaged in warfare with rebel groups in Afghanistan in its search for the leaders of al-Qaeda (the terrorist group responsible for the 9/11 attack on the United States) as well as in an all-out war in Iraq, neither the executive nor the legislative branches of the US government, let alone the Pentagon, would have ever countenanced such an idea.

53 Human Rights Watch, "Darfur Destroyed: Ongoing Crimes in Darfur, Sudan," Dev-Witness, 2004, http://dev.witness.org/option,com_rightsalert/Itemid,178/task,view/alert_id, 6.

54 U.S. State Department, "Fact Sheet: Sudan: Death Toll in Darfur," Bureau of Intelligence and Research, 25 March 2005, http://www.state.gov/s/inr/rls/fs/2005/45105.htm. Emphasis added.

55 Ibid.

56 "Darfur's Real Death Toll," Washington *Post*, 24 April 2005, http://www.washingtonpost.com/wp-dyn/content/article/2005/04/23/AR2005042301032.html.

57 Representative Henry Hyde et al., Darfur Peace and Accountability Act (HR 3127/S. 1462), United States House of Representatives, 25 June 2005, http://www.genocideintervention.net/advocate/docs/HR_DPAA.pdf.

58 Spiegel Online International, "John Bolton Doesn't Want to Hear about Darfur," *Spiegel's Daily Take*, 18 October 2005, http://www.spiegel.de/international/0,1518,380360,00.html.

59 Joel Brinkely, "Surge in Violence in Sudan Erodes Hope," New York *Times*, 7 November 2005, 1.

60 Ibid.

61 "US Backs Away from Genocide Charge in Darfur," Agence France Presse, 3 February 2006, http://www.genocidewatch.org/SudanUSbacks awayfromgenocidechargeinDarfurFeb06.htm.

62 Sam Brownback, "Brownback, Biden Urge President to Act to Stop Genocide in Darfur," Senator Sam Brownback's Washington D.C. Office Press Release, 17 February 2006, http://brownback.senate.gov/pressapp/ record.cfm?id=251728.

63 Jim VandeHei and Colum Lynch, "Bush Calls for More Muscle in Darfur," Washington *Post*, 18 February 2006, http://www.washingtonpost.com/wp-dyn/content/article/2006/02/17/ AR2006021701935.html.

64 Sue Pleming, "U.S. Tells U.N. to Hurry up with Darfur Planning," Reuters AlertNet, 21 February 2006, http://www.redorbit.com/news/ international/400709/us_tells_un_to_hurry_up_with_darfur_planning/ index.html.

65 Reeves, "Report of the International Commission of Inquiry," 12–13.

66 Brinkley, "Plan to End Darfur Violence Is Failing, Officials Say."

CHAPTER EIGHT

Visual Advocates: Depicting Darfur

CARLA ROSE SHAPIRO

The exhibition medium is increasingly being harnessed to support social justice causes, including genocide awareness. The crisis in Darfur is the subject of several significant travelling and permanent exhibitions, two of which will be explored in this chapter – *The Smallest Witnesses: The Conflict in Darfur Through Children's Eyes*, and *Darfur/Darfur*. Both are highly original and creative public displays that engage traditional and new media methods of communication. By describing the content of these exhibitions and critiquing their visual and textual elements, I will examine how exhibition methodologies contribute to the overall construction of meaning and how representational forms create and reinforce particular types of knowledge. I will also query the complicated artistic, ethical, and historical debates surrounding the representation of genocide in general and the Darfurian tragedy in particular. This study reflects on how the representation of the Holocaust and the Rwandan genocide – and their inscriptions in exhibitions – has informed the ways in which the Darfurian genocide[1] is depicted. While exhibitions are often employed to bring awareness to the public about genocidal events, I will consider whether such exhibitions are efficacious in moving the public discourse about genocide to more active and participatory forms of social engagement.

The manner in which the Darfurian tragedy came to be depicted in exhibition format is the offspring of two concurrent trends in museology and the field of Holocaust studies, trends that are both founded on notions of inclusion. Historically, exhibitions usually told uplifting stories and emphasized the positive side of history, including the benevolence of science and technology and the creative achievements of cultures and individuals.[2] This is beginning to change. Conservative and edifying museological visions have grown more expansive as exhibition visitors increasingly demand that exhibits ask essential and critical questions about social issues. And so, as exhibitions become more democratized and inclusive spaces, we see with greater frequency exhibitions that "reflect issues and people that have been marginalized by mainstream society" and that are often accompanied by an "activism that embraces community issues and aspirations, in an effort to provide value and meaning."[3] An exhibit panel that once posed the question, "what is history?" now more commonly morphs into content that asks, "what can history do to improve the world?"[4] Currently, exhibitions are frequently employed to foster awareness and activism in relation to social justice and human rights issues, including crimes against humanity. This genre is founded, in part, on the popular reception of Holocaust-themed exhibitions (particularly those housed in Holocaust museums), which provide a representational template for the depiction of genocide and reinforce the notion that audiences are receptive to viewing exhibitions about the grim subject of atrocity crimes.

The Holocaust, rightly, continues to exert an impact on contemporary culture. While debates still abound about the uniqueness or universality of the Holocaust along the continuum of genocide, the unique stature of the Holocaust as an object of musealization is not disputed. The Holocaust's status as iconic symbol of humankind's destructive impulse has endured within its unparalleled representational currency. Holocaust museums and exhibitions have proliferated in the past fifteen years, playing a key role in how the general public understands the Holocaust. More than twenty-five million people have visited the United States Holocaust Memorial Museum (USHMM) since its opening in 1993. And the Holocaust exhibition at the Imperial War Museum in London has received more than two million visitors since opening in 2000.[5]

Until very recently, scant attention was paid to more recent genocides. The interest stirred in the subject of the Holocaust with the opening of the USHMM and the release of the film Schindler's List, both in 1993, came too late for the victims of the Rwandan genocide, and there remains a conspicuous dearth of museums and exhibitions addressing other genocides. That said, at the beginning of the twenty-first century, we are starting to witness a sea change in this representational divide, spawned in part by the tremendous and somewhat surprising "success" of the Holocaust museum in attracting audiences to their galleries. Evident is a subtle but perceivable shift from the singularly focused Holocaust museum and exhibition to Holocaust museums and exhibitions that address other genocides and human rights violations. The Museum of Tolerance (MOT) in Los Angeles and a major new national museum project in Canada, the Canadian Museum for Human Rights (CMHR), are two such examples.

A marked transformation within many organizations devoted to Holocaust education can also be perceived; the "lessons" of the Holocaust are being placed in more global contexts as educators' mandates increasingly consider the study of the Holocaust alongside genocide and human rights. Efforts to combine Holocaust education with genocide awareness – including, in particular, information about the Rwandan and Darfurian genocides – reflect the desire of such organizations to make the Holocaust more relevant to younger and more diverse audiences. There are important ethical and theoretical considerations in the bridging of Holocaust and genocide awareness. The commitment to oppose genocide in all forms seems especially prescient for Jewish communities, which themselves have been targets of genocide. As Sara Horowitz suggests, "the Holocaust reminds us not only of our own unspeakable tragedy, but also provides a moral imperative – not to be bystanders, not to be those who, during the Shoah, passively allowed the Nazis and their cohorts to murder most of Europe's Jews."[6] The indifference of the world during the Holocaust led to millions of lives lost; such indifference can lead to the same fate in Sudan. The events in Darfur now demonstrate "the need to understand that cry for 'Never Again' as a challenge, rather than a promise, and certainly not as a fact."[7]

The USHMM, whose internal debates about maintaining the uniqueness of the Holocaust as a historical event have been well documented,[8] has recently shown more openness to the inclusion of other genocides. The museum's Committee on Conscience (COC) bases its work on the definition of genocide found in the United Nations 1948 Convention on the Prevention and Punishment of the Crime of Genocide, and it attempts to uphold its mandate of "Responding Today to Threats of Genocide ... to insure that such a totally inhuman assault as the Holocaust – or any partial version thereof – never recurs."[9] In July 2004 the COC declared a "Genocide Emergency for Darfur." Indeed, according to Gérard Prunier in *Darfur: The Ambiguous Genocide*, the COC, and other vocal Jewish and Protestant groups, joined the early chorus of protests in Washington about Darfur.[10] The COC has held educational programming on the Darfurian genocide and hosted two national conferences; it also offers a weekly podcast series and posts a blog called "Voices on Genocide Prevention." The USHMM's Darfur exhibition, *Genocide Emergency – Darfur, Sudan: Who Will Survive Today*, is a substantial exhibition in terms of the resources and space (text panels, documentary photographs, narrated videos, edited news-footage sequences, and vitrines holding a small number of artifacts from homes destroyed in the violence) that have been dedicated to it. The COC's lead in bringing *Darfur/Darfur* to the walls of the USHMM – a project unlikely to have found a venue at the USHMM when the museum first opened its doors – is also suggestive of the USHMM's increasing receptivity to exhibiting other genocides.

Unlike the Rwandan genocide, the Darfurian genocide is happening at a time when anti-genocide advocacy networks and partnerships are established, online global communities are in full gear, and the human rights potential of the exhibition medium is more fully realized. Eyeing the popularity of the Holocaust museum, networks and communities devoted to genocide awareness began to see exhibitions as an important tool for their campaigns, mediums of awareness and information and, potentially, conduits for direct social action. Accordingly, there were new partnerships forged between non-profit organizations, non-governmental organizations (NGOs), and Holocaust education organizations for the purposes of creating and distributing exhibitions about the genocide in Darfur. Established Holocaust education-oriented entities offered something to anti-genocide advocates interested in accessing the public through visual-culture projects, namely, an already engaged constituency and established exhibition spaces.[11] Holocaust museums and education centres, and Jewish museums, have partnered with human-rights- and anti-genocide-related NGOs to produce exhibitions about the Darfurian genocide. For example, when *The Smallest Witnesses* was exhibited at Washington University's Odegaard Library, sponsoring organizations included Human Rights Watch (HRW), the American Jewish Committee, and the Washington State Holocaust Education Resource Center, among others. Hundreds of extant university gallery spaces, art galleries, and artist-run centres, many receptive to hosting human-rights-themed exhibitions, provided further loci for igniting activism.

The ascent of the Internet has created limitless virtual exhibition spaces. Where once the possibilities for exhibiting genocide were limited to a few venues with small and very specific audiences, suddenly hundreds of organizations were looking for, or were receptive to, genocide-themed exhibitions to fill their websites and virtual gallery spaces. Online exhibits and a whole host of images, audio, and video about the Darfurian genocide are features of many Darfur advocacy organizations, including NGOs such as the International Crisis Group and Amnesty International, both of whom first picked up on the Darfur story and were instrumental in bringing the crisis out of the shadows.[12]

The USHMM set the standard by which other Holocaust and human-rights-related exhibitions are measured. The permanent galleries at that museum have stood the test of time and, for the most part, public and critical scrutiny in appropriately translating into an exhibition format the destruction of European Jewry – the dehumanizing process of racially based identification and separation, the inexpressible suffering caused by ghettoization and deportation, and the murder of six million people. But how can a museum depict the brutality of the crimes of the Hutu militia in Rwanda, where 800,000 Tutsi and thousands of Hutu moderates were killed? Or, in the case of Darfur, how can one represent the suffering of the hundreds of thousands of people who have died, and the more than two million people displaced and left homeless since the conflict began in February 2003?[13]

For some, the gravity and scale of these tragedies defy the very possibility of historical and aesthetic representation. Elie Wiesel's oft-quoted personal plea that the Holocaust is an event beyond imagination, language, and visualization, and Theodor Adorno's dictum that writing poetry after Auschwitz is barbaric, have been endlessly countered. Despite the ethical presumption of genocide's radically unassimilable nature, it remains true that, as with any other significant historical event, attempts at representation and interpretation are not only possible but abound, and the question of the impossibility of representing the Holocaust has lost much of its pervasiveness. In the twenty-first century, no similar critical debates have ensued regarding the representation of the genocides in Rwanda and Darfur. However, the debates that accompany the conceptualization of the "limits" of representing the Holocaust are also present in the context of the Darfurian genocide. Are some kinds of exhibitions unacceptable insofar as they betray an intrinsic limit set by the radical nature of genocide?

In *Probing the Limits of Representation*, Saul Friedlander refers to the Holocaust as an "event at the limits."[14] What constitutes a breach of this limit, however, is not easily defined, even if such a definition could be determined at any one time as a standard within a particular community. An even greater challenge exists in determining a standard within the conflicting writings and rewritings of events that serve the needs of different communities of memory. Is there a "limit of representation" when depicting the Rwandan genocide or the conflict in Darfur, and how and why do these limits differ? Some of the cultural discourses on Nazism that Friedlander describes transgress an intangible boundary, "some inchoate yet intractable sense of decency, propriety, and limit."[15] In his judgment of limits – which he says can be easily breached by intuition and feeling – Friedlander suggests that one can sense when a particular representation is amiss.[16] Can the same be said for Rwanda and Darfur, where incommensurability can no longer be upheld as a measure for the representation of these tragedies? Exhibitions are one of the "texts" through which knowledge about the Darfurian genocide is gleaned. Yet, in accessing the history of a particular genocide through this medium, there exists the danger of presenting these events in ways that are inexact. Exhibitions do not simply present history; they shape the "random" material of history through an often complex arrangement of text, documents, and images. The artifices of exhibition construction – selection, stylization, and narrativization, among other considerations – are all prone to imposing unreliable and untruthful structures that occlude the historical veracity of the events being depicted.

In spite of these representational challenges, our moral obligation to understand and remember genocide demands that the reality of mass, planned destruction must be transmitted only through historically accurate frameworks and via visual and textual languages that are suitable and sensitive to expressing the atrocities that have occurred. The enormity of these tragedies demands that all acts of representation be judiciously conceived and created; representations must "remain true to the historical truth and memory of the event."[17] However, exhibitions about genocide are constructed in ways that are accessible to and engaging for varied contemporary audiences. If the primary goal of any of these representational forms is that a genocide be remembered or known by as large a public as possible, then unconventional, experimental, and new media forms, with their appeal to contemporary spectators, particularly the younger generation of viewers, may be most efficacious. As Dominick LaCapra notes, "for memory to be effective on a collective level, it must reach large numbers of people."[18]

Exhibition visitors come to view the Darfurian genocide through the lens of documentary photography. But how are the images of Darfur we encounter in exhibitions "selected"? Is the exhibition content chosen on the basis of the perceived palatability of such images for mainstream audiences? Or are more charged images chosen based on their ability to draw audiences into the narrative of genocide? Some critics, who claim that there is potential for the "repetition of the imaginative and ethical error that defamed the victims,"[19] have struck a cautionary note about the exploitative capacity of the visual documents of genocide. Recalling the victims of genocide through abject documentary photographs recording the last vestiges of an individual's physical destruction, or through graphic post-mortem images, holds potential disrespect for the victims themselves. The radical de-subjectification of victims through the perpetuation of images of their denigration and death raises questions about the use of such charged images within exhibitions. In a range of exhibition practices, we see those that draw upon the visual record of atrocity, those that consciously react against its use, and those that take a middle position. Verisimilitude in the depiction of genocide is often equated with images of graphic violence; exhibitions about genocide must always be cautious about spectatorial reception, for in it lies the possibility that violent images will lure viewers through awed fascination – an ever-present danger when using Nazi imagery. Photographs of charred and desiccated remains of the Darfurian dead, or a dying refugee child slashed by Janjaweed marauders, risk blurring the boundary between historical/humanitarian inquiry and a voyeuristic gaze preoccupied with death.

For those genocides whose visual culture has not become part of the collective Western conscience, the question of when and how to use graphic images of atrocities is less clear. Working with Rwandan survivors for a travelling exhibition project, *Portraits from the 100 Days*, confounded my own assumptions about using extremely graphic images of mass death and detailed photographs of post-genocide exhumations. Several survivors featured in the exhibition insisted that such images be shown – even where evidence of Hutu crimes involved their own family members. The survivors maintained that these photographs would not only provide concrete evidence of the nature and scale of the crimes committed but also honour the memory of the dead.[20]

Considering the different religious and cultural backgrounds of Darfurian witnesses, one could not assume they would hold the same

representational wishes. Indeed, the fact that only one travelling exhibition about the Darfurian genocide (Aegis Trust's *Darfur* exhibition)
employs survivor testimony as a significant part of the textual material raises another question about representing genocide: To what
extent are genocide survivors themselves, both as individuals and as a
community, engaged in the process of self-representation? How much
agency are Darfurians afforded in the telling of their own experiences?
Without a textual or participatory voice assigned to the survivors,
the spectre of the museum's old ways is raised, where "the selection
of knowledge and the presentation of ideas and images are enacted
within a power system."[21] The hierarchical implication is that the
authority of such presentations is placed outside the sphere of those it
purports to represent. In a much subtler variant of the charges levied
against colonial collections in museums, do exhibitions risk establishing "positions of authority, dominion, and social imperialism over the
collected "other"?[22]

As the evidentiary needs of Holocaust museums have waned over
the decades, graphic images of atrocities committed during the Holocaust appear on exhibit walls with less frequency; descriptions of the
crimes committed are instead assigned to the text panels of exhibits
and to audio- and video-based survivor testimony. European Jewish
civilization tends to be evoked through precious family photographs
and objects of material culture from the rich European history that preceded the Holocaust. It is by viewing images and artifacts from thriv-
ing Jewish communities that exhibition visitors come to understand
what was lost during the Holocaust. The idea here – in re-humanizing
the survivors – is that we re-humanize the murdered victims as well
and in doing so also offer a place of intersubjectivity between the exhibition visitor and the victims being depicted.

However, such approaches may not be feasible or desirable in the
case of Darfur. *The Smallest Witnesses* and *Darfur/Darfur* both display
less interest in examining the hermeneutics of memory than in documenting the actual events, and the evidentiary pull of documentary
media predominates. Unlike many Holocaust survivors, or middle-
class Rwandan survivors, few Darfurian survivors possess family
photographs and objects of material culture from which to represent
their lives before the genocide.[23] Where photographs and personal
effects may have existed, the rapidity of Janjaweed and Government of
Sudan (GOS) attacks and the total incineration of Darfurian villages
made the majority of such precious items lost for posterity. Thus, it is

more difficult to construct the normalizing, or nostalgia-producing, "before" from which exhibition visitors can forge empathetic bonds. It would, however, be remiss to address this dearth of photographs by substituting tribalizing or exoticizing depictions, an easy and oft-used representational default setting that marked the representation of the Rwandan genocide in 1994. Such an approach would risk repeating eighteenth- and nineteenth-century representational strategies that "generally reinforced colonial politics; this was achieved through representations of the 'other' as being in a state of 'arrested development' ... both intellectually and culturally."[24]

Unlike the Holocaust, the Darfurian crisis is not an already highly mediated historical event and the scant visual record of the atrocities there may present a creative representational opportunity. Those who engage in acts of representation commence their projects virtually tabula rasa, almost unfettered by past constructs. This relative freedom does not suggest that Darfur is completely free of clichés, or that a representative photographic record does not exist. The materials used to depict Darfur have their own culturally available and assimilable signs; we see the ubiquitous dying African baby, the close-up portraits of character-laden African faces, the dusty refugee or internally displaced persons (IDP) camp teaming with women and children, and the rich colours of African tapestry worn by Darfurian women. With reference to some of the more vibrant and playful images from the refugee camps, such photographs may restore positive features to Darfurian individual and collective identity, creating empathetic connections between viewers and victims, and recovering from the impersonal machinery of destruction an individual glimpse of displaced lives. However, much like the perils of representing the Holocaust, within this familiar "narrative" of the horrible aftermath of the genocide in Africa – the pictures of women and children in refugee camps and the distribution of humanitarian aid – there runs the danger of aesthetically "resolving" atrocity and providing a form of redemptive closure. The entrance of violence into narrative may facilitate another type of normalization. Much like the Holocaust, the once unfathomable crimes in Darfur assume a similar "mantle of coherence that narrative necessarily imposes on them, and the trauma of their unassimilability is relieved."[25]

At the same time, some photographer's and curator's approaches to visualizing the genocide challenge yet another limit of representation: Can a visualization of an event show too little? Instead of tangled masses of anonymous bodies, we might see the bullet-punctured surface of a village hut, a battle-worn foot, or a textile-wrapped form. Both graphic and more evocative representations offer different lenses through which to debate the limits and propriety of visually depicting genocide. Do these more abstruse photographs present a trope of tragedy, devastation, and loss, more sensitively depicting the vast crimes perpetrated by the GOS and the Janjaweed? Both the graphic and more evocative approaches beg the same questions: Do exhibitions about the Darfurian genocide provide insight into the causal factors that have enabled genocide to occur? Do we come to know something of the culture and politics of the region? Museological attention is no guarantor that the facts of Darfur's history will be known or its significance understood, or even that pondering these displays will offer the viewer any insight into the events that are taking place in the Sudan. Exhibitions are, like other forms of mass communication, frequently charged with purveying simplistic awareness rather than true confrontations with the present and past.

The exhibition format depends on a variety of historical and documentary media to represent subject matter. Reporting and conducting research in Darfur has proved to be challenging. Geographically, and otherwise, Darfur is in one of the most inaccessible and inhospitable areas of the world; violence, intimidation, and insecurity reign.[26] The question of access has implications for exhibitions because exhibit content finds its source in those aspects of the tragedy that have been recorded or collected. Darfur has been covered extensively as compared to the Rwandan genocide, at the time of its unfolding, and as compared to most stories about Africa. This groundswell of interest in Darfur has waxed and waned, tempered by other significant world events. Darfur has to contend with the effects of compassion fatigue of the variety that can be shaken only by massive violence on the scale of the Rwandan genocide – and massiveness that can be expressed visually. As veteran war correspondent Donatella Lorch notes: "Tents and dust do not translate well in trying to arouse the interest of the world."[27] There are virtually no publicly available photographs and little footage of Janjaweed militias or Sudanese soldiers attacking villages. And, unlike the Rwandan genocide, "[Darfur] does not have the fields of bodies of Rwanda. It does not have everyone starving to death like Somalia. It has refugee pictures, but as far as trying to bring across the horror or the impact of genocide or a holocaust, it does not have those pictures."[28] Much of the tragedy of Darfur – the killings and the destruction of villages – has taken place beyond the view of cameras. Although a less important factor in exhibitions than in the journalistic genre, this lack of photographic documentation of all facets of the crimes of the GOS and the Janjaweed makes the creation of engaging and compelling exhibition narratives more difficult.

The complexity of the historical origins of the Darfurian conflict, and the more recent events that ignited the genocide in 2003, present numerous interpretive challenges for exhibition curators. Historical background in exhibitions is typically provided in text panels, but such panels function best when they are succinct. How can an overview of the Darfurian genocide be achieved vis-à-vis exhibition text panels, considering the limitations of space; the presence of multiple causal explanations for the occurrence of the genocide, which in turn negates the possibility of employing a single overarching exhibition narrative; and the fact that several key points of interpretive contestation exist?[29] In Prunier's *Darfur: The Ambiguous Genocide*, no less than *four* explanations are given for the violence in Darfur – tribal conflicts exacerbated by drought, a counter-insurgency campaign gone wrong, ethnic cleansing, and genocide.[30] Each one of these interpretations has grains of truth and invention, and all involve explications that require expert knowledge. To grasp the contemporary conflict, one must also look to colonial legacies (the "benign neglect" under the Anglo-Egyptian Condominium[31]), Chadian revolutionary movements and Libyan interest in the Arabization of the region, many years of administrative disregard by the government in Khartoum, the very contemporary interests of China, Russia, and the United States, and the impact of years of drought and desertification. To compound the difficulties in presenting intricate and multifaceted causal explanations for the crisis in Darfur, exhibition visitors in North America are likely to lack even basic knowledge about the culture and politics of this part of Africa.

Unlike the Holocaust and the Rwandan genocide, the Darfurian genocide is not a historical event. Exhibitions about the crisis in Darfur explore ongoing crimes rather than tragedies of the past. Exhibition narratives are thus constructed with a palpable representational urgency. By examining *The Smallest Witnesses* and *Darfur/Darfur* in greater detail, we can see how these two exhibitions engage with some key representational concerns.

The Smallest Witnesses: The Conflict in Darfur Through Children's Eyes

The Smallest Witnesses is a travelling exhibition produced by Human Rights Watch. In The Smallest Witnesses, drawings of children are the primary medium of expression, giving voice to the youngest victims of the crisis in Darfur and standing as graphic testimony about the atrocities these children have witnessed and experienced. The precious sketches that document these child-survivors' experiences are concrete evidence of their lives and struggles and an expression of their need to bear witness to the catastrophe that befell individuals, families, and entire communities. It is this clarity of purpose that we see in the children's drawings that comprise The Smallest Witnesses. These disturbing and vivid images of violence are one of the few extant visual records created by witnesses of the Darfurian genocide. Theirs is a language that approximates the horrors of the genocide, a "unique visual vocabulary of war"[32] that includes scenes of GOS and Janjaweed-perpetrated attacks and the aftermath of the destruction.

On a research trip devoted to assessing the issue of sexual violence, Dr Annie Sparrow, a pediatrician, and Olivier Bercault, a HRW lawyer, visited seven Darfurian refugee camps along Sudan's border with Chad and the border town of Tine. Sparrow and Bercault gave children paper and implements for drawing while their parents, teachers, or guardians were being interviewed.[33] The children were not prompted to draw; the drawings happened spontaneously, without any instruction or guidance. Sparrow and Bercault also visited schools located in these refugee camps, where many children shared the drawings they had sketched in their notebooks. It is from all these sources that the drawings in The Smallest Witnesses are gleaned. The first version of the exhibition included twenty-seven original drawings – a representative sample out of the hundreds of drawings collected by HRW researchers during their field research in Sudan and Chad.[34] The scale of the exhibition was determined by the size of the original drawings, which have their source in typical school notebooks and similarly sized individual sheets of paper; each notebook page or sheet was readied for display by first being mounted and then framed.

The drawings are accompanied by captions, more extensive text and background information about the conflict in Darfur, an account of how the drawings were collected, interpretive material related to the content of the drawings, and excerpts of testimony providing context about the artists' renderings. Supporting the in situ exhibition materials is an exhibition catalogue, available both in hard-copy form and as a downloadable PDF document on the HRW website. It is interesting to note that the exhibition text does not refer to the ethnic cleansing and human rights crisis occurring in Darfur as genocide.[35] The exhibition catalogue is loosely divided into several thematic sections – *laws of war, attacks on civilians, sexual violence, inhumane treatment,* and *forcible displacement* – and, while the exhibition itself contains imagery that depicts each topic, the content is not ordered according to this basis. Each theme is illustrated with examples of the children's drawings and their first-person accounts. In the exhibition catalogue, the drawings and accounts are set beside passages from the Geneva conventions or the Additional Protocols that correspond to the violation being depicted. The background textual information is densely worded in contrast to the brief testimonial excerpts, but it is scant in detail about the cultural and religious traditions of the region.[36]

Language is not a significant part of these children's artistic expressions; where language does appear on the "canvas," there are just a few words in Arabic. Perhaps this absence of language indicates that drawing, rather than words, was a more accessible vehicle of expression for the victims of this genocide. As Robin Goodman, psychologist and art therapist, notes: "Creative activity is incredibly powerful, especially for responding, or as an antidote, to a destructive act."[37] Art is a non-threatening medium that is empowering to children because they are able to set their own representational and creative boundaries. This sense of safety in the art allows them to render and express their experiences, helping to make whole what has been shattered by trauma.[38] The children who contributed their artwork were provided with an even greater sense of safety by knowing that pseudonyms would be used to preserve their anonymity.

While the children's communicative powers are drawn from the resonance of the drawings, *The Smallest Witnesses* includes explanatory and contextualizing passages, including excerpts from testimonies collected by HRW researchers. These testimonial fragments are the full extent of the biographical information provided to exhibition goers. Where testimony is included, it is limited to descriptions of violent encounters, thus reducing individual identities to their association with acts of genocide. These first-person accounts, albeit brief and limited in scope, are riveting and powerful documents in themselves and offer viewers further insight into the events being depicted in the drawings. Much more discursive space is given to the Geneva conventions and their protocols, which appear as textual inserts alongside witness testimony in the catalogue. It is curious that HRW researchers and exhibition curators did not provide more details about the children who created the drawings – their lives before and after the conflict – considering the greater empathetic connections and heightened sense of relatedness that could have been provided for exhibition visitors.[39] An opportunity for further contextualization, via first-person accounts attached to individual drawings, seems to have been missed. However, the researchers and curators may have considered the children's subjectivity in synchronic and collective terms rather than through the prism of individual biography or through situating the artworks more diachronically.[40]

The drawings are valued less for the quality of their rendering than for the unique glimpses they offer of the perceptions of child survivors of the Darfurian genocide, and for the detailed and specific references they provide about the perpetrators of these crimes and their means and methods of mass murder. A range of artistic and drafting skills are presented; many drawings are quite elementary – stick figures and rough outlines of objects – while others show a more sophisticated graphic quality. But the technical rendition does not take away from their power to convey essential truths. The drawings have a raw, unedited quality that conveys an organic genuineness. It is their very simplicity that makes their messages universal, and it is their candid quality that adds to their emotional resonance. In a universe filled with graphic images of violence, these drawings still have the power to shock, but with none of the sentimentality to which they were surely prone. While emotionally moving, they are never maudlin, nor do they appear to seek such forms of attention.

There is no mistaking that these drawings were made by the hands of children. From a distance we see features typical of all children's art – roughly hewn figures, skewed spatial relations, virtually absent perspective, colours that seep beyond bold and uneven lines. With few exceptions, the palette is muted, punctuated only by swaths of colour denoting violence and fear – the blood from a corpse, the amber light of burning huts, aggressive tones beside victims being raped, and sometimes a bright green of a soldier's uniform. What is atypical for children's art are the subjects of these compositions, which quickly makes obvious that these "artists" are the victims of war. The images are painfully vivid and direct, affording little room for interpretation beyond the obvious gravity of the scenes of destruction being depicted.

The drawings include common representational motifs in art created by children who have experienced trauma. Children of war tend to draw airplanes as symbols of power, burning houses, projectiles, trajectories, and cadavers.[41] Such things are common in the Darfur drawings: planes and helicopters raining down bombs upon village huts, machine-gun-clad Janjaweed militia, figures suggestive of mass fleeing, and other forms – fallen, outstretched, sometimes bloody – which suggest death. For the few compositions where the imagery is ambiguous or difficult to read, accompanying first-person accounts clarify the subject matter. What, at first glance, appears to be a picture of men dancing with women actually portrays Sudanese soldiers taking women away to be raped.[42] In compositions that are purposefully more abstract, one senses that these less defined, more fluid lines are expressive of the chaos of the moment of Janjaweed violence – swirls in one drawing represent Janjaweed running after a screaming family, torn apart in this moment of terror.

The 'visual vocabulary of war' evident in *The Smallest Witnesses* is expressed as five broad themes that predominate in these compositions: the bombing of villages, civilians fleeing for their lives, the rape of women and girls, corpses, and the actions of the Janjaweed. Several of the drawings picture scenes of villages being bombed by planes and helicopters and then burned to the ground. Musa, age fifteen, and his cousin Zania, eight, both show the aftermath of an Antonov aircraft bombing their village; Musa's mother, father, and brothers were all killed in the attack. The cousins depict the same scene with striking similarity – simple line drawings show a series of triangular huts; plane and Janjaweed attacks set the huts ablaze in shades of yellow, orange, and red.

Another genre of drawing depicts groups of civilians fleeing for their lives. The trauma of witnessing mass death, and subsequent exile and separation, are expressed through these drawings via a powerful simplicity of means. Taha, age thirteen, from North Darfur, drew such a landscape – planes showering bombs across a village, causing wide chaos, destruction, and death. The figures that appear are punctuated by broad strokes of red crayon, suggestive of those who did not make it. The accompanying first-person account reads: "In the afternoon we returned from school and saw the planes. ... Then they began the bombing. The first bomb [landed] in our garden, then four bombs at once in the garden. The bombs killed six people, including a young boy, a boy carried by his mother, and a girl. In another place in the garden a woman was carrying her baby son – she was killed, not him. Now my nights are hard because I feel frightened. We became homeless. I cannot forget the bad images of the burning houses and fleeing at night because our village was burned."[43] In another drawing, Amani, age eight, shows villagers fleeing from the Janjaweed and GOS planes. Amani reveals in the testimonial account that they ran to a riverbed for protection, and then to Chad. The monochromatic, ochre–stained, roughly drawn figures of varying shapes and sizes indicate families being displaced en masse.

Just as rape and sexual violence against women and girls has been a pervasive feature of the genocidal campaign carried out by government forces and militias, so too is rape a prominent theme in the children's drawings. Mahmoud, age thirteen, shows uniformed soldiers seizing women amidst the destruction of homes and the murder of villagers. Salah, age thirteen, of West Darfur also recalls such a scene. Two groupings of figures, large in scale, convey an ominous tone. The first pictures a vulnerable horizontal positioning of a female figure; the second features another female figure, wearing an indistinct partial textile reminiscent of a dress, with a soldier's gun pointing in her direction. Ala, age thirteen, depicts the sexual violation of men. In his drawing, a Darfurian rebel fighter is executed by a Janjaweed attacker through a purposeful act of emasculation – gunshots to the groin. Another portrait, by Doa, is a reminder that these crimes are taking place in the *present*; one rape victim is shown sprawled on the ground, clutching her cellular phone in a futile gesture for help.

Corpses also figure prominently in the children's drawings, replete with detail of the violent acts that befell the victims. In the upper-right side of a drawing by Isma, age eight, a lifeless figure lays on the ground, her head streaming red. Near the middle of the page, there is a large green vehicle, a man clad in clothing of a similar colour, and a multi-coloured circular burst of energy. Referring to the listless woman, Isma recollects:

Human Rights Watch Researcher: "And what is going on here?"
Isma: "My hut burning after being hit by a bomb. This man in green is a soldier from Sudan."
HRW: "And here?"
Isma: "It's a woman. She is dead."

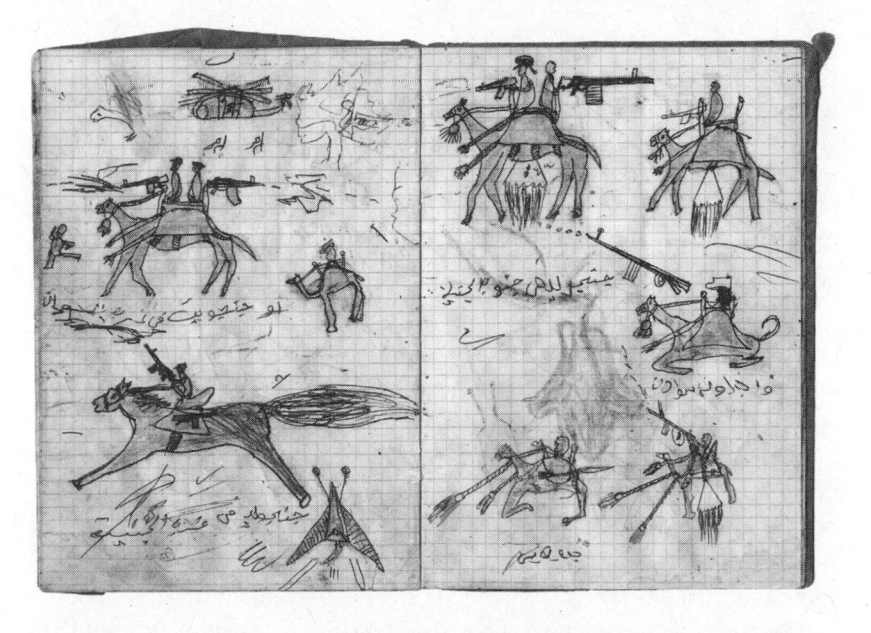

Abd al-Rahman, age thirteen: "I am looking at the sheep in the *wadi* [riverbed or oasis]. I see Janjaweed coming – quickly, on horses and camels, with Kalashnikovs – shooting and yelling, 'kill the slaves, kill the blacks.' They killed many of the men with the animals. I saw people falling on the ground and bleeding. They chased after children. Some of us were taken, some we didn't see again. All our animals were taken: camels, cows, sheep, goats. Then the planes came and bombed the village." (Credit: Human Rights Watch)

HRW: "Why is her face colored in red?"
Isma: "Oh, because she has been shot in the face."[44]

It is the actions of the armed Janjaweed, on horses and camels, that, by far, dominate in the mind's eye of *The Smallest Witnesses* artists. The Janjaweed are most expressive of the children's subjectivity, for it is in these menacing figures, their automatic rifles spraying bullets at unarmed villagers, that the viewer most acutely senses the fear these children experienced. In the notebook belonging to Abd al-Rahman, age thirteen, from West Darfur, there are numerous stylized Janjaweed, one or two riders atop horses and camels, the grip of their guns and their postures signalling a "hunt" for their victims. The Janjaweed loom large in Abd al-Rahman's memory; by comparison, one victim appears as a minute presence on the very edge of the page. Abd al-Rahman recalls: "I am looking at the sheep in the *wadi*.[45] I see *Janjaweed* coming – quickly, on horses and camels, with Kalashnikovs – shooting and yelling, 'kill the slaves, kill the blacks.' They killed many of the men with the animals. I saw people falling on the ground and bleeding. They chased after children. Some of us were taken, some we didn't see again. All our animals were taken: camels, cows, sheep, and goats. Then the planes came and bombed the village."[46]

The Smallest Witnesses drawings reflect real-life witnessing rather than imaginings. The children's visual recollections are entirely in accordance with the historical record. That they are translations of actual lived experiences is evident in the consistency of their detail and the plausibility of the visual descriptions, and is corroborated by other evidence. In common with the drawings by children affected by other wars, *The Smallest Witnesses* is characterized by "very factual recordings of war events, not the sensationalized, fantastic version that is pictured by those who have never experienced it."[47]

The significance of the images the children share goes beyond their value as personal expressions of trauma and compelling works of art; these drawings are an evidentiary visual record. The drawings corroborate eyewitness testimonial evidence and the documentation of the crimes committed by the GOS and the Janjaweed as collected by HRW and other NGOs that have a presence in the region. The children's drawings display an uncanny familiarity with the military aircraft, artillery, and guns they have seen used (MiG-21s, Anatov aircraft, AK-47s, FAL rifles, and Kalashnikovs), and, rather than drawing generic armaments, some sketches include enough detail to identify the actual weapons, as determined by arms experts who have reviewed the artwork. It is also noteworthy that a series of these drawings has been submitted to the International Criminal Court (ICC) for consideration.[48]

The drawings illustrate aspects of the crisis in Darfur that have evaded photographers and television crews. For example, these drawings portray Sudanese government officials and Arab militias attacking villages together. The fact that the Sudanese soldiers are clearly distinguished from the militia fighters by their dress – the soldiers wear uniforms, the militiamen do not – further underscores the accuracy of the children's portrayals. The children's sketches also refute the GOS's claim that this war is a tribal conflict between the Africans and the Arab militia. The Janjaweed have only horses and camels and various types of assault rifles; the presence in these drawings of planes bombing civilians and villages, tanks, Antonov planes, MiG fighter planes, and armoured personnel carriers is evidence of the participation of government forces.[49]

In the exhibition catalogue, articles from the Geneva conventions and protocols preface many of the drawings, providing an additional narrative framework for *The Smallest Witnesses* – that the laws of war are repeatedly being violated. For example, the exhibition quotes Protocol II, Article 13 on the Protection of the Civilian Population: "The civilian population as such, as well as individual civilians, shall not be the object of attack. Acts or threats of violence the primary purpose of which is to spread terror among the civilian population are prohibited." Below this article is Taha's drawing of plane attacks on huts and civilians accompanied by a passage from her first-person account. Mahmoud's drawing of women and girls being dragged away by soldiers intent on raping them is exhibited beside Protocol II, Article 4 on Fundamental Guarantees: "Civilians and captured combatants shall be protected against outrages upon personal dignity, in particular humiliating and degrading treatment, rape, enforced prostitution and any form of indecent assault." The exhibit also brings to mind the specific human rights of children. The opportunity to complement the children's drawings with passages from the UN Convention on the Rights of the Child and the Rome Statute of the International Criminal Court, where definitions of war crimes are enshrined, seems to have been missed. The perpetrators of the conflict in Darfur are clearly not adherents to the important principles laid out in the Geneva conventions, the Convention on the Rights of the Child, or the Rome Statute, and a more fitting narrative may have better served the human rights agenda of this exhibition.

From the exhibited works we are given few glimpses of the optimism present in the drawings of child survivors of other conflicts. The drawings in *The Smallest Witnesses* show, without reserve, the legacy of trauma held by children exposed to genocidal violence – depictions of loss: loss of childhood, loss of identity, and loss of family and community. The children's compositions are distilled into stark, acute, life- and-death struggles. There is no apparent place for escapism or decoration. Noticeably absent are birds, butterflies, hearts, and other life-affirming images found in drawings by children of other wars.[50] The figurations of the Darfurian artists are literal – bombs, fire, and utter devastation. One recalls here that these drawings were made mere weeks or months after the children's encounters with violence; they are not visual reflections years after the conflict. The creative processes and products of these child-artists mostly reveal their painful memories and fears rather than their sense of strength and hope for the future. There is an implicit message of pessimism expressed in these drawings: the children perceive the world as silent. Audiences of *The Smallest Witnesses* see little of these children's lives in times of relative peace, before the conflict began, or their hopes for life after it. Only occasionally, such as in the drawing by Nur, age nine, from North Darfur, does one see aspirations for the future. Nur's picture includes an image of colourful books floating over the head of her brother – an expression of his desire to go to school. The memory of the village school also reveals the children's tenuous position within the refugee camps, which do not appear in these drawings as temporary havens but merely as a continuum of displacement and deprivation. Ironically, this pessimism may have been somewhat tempered by the drawings themselves, since the sketches found their way back to the refugee camps. Sudanese lawyer and human rights activist Salih Mahmoud Osman took exhibition brochures with him while visiting Darfurian children in refugee camps. The existence of the exhibition and its international stature illustrated to the children not only that their stories were being heard but also that their drawings were contributing to global awareness about the plight of Darfurians.

The drawings that comprise *The Smallest Witnesses* speak with poignant immediacy about the human cost of the Darfurian genocide. These compelling sketches function on multiple levels – as works of art, as historical documents, and as avenues of catharsis. While fear and political uncertainty do not permit the children to put their names to their artwork, each drawing gives a human and individual expression to the overwhelming tragedy of genocide. The drawings are also a collective and comprehensive condemnation of the crimes perpetrated by the GOS and the Janjaweed. If, in our contemporary familiarity with images of violence, we have become inured to tragedy, *The Smallest Witnesses* invites us to look at the human cost of genocide in a new way.

Darfur/Darfur

Darfur/Darfur is a travelling exhibit of digitally projected documentary photographs taken in Darfur and Chad by former US Marine

Brian Steidle and seven photojournalists: Lynsey Addario, Mark Brecke, Hélène Caux, Ron Haviv, Paolo Pellegrin, Ryan Spencer Reed, and Michal Safdie. It was conceived and curated by Leslie Thomas, a Chicago-based architect, who was inspired to take action after reading about the scale of civilian casualties in Darfur. She was joined by a collective of concerned citizens, artists, and photographers, all of whom were inspired to employ documentary photography as a vehicle to promote international awareness about the Darfurian genocide. The goals of *Darfur/Darfur* are manifold and ambitious. Like *The Smallest Witnesses*, the exhibition's primary objective is to bring greater public attention to Darfur and to prompt international humanitarian efforts. Its stated visual scope, however, is wider than *The Smallest Witnesses*: to demonstrate how the ongoing violence and mass killings have devastated the region; to provide visual education about the culture and politics of the region; and to show the destruction of Darfurian cultural heritage.

The more than 100 documentary images that comprise *Darfur/Darfur* are exhibited in two formats: as large-size projections on the exterior walls of buildings, or as a projected in-gallery series.[51] A book of photographs based on the exhibition content, entitled *Darfur/Darfur: Life/War*, was published in 2008; the exhibition also has an online presence. *Darfur/Darfur* was first exhibited on 18 September 2006 at the James Cohan Gallery in New York City and had its premiere large-scale projection one month later in Los Angeles at UCLA's Hammer Museum. The installation is currently travelling to a host of international cities.[52] *Darfur/Darfur* was also shown at the Michael Lee-Chin Crystal of the Royal Ontario Museum (ROM) in Toronto from 8–17 September 2007. What follows is a description of the series as it appeared at the ROM.

The large-scale photographs that comprise *Darfur/Darfur* were projected onto the upper portions of the north exterior façade of the ROM, with three sections of the highly faceted glass surface serving as individual tripartite "screens." A discrete, looped series of images was presented onto each of the screens accompanied by traditional Sudanese music. In addition to the documentary images, the easternmost screen featured creative and technical credits and a few lines of introductory text: "In a multicultural region of Sudan where 12 languages are spoken hundreds of thousands of people have perished. Experience the rich culture that is being erased and learn what you can do to help."

The "sequentialization" of *Darfur/Darfur*'s images lends movement and dynamism to the once more static images, and the exhibition takes on a dialogical and performative quality that engages the viewer's imagination and responsiveness more fully. This photographic space is constructed as an entry into the experiential, and the photographs aspire to operate as a form of vicarious witnessing through both identification and positioning. However, the "slide-show" technique also lends an air of ephemerality to the exhibition because the viewer is not given the opportunity to stay with these images for any significant length of time and contemplate them further.

The projected photographs assume a monumental scale, with their massive visual bearing amplifying what Roland Barthes refers to as the photograph's "certificate of presence."[53] The amplitude and scale of the images command attention, making it difficult for passersby to disregard the installation. By capturing the notice of diverse viewers, those who intentionally set out to view the installation and those who happened upon it, *Darfur/Darfur* reaches a wide audience. At the same time, the surface of the "screen" makes the images less distinct, and from time to time the images take on the form of a ghostly revenant. This spectral superimposition is reminiscent of the digital projections of artist Shimon Attie, in particular his series *Writing on the Wall*, in which he projected archival photographs of the inhabitants of Berlin's Jewish past onto now-gentrified storefronts. The past and present images in *Writing on the Wall* are bound together in a representational embrace, but they are also bound by shared location. *Darfur/Darfur* presents a more attenuated relationship between past and present; while the historical events are similarly separated by time, they are also dislocated in space. Such space between past and present was collapsed only when *Darfur/Darfur* was projected onto the walls of the USHMM and the Jewish Museum in Berlin, where images of Darfurian life and death and the evocation of the destruction of European Jewry appear bound by a shared genocidal fate and world indifference. As projections on the walls of the ROM, however, the colonial legacies of the museum's African collections are implicitly evoked.

No original visual content was produced for *Darfur/Darfur*; the projected photographs were selected from existing Darfur-related documentary projects of the participating photographers. The photographs, all taken in Darfur and Chad, offer glimpses of regional culture and geography, but the primary focus of the camera is on the struggles of the survivors, post-genocide, and the effects of the ongoing humani-

Darfur/Darfur exhibit at the Royal Ontario Museum (ROM) in Toronto, September 2007. (Credit: C. Peter Morgan, 2008 / http://www.flickr.com/photos/pmorgan)

tarian crisis. The collage of photographs is not organized thematically, or by artist, but rather move according to the curator's chosen patterning. While some sequences appear more randomly drawn – portraits of Darfurians are interspersed with photographs of destroyed villages, ramshackle IDP dwellings, and Sudanese Liberation Movement/Army (SLM/A) rebels – other sequences appear more methodically constructed. We see a number of portraits – bruised, weary, and worn faces followed by more stoic expressions and then contemplative countenances. In another series, overhead photographs of burning villages are followed by ground shots of the charred remains of homes and possessions. Severely malnourished babies are seen clinging to life; the next photograph in the sequence is that of a funeral.

The photographs included in *Darfur/Darfur* vary from venue to venue because of format and space requirements and as new work is added, but they maintain an overall continuity. The photographic content falls into several distinct themes that provide the general visual narrative of the exhibition: the devastation of Darfurian villages; the social lives of individuals and the fabric of changed communities in the aftermath of this destruction; conditions in the refugee and IDP camps; portraits of members of the SLM/A and other rebel groups, and their training and movements. Portraiture featuring women, children, and the elderly is a mainstay of the series, as are more panoramic glimpses of Darfurian landscapes. The malnourished, injured, deformed, wounded, traumatized, bandaged, bedridden, and hospitalized also appear throughout the sequences, but do not predominate. Unlike the projection at the USHMM, the Toronto installation contains a few photographs of the dead but does not dwell on these images.

Each of Darfur/Darfur's contributing photographers lends his/her distinctive vision to documenting the crisis. Brian Steidle's photographs show the physical destruction brought on by the GOS and the Janjaweed: the charred remains of the village of Aliet; an aerial photograph of the burning of Um Zeifa; and a reportage-style photograph of two Sudanese soldiers looting the town of Marla. A conventional portrait of a Darfurian child in El Fashir, the capital city of North Darfur, and an image of the IDP camp of Al Geer – a quizzical tangle of plastic, metal, and textile – offer a counterpoint to the ruinous Darfurian villages.

Between September 2004 and February 2005, Steidle, an unarmed military observer, took hundreds of photographs documenting atrocities in Darfur. As a member of the African Union team monitoring the conflict, he had access to areas off-limits to journalists. He travelled in helicopters, which afforded him aerial views of burning villages and the devastated aftermath. He returned to the United States in February 2005 with hundreds of images, which he made public despite US State Department policy prohibiting the publication of such materials. The most graphic of these photographs – a castrated man left to bleed to death, people with their ears cut off and eyes plucked out – were not included in the series which was projected onto the walls of the USHMM.

Mark Brecke's high-contrast, stark black-and-white photographs are focused on human subjects: a group of concerned-looking Sudanese women and children; a child, in desperate need of medical attention, perched in the arms of a guardian; in a tent put up by the United Nations High Commissioner for Refugees (UNHCR), teeming with the indigent, a village elder displays an identity card; a contemplative figure lays on a bed, his eyes trying to express what his battle-scared body has experienced; and a group of heavily armed SLM/A rebels posed in and on their vehicle. Brecke took these pictures from October to December 2004, when he visited the refugee camps of eastern Chad and travelled in Darfur with the SLM/A.

Ron Haviv's carefully composed colour photographs combine portraiture, abstraction, and texture. His camera, focused from above, looks to the ground, where hands belonging to seated figures hold writing instruments to their Arabic notebooks; two children play near the belly of an aircraft which has landed in the town of Fina; young Sudanese women in richly coloured traditional dress walk through the desert in search of firewood; veiled by the blue mess of a makeshift tent at the Abu Shouk IDP camp, a mother attentively looks at her sleeping baby at the Action against Famine's feeding centre; and a young girl wearing flip-flops squats in a mud hut at the Kass camp.

Hélène Caux's lens focuses on daily life struggles in the refugee and IDP camps of Chad and Darfur. Women and children figure prominently in a world that is not black and white but imbued with colour. While free of any illusions about the gravity of the humanitarian crisis, Caux's landscapes are inhabited by markers of courage and resistance: a child plays by a sun-drenched wall riddled with war graffiti; women assume dignified postures in their brightly coloured dresses; traces of happy, smiling faces of girls appear in the foreground of a makeshift tent. Caux's projected photographs offer glimpses of normal life amidst appalling conditions.

Paolo Pellegrin's haunting black-and-white photographs suggest the loneliness and sorrow of the refugee journey. Using soft focus, chiaroscuro, and shallow depth of field, Pellegrin captures sparse and dramatic moments that he describes as "unfinished." In Pellegrin's Darfur-cased oeuvre we see the suggestive environs and figures of a refugee camp during a rainstorm in Zelingei; a South Darfurian girl caught in a rainstorm; a severely disabled girl struggling on the barren ground in Nyala; the stark interior of a hospital in Kass where a boy is recovering from a gunshot wound in the leg; and an elderly refugee woman sitting on a table in the South School refugee camp in Kass.

Lynsey Addario uses saturated colour, angled perspectives, and blurred focus to express dislocation and chaos. Barely discernible figures roam a blurry desert landscape, as if to imply that what was lost in this conflict cannot truly be captured. In another image, scorched ochre earth that once held Tama's village huts still smoulders after attacks the previous week, the smoke so thick the blue sky appears heavy with clouds. Addario also pictures an SLM/A soldier perched beside a charred beam of a structure that once stood on that spot before the village of Hangala was burned by the Janjaweed; the soldier stands angled like one of the twister lumbers. The bright yellow and green fabric worn by the SLM/A soldiers and the softness of their expressions surprises us; this is not the typical iconography of warfare.

The very close-up and panoramic black-and-white photographs employed by Ryan Spencer Reed reveal essential details about the victims of war. Row upon row of UNHCR tents stretch to the horizon, communicating the vastness of the refugee crisis in Darfur. Lines of refugees cross deep, muddy streams to make their way to safety. There is enough character on a sandalled foot to speak volumes of a perilous journey.

The youngest and oldest victims of war are the focus of Michal Ronnen Safdie's contribution to *Darfur/Darfur*. In their stillness, and in the weariness of expression in their postures and eyes, we can sense the Darfurian victims' profound distress and shock. What might seem perfectly natural in another context – portraits of grandmother and child, brother and sister, a girl and two babies – assumes a more ominous character in these photographs, which were taken at the Bahai Refugee Camp on the border of Darfur and Chad. With absent or deceased parents, grandmothers and older children take care of the young. The photos are grim and foreboding; the children are too thin, the grandmothers too tired, the faces too overwhelmed.

Darfur/Darfur takes a mostly allusive approach to the limits and propriety of representing the crisis in Darfur by focusing on visual texts that are not explicitly about the genocide but rather reveal the traces and voids left behind in its aftermath.We see physical environs where scarred geographical and cultural landscapes refer to the life of the community that once inhabited these spaces, a metaphorics of loss in which the photographic images capture a sense of overwhelming fragmentation and displacement. The surfaces of the present suggest the horrors of a recent past as topographical photographs are sequentially linked to photographs of the previous inhabitants of these lands, dislocated by their status as refugees. The spaces occupied by the living subjects of these photographs are interrupted only occasionally, and fleetingly, by reminders of those even less fortunate.

The primary subjects of the photographer's lens are the victims of the Darfurian genocide as they attempt to convey "the human experience of otherwise anonymous 'processes' and the empathy it inspires towards subjects otherwise rendered unfathomable and impersonal because of their vastness."[54] Many of these images offer a poetic, subjective telling of events that shows Darfur as a human tragedy that has claimed the lives of individuals and communities. The sum of the photographs in *Darfur/Darfur* creates a tension between the numbing totality of mass destruction and the visual testimonies of individual victims, families, and communities. The people pictured are the community remnants, the "lucky" ones who have escaped death. We see the "defeated" and we see those with more reserves, whose acts of resistance involve retaining some sense of normality despite their desperate situation. Photographic absences make reference to "the missing" and, by implication, the other realities of genocide, while brief but poignant appearances of the dead confront exhibition viewers. In its balanced approach to representing the aftermath of genocide, *Darfur/Darfur* pays respect to those whose lives have been lost and their families while promoting notions of justice and accountability. But what do we make of the other "missing" photographs – such as the most graphic photographic evidence of genocidal death in Steidle's series, *In Darfur, My Camera Was Not Nearly Enough* – that were deemed too gruesome for public display on the walls of the USHMM? According to *Darfur/Darfur*'s curator, Leslie Thomas, requests by host institutions to omit specific images are considered on a case-by-case basis. For a handful of venues, the editing of certain graphic sequences was deemed appropriate in response to parental and community concerns. Turning the camera's lens on the aftermath of mass murder is perhaps the most obvious illustration of photographic objectification. The strategy being employed in *Darfur/Darfur*'s more oblique use of documentary photography lies not in approximating the "real event" but in positioning these images within a wider interpretive structure.

Few of the photographs in *Darfur/Darfur* assume a purely descriptive or evidentiary function, although all provide an evidentiary affirmation of the circumstances of the subject depicted. Through the "present," we access some facets of the experience of surviving genocide and the harsh conditions that Darfurian refugees face. In particular, the portraits of *Darfur/Darfur* support these subjects in their function as witnesses to genocidal events. While images of faces "affect us viscerally, evoking emotional, parasympathetic responses,"[55] the photographic portraits are not invitations to sentimentality. The evocative powers of the human face, in particular a child's face, are meant to collapse the distance between self and other. By engaging each viewer's sense of recognition and identification with these subjects, by obscuring "otherness," *Darfur/Darfur* creates a site of intersubjectivity; the observer and the witness are meant to merge in a confrontation with the genocidal present. The potentially neutralizing language of the documentation of death is silenced by faces and story portraits.

However, these evocative compositions, when projected, offer virtually no explanatory text or historical background. A square kiosk constructed for the exhibition, lined with didactic panels, stood in front of the ROM's Lee-Chin crystal. The stand was diminutive in comparison with the projections and easily missed by passersby. One side of the kiosk explained: "This exhibition endeavors to place the brutal realities faced in Darfur in context with its vibrant culture and people. We hope to put a human face on the continuing atrocities and prompt international support for the prevention of further destruction of life." The next panel provided historical background from the post-independence political conflicts and the north-south civil war up to the present. Another section of the panel directed readers to international and Canadian advocacy organizations and charities working in Darfur. But such general information is disconnected from the specifics of the photographs being presented.

Photographs can be difficult to decipher if exhibited without toponymic descriptors and further contextualization. What do we know about the landscapes and faces that are pictured without captions? For example, Ron Haviv's brilliant photograph of the beautiful young Darfurian women walking though the desert has a pleasant air about it – the contented expressions, the rich textiles, the cloudless blue sky. This image seems to offer the viewer a sense of comfort and safety. However, the photograph alone belies the truth of the dangers that lurk just beyond the edges of the frame. A caption accompanying the image might inform viewers that the pictured women have been sent to collect firewood. As Brian Steidle recounts: "Every day, women are sent outside the IDP camps to seek firewood and water, despite the constant risk of rape at the hands of the *Janjaweed*. Should men be available to venture out of the camps, they risk castration and murder. So families decide that rape is the lesser evil. It is a crime that families even have to make such a choice."[56] The IDP camps are certainly not glorified in these photographs, but their squalour and haphazard quality tell only part of the story.

The photographs that appear in *Darfur/Darfur* without proximate captioning risk promoting a cursory form of spectatorship. Unlike *The Smallest Witnesses*, *Darfur/Darfur* does not integrate survivor testi-

Young girls leave a camp for internally displaced persons to gather firewood. (*Darfur/Darfur* exhibit). (Credit: Ron Haviv / VII)

mony or other text-based explications into the projected exhibition – an approach that would offer audiences more insight into the images they are observing. Nor do exhibition visitors learn anything of the identities and background of those pictured. *Darfur/Darfur* presents an essentially mute, nameless series of photographs, whose indeterminations are heightened by the rapidity of the sequentialization. This visual muteness creates an innate tension between the silence that describes the rupture and the contiguous images that attempt to bridge this silence. Or is the strength of this project bolstered by its insistence on the suggestive power of the photograph alone?

The portraits of *Darfur/Darfur* represent one world of memory – *the after*. Picturing *the after* of the Darfurian genocide does not approximate the experience of genocide. In these Darfurian portraits do we see a reliance on visual conventions that obscure genocidal reality? Or do these photographs trace an alternative and parallel aspect of truths revealed in the genocidal abyss? Susan Sontag, in her noted book *On Photography*, suggests that there "is something predatory in the act of taking a picture. To photograph people is to violate them ... it turns people into objects that can be symbolically possessed."[57] Indeed, in

Darfur/Darfur, certain photographs, such as Paolo Pellegrin's photograph of the disabled child, approximate the Barthian conflation of photography with death.[58] For the victims of the Darfurian genocide, this symbolic possession assumes more extreme implications because the causalities of such crimes "have no means to represent to themselves the abjection and the extermination of which they are the victims."[59] Does the frozen moment of horror and misery captured in the documentary record of genocide serve its victims? Documentary images are often all people see and remember of the once rich traditions of cultures felled by genocide because rarely are corresponding images of life before or after the catastrophe included. If the intention of the génocidaires was to dehumanize their victims, to destroy the very notion that the victim was a human being, then the use and reuse of graphic photographic depictions of atrocity serve to perpetuate the génocidaires' model.

By limiting the use of in extremis images, perhaps it is the intention of *Darfur/Darfur* to express tragedy through evoking loss, not degradation. The exhibition visitor rarely looks at the atrocities directly; references to genocidal acts are implicit, and the tragedy of Darfur is shown more obliquely. The exhibition thus avoids re-victimizing the subjects of the Darfurian genocide. *Darfur/Darfur* might thus be understood as an attempt to restore a positive memory of Darfurian individual and collective identity through reversing the process of photographic objectification. Alongside the suffering of the victims, it is the humanity of the survivors that many of the photographers capture. The young woman whom Hélène Caux finds in the middle of a vast, barren landscape, seemingly alone, with a few meagre possessions behind her, still offers a dignified presence to the camera and something of her subjectivity is preserved.

Darfur/Darfur does not fully transcend the inescapable representational trap – that visual documents of genocide concomitantly function as aesthetic objects. Michal Ronnen Safdie describes the tension between the beauty of photographic composition and the reality of genocide: "Wars occur on regular days, while the sun is shining and the sky is blue ... Even the most terrible situations can be photographed beautifully. We have to respect every person. Every human being deserves to be shown in the best way."[60] Ron Haviv also rejects those who complain that such photographs glamorize – and so deflate – tragedy: "It's difficult to get people to look at horror," he says. "It's important to engage the viewer as much as you can. Only once there's emotional involvement can content be absorbed."[61]

Considering the public's familiarity with the visual culture of tragedy, can the more subtle – or sometimes pleasing – imagery of *Darfur/Darfur* maintain the power to communicate substantive truths about the genocide in Darfur? It is in the post-liberation photographs of the Nazi death camps that we find an extreme reference point for the evils of human history, a memento mori of the twentieth century. More recently, another representational nadir was found in the photographs and videos of huddled masses of dead bodies in the churches and schools of Rwanda that were discovered and documented in the aftermath of the one-hundred-day genocide. Do the photographs that appear in *Darfur/Darfur* – burning villages, refugee camp life, portraits of victims, babies in ill health – have the same visual resonance as atrocity photographs from the Holocaust or the Rwandan genocide? Have the artists who have contributed to *Darfur/Darfur* "given people images of Darfur they can hold onto"?[62] The representational ante for genocide is high; even the gravest of Steidle's photographs, or the most poetic of Pellegrin's, may not be enough to rustle the public out of its compassion fatigue.

There is a fundamental question still associated with these exhibition projects: What does the public do with all its new information and enhanced awareness? How exactly do these exhibitions function as visual advocates of peace in Darfur? Will these children's drawings, documentary photographs, and didactic panels spur more people and nations to act to help save Darfurian lives? For one Darfurian refugee, Omer Ismail, the stated goals of the exhibition medium are quite modest. If the pictures "stir some sort of curiosity in the average person as they go by and see it, then the job is done ... They will go out and ask, Why?"[63] For others, such as photographer Hélène Caux, the goals of the representational impulse are also straightforward, but more ambitious: "My main goal with the pictures was to document human rights abuses and the catastrophic humanitarian situation. For me, it's a way of making people aware of what's happening in the world so they get out of their daily routine and try to maybe make a difference by joining the humanitarian organizations, funding the humanitarian organizations, by talking about what's happening in Darfur in schools ... I see my work in a way as a duty of history to document what has happened at a certain time so that people don't forget."[64] There are those who suggest that a visual culture of atrocity can achieve more lofty goals. In reference to Brian Steidle's photographs, David Del Conte, an American humanitarian worker who met Steidle in South Darfur, stated: "He moved Darfur onto the front page. He saved thousands of lives."[65]

By examining the educational programs and social justice initiatives that these exhibitions support, one can see how exhibits function as embarkation points for historical learning and for larger discussions about genocide prevention and humanitarian intervention. Through direct, or more tacit, means, each exhibition prompts visitors to more active forms of anti-genocide advocacy.

The Smallest Witnesses has been displayed in North America and Europe – primarily at Jewish museums, Holocaust museums, community organizations, and universities. Human Rights Watch prepared supporting materials to accompany the exhibition including two flyers, one providing general background information on the crisis in Darfur and the other detailing the issue of sexual violence against women and children in the Darfur region. The latter flyer outlines "What Should have Been Done" and "What Has Been Done" and includes a highlighted textbox "What You Can Do." HRW also provided exhibition goers with a *Smallest Witnesses* postcard. A children's drawing appears on the front of the postcard; the back provides a space for the reader's name and signature and is addressed to President Bush with an appeal to support the United Nations-African Union force in Darfur, to closely monitor the actions of the GOS, and to impose further sanctions should the GOS fail to meet stated fundamental obligations. Some venues provided their own supplementary information; for example, Eastern Washington University promoted a direct connection between viewing the exhibition content, continued learning about Darfur, and social action, stating online in its introduction to the exhibition: "As you view the drawings their message becomes clear; acts of genocide still happen in the world and the world remains silent."[66] The exhibition visitor is directed to the Genocide Intervention Network's "Ten Things You Can Do about Genocide."[67] There is a comprehensive reading list and links to Darfur resources at Amnesty International, Physicians for Human Rights, and Human Rights Watch. Similar pamphlets of "action items" have been distributed at other exhibition sites. "Never Forget: Save Darfur," a social justice initiative from Hillel: The Foundation for Jewish Campus Life, suggests that visitors follow their viewing of HRW's *The Smallest Witnesses* with a letter-writing campaign to "congressional representatives, senators, President Bush and United Nations Secretary General Kofi Annan and a fundraising drive to benefit Sudanese relief organizations.[68] To those interested in making a financial contribution to anti-genocide efforts, *Darfur/Darfur* directs their attention to NGOs working on the ground in Darfur and Chad that provide emergency medical and social services. Some exhibition venues distributed postcards for the *Million Voices for Darfur*, a campaign to gather one million physical and electronic post cards urging President Bush, his administration, and Congress to demand a stronger and more effective US response to the crisis in Darfur. The verbiage associated with such campaigns is often quite simplistic, usually stated as government support for a larger, stronger, multinational force to protect the civilians of Darfur. Visitors to *Darfur/Darfur* are also encouraged to put constituent pressure on elected officials in Washington and Ottawa via letter-writing campaigns; the "Write a Letter, Save a Life" initiative provides more guidance on the nature of the text to be included in the letter, and directions on where to find the addresses of appropriate representatives in Congress.[69]

Exhibitions are one part in a greater movement of genocide awareness – a movement intent on channelling and then sustaining the power of the media as a catalyst for influencing governments, which, in turn, holds at least the promise of mobilizing political will. That the exhibition medium is an effective tool for rousing public interest in the Darfurian genocide is not debatable, but how does this translate into action by policy makers? The curators, artists, and photographers who have forged exhibitions about the crisis in Darfur are motivated by the same passions as the scholars of genocide – "to learn from the past to prevent recurrences in the future."[70] Despite the rhetoric of "never again" following the Holocaust, and then Rwanda, and despite the failure of the international community to intervene in Darfur, exhibitions will continue to play a part in resisting indifference to human suffering.

Notes

1 The crimes taking place in Darfur have been described in many different ways: as war crimes, crimes against humanity, ethnic cleansing, large-scale massacres or atrocities, or genocide. The fact remains that

death and violence on a massive scale are occurring in this region, and many elements of what constitutes genocide are present.

2 Michael Ames, *Cannibal Tours and Glass Boxes: The Anthropology of Museums* (Vancouver: UBC Press 1992), 7.

3 Robert R. James and Gerald T. Conaty, "Introduction," in James and Conaty, eds., *Looking Reality in the Eye: Museums and Social Responsibility* (Calgary: University of Calgary Press 2005), 3.

4 Ruth J. Abram, "History Is as History Does: The Evolution of a Mission-Driven Museum," in James and Conaty, eds., *Looking Reality in the Eye*, 19. However, with many larger museums and galleries shying away from the potentially controversial subjects associated with social justice, museums and exhibition spaces specializing in various aspects of the human rights story – civil rights, women's history, and the Holocaust – were created to fill the void.

5 The USHMM website notes that there were sixteen million non-Jewish visitors to the museum from April 1993 to January 2005: http://www.ushmm.org/research/library/index.utp?content=faq/right.htm, 12 March 2005. The Imperial War Museum's statistics were found at http://london.iwm.org.uk/server/show/nav.00b005008, 13 March 2008.

6 Sara Horowitz quoted in the *Jewish Tribune*, 9 November 2006, 20.

7 Stated by Bridget Conley during a presentation at the USHMM; transcript available at http://www.ushmm.org/conscience/analysis/details.php?content=2005-06-28&page=1&menupage=, 23 May 2007.

8 See Edward T. Linenthal, *Preserving Memory: The Struggle to Create America's Holocaust Museum* (New York: Columbia University Press 2001).

9 From the Committee on Conscience (COC) website, http://www.ushmm.org/conscience/about/, 17 March 2007.

10 Gérard Prunier, *Darfur: The Ambiguous Genocide* (Ithaca, N.Y.: Cornell University Press 2005), 139.

11 The Association of Holocaust Organizations (AHO) lists over 150 member organizations in the United States and over 50 international associates: http://www.ahoinfo.org. The Council of American Jewish Museums (CAJM) lists over seventy-five institutional members in the United States and Canada according to figures available at http://www2.jewishculture.org/cultural_services/museums/cajm/, 26 April 2007.

12 Prunier, *Darfur*, 127.

13 According to United Nations figures: http://www.un.org/apps/news/story.asp?NewsID=21035&Cr=sudan&Cr1=, 17 December 2006. In "Darfur and the International Abandonment of a 'Responsibility to

Protect,'" Eric Reeves quotes figures much higher, 500,000 dead and 4.5 million conflict-affected persons in Darfur and Eastern Chad: http://www.sudanreeves.org/Article144.html, 3 January 2007.

14 Saul Friedlander, "Introduction," in Friedlander, ed., *Probing the Limits of Representation: Nazism and the "Final Solution"* (Cambridge, Mass.: Harvard University Press 1992), 3.

15 Cited in Lisa Saltzman, "Avant-Garde and Kitsch Revisited: On the Ethics of Representation," in Norman L. Kleebatt, ed., *Mirroring Evil: Nazi Imagery/Recent Art* (New York: The Jewish Museum, 2001), 56.

16 Friedlander, "Introduction," 4.

17 Omer Bartov, *Murder in Our Midst: The Holocaust, Industrial Killing, and Representation* (New York: Oxford University Press 1996), 125–6.

18 Dominick LaCapra, *History and Memory after Auschwitz* (Ithaca, N.Y., and London: Cornell University Press 1998), 139.

19 Ibid., 331.

20 Interviews with Rwandan genocide survivors by Carla Shapiro in Toronto, January–March 2004, for the exhibition *Portraits from the 100 Days*.

21 Ivan Karp, "Introduction," in Ivan Karp, Christine Mullen Kreanmer, and Steven D. Lavine, eds., *Museums and Communities: The Politics of Public Culture* (Washington, D.C.: Smithsonian Institution Press, 1992), 1.

22 Christine Mullen Kreamer, "Defining Communities through Exhibiting and Collecting," in ibid., 368.

23 At the time this article was written, only one exhibition, the USHMM's *Genocide Emergency – Darfur, Sudan: Who Will Survive Today*, displayed any original objects of material culture. Even in this exhibit there was no thorough material-culture interpretation that embodied artifactual witnessing, and the objects did not effectively express survivor and refugee experiences. The impetus for a *60 Minutes* segment about Darfur by correspondent Scott Pelley was a boy's notebook on display at *Genocide Emergency*. The story of the Darfurian genocide in this documentary is told through the search for Jacob, the boy to whom this book belonged.

24 Christine Mullen Kreamer, "Defining Communities," 368.

25 James E. Young, *Writing and Rewriting the Holocaust: Narrative and the Consequences of Interpretation* (Bloomington: Indianapolis University Press 1988), 16–17.

26 Brian Steidle's article, "In Darfur, My Camera Was Not Nearly Enough," offers a detailed and vivid account of the challenges he faced in attempting to photograph the atrocities he witnessed: http://www.washingtonpost.com/wp-dyn/articles/

A48943-2005Mar19.html, 20 March 2005. See also Rick Hampson, "Through Lens in Darfur, 'I was a Witness to Genocide," *USA Today Online*, 27 September 2006, http://www.usatoday.com/news/world/2006-09-27-darfur-cover_x.htm.

27 Donatella Lorch quoted at http://www.ushmm.org/conscience/analysis/details.php?content=2005-06-28&page=1&menupage=, 2 February 2007.

28 Lorch: http://www.ushmm.org.

29 There are no simple reasons for the violence in Darfur. Religious conflict cannot be the explanation, since both the "African" and "Arab" tribes involved are Muslim. And, while distinct ethnic groups exist, this does not mean that what is happening is necessarily an ethnic conflict either.

30 Prunier, *Darfur*, 152–8.

31 Sudan was known as a 'Condominium' following the 1899 agreement between Britain and Egypt to hold joint authority over it. Ibid., 29.

32 This is a description used by H R W in its introduction to the online exhibition: http://www.hrw.org/photos/2005/darfur/drawings/introduction.htm.

33 An account of the process of how the pictures were procured is provided in the *Smallest Witnesses* catalogue (p.5) and on the websites of H R W (http://www.hrw.org/photos/2005/darfur/drawings/introduction.htm) and the U S H M M (http://www.ushmm.org/conscience/analysis/details.php?content=2005-06-03&page=1&menupage=Sudan), 14 March 2007.

34 As described by Liba Beyer, H R W outreach director, phone interview, 8 August 2007. In response to a tremendous outpouring of interest and requests from numerous venues for the travelling exhibition, other variations of the exhibition have also been circulated, including a version with thirteen original sketches and a completely digital version which includes twenty-seven high-resolution digital scans. Via this digital media, organizations could produce material of their choosing, in multiple formats. Both original and digital versions of the exhibition included captions and other supporting materials.

35 H R W has chosen not to use the term "genocide" in this case since thus far it has not had access to sufficient evidence to show all the elements of genocide as the word is defined in international law. That is not to say that H R W has determined that the crimes do *not* amount to genocide, only that it cannot determine this based on evidence currently available. Explanation provided via e-mail by Selena Brewer, Sudan researcher, Human Rights Watch, 3 October 2008.

36 Reference is made, however, to the common religion shared by victims and perpetrators of the conflict: "The *Janjaweed* militias, Muslim like

the groups they attack, have destroyed mosques, killed Muslim religious leaders, and desecrated Qur'ans belonging to their enemies." Quoted in HRW, *Smallest Witnesses* PDF catalogue.

37 R. Goodman and A. Fahnestock, *The Day Our World Changed: Children's Art of 9/11* (New York: Harry Abrams 2002), 14.

38 Deborah Golub, "Special Media Review," *Journal of Traumatic Stress*, vol. 7, no. 2 (1994): 333.

39 This could have been done while still refraining from revealing any particulars of the child's individual identity that might be endangering.

40 Nicholas Stargardt, "Children's Art of the Holocaust," *Past and Present*, 161 (November 1998): 234.

41 N. Lambert, "Art Education for Children in Crisis," *Drawings of War and Peace: International Society for Education through Art*, vol. 1, no. 2 (1994): 12–16.

42 "Darfur's Smallest Witnesses," PBS's Newshour, interview with Dr Annie Sparrow: http://www.pbs.org/newshour/bb/africa/july-dec05/darfur_9-27.html, 11 April 11 2007.

43 HRW online exhibition material: http://www.hrw.org/photos/2005/darfur/drawings/2.htm.

44 HRW, PDF of the *Smallest Witnesses* catalogue.

45 riverbed, or oasis.

46 HRW, PDF of the *Smallest Witnesses* catalogue.

47 Lisa Lefler Brunick, "Listen to My Picture: Art as a Survival Tool for Immigrant and Refugee Students," *Art Education*, vol. 52, no. 4 (1999): 16.

48 Interview with Liba Beyer.

49 A position presented by Olivier Bercault, quoted in Marissa Muller, 'Children's Art Imitates Horrors of Darfur," CNN Online, http://www.cnn.com/2005/WORLD/africa/08/04/sudan.drawings/index.html, 4 August 2005.

50 E.R. Tanay, "Croatian and Bosnian Children's Art in Times of War," *Journal of Art and Design Education*, vol. 13, no. 3 (1994): 237. The drawings in *The Smallest Witnesses* are also reminiscent of the children's drawings of the Terezin Ghetto, which are considered among the most poignant documents of the Holocaust. Selections from the collection of Terezin Ghetto children's drawings are published in Hana Volavková, *I Never Saw Another Butterfly: Children's Drawings and Poems from Terezín Concentration Camp, 1942–1944* (New York: Schocken Books, 1978). Another project based on children's drawings related to the witnessing of war – the archive of original children's drawings created during the Spanish Civil War – has been published in Anthony L. Geist, *They Still Draw Pictures: Children's Art in Wartime from the Spanish Civil War to Kosovo* (Urbana: University of Illinois Press 2002).

51 A print exhibition on fabric containing thirty images was recently produced.

52 Tour dates and venues can be found at http://www.darfurdarfur.org.

53 Roland Barthes, *Camera Lucida: Reflections on Photography*, trans. Richard Howard (New York: Hill and Wang 1981), 87.

54 David Cesarani, "Memory, Representation and Education," in John Roth and Elisabeth Maxwell, eds., *Remembering for the Future: The Holocaust in an Age of Genocide*, vol. 3, *Memory* (Hampshire, U.K., and New York: Palgrave 2001), 232.

55 Young, *Writing*, 163.

56 Steidle, "In Darfur, My Camera Was Not Nearly Enough."

57 Susan Sontag, *On Photography* (New York: Doubleday 1989), 14–15.

58 Barthes, *Camera Lucida*, 14–15.

59 Jean-François Lyotard, *Heidegger and "the Jews,"* trans. Andreas Michel and Mark S. Roberts (Minneapolis: University of Minnesota Press 1988), 27.

60 Michal Ronnen Safdie quoted in Pat Sherman, "Dying in Living Color" (review), *Jerusalem Report*, 12 August 2006, 35.

61 Ron Haviv quoted in Suzanne Charle, "Capturing Compassion," *The Nation Online*, http://www.thenation.com/doc/20061113/charleacute, 27 October 2006.

62 Hampson, "Through Lens in Darfur."

63 Quoted in David Montgomery, "The Darkest Light," Washington *Post*, 4 March 2007, http://www.washingtonpost.com/wp-dyn/content/article/2006/11/21/AR2006112100275.html?nav=emailpage. Also, "Outside the Holocaust Memorial Museum, the Genocide in Darfur Is Illuminated in a Nightly Photo Exhibit," Washington *Post*, 21 November 2006, C01.

64 Hélène Caux quoted in Hillary Mayell, "Surviving Darfur: Photographer on Life in the Camps," *National Geographic News*, http://news.nationalgeographic.com/news/2005/06/0620_050620_darfur_2.html, 20 June 2005.

65 Hampson, "Through Lens in Darfur."

66 From an introduction to *The Smallest Witnesses* on Eastern Washington University's website: http://www.ewu.edu/x23579.xml, 24 February 2007.

67 http://www.genocideintervention.net/advocate/tenthings.php, 3 March 2007.

68 Hillel: The Foundation for Jewish Campus Life, http://www.hillel.org/tzedek/initiatives/darfurcampus.htm, 18 July 2007.

69 The text reads: "You want the African Union troops supported until they can be bolstered by the United Nations. You want the United

Nations peacekeeping troops to be able to fulfill their mandate to protect civilians in Darfur. You want political pressure on Sudan by the
United States and our allies until they stop sponsoring mass murder."
See http://www.darfurdarfur.org/.
70 Gerald Caplan, "The Genocide Problem: 'Never Again' All Over Again,"
The Walrus, 16 July 2007, http://www.walrusmagazine.com/articles/
sudan-genocide/.

CHAPTER NINE

Rhetoric, Rights, and the Boundaries of Recognition: Making Darfur Public

DANIEL LISTOE

In May 1994 the United States assistant secretary of state for African affairs, George Moose, appeared before Congress to outline the State Department's five-point strategy for responding to the genocide then under way in Rwanda.[1] First point: "stop the killings." This seemingly inarguable goal was undercut, however, by the US priority of returning Rwanda to its delicate political balance of 5 April 1994, when a tentative ceasefire and power-sharing agreement between Rwandan Hutu leadership and the Tutsi-led Rwandan Patriotic Front was in place. In other words, Moose was there to argue for a diplomatic strategy that the death of Rwandan President Juvénal Habyarimana in a downed plane, and the subsequent assassination of the moderate prime minister Agathe Uwilingiyimana, had made obsolete.

As if acknowledging the disastrous cost of such a policy, Moose also testified to the plans to tend to the "humanitarian crisis" that was already, at that point, stark, clear, and growing. Before the assembled representatives, "Moose testified that 'conservative' estimates put the death toll from Rwandan violence at 100,000. The number of deaths may run as high as 500,000, Moose said, but it was not possible to corroborate that figure. Moose said the Clinton administration is applying diplomatic pressure to end the slaughter. The United States has pledged about $30 million in aid for the estimated 300,000 refugees from the crisis, most of whom have fled to neighboring Tanzania. Subcommittee Chairman Harry A. Johnston, D-Fla., told Moose, 'It is unforgivable and shameful to watch a whole generation of (Rwandans) be slaughtered in cold blood.'"[2]

Almost ten years later, Moose addressed the causes of that *unforgivable and shameful* political position. In doing so he did not argue for the rightness of the policies and claim that the calculations had been made according to a clear sense of national interest. Nor did he suggest, as many did, that the true nature of what was happening in Rwanda had been blurred by the speed of events in the small and distant African nation. Rather, he claimed that the administration's *willingness to watch* stemmed from something far more difficult to account for within the political sphere of institutions. Explaining how it was that the killings that happened in Rwanda in the spring of 1994 could be counted and yet not truly acknowledged, Moose said simply, "We were psychologically and imaginatively unprepared."[3]

It is almost impossible not to hear in his admission another self-serving exculpation. But what if the formulation were to be taken seriously? What does it mean to be psychologically and imaginatively unprepared to recognize, with facts in hand, something like the Rwandan genocide or the ongoing crisis in Darfur? How does one take into account the psychological and imaginative incapacities that must be overcome for facts to become understanding, understanding a basis for engagement, and far-off catastrophes, matters of life and death, to become matters of shared concern?

Those witnessing the carnage first-hand needed no intermediary to teach them the terrible facts. For example, the director of the International Committee of the Red Cross (ICRC) mission in Rwanda, Philippe Gaillard, spent those crucial months in the spring of 1994 trying to save the dying. He tended to the shocking scores of people who were slashed, shot, and hacked, to those whose hands were gone and whose heads were sliced open. When he used the media to further the operations of his Red Cross hospital in Kigali, he could only anticipate the wide dissemination and clear reception of the facts.

Gaillard himself spoke of using the press when a Red Cross vehicle with staff and victims was attacked on 14 April 1994, leaving six people dead. Consulting with Geneva, he decided to break with the ICRC's well-honed practice of silence and neutrality and "make it public." The "following day," he says, "[the news was on] BBC, Reuters, Radio France Internationale – it was *everywhere*." The circulating report of those victims was enough, it seems, to bring a kind of halting shame to the génocidaires, at least as far as ICRC transits were concerned. Gaillard's hospital kept functioning and managed to save a great number of people. Understandably, he dismisses the notion of anyone's ignorance: "Everybody knew every day, live, what was happening in [Rwanda]. You could follow that every day on TV, on radio. Who moved? Nobody ... They cannot tell us or tell me that they didn't know. They were told, every day, what was happening there. So don't come back to me and tell me, 'Sorry, we didn't know." No, no. No, no. No, no. Everybody knew. They knew. Everybody knew. It was on TV, in the papers, you cannot tell me they didn't know."[4]

The news emerging from Rwanda, however, could also reinforce notions of an inalterable situation. The report that Gaillard's Red Cross hospital had to suspend its operations because of the violence became just another point in a plot of inevitable and uncontrollable destruction: Rwanda as tragedy. As Gaillard said at the time, "It is machete massacres ... More and more the civilian population armed with machetes is ruling the streets. The army cannot control them. You want to hold back those people when you are witnessing it, but you have your blue beret and there's no respect for it."[5]

Looking back on the moment of breaching the ICRC ethic of neutrality, Gaillard articulates the privilege granted to testimonial power: "The International Committee of the Red Cross, which is a 140-year old organization, was not active during the Armenian genocide, shut up during the Holocaust. Everybody knew what was happening with the Jews. In such circumstances, if – if you don't at least speak out clearly and – you are participating [in] the genocide. I mean, if you just shut up when you see what you see – and morally, ethically, you cannot shut up! It's a responsibility to talk, to speak out." We have, then, Gaillard poignantly talking about the moral impulse to speak out, to betray the temptations of silence and complicity, and, in so doing, indicting the institutions that did nothing. Publicizing attacks on his ambulances may have deterred attacking Hutu, but little else seemed to have mattered, particularly in the realm of diplomats like George Moose, where reception of the facts mattered most and yet where there was at best confusion, and at worst indifference.

In an age when human rights are defined as much by the problematic practice of media advocacy as by a set of principles and values,[6] it may seem that between the plaintive cry of the victim and recognition is a gulf of experience and investment that no representation can close. The most generous description of this idea is that the more horror-inducing the message from within a set of unbearable circumstances, the more potent the temptation of those outside that realm to deny and deflect the realities. Primo Levi defined this unbridgeable divide of the concentration camps and the world, drawing the distinction between those who, like himself, suffered and those who witnessed from outside. "We were denied the screen of willed ignorance," Levi says of being trapped within the wire. "It was useless to close one's eyes or turn one's back to it, because it was all around, in every direction, all the way to the horizon." For those beyond that border, those with the privilege of turning from such knowledge, "it is enough not to see, not to listen, not to act."[7]

If Rwanda weakened faith in the capacity of human rights advocacy to protect civilians, Darfur has likely shattered it. For once again we have seen how a "peace accord" – more symbol than substance – becomes the focus of policy debates, leaving the human catastrophe as a "humanitarian" supplement to strategic alignments. As Secretary of State Colin Powell said before the US Congress, "In the intermediate and long term, the security of Darfur can be best advanced by a political settlement at Abuja and by the successful conclusion of the peace negotiations between the SPLM and the Government of Sudan."[8] Because such negotiations in Sudan have proven to be war by other means, people remain caught in spasms of terror and killings. Darfur has demonstrated the thoroughly troubled rhetoric of human rights, enmeshed as that language is in the institutional and state-level articulations that can so easily betray any effective recognition. In this sense, politics becomes a series of objectives rather than a process to tend to real objects, real things, real concerns, and real people dying.[9] What is *unforgivable and shameful* remains familiar forms of an institutional language that traffics in facts and reports only to produce postures and policy statements.

Compressed into only one hundred days, the Rwandan genocide did, perhaps, leave room to claim, as many did, that they could not, in Moose's terms, imagine the depths of the truth. Darfur, on the other hand, has been a slow, relentless refusal, one measured in unfolding years, seemingly without end. The dead and the displaced, those entrenched in the internally displaced persons (IDP) camps and scattered into Chad, live through the brutal cycles of war, assault, killings, burnings, rape, starvation, and traumatic shock. The victims' experiences have been represented and disseminated around the world, but those representations circulate outside the economy of talk that shapes Darfur as a matter of political discussion, debate, or concern.

There are certainly individuals trying to show the devastating damage done to Khartoum's victims. Testimony and analysis trickle out at a steady pace; those working to get the story "out" are surely trying to initiate an interventionist and protectionist response by the "international community." Thus far, that "international" audience has demonstrated the desperate need for a linguistic currency that is effective when used within parliamentary walls and adapted to move across the very different borders of non-governmental organizations (NGOs), interested governments, disinterested governments, and various legislative bodies.[10] As for the victims far from the rhetorical field into which their condition is given shape inside parliaments – as a numerical measure of the dead, as a representative tale of pathos – they remain trapped and exposed in "bare life": "subjugated, starved, or shot without compunction."[11]

In addition to Levi's theory that those who have the capacity to turn away will do so, a key component of maintaining such a difference between reality and rhetoric is the effect of what Mike Davis calls "definitional firewalls."[12] United Nations resolutions, peace negotiations, legalistic determinations of genocide, the play of international oil interests, campaigns for divestment, and the desperate pleas for care and assistance all move along well-established routes that govern responses and possibilities. Even empathy becomes practised, limited, and performed in response to – without actually responding to – the disaster; they serve only the purpose of their place, which is a place apart. In his *Late Victorian Holocausts* Davis uses the concept of "definitional firewall" to mark the impenetrable barrier between a language of appraisal by those in power and a language of plight used by vulnerable victims and their advocates.

Davis draws on Alex de Waal's attempt to move the category of famine in Africa beyond the limited Malthusian concept of starvation and mass death. De Waal puts into play "the broader spectrum of meanings, including hunger, destitution and social breakdown, encompassed within traditional African understandings." Davis, in turn, suggests that the gap between those outside the experience and those "on the ground" can be summarized this way: "Local people, like [de Waal's] Darfurian friends in the western Sudan, do not build definitional firewalls between malnutrition and famine, poverty and starvation. Nor do they fathom the moral calculus of wealthy countries who rush aid to certified famines but coolly ignore the chronic malnutrition responsible for half the infant [mortality] on the planet. And they are rightly suspicious of a semantics of famine that all too often renders 'ordinary' rural poverty invisible."[13]

During the Rwandan genocide, the obvious symbolic firewall was a refusal to classify the systematic killings of targeted innocents as "genocide." The Clinton administration's *signature* gesture during the spring of 1994, for instance, was to reference only "acts of genocide."[14] Its strategic naming, in effect, rewrote the violence as the by-product of a civil war, thereby barring from consideration the trigger of obligation – an obligation outlined in the United Nations' 1948 Convention on the Prevention and Punishment of the Crime of Genocide, which declares a signatory bound by articles 1 and 8 to act in the *prevention* and *suppression* of genocides where they occur. While the United States was not so moved, the Clinton administration at least understood the perils inherent, at the level of appearances, in publicly refusing that obligation while acknowledging the truth of the situation.[15] If nothing else, there was an appreciation that the convention itself could not be contradicted so brazenly, that somehow the convention *itself* needed protection.

In the case of Darfur, not even the promise of the convention, however unfulfilled, remains intact. In July 2004, more than ten years after Moose's appearance, the US Congress passed a resolution that urged the Bush administration to acknowledge Darfur as a genocide. Colin Powell and the State Department, as well as President Bush, obliged in public. When Powell testified before the Senate Foreign Relations Committee, however, he emphasized that classifying Darfur as a genocide would not, contrary to expectations, initiate any action that would lead to prevention of the murders. Powell argued, in essence, that the designation was meaningless for those at risk of being killed with impunity, and that it would be relevant only for the government of Sudan, should certain members of that government be held responsible for crimes against humanity. "Before the Government of Sudan is taken to the bar of international justice," Powell warned, "let me point out that there is a simple way for Khartoum to avoid such wholesale condemnation. That way is to take action." Framing the issue in terms of Sudanese criminality as distinct from the situation of their victims, Powell severed the bind between US acknowledgment, designation, and action: "Mr. Chairman, some seem to have been waiting for this determination of genocide to take action. In fact, however, no new action is dictated by this determination. We have been doing everything we can to get the Sudanese government to act responsibly." In other words, the sovereign state of Sudan, no matter its actual fractured condition and vicious intent, was reinforced as the final source of human rights protection in Darfur. "So let us not be preoccupied with this designation of genocide," Powell concluded. "These people are in desperate need and we must help them. Call it a civil war. Call it ethnic cleansing. Call it genocide. Call it 'none of the above.' The reality is the same: there are people in Darfur who desperately need our help."[16]

Despite the concluding gloss of their "need" and "our help," the proposed assistance is outlined as a partnership with the very country perpetrating the crimes: "Specifically, Mr. Chairman, the most practical contribution we can make to the security of Darfur in the short-term is to increase the number of African Union monitors. That will require the cooperation of the Government of Sudan." Powell's position comes from the clear calculation of the possibilities for "success." It could therefore be called sober and realistic, and above all cognizant of the political, diplomatic, and economic limitations in influencing the Sudanese government "to act," or to dilute its own power. Here Powell is in fact being true to a particular strand of human rights thought, which holds the following positions simultaneously. The first lays out the principles to be defended: "The most essential message of human rights is that there are no excuses for the inhuman use of human beings. In particular, there is no valid justification for the abrogation of decency and due process on the grounds of national security, military necessity, or states of siege and emergency. At most, rights protections can be suspended in cases of ultimate necessity, but these suspensions of rights must be justified before legislatures and courts of law, and they must be temporary."[17] The second and related point is meant to protect the above principles by holding in strict reserve the interventionist impulse, which, when practised, is subject to both inconsistency and ineffectiveness: "Western governments watching the slide of [regions like the Great Lakes of Africa] into endemic civil war are justified in concluding that restoring stability – even if it is authoritarian and undemocratic – matters more than either democracy or human rights. Stability, in other words, may count more than justice."[18]

The protection of rights by protecting the very state structures that make them invisible is one of the more obvious fault lines between the ideal of rights and their actualization, and Darfur has thoroughly demonstrated the degree to which the protection of the appearance of rights can take absolute precedence. The UN tries desperately to appear potentially relevant by retreating from anything that may expose its inability to marshal international cooperation, leaving the International Criminal Court (ICC) to follow through on Powell's threat in July 2008, when it indicted the Sudanese President Omar Hassan al-Bashir for genocide, crimes against humanity, and war crimes.

The relationship of rights and states is the long-standing paradox articulated by Hannah Arendt in *The Origins of Totalitarianism*. Rights culture developed in the aftermath of the Holocaust, Arendt explains, because for the first time the solemn proclamations in the Rights of Man had to face a real, European catastrophe. The stateless survivors, crowded into displaced persons camps after the war, created a crisis of citizenship, exposing the truth that the inalienable rights promised were nothing without the status of citizenship and the protective recognition of a nation-state. Arendt's formulation has it that existence is more than "bare life," requiring a political orientation of being: the capacity to hold an "opinion," to contribute to political action. Without that one was cast out of humanity itself and left exposed in "abstract nakedness."[19] For refugees, being stateless was to be vulnerable to "political" violence; the rights once offered as inalienable crumbled at precisely the threshold that called them to presence. Those who found themselves forced to dwell "outside the scope of all tangible law" and deemed the "scum of the earth" were without any government, institution, or political body to ensure the recognition of rights that were wholly dependent on such recognition.[20] All this is to say, "the Rights of Man are the rights of those who have not the rights that they have and have the rights that they have not."[21] *These people are in desperate need and we must help them,* Powell said. And yet this translates into the need and threat of state protection, the very coordination of state-level politics that makes them vulnerable. In the end, in the focus on the prosecution of al-Bashir and Khartoum, and in the need for cooperation in a state-to-state partnership required for even considering the future role of humanitarian assistance, we have the effective disappearance of the persecuted.

Talal Asad, for one, has traced the rhetorical forms that keep the imagination at bay by confining those killed to different domains of violence, some sanctioned and others seen as a violation.[22] Asad's focus is not on "cruelty as such but with how, in a secular system like human rights, responsibility is assigned for it."[23] What are the degrees of difference, he asks, between people killed through state-practised torture, "tribal" warring, and state-sponsored ethnic cleansing or systematic rape, as well between the dead discarded as "collateral damage" by intervening forces and those suffering the long-term effects of economic sanctions, or even those who perish through the "necessities" of economic development? Which cases earn the name of a human rights violation? Of genocide? Which naming, in turn, is heard and recognized? And what does it matter that "the suffering that the individual sustains as citizen – as *the national of a particular state* – is distinguished from the suffering he undergoes as a *human being*"? The result of these various formulations can be vividly recognized in the logic Powell presents on Darfur. *"These people"* becomes an otherwise empty institutional category standing for those in Darfur. No matter the supposed moral norms or universal values posited as forces beyond each nation-state or an assembly of nations, writes Asad, for "the identification and application of human rights law has no meaning independent of the judicial institutions that belong to individual nation-states (or even to several nation-states bound together by treaty) and the remedies that these institutions supply – and therefore of the individual's civil status as a political subject."[24]

One possible response to this is to take Asad's parenthetical and Powell's claim together to argue that Darfur "provides a good test of whether the 56-year old Genocide Convention, created in the aftermath of the Holocaust, can make good on its promise to 'never again' allow the targeted destruction of a particular ethnic, racial, or religious group."[25] The problem, however, is not with the convention itself but with that approach to politics and rights which sustains the dominant place of the convention. *It* does not include the categorical imperative of "never again" and cannot, as a statement, uphold a "promise" independent of its signatories. The problem resides in the *institutional determinations of* the language of appeal, recognition, and judgment, which is to say, the institutional domination of the rhetorical situation in which rights are mobilized.

These determinations exacerbate the privileging of, and over-reliance on, such documents, as if their mere existence could affect outcomes, as if their language alone should define, make visible, and govern action for a situation like Darfur. In the words of Kirsten Hastrup: "Because human rights are cast in the genre of legal language, they rely heavily on their form for authority. Their nature is form and, along with other genres that depend on form, the law also legitimately exercises a violence of the freedom of interpretation. It is in the nature of legal strategy to impose a particular form, though which the 'consecrated works impose the terms of their own perception.'"[26]

Given the reach of these forms, the power of consecration, and the frustration of witnessing Darfur suspended in its agony – while diplomatic distractions leave people to rot – there is clearly the need for a sense of representation that commands the recognition of the very existence of those in need. Gérard Prunier, for one, risks a great deal when he takes a step in this direction, titling his impressive work *Darfur: The Ambiguous Genocide*. It sounds as if it is intended to deflect understanding and possibly argue for a complexity that bleeds into some ultimate uncertainty, precisely the kind of tactic Khartoum or its defenders might employ. Prunier, however, not only gives a detailed and subtle portrait of Sudan's long wars and Darfur's place within them, he engages the very formulations through which human rights, their violations, and the prospect of their protections are stringently filtered.

"Genocide," obviously, is not simply a legalistic determination, even as its etymology and function supposedly serve a precise purpose for international law. Just as important to keep in mind is the term's aura of magnitude, its measure of *historical* significance. Prunier outlines the dangers of that aura and charts how the idea of Darfur as genocide has interfered with recognizing the actual violence and human destruction. His polemic targets the ways magnitude becomes an issue in its own right, turned into a "semantic quarrel" and thereby a deflection and disengagement from what *is happening*.

Here we see how a terminology that stirs the media can do so at the expense of the complexities that cases like Darfur, or Rwanda, rightly pose.[27] Furthermore, we can use this opening to question whether or not the media coverage that emerged about Darfur in 2004 simply treated it as a repetition of the Rwandan genocide that had occurred ten years prior. Prunier suggests that the representations depended upon a ready-made template and an underdeveloped parallel to lend the story of Darfur an inherent momentum and historical "newness": where there had once been Hutu killing Tutsi, now we were seeing, in a narrative ripened for the post-9/11 mindset, Arabs killing Africans, a formulation that seduces with what Prunier aptly calls a "misleadingly 'evident' explanatory power."[28] This was not only a simple and convenient means of making sense of the violence in the Sudan, but also a justification for the coverage itself (as if anything other than "genocide" would not warrant the attention). Violence as violence was not enough to put Darfur "on the map." As Prunier puts it, "it is in fact a measure of the jaded cynicism of our times" that "simple killing is boring, especially in Africa."[29]

Such a conclusion is borne out by the response to the report of the International Commission of Inquiry (COI) on Darfur. On its submission to the UN, the COI's report was widely criticized for its findings that there was not genocidal "intent" on the part of the Sudanese government. At the same time, issue at hand, regardless of the COI's genocide conclusion, there remained this basic definition of Darfur: "Government forces and militias conducted indiscriminate attacks, including killing of civilians, torture, enforced disappearances, destruction of villages, rape and other forms of sexual violence, pillaging and forced displacement, throughout Darfur. These acts were conducted on a widespread and systematic basis, and therefore may amount to crimes against humanity."[30] These are, as Eric Reeves says so succinctly, "the conspicuous realities."[31]

For Reeves, the "genocide debate," whatever its limitations, serves as a vital, unavoidable component of coming to terms with Darfur. "The time and energy devoted to debating whether or not genocide happened in Darfur has hardly been incapacitating," he writes, describing the obligatory process that led to the UN inquiry.[32] But one wonders what appreciation and acknowledgment might develop if those "conspicuous realities" were at the forefront of our attention rather than the debate about genocide as a legal determination, a debate that "betrays only a peculiar fixation on a particular form of documentary evidence."[33] Would being wary of a packaged "genocide" narrative turn us towards the complicated structure of events and move our imagination past the limitations Hastrup calls *the impositions of a particular form?*

In Prunier's writing, the events of Darfur belie easy definition. The complexities of insurgency suppression, a government's genocidal actions, the Janjaweed's terror tactics, systematic rape, and the mobilization of latent ethnic difference – creating a self-generating and murderous conflict within the region – flood any single definition or solution. Instead, we begin to see the outlines of multiple narratives layered atop one another, overlapping and shifting with each year. In a crude approximation of Prunier's timeline, what was genocidal terror in 2003 became "ethnic cleansing" in 2004 and then the period of devastating attrition encapsulated by the acronym CMR, or "crude mortality rate." In other words, when the rains and Sudanese interference cut off humanitarian assistance, the Janjaweed militia did not have to kill actively but could herd victims into the desperate and disparate camps and make sure they died far from the "aid agencies" and "without benefit of the label."[34]

If the ready-made labels have proven insufficient, Darfur's representations have fractured. On the one hand, there are recurrent public references to the region; on the other, these references are more likely to focus on the political strategies of the United States, the United Nations, the African Union troops, China, the "progress" or plight of humanitarian activism, and the indictment of al-Bashir rather than on the *realities* of those dying in Darfur. This follows a general cultural trend where each "crisis" has its niche market, its gallery space, its eleven minutes of allotted yearly news coverage. As Reeves points out, when Darfur was four years into the annihilation, instead of becoming more coherent as a matter of concern, it was increasingly illustrated only by a "specialist literature," a literature likely to reinforce the very limiting formulations already at work.

There are facts to glean from UN reports, the small stories in the international press and aid-agency updates, and the relentless archiving work of attentive scholars like Reeves. But, since Darfur denotes ineffable cruelties and a massive "humanitarian crisis," to come to the substance of that *thing*, one must break free from what Reeves rightly calls "perceptions ... imprisoned in sloganeering advocacy, and increasingly irrelevant caricature of the nature of violence on the ground, and disingenuous political posturing."[35] Even using a phrase like "humanitarian crisis" becomes unsettling because the words make a readily absorbed combination of sounds that bypasses judgment for the sad eloquence – affective and affected – that former Médecins sans Frontières director Rony Brauman says has come to be the language of disasters. Of that well-worn phrase, he says, "The UN as well as governments, the press and NGOs are constantly using this formula, which leads me wonder if Auschwitz would be considered a 'humanitarian crisis' were it to happen today."[36]

The prevalence of the formula needs to be understood in all its dimensions. It is one thing to critique media representations or, with more subtlety, ask about how it is we *regard the pain of others*.[37] Reeves's remark and Brauman's complaint, however, also ask that we add the effects of a language of advocacy and determination. For an NGO representative, the economy of humanitarian aid means, at times, feeding the media machinery – as Philippe Gaillard suggested when looking back at his availability to the press that remained in Rwanda during the genocide. But NGOs do more than respond to, and draw attention to, catastrophes. They also shape them from within, as when performing the task of naming who is granted "refugee" status. The Office of the United Nations High Commissioner for Refugees, the Human Rights Association, and the ICRC all utilize language constructions as a means both of aid and of determining who will receive it. Each of these organizations relies at times on certain speech acts to determine the fate of those seeking asylum and sanctuary. The work on the borders between states, designed to shepherd individuals from the legal category of citizen to that of a state-acknowledged "refugee," is vital, demonstrating the dangers for those whose performance of need are not enough, or of the wrong kind, to secure sanctuary or status.[38]

Conversely, human rights activists outside such positions of direct control but seeking relief for the suffering, and protection for themselves, attempt to educate and enlighten with the requisite foundational faith that *seeing must mean believing*. Meg McLagan suggests, "This axiom underpins the reliance on a kind of documentary visuality that characterizes the new human rights communications infrastructure, with its emphasis on bringing what is hidden into the light, and its realist insistence on the universal legibility of visual facts."[39] Such strategies, ideally intended to quicken an interventionist act by the "international community," can readily become another form of limited, passive engagement which potentially shapes the event from within. In Darfur, we have seen this tactic in the reliance on vulnerable African Union "monitors." Before the Rwandan genocide began, the then head of UN peacekeeping, Kofi Annan, deployed this same strategy of non-interventionist monitoring, even with the United Nations Assistance Mission in Rwanda (UNAMIR) in place. Knowing that direct engagement was impossible, the UN was reduced to a desperate faith in "shining light on ... things." According to Annan, "telling those planning [crimes against humanity] at a governmental level that, 'The international community knows what is being planned, we are monitoring, we are going to deal with you harshly and we know what you are up to' – sometimes it's a very good deterrent."[40]

The Catholic church at Nyarubuye, Rwanda, is a memorial to the results of that tactic of the shining light, the mode of the distant transmission. It is the site of human ruin. During the killings, Tutsi seeking sanctuary were contained within its fortifications, where they were all the more readily chopped down by the génocidaires. Long after, it held the remnants of the dead: corpses heaped and spread over the grounds, unburied, unavoidable. When the author Philip Gourevitch travelled to Rwanda in 1995 to try to make sense of what had happened, he – like many heads of states, dignitaries, and other journalists – went to Nyarubuye. What is striking about his encounter with the space is not a response of remorse or a promise of "never again." Rather it is the testimony that to see what lay before him required great work. In the church itself, around its parameters, around its cloistered courtyard behind, he walked over the massacre of between two and three thousand people. The death was not only palpable but also living on, evolving with the entropic effects of earth and air. There was no need for epitaphs when he found the site holding the reverberating stillness of so much human destruction in all its awful actuality. Nyarubuye had become, in this way and with time, a delicate, dissolving reality, and, as such, a synecdoche of the genocide. Fittingly, Gourevitch opens his book – *We Wish to Inform You That Tomorrow We Will Be Killed with Our Families* – with the imperative of that space.

His description is worth examining in some detail because it provides an object lesson in the imagination struggling to recognize what is there before the eyes as an unavoidable fact, and nonetheless demanding some translation, even when the distance of space has been closed and one has allowed the tempering effects of time.[41] Rather than reduce the scene to measure, to category, to evidence of the crime, he explores his own reception and the work required to close the distance, even as the object is the very ground he stands upon. He thereby demonstrates the necessities of making sense of the apparent, of engaging in the labour of recognition that does not rely on the given form. While representatives of governments or organizations have routinely placed themselves in such sites of memory as necessary gestures, a writer like Gourevitch went seeking something else, and he goes with what he calls a "properly disturbed curiosity."

Stepping through the strewn skeletons and heaped corpses, meeting the bodily remains "intimately exposed," he finds a place where the unfathomable horror has been replaced by an uncanny beauty. Encased in the dramatic numbers of media representation, or congressional testimony, the victims become all the harder to imagine as alive, as human beings with rights, as people with names. Amassed in death, for the one who walks over them, they also signify the privileged safety of the northern writer. And still, having come to witness these remnants and face these signs, he too is exposed. Without the insulating effects of the institutionalized language of rights, he is susceptible to his own struggle to recognize the victims as victims, as beings who held their rights to life up to the moment they were killed. Beneath him he sees the "skin" of the dead polished by time, hardened past rot and stench, taking on a surreal sheen, and he has to adjust against the impositions of form, the aesthetic expectation of witnessing "the dead": "The dead looked like pictures of the dead," he writes. "They did not smell. They did not buzz with flies." Several severed heads have rolled away. The bodies and skulls are close together and he has to work hard not to step on them: "Looking at the buildings and the bodies, and hearing the silence of the place, with the grand Italianate basilica standing there deserted, and beds of exquisite, decadent, death-fertilized flowers blooming over the corpses, it was still strangely unimaginable. *I mean one still had to imagine it.*"[42] Faced with the unavoidable corporeality, the imagination buckles against an appraising reason, struggling with ghostly impressions rightly beyond an outsider's sensations. The moral strain for a fitting responsiveness is itself a sign of recognition, and that it remains in that instant an uncertain response is owing to the imagination's necessary labour, signalling the difficulty of truly encountering the awful loss.[43]

If this is the difficulty of imagining the horror beneath one's feet, what hopes can there be for translating the continuing presence of the dead and dying into our political spaces, given the current orientations and procedures of those spaces? Trying to summon a sense of the seeming indifference of the United Nations to UNAMIR's plight in Rwanda, Major Brent Beardsley, an assistant to Colonel Roméo Dallaire, the Canadian officer who headed the UN peacekeeping forces in the country, once remarked: "It made no difference what you said or how you said it. We could have packed up dead bodies, put them on – flown to New York, walked into the Security Council and dumped them on the floor in front of the Security Council, and all that would have happened was we would have been charged for illegally using a UN aircraft."[44] Beardsley's palpable animus towards the institution that abandoned UNAMIR notwithstanding, it would be a mistake to take this despairing image as mere hyperbole. Beardsley's impossible, unrealistic scene truly captures the stark discrepancy between institutional frames of representation and the bodily matters supposedly addressed by human rights.

Imagine the dead there, in the middle of the horseshoe arrangement of the Security Council. Those dead would indeed be absolutely ineffective, for *they would still have to be imagined* – imagined as once-living beings, as those whose rights were violated, and, beyond that, as representative of the lives still vulnerable to assault and death. Could diplomats, encountering the dead, respond any differently as diplomats if they had to see the dead there and begin to imagine the causes and the futures of others? Would their institutional roles allow any greater acknowledgment of the real dimensions of what comes before them if that issue was indeed dumped down as evidence? Could they ever be, psychologically and imaginatively, prepared to translate the rhythms of representative politics and policy into perception of such grave matters? Insofar as it is impossible, Beardsley's image comes to stand as the great lesson of both Rwanda and Darfur, emphasizing the conditions under which grave matters fail to matter, and how matters of the body, the bare life of the human, which should speak the manifestation of rights, are shifted beyond political concern.

This language of *political possibility* is borrowed from Bruno Latour's recent work on democracy and representation. His essay, "From *Realpolitik* to *Dingpolitik* or How to Make Things Public," is a polemical call for an "object-oriented democracy." By redirecting our attention from the communicative norms that are the process of politics to determining the truthful dimensions of the objects that concern us, we might, he says, discover a politics responsive to the world we actually inhabit. Should matters that matter – and could there be any *matter* more pressing than what we choose to call a "humanitarian crisis"? – come to occupy the centre of our political deliberations, we might discover in each case "a hidden coherence," a constellation of interested parties capable of offering "new ways of achieving closure without having to agree on much else." As Latour says, "objects – taken as so many issues – bind us all in ways that map out a public space profoundly different from what is usually recognized under the label of 'the political.'"[45]

Representation, he reminds us, has a twofold meaning in politics and we have developed a tradition that privileges the process over the subject of deliberation. The first meaning refers to representative bodies that come together within a structure, whether it is the Canadian House of Commons or the US Congress, the United Nations, or the European Union's Parliament. These bodies are representative to the extent that they have been deemed legitimate and structured to govern; their declarations emerge only according to "the right procedures." They are thus ideal embodiments of the structural spaces they inhabit, parliaments architecturally "devised to assemble the relevant parties, to authorize them to contract, to check their degree of representativity, to discover the ideal speech conditions, to detect the legitimate closure, to write the good constitution." The second meaning, too often clouded in politics, concerns the faithfulness of the representations. A proper representation is "said to be good if the matters at hand have been accurately portrayed."[46] Yet, if the sphere of politics is limited to the given structures – the rules of assembly and the regulative procedures of assemblies, or the first sense of representation – the result is the enervation of that second sense of representation, so much so that we have all but forgotten the possibilities of persuasion through proof, through rhetoric, through eloquence and the introduction of materials that must be imaginatively assembled. Where once there was the dream of a communal effort at knowing what could be known – and, in the case of genocide, cruelty, and crimes against humanity, the boundaries can be extreme – now we have the vast distance between things in the world and the merely political language that seems so far removed from engaging those *things*.

Latour's most vivid illustration of this distancing and its deadly consequences takes us back to that same United Nations setting conjured by Major Beardsley. Again, it is US Secretary of State Colin Powell speaking, this time on 5 February 2003, just as the catastrophe of Darfur was beginning. On that day, however, Powell was there for a far different purpose. He was presenting – in word and image – the now infamous catalog of ominous "facts" of Iraq's threat to the world. It was a performance that condemned Iraq to sanctioned invasion. Pitting the indisputable against mere rhetoric, assertion, and claim, Powell demanded acquiescence to the American policy. His presentation implied that "matters of fact," determined by Intelligence, would be the provenance of the few entitled to possess it. "On the one side," writes Latour, "would be the truth and no mediation, no room for discussion; on the other side would be opinions, many obscure intermediaries, perhaps some hecklings ... Those who remain unconvinced prove by their resistance how irrational they are; they have unfortunately fallen prey to subjective passions."[47]

Counter to such an approach is rhetoric as entreaty, as claim and proof in the Aristotelian sense. To borrow briefly from those categories of Aristotle, we can say that rather than a merely functional discourse – *sloganeering advocacy, irrelevant caricature,* and *disingenuous political posturing* – there should emerge something like a rich reliance on the possibilities of the forensic; a critical engagement with issues through the deliberative; and the censuring of creations of the epideictic.[48] The hope is for a richer and more textured treatment of our political objects, approaching objects of worry with the expectation of tracing and using their "multiple entanglements":[49] "For too long, objects [of worry] have been wrongly portrayed as matters-of-fact. This is unfair to them, unfair to science, unfair to objectivity, unfair to experience. They are much more interesting, variegated, uncertain, complicated, far reaching, heterogeneous, risky, historical, local, material and networky than the pathetic version offered for too long ... Rocks are not simply there to be kicked at, desks to be thumped at. 'Facts are facts are facts'? Yes, but they are a lot of other things *in addition*."[50] The tone here may not immediately suggest that these hopeful ideas of arrangement are apt for a dire situation like Darfur. But is not that a site where *the variegated, the uncertain, the complicated, the far reaching, the heterogeneous, the risky, the historical, the local, and the material* demand, more than any other, to be forged into a working assemblage?

What is needed, then, certainly is something *in addition*.[51] As a sample of what one small part of such a fuller representation might look like, we should turn, I believe, to an essay written about the Sudanese war before Darfur. Written by a northern writer, it openly wrestles with the dynamics of reception and recognition, with the difficulty of making sense of such madness. It does so without explaining away the situation, or romanticizing the inadequacies of its language, or rendering its subject as a purely historical event. Instead, it exposes the *textures* of the devastation found there – in this case, the Sudanese war in the south and the mass assault on the Nuba, which proves now the genealogy of Khartoum's genocidal practices. It comes from an unlikely source to be certain, for its author is more notorious than trusted. If Gourevitch's attempts to write the aftermath of the Rwandan genocide illustrated the strain required for recognition, Bernard-Henri Lévy's essay, "The Pharaoh and the Nuba," can be read as a foreshadowing of the difficulty, and possibility, of making Darfur public.

Whatever political postures one associates with Lévy, his writing about the Sudan suggests that what he saw there defeated any attempts to impose a ready-made narrative, or affirm an established world view. And, as we think of what helps to make things public, both the grand stylization that marks Lévy's prose and the pose that has created and fostered his own persona become important for highlighting that rhetoric and aesthetics are necessarily at work.

His essay describes a scorched earth salvaged for oil production, wretched wanderers weaving with hunger, abandoned camps of the NGOs driven out by the fighting, and craters left by the government's assaults on the Sudanese People's Liberation Movement/Army (SPLM/A) – where the "tactic" of bombing with munitions-filled oil barrels dumped out the back of a Russian cargo plane got its start. At the heart of "The Pharaoh and the Nuba," however, is a series of uneasy encounters: with abject annihilation, with perverse images of strength and power, with quixotic hopes. Through it all we are allowed to see that, even in the midst of such destruction, an essential aesthetic is at work. It is not that of spectacle, or of the writer turning the horror into the setting for an adventure. Instead, there is the perception that the horror can be caused by aesthetic constructions, an aesthetic that is essential in the process of destruction. This can bring us closer, for instance, to understanding the logic of the Janjaweed, who develop from ad hoc mercenaries to cohorts with uniforms, insignias, and names for their units – for example, "The Quick and the Horrible" – which, while chilling in its combination of murderousness and juvenilia, also suggests a motivation to move from being "irregulars" to forging, in the chaos, a system, an association of identity: the symbol of *something*.[52]

There is also, in the essay, a series of moments in which people come together over an aesthetic construction so as to share an act of apprehension, or sense-making in the delirium. For reflecting such tasks, Lévy's rhetorical stance is openly and appropriately *eloquent*. Through it he shows the witnessing of a northern journalist who cannot be too certain of what he is seeing; his conclusions are tempered by an uncertainty that inevitably works its way into the scenes.

For example, when he meets the then SPLM/A leader, John Garang, there is talk of an end to the war through Khartoum's capitulation; the dream of the periphery entering the centre of power. Garang literally illustrates his hopes. Lévy describes him pulling from his pocket, the one marked "CDR. Dr. John Garang of Mabior," a folded piece of paper exhibiting "a whole series of circles and ovals ... and from the former to the latter, arrows." Garang explains his preference for the second of the many diagrams that demonstrate potential relationships between north and south, and, through the diagram, his belief in the people's power to impose the change on Khartoum:

All the officers present, including me, our eyes open wide, lean toward the graphics ... The guerilla leader, this man who, for almost twenty years, has known no other law than that of the armies, in the process of saying that his life, his fate, his combats, are reducible to childlike diagrams ... Does he really believe what he's saying? Does he truly believe that the SPLA, his party, is on the verge of provoking this general insurrection and of winning? As just now ... I am struck by his air of credulity: the effect, perhaps, of this strange life, cut off from everything and everyone, in the brush: twenty years of secrecy, guerilla warfare as a job and a destiny – and political judgment which, necessarily, has to lose all its points of reference.[53]

This is a seductive moment, with the allure of the diagram, the guerilla who would bring the burnt edges of the Sudan into the power and economic centre of a nation. It comes, though, at a cost that must also be measured. If Lévy's prose seems more often than not driven by the doctrinaire, here the "just now" of the moment presented overwhelms even the idea of a greater frame of reference. "Does he really believe what he is saying?" Is that only a question for John Garang? Is it not asked of Lévy himself? Can this not also be a warning not to believe too quickly, in isolation, what we are reading? Does it not suggest that the events cast some shadow upon the writing? What does that diagram define but the necessary, inevitable reduction that is bound to happen when pen meets paper? That single condensation finds its essential quality, then, in the tone "perhaps," in that hesitancy of the struggle to situate understanding in imposed, and possibly refused, points of reference.

The struggle to situate Sudan's war in a larger diagram of concern is illustrated by Lévy when he travels to the "city" of Gogrial. Once a government administrative centre, then overrun by the SPLM/A and emptied of its inhabitants, it is at the time of his visit used to garrison troops. Refugees from government-sponsored raids in the south gather across the river. Lévy, however, glosses over its strategic import and instead fills the passage with ellipses, the crumbling of his own perception leaving a gagging prose. He writes, "I have already seen phantom cities. I've seen Kuito, in Angola. El Quneitra, on the Golan Heights. Vukovar, of course, in Croatia. But this ..." The *this* has no equivalent and the choking rhetoric helps define the imagination's rush to catch up with the presence of so much absence: "This ... This desolation ... This desert ... These little piles of mud which had been houses ... These bricks with which they've made bunkers ... These fires ... These tents ... These nests of snakes ... This filth ... This rotting smell of shit and corpses intermingled ... These weird dogs, too fat, who are no longer afraid of humans ... This immense space ... This square ... Yes, you can see it had been a square ... You can see, from the skeletons of the structures, bordering it, that it was a large square, home to official buildings."[54] Finally, he begins to sketch the outlines of the known: "You can see." The remnants become an image: "It had been a living, animated square, full of the good life of normal cities, and now it looks like the devastated amphitheater of an ancient city, testimony of a vanished civilization."[55]

The essay ends with another fight against an object of concern vanishing from view, this time in the Nuba Mountains. In a region cut off from the world's attention or assistance and subject to government assaults, the Nuba, he tells us, are rounded up into "peace camps" controlled by the government. Those in the mountains are bombed, and often starving. Some are sold into slavery. There, the "system" of Darfur's disaster was first apparent in the total war of violent containment, destruction, and "famine as a weapon." Again, Lévy uses a layering of representations, a collection of perspectives to draw us into the life-and-death conditions there, conditions that must be seen anew, through the representation of representations.

To the squadron leader, Abdel Aziz Adam al-Halu, Lévy brings a curious gift: an infamous book of photographs. They are of the Nuba, taken by the one-time Nazi image-maker, Leni Riefenstahl. Picturing Riefenstahl picturing the Nuba the way she does seems surreal now, as if her book is the moment of equidistance between two disasters – long after the European and just before the dawn of the ravages Lévy encountered later in their green-hilled graveyard. And perhaps that is what he tries to measure by bringing those images. His choice to bring it there and include it as the essential moment of this essay reminds us that the West comes to a place like the Nuba Mountains looking to invest. That investment may be in the form of the oil production then run by Canada's Talisman, or for the sake of rehabilitation, as with Riefenstahl. It may be to test and reaffirm something of the Rights of Man for a French celebrity. Whatever the initial motivation, the encounter will have to be allowed its influence, the object its dimensions.

The squadron commander, Aziz, begins to leaf through the book of pictures, "as if it were familiar to him." What role do these images serve? Are they epitaphic for him? After all, even if the children die of "forgotten illnesses they no longer know how to cure," Aziz still argues for the greatness of the Nuba, telling Lévy of the many languages spoken, the great Babel of the people; the rituals held in memory if not in practice; their culture, its remnants suspended in the suffering of the people who are now dying before his eyes: "'Look what they've done to us,' Aziz murmurs, leafing through the book. 'Look.' It's the photos he's showing ... the legendary Nuba in well-composed photos, by the filmmaker. But it's the others he wants me to look at, the real Nuba, his own, with their emaciated faces, their rags, who no doubt seem to him, at this instant, the shadow of these shadows." And just as the assembled officers crowded around Garang's drawing of the dreamt future of the Sudan, all of its complexities written out of a diagram, here Aziz's officers "come very close, very close to the photos," as do the children, who "slip, very excited, among the squadron leaders," and their teacher, as well as "the peasant who had climbed up on the wing of the plane to help the pilot recharge his fuel and who chuckles with joy at the sight of these elder brothers, naked and scarified." All heed the imperative to look and we can tell that each will take from them according to a necessity. Do they really admire them, the photographs? Can they see the Nuba as they once were in the camera eye of a mythmaker?

Lévy looks "very carefully" at the wounded and suffering Aziz wants him to see, the people, "together, almost superimposed, the shadows and the shadows of the shadows": "But I see the opposite in them, it seems to me, of what he was inviting me to see. Not the degeneration of icons. But, miracle of art or of life, I don't know, a stubborn faithfulness to the finest quality the photos had, of which, I'm sure they have only captured a vibration; a force risen from the depth of the ages; an indomitable courage that, today as well as yesterday, emanates from these ashen faces; miserable, abandoned, pawns for all the governments, the great forgotten ones of this forgotten war, men whose tragic grandeur compels us all the more since their disappearance wouldn't affect the world's economy in the least."[56] The solider and the children, the teacher and the humanitarian aid worker, a pilot and a peasant, a celebrity-journalist-philosopher and soldiers, with cannon fire in the distance, crowd together: an assemblage with a set of representations between them. The photos are the barest truth of what was, but they offer an occasion: an object around which to assemble and look with entangled needs and desires – here, at what was once an aesthetic rendering of the immemorial grace of power, now another kind of scarification, shadows upon shadows.

At this period when Lévy was in Sudan, the cruel shape of Darfur was in many ways already present in the civil-war imagination of those in Khartoum: the means for draining life from the western region of the country already tested; the capacity to undercut the humanitarian efforts already understood; the disregard of a weak, inconsistent, or fraudulent "international community" already entrenched. In this light, Lévy's claims for the "stubborn faithfulness to the finest qualities" can be read against the grain of his world view. For the pronouncements he makes are not as vital as the moments of "perhaps," the scenes of ad hoc assembly where human eyes struggle to measure the past and hold to a future and expose an object to the variations of perception around a shared issue of concern. Each in the assembly knows without seeing, and that is all that is needed to begin to make something become something to be seen truly. It explains the necessity – if rights are to find their meaning in language – of the tentative alliance. For, if those rights are to be imagined as belonging to living beings, then recognized as a matter of concern, they will have to come through such a demanding, provisional alliance, one formed despite the bombs and camps and disease and distance, and all those other crippling impositions of value that are now determined by the architecture of the powerful assemblies, or driven more quietly in the viciousness of the world's economy.

Notes

1   *US Department of State Dispatch*, vol. 5, no. 21 (23 May 1994): 341.
2   *Congressional Quarterly Weekly Report*, vol. 52, no. 18 (7 May 1994): 1138.
3   See Samantha Power, "Bystanders to Genocide," *Atlantic Monthly*, vol. 288, no. 2 (2001): 84–108.
4   Gaillard was interviewed for the film *Ghosts of Rwanda*, dir. Greg Barker, Frontline Films, 2001. All quotations from him are from this film unless otherwise indicated.
5   Donatella Lorch, "U.N. in Rwanda Says It Is Powerless to Halt the Violence," New York *Times* (Late Edition [East Coast]), 15 April 1994, A3.
6   Thomas Keenan, "Mobilizing Shame," *South Atlantic Quarterly*, vol. 103, nos. 2/3 (2004): 435–49.
7   Primo Levi, *The Drowned and the Saved*, trans. Raymond Rosenthal (New York: Vintage 1989), 65–6.
8   "Powell Reports Sudan Responsible for Genocide in Darfur," US Department of State, 9 September 2004, http://usinfo.state.gov.

9 Bruno Latour, "From *Realpolitik* to *Dingpolitik*, or How to Make Things Public," in Bruno Latour and Peter Weibel, eds., *Making Things Public* (Cambridge, Mass.: MIT Press 2005), 14–41.

10 For a rich analysis of the interplay between these political spheres, see James G. Ferguson, "Transnational Topographies of Power: Beyond 'The State' and 'Civil Society' in the Study of African Politics," in Bill Maurer and Gabriele Schwab, eds., *Accelerating Possession: Global Futures of Property and Personhood* (New York: Columbia University Press 2006), 76–98.

11 Julie Flint and Alex De Waal, *Darfur: A Short History of a Long War* (London: Zed Books 2005), 134.

12 Mike Davis, *Late Victorian Holocausts* (New York: Verso 2001), 21.

13 Ibid., 21. The divide between the "local people" and state-level governments may have become radically reconfigured through the groundwork of NGOs, and, while we may begin a study of rhetoric and human rights by outlining the distinctions between those appealing for rights and those recognizing them, we do well to keep in mind that the local too borrows from and plays upon the "moral calculus" at work in bodies like the United Nations and the African Union. For it may be that, despite the seeming dissolve of state sovereignty, through the root-taking of international organizations (especially in Africa), the firewalls only entrench further. Again, see Ferguson, "Transnational Topographies."

14 The International Commission of Inquiry on Darfur used the formulation in its report, asking "Have acts of genocide occurred?" This form of inquiry allowed the report to present findings of gross human rights abuses while downplaying genocide, which, while perhaps committed, never rose to the level of Sudanese policy.

15 Samantha Power, *A Problem from Hell* (New York: Harper Collins 2002), 358–64.

16 "Powell Reports Sudan Responsible for Genocide in Darfur."

17 Michael Ignatieff, *Human Rights as Politics and Idolatry* (Princeton, N.J.: Princeton University Press 2001), 16.

18 Ibid., 25.

19 Hannah Arendt, *The Origins of Totalitarianism* (New York: Harcourt Brace Janovich 1951), 297.

20 Ibid., 293.

21 Jacques Rancière, "Who Is the Subject of the Rights of Man?" *South Atlantic Quarterly*, vol. 103, nos. 2/3 (2004): 302.

22 Talal Asad, *Formations of the Secular* (Stanford, Calif.: Stanford University Press 2003), 143.

23 Ibid., 129.

24 Ibid.
25 Scott Straus, "Darfur and the Genocide Debate," *Foreign Affairs*, vol. 84. no. 1 (2005): 123–33.
26 Kirsten Hastrup, "Representing the Common Good: The Limits of Legal Language," in Richard Ashby Wilson and Jon P. Mitchell, eds., *Human Rights in Global Perspective: Anthropological Studies of Rights, Claims and Entitlements* (London: Routledge 2003), 24; Pierre Bourdieu, *Language and Symbolic Power* (Cambridge: Cambridge University Press 1991).
27 See Johan Pottier, *Re-Imaging Rwanda: Conflict, Survival and Disinformation in the Late Twentieth Century* (Cambridge: Cambridge University Press 2002).
28 Gérard Prunier, *Darfur: The Ambiguous Genocide* (Ithaca, N.Y.: Cornell University Press 2007), 127.
29 Ibid., 156.
30 *Report of the International Commission of Inquiry on Darfur to the United Nations Secretary-General* (January 2005), 3.
31 Eric Reeves, "Watching Genocide, Doing Nothing," *Dissent* (fall 2006), 7.
32 Ibid., 7.
33 Ibid.
34 Prunier, *Darfur*, 119.
35 Reeves, "Watching Genocide," 5.
36 Rony Brauman, "From Philanthropy to Humanitarianism: Remarks and an Interview," *South Atlantic Quarterly*, vol. 103, nos. 2/3 (2004): 411.
37 Susan Sontag, *Regarding the Pain of Others* (New York: Farrar, Strauss, Giroux 2003).
38 See James Dawes's first-hand account of this work in "Atrocity and Interrogation," *Critical Inquiry*, vol. 30, no. 2 (2004): 249–66.
39 Meg McLagan, "Introduction: Making Human Rights Claims Public," *American Anthropologist*, vol. 108, no.1 (2006): 192.
40 *Ghosts of Rwanda*.
41 For a description of distance, time, and appreciation, see Carlo Ginzburg, "To Kill a Chinese Mandarin: The Moral Implications of Distance," *Wooden Eyes*, trans. Martin Ryle and Kate Soper (New York: Columbia University Press 2001), 157–72.
42 Philip Gourevitch, *We Wish to Inform You That Tomorrow We Will Be Killed with Our Families* (New York: Picador 1998), 16. Emphasis added.
43 For a critique of Gourevitch's eventual adoption and repetition of the Rwandan Patriotic Front perspective, see Pottier, *Re-Imagining Rwanda*.
44 *Ghosts of Rwanda*.
45 Latour, "From *Realpolitik* to *Dingpolitik*," 15.
46 Ibid., 16.

47 Ibid., 19.

48 Aristotle, *Art of Rhetoric*, trans. J.H. Freese (Cambridge, Mass.: Harvard University Press 1926).

49 Ibid., 41.

50 Ibid., 20–1.

51 Latour calls this a "renewed empiricism," or a critical approach ready for the public realm in which uncertainty can be marshalled as the end of thought rather than the spur for interpretation. See his "Why Has Critique Run out of Steam? From Matters of Fact to Matters of Concern," *Critical Inquiry*, vol. 30, no. 2 (2004): 225–48.

52 Prunier, *Darfur*, 98.

53 Bernard-Henri Lévy, *War, Evil, and the End of History*, trans. Charlotte Mandell (Hoboken, N.J.: Melville 2004), 100–1.

54 Ibid., 94–5.

55 Ibid., 95.

56 Ibid., 108.

CHAPTER TEN

Preventing Genocide and Crimes against Humanity: One Innovation and New Global Initiative*

H. PETER LANGILLE

What can be done to stem the ongoing crisis in Darfur? For years, the Government of Sudan (GOS) and the Janjaweed militia have committed a campaign of systemic mass-murder, gang rape, ethnic cleansing, "scorched earth" tactics, and frequent cross-border incursions to kill Darfur refugees in Chad. Officials in many, if not all, national capitals know that even after signing the Darfur Peace Agreement in May 2006, the GOS unleashed yet another offensive to conclude its efforts to "cleanse" the region.[1] Yet, rather than the rapid reaction required in a serious emergency, the wider response to Darfur reflects a recurring pattern: routine delays, "too little, too late, too lame," and the increasingly dubious promise of "never again." Following Rwanda and Srebrenica, few can be confident that our existing arrangements are sufficiently reliable to save succeeding generations from the scourge of armed conflict and genocide. Regrettably, there has been little tangible progress in addressing four related challenges:

1) the prevention of armed conflict, including genocide and gross violations of human rights;
2) the protection of civilians at high risk;
3) rapid deployment for prompt start-up of demanding peace operations; and
4) the delivery of humanitarian assistance in a volatile environment.

Once again, we are confronted with familiar questions. First, why are current arrangements insufficient to prevent, stop, or effectively manage armed conflicts? Can any existing service provide an assurance of prompt, appropriate help? Second, given the consistent failure to stop or mitigate such atrocities again and again, what sort of strategy might actually work? Is there a more promising alternative?

This chapter commences with a review of the existing arrangements assigned to help victims of genocide, followed by an overview of strategies that might improve our capabilities to intervene effectively. I argue that our existing "tool box" is far from adequate in addressing the crisis in Darfur or any of the four noted challenges. There is an urgent need to expand our range of instruments and options, and I suggest one key innovation: a permanent United Nations Emergency Peace Service (UNEPS) that has the capacity to respond to similar crises ahead in a far more reliable, rapid, and cost-effective manner.

Existing Arrangements

THE AFRICAN UNION STANDBY BRIGADES

The initial deployment of African Union (AU) soldiers to the African Union Mission in Sudan (AMIS) represented an attempt to deal with a fast breaking crisis on their continent, reflecting both a Western desire to offload a shared responsibility by demanding "African solutions to African problems" and an effort at a compromise that would be acceptable to Sudanese officials in Khartoum. The exercise was premature and flawed. The AU had been formed in 2002, and the development of the AU Standby Brigades was announced the same year. Even before the start of their Sudan mission in 2004, there were legitimate concerns that the AU forces were not ready for such a demanding operation.[2] Those nations participating in the AU simply lacked too many of the required resources: well-trained, well-equipped soldiers; transport and support; and a mandate to protect civilians.

Given the scope and scale of the Darfur crisis already under way in 2004, the AU forces that joined AMIS were essentially assigned a "mission impossible."[3] Darfur is often described as being nearly the size of France or Texas, and this region would pose serious challenges for any multinational force. There is only one major paved road through 200,000 square miles of vast territory. Only those forces with extensive air and land transport, backed by substantive support in communications, surveillance, and logistics, could monitor and patrol such an area.[4] International efforts were made to provide AMIS with modest military resources, but, even if combined, these efforts were hardly sufficient.[5]

Gradually, AU forces in AMIS were expanded in response to widespread pressure over a deteriorating catastrophe in Darfur. The initial deployment should have alarmed all from the start: 60 military observers and 310 protection troops (to monitor and observe the compliance of the parties to the Humanitarian Ceasefire Agreement of 18 April 2004). On 20 October 2004 the AU contribution increased to 2,431 military personnel and 815 civilian police to monitor and observe compliance with the agreement and to contribute to a secure environment for the delivery of humanitarian assistance and the return of refugees and internally displaced persons. With persistent attacks and a precarious situation, on 28 April 2005 the AU Peace and Security Council bolstered the AMIS force to 6,171 military and 1,560 civilian police.[6] At this strength, the AMIS force could conduct daytime observation, monitoring, and reporting in some sectors. But it was hardly enough. While the AU troops attempted to help the suffering inhabitants and facilitate the delivery of humanitarian assistance, they frequently could do little more than protect themselves.

As to be expected, the AMIS force also attracted international concern and even hostility. Despite its efforts, AMIS represented a bad political decision, a token contribution that could provide only occasional help to over two million refugees and internally displaced people suffering in squalid camps and thousands in hiding, fearing worse. Inevitably, criticism arose from individuals and organizations attempting humanitarian operations in Darfur; some viewed AMIS as far too conservative in asserting its presence, conducting patrols, monitoring villages, and, in particular, protecting people at high risk.[7]

Notably, the number of AU member states providing troop contributions to AMIS was hardly representative of the far larger AU, with Nigeria and Rwanda providing the majority of the protection forces. Smaller military contingents were supplied by Gambia, Senegal, South Africa, Togo, and Kenya, and twenty-five AU countries sent military observers. Increasingly, those providing the major funding to the mission were dissatisfied with the return on their investment, and several countries were inclined to curtail the funding as AMIS continued to struggle with even the limited tasks assigned.

The AU had neither the mandate nor the capacity to stop the Janjaweed militia, the Sudanese armed forces, or the ongoing, often joint operations of both.[8] At best, the AU contribution in Darfur might be considered partially helpful. In no circumstances could any informed observer deem it adequate to stop this catastrophe. Yet, while it is unprepared for the crisis in Darfur, the AU should not be prematurely dismissed for its potential to help in the future. There appears to be a deep commitment in Africa to do more and to be far more prepared.[9] The AU members are engaged in planning five multinational, regionally dispersed, high-readiness brigades for peace operations authorized by the UN Security Council.[10] The brigades will be developed by member states within the AU's five regional economic commissions (RECs), with guidance from an AU planning element and a central AU headquarters. Each brigade will include its own planning elements and its own mobile mission headquarters. Of equal, if not greater, promise is that some also plan to include not only military brigades but smaller task forces, reserve forces, and air and naval forces, as well as police and civilian elements.[11] Combined, these efforts appear to be encouraging steps towards ensuring a more comprehensive, well-integrated response to diverse operations. AU reports indicate that all brigades will be listed within the United Nations Standby Arrangements System (UNSAS), which also needs help.

The AU brigade system is still a new arrangement, and its first substantive test continues to be negotiated and coordinated while under trial in a very tough mission in Darfur (where a slow and insufficient deployment should have been anticipated). Irrespective of the shortcomings of AMIS, however, the UN and international capitals continue to support the development of these AU brigades. On paper, the new brigades do look quite impressive. However, as one close to the plans noted, "the devil is in the details."[12] The effort involves numerous countries with divergent interests, as well as different cultures with different military standards and practices. At this stage, there is little assurance that the AU standby brigades will actually come together as planned or with a modest degree of cohesiveness, interoperability, and unity of purpose.

At the outset of the AMIS operation, there was a concern among UN officials that it would not be too long before their organization was assigned the task. There was also a fear that the AU would be "scapegoated" first and the UN second.[13] Following the Darfur Peace Agreement (DPA) signed on 5 May 2006, there were widespread expectations that the horrid suffering would end. Yet officials were also aware that the AU contribution would not come to a close promptly. Even if a new operation were launched, it would still be largely dependent on

Africans.[14] Although scheduled to conclude in September 2006, AMIS was extended until year's end, with a modest expansion of the force. For the worst reasons, AMIS had become the preferred option of the Sudanese government; officials in Khartoum knew that AMIS could do little to alleviate the crisis in Darfur.

THE UNITED NATIONS

The United Nations retains unique authority and legitimacy as the one universal organization dedicated to advancing peace and collective security, human rights, health, sustainable development, environmental protection, international law, and wider well-being. Numerous UN departments, agencies, and officials, at all levels, have worked tirelessly over the course of the Darfur crisis. Their efforts extend far beyond consulting, negotiating, mediating, briefing, gathering information, ensuring support for AU participants in AMIS, providing food and shelter, coordinating humanitarian relief, raising awareness of the situation, and facilitating the DPA.[15] As early as 2004, officials in the UN Department of Peacekeeping Operations (DPKO) engaged in contingency planning and exercises to help prepare for a potential deployment. Subsequent efforts were made to facilitate the transition from the AU mission to a UN peacekeeping operation.

Unfortunately, within the current UN system, there remain several prominent impediments to the type of response urgently required in Darfur: Security Council authorization; an agreement from national governments to contribute the necessary resources; sufficient national capacity, with appropriately trained and equipped personnel; and competent prior planning and preparation to ensure that everything required is ready.

On issues of peace and security, it helps to recall that the UN is the sum of its parts, including 192 diverse member states and a Security Council dominated by the permanent five (P5) members (China, France, the Russian Federation, the United Kingdom, and the United States).[16] At present, the "sum" is seldom united in perspective, in institutional preferences, or in a desire to move towards prompt responses to international conflict. [17] Genocide, war crimes, crimes against humanity, and cross-border aggression are unequivocal violations of international law; in Darfur, over three million people have been the victims of such heinous crimes. On such issues, the UN Security Council has the primary responsibility to authorize action.

If in agreement, the council has several potential ways to respond to these crimes, including a peacekeeping operation under Chapter VI of the UN Charter or a more robust peacekeeping operation – or even a collective-security operation – under Chapter VII.

Over the past six years, robust peace operations authorized under Chapter VII have become the norm, providing peacekeepers with a mandate to use "all necessary means," including the use of force to protect themselves, the mission, and, frequently, civilians at risk. Force compositions are designed to be strong, with a deterrent capacity to repel or, if necessary, stop violent belligerents. Rules of engagement now offer more flexibility to ensure that peacekeepers can, at least, conduct their assigned tasks without having "one arm tied behind their back."[18]

Although there has been a marked improvement in UN peacekeeping, valid concerns remain over how this system functions when confronted by a crisis such as Darfur. As stressed by the 2005 Report of the High-level Panel on Threats, Challenges and Change:

The biggest source of inefficiency in our collective security institutions has simply been an unwillingness to get serious about preventing deadly violence. This is a normative challenge to the United Nations: the concept of State and international responsibility to protect civilians from the effects of war and human rights abuses has yet to truly overcome the tension between the competing claims of sovereign inviolability and the right to intervene. It is also an operational challenge: the challenge of stopping a Government from killing its own civilians requires considerable military deployment capacity.[19]

... The biggest failures of the United Nations in civil violence have been in halting ethnic cleansing and genocide.[20]

... Prompt and effective response to today's challenges requires a dependable capacity for the rapid deployment of personnel and equipment for peacekeeping and law enforcement.[21]

With the world summit of 2005 prompting the UN General Assembly to endorse the Responsibility to Protect, followed by the endorsement of the Security Council, public – if not diplomatic – expectations were high. Yet it may have premature to assume that any political agreement over a new principle, or even a doctrine, of protection would immediately change long-standing preferences and practices.

To secure broad-based agreement on a contentious issue, the International Commission on Intervention and State Sovereignty had deliberately avoided the more controversial questions of "how" and with "what" to protect.[22] Protecting civilians was a new, largely unexplored task for governments and national defence establishments. Few, if any, aside from independent academics and organizations, had even contemplated the operational or tactical requirements.[23]

After three years of the growing crisis in Darfur, the UN Security Council managed to break a lingering deadlock, with a relatively strong resolution (1709) on 31 August 2006.[24] In brief, the council determined that:

- the situation in Darfur continued to constitute a threat to international peace and security;
- the UN Mission in Sudan (UNMIS) mandate and objectives should be expanded;
- efforts should be made to arrange the rapid deployment of additional capabilities;
- UNMIS should be strengthened by up to 17,300 military personnel and an appropriate civilian component, including 3,300 civilian police and up to 16 police units;
- these elements should begin to be deployed no later than 1 October 2006 to effect the transition from AMIS to UNMIS in Darfur; and
- the mandate would be to support the DPA in twelve general tasks, supplemented by new ones, several authorized under Chapter VII: namely, to use all necessary means in areas of deployment, to protect civilians under threat of physical violence, to prevent disruption of the DPA, to seize or collect arms, and to take strong measures against any individual or group violating or attempting to block implementation of the DPA or committing human rights violations.[25]

The decision to expand the UNMIS mission and move it to Darfur (to effect the transition from AMIS) initially appeared brilliant and, for many, unanticipated. Aside from already operating within Sudan, UNMIS was concluding its assigned task of overseeing the two-year ceasefire agreement between Khartoum and Southern Sudan.[26] Furthermore, personnel within UNMIS were familiar with the environment, and the demanding task of mission-start-up was largely completed, albeit in a different location. Relatively secure lines of communication and supply (logistics) were in place.

On 31 July, UNMIS had a total of 10,253 uniformed personnel, including 8,909 troops, 689 military observers, and 655 police, supported by 696 international civilian personnel and 1,228 local civilians. With a protection force of 4,000 troops, it was, at least, a bridgehead until augmented. If increased to the newly authorized strength, UNMIS would definitely be a robust UN presence, with up to 27,300 military personnel, 4,015 police, 16 police units, and an appropriate civilian component. UNMIS already included very wide representation from sixty-one UN member states.[27] If inclined to stay and rapidly increase their contribution of personnel and resources, the member states within UNMIS might have been adequate to stem the crisis in Dafur, barring any major escalation or threat. From the perspective of operational planners, the expansion of UNMIS likely appeared feasible, if not the only conceivable option, given a very difficult situation.[28] Yet senior diplomats, particularly the P5 members of the Security Council, had to realize that their option was far too vulnerable to stalemate. However appropriate or promising Resolution 1709 appeared on paper, it was too late and it included too many exploitable conditions. The Security Council's delay in authorizing UNMIS limited the UN's prospects in acquiring the necessary assistance to extend the operation. It would also adversely influence any prospect for a prompt expansion of the UNMIS.

With several years of ongoing deliberation and debate, squabbles and trade-offs, reluctance from Russia, and even the threat of a veto from China, the Security Council effectively made it known that any UN response to Darfur would be awkward and slow. In any conflict, such signals reduce pressure on belligerents and officials engaged in violence, who can read it as permission to continue their behaviour or even to become more aggressive. Conversely, these signals may also reduce the pressure on supportive member states to contribute in a timely manner or to contribute at all if the mission is deemed to constitute an unacceptably high risk.

Seldom have the effects been so evident. By the spring of 2007, officials in the Government of Sudan had yet to respect the terms of any of the numerous agreements it made to help stem the crisis in Darfur.[29] With the killing and rapes intensifying in June 2006 (following the signing of the DPA), the UN Security Council rushed a senior delegation of diplomats and ambassadors to Sudan in an attempt to secure approval for the extension and redeployment of UNMIS. This delegation assured the Sudanese president, Omar al-Bashir, that the full sovereignty of Sudan would be respected, that the UN would not deploy an intervention force, and that al-Bashir's consent was essential for the UN to do anything. Having been well briefed on his options, al-Bashir promptly vetoed the proposed UN force, specifically any robust operation authorized to protect civilians. [30]

Within weeks, al-Bashir also warned that any UN deployment would not only be opposed at the political level, it would also be fought by his armed forces. This warning could not be easily dismissed. As UN Secretary General Kofi Annan stated, "The Sudanese Government ... has ably played on Western fears of entering a military quagmire ... exploiting some of these issues, saying, 'If you want to have another Iraq, come,' and this scared away governments."[31] For officials in the various member states who may have been considering a further contribution to UNMIS, the risks were now clear and far higher. As reported, "without Khartoum's permission, no nation will send troops to Darfur and risk a battle with the Sudanese military, which has increased its troops and aircraft in Darfur."[32] Equally problematic, national officials now had another plausible justification to add to what were frequently their long lists of dubious excuses for ignoring UN requests for help.[33]

Irrespective of the Sudanese warning or the less-than-compelling diplomatic effort, it was already evident to a few senior sources that the UN would encounter serious difficulties in assembling the more substantive UN force needed for Darfur. Prior to the signing of the DPA on 15 May, quiet consultations between UN officials and various governments were under way in an effort to identify and solicit contributions of the necessary troops and resources. To its credit, on this occasion the UN Security Council responded very promptly with Resolution 1679, formalizing the initial process on the following day, 16 May.[34] Darfur needed immediate help and that meant it was critical to avoid the last-minute, ad hoc, improvised response characteristic of peacekeeping in the early to mid-1990s.

On 18 May, the UN under-secretary general (U-S-G) for peacekeeping operations, Jean-Marie Guéhenno, publicly stated that "if there is an operation in Darfur, then it would be a U.N. force, and a U.N. force which would comprise forces from – should comprise forces from all continents, to really show that the world is coming together."[35] Guéhenno definitely had to try to obtain the additional contributions, but he also had to know that this would be a slow, uphill struggle.

The response from national governments was far from encouraging. Most of the northern member states were either already worried about being overstretched in contributing to the NATO operation in Afghanistan and/or the American-led war in Iraq, or they were under NATO and American pressure to do more in one of these wars. Most of the southern troop contributors were also heavily stretched in helping the UN with a major surge in peacekeeping operations. Furthermore, for sixteen years the UN has also been confronted with a challenge to do far more with much less.[36] To date, the member states have refused to provide the UN with anything comparable to a national-security headquarters or any permanent UN force or dedicated service for responding to violent challenges. Article 47 of the UN Charter stipulates that member states are to provide the necessary support for maintaining international peace and security, but, while it remains an obligation, few, if any governments, are willing to abide by it.[37]

Prior to initiating any peace operation abroad, the UN still has to plead to borrow personnel and equipment from governments; this process tends to be more cumbersome, complicated, lengthy, and difficult than organizing any sheriff's posse at the last minute.[38] With enthusiasm for the UN waning in Washington (following the American failure in Somalia), competition arising from NATO (following the end of the Cold War), and the Non-Aligned Movements' demand for equitable regional representation in the UN's Department of Peacekeeping Operations (1997), the governments and defence establishments of the northern hemisphere simply "jumped ship," leaving the UN with only token troop contributions.[39] An undue share of the burden in UN peacekeeping was pushed onto those in the south,[40] in effect creating a two-tiered, slow system.[41] Even the UN Security Council acknowledged a "commitment – capacity gap," where those with the capacity seldom contribute and where those contributing frequently suffer from insufficient capacity.[42]

Would there be sufficient capacity committed to expand UNMIS? Unlikely! Even for the UN and those member states inclined to help, the timing could hardly have been worse. For two years, the UN had been coping with a major surge in peace operations. In May 2006 the organization had almost 90,000 personnel serving in 18 UN DPKO-led operations on four continents in ten time zones.[43] Within four months, the UN was heavily challenged by an unprecedented surge in peace operations, with urgent demands for more. In August 2006, confronted with escalating violence in East Timor, war in Lebanon, and a new offensive in Darfur, the Security Council authorized an increase of 40 per cent in the overall size of operations.[44] Even without UNMIS, this increase would be the largest effort at UN peacekeeping in the sixty-one-year history of the organization, with more than 100,000 troops and police to be deployed by year's end. By 2007, the total was expected to exceed 140,000 personnel, stretching the UN – particularly the DPKO and supportive national contributors – beyond anything previously experienced.[45]

The short-term implications for UNMIS were serious. Acknowledging a high risk of political neglect, Under-Secretary General Guéhenno conceded that "Darfur could be a victim of that overstretch."[46] At a meeting with forty-nine potential troop contributors for UNMIS on 25 September 2006, the UN received pledges of support for additional troops from only five member states: Bangladesh, Nigeria, Norway, Tanzania, and Sweden.[47] Yet, within ten days, fearing the beginning of a process that might expand to represent a problem, the Sudanese ambassador to the UN responded with a uniquely intimidating letter to potential troop contributors, stating, "In the absence of Sudan's consent to the deployment of UN troops, any volunteering to provide peacekeeping troops to Darfur will be considered as a hostile act, a prelude to an invasion of a member country of the UN."[48] This threat created a modest diplomatic storm, with numerous official protests but little more. Once again, the intentional intimidation actually worked and few governments would volunteer to help with the crisis.

The UN system for peace operations has many limits, many that are not easily or quickly overcome, particularly when the organization must deal with diverse emergencies. Numerous reports and studies over the past sixteen years have encouraged an array of necessary reforms for peace operations, preventing armed conflict, and protecting civilians.[49] While more ambitious ideas may attract headlines, the official preference is for pragmatic incremental steps to modify existing arrangements.[50] This protracted approach appeals to the majority of governments – including those of the P5 – because they tend to be very leery of any bold, new shifts entailing a substantive change, especially one that might affect national interests, sovereignty, or control.[51]

Overall, the results of the incremental reform process are mixed. On the positive side, the UN now has a larger department of peacekeeping operations, with six hundred staff who are increasingly capable of planning, organizing, and supporting operations worldwide. Strategic deployment stocks and mission start-up kits are readily available at the UN logistics base in Brindisi, Italy. A forward-thinking Lessons-Learned Unit has helped to institutionalize much-needed change in peace operations. Increasingly, the emphasis has been placed on integrated analysis and planning to ensure well-integrated, multidimensional operations, with civilian, military, and police elements. With the shift to robust operations authorized under Chapter VII of the UN Charter, mandates, rules of engagement, and force compositions have been revised to ensure an adequate deterrent capacity. Such disincentives to non-cooperation are frequently twinned with incentives to cooperation. By addressing critical human needs with quick-impact projects and peace-building efforts, people in need receive help and hope, as well as an interest in sustaining the peace process. Because of the complex nature of contemporary armed conflict, various operational requirements are sequenced throughout the short, medium, and long term.[52] A 24/7 operations unit now maintains contact with those in all operations, channelling information, early warning, and requests to and from appropriate offices in the wider UN system. A standby cadre of civilian police and a strategic reserve of multinational forces were proposed to augment operations needing prompt assistance. The latter would have been very helpful in expanding UNMIS, but it was opposed by the Bush administration.

The UN Standby Arrangements System was repeatedly modified over the past decade to attract additional contributions at higher levels of readiness and competence. This was modestly helpful in informing potential contributors of UN expectations and in generating a list of what *might* be available. These efforts are among the diverse reforms that have helped to improve current UN peace operations. However, there remain inherent limitations in many critical areas.[53] To cite one example, the UNSAS is an entirely conditional arrangement, one that places no binding obligation on any government to contribute help. Numerous governments volunteer assistance only when they have direct interests or when they are pressured to by major powers. Rather than rapid deployment, this system is chronically plagued by routine delays – averaging four to six months but often longer – irrespective of what is happening to people in harm's way. Even with a new offensive, officials expect that Darfur will be another situation in the category of the slow "routine." Despite the Security Council resolution for rapid deployment to expand UNMIS by 1 October 2006, Jean-Marie Guéhenno was forced to announce that the planned deployment would have to be delayed until at least January 2007.[54]

Experience over the past thirteen years has clearly demonstrated that the UN's member states are either unwilling or unable to provide a reliable, effective, rapid response to diverse emergencies. Although the situation may change, the early indications for UNMIS and the people of Darfur are not comforting. Given the intransigence of the Sudanese government and the related reluctance of UN member states, there was little prospect of UNMIS promptly assuming the lead role in Darfur. In response, the African Union authorized an extended timeframe for AMIS (until the end of 2006). Two days later, the UN Security Council extended the mandate for UNMIS.[55]

Sudanese officials appear to have calculated correctly in assuming more talk than action, at least in the short term. They understood that governments could simply ignore UN Secretary General Annan's warning in September 2006 that "Darfur is heading toward disaster unless UN peacekeepers are allowed in." Chad had also attempted to raise the stakes in warning the UN General Assembly that the crisis in Darfur threatened to destabilize the entire region.[56] In a modestly different political environment, this might have prompted a powerful collective response.

Over a three-year period between 2003 and 2006, the Sudanese government has definitely had to worry about increasing public awareness and political pressure for stemming the crisis in Darfur.[57] Yet, in the absence of clearly specified demands targeted at UN member states with available capacity, Western public pressure was little more than a protest coupled to general support for doing *something more*. Arguably, decision makers in Khartoum, Beijing, and Moscow were initially willing to continue with a high-risk strategy because they were confident they could. However, over an extended period, political environments occasionally shift, public pressure can push reluctant governments, dubious deals can become embarrassingly problematic, and the confidence of partners can diminish, prompting a different approach.[58] Most governments also know that there are worse options than consenting to a UN peacekeeping operation, particularly when government officials are still in a position to influence the terms on which consent is given.[59]

On 16 November 2006 the Sudanese government agreed in principle to allow a joint UN-AU peacekeeping force into Darfur.[60] The tentative agreement was for a modestly smaller joint force (17,000 troops and 3,000 police officers). A joint UN-AU force was not explicit in Resolution 1706, but it had been central to the planning for UNMIS. If it was deemed a viable compromise, it might have started a promising process. However, officials in Khartoum had simply floated another tentative agreement in order to assess international response. As soon as it became apparent that the UN would encounter problems in raising credible capacity, Sudan's president reverted to his obstinate opposition to any UN force.

THE STANDBY HIGH-READINESS BRIGADE

The multinational Standby High-Readiness Brigade (SHIRBRIG) was twice warned to prepare for a UN deployment to Darfur. Yet the requests to prepare promptly were just as promptly cancelled.[61] SHIRBRIG is deemed to be the most advanced formation available for UN peace operations.[62] The initial objective of the participating member states was to be able to deploy 4,000–5,000 well-trained, well-equipped, self-sufficient troops within two weeks in a coherent, pre-coordinated formation.[63] Furthermore, SHIRBRIG has an integrated mission headquarters and planning element, which is maintained for and dedicated to UN operations.[64] Fifteen countries now participate in the brigade, with a number of others taking part as observers.[65] Overall, it has a relatively broad geographic and cultural mix of participants.

The commanding officer, Canadian Brigadier-General Greg Mitchell, supported the prospect of SHIRBRIG's deployment to Darfur, as did his multinational staff.[66] After participating in the critical start-up phase of the earlier UNMIS, they were confident in knowing both the conflict and the key participants. Likewise, they had already conducted contingency planning and exercises for such a deployment with officials in the UN Department of Peacekeeping Operations. Arguably, if supported for deployment to Darfur, SHIRBRIG would have been a very useful complement in the initial expansion phase of UNMIS. Most participants already have experience in demanding Chapter VII operations. Most have a high degree of professionalism and competence, as well as general and specialized military assets. If combined in a sound division of labour as planned, these would provide useful synergies, a very competent mission headquarters, a highly mobile vanguard, and a robust protection force.

Unfortunately, the SHIRBRIG arrangement also looks better on paper than it has in UN operations. Experience in the latter indicates a mixed record, with modest success to date.[67] Since its inception, SHIRBRIG has not managed a deployment at anywhere near brigade strength. At present, there is not sufficient political will or leadership among the participating members to make SHIRBRIG work as intended.[68]

A relatively small SHIRBRIG team had helped to establish the planning and critical early-mission management for monitoring the ceasefire agreement between north and south Sudan in UNMIS. The participating members had a long lead-time to prepare for that mission. Yet, from ten full members and eight aligned members, the UN secured a rather modest commitment of a mission headquarters (approximately 120 officers) and two security companies (240 troops) to protect it.

Among numerous problems, one constraining fact remains: SHIRBRIG is another conditional standby arrangement. Each participating government retains decision-making authority over any deployment of its national armed forces. Many share a concern over contributing from limited resources, particularly when already committed to allied operations elsewhere. SHIRBRIG is also a very low defence priority of most, if not all, of the participating member states, and even a lower priority of national defence establishments. Another factor compounding the problem is that many of the governments that initially agreed to participate in this arrangement are no longer in power. Their successors appear to share a limited understanding of SHIRBRIG, and less interest in making it work.

Without a political profile or public awareness of SHIRBRIG, the participating governments face little, if any, pressure in domestic or international politics to commit to a deployment. Only a few academics, officials, and journalists were sufficiently informed to raise the SHIRBRIG option as potentially helpful in response to the crisis in Darfur.[69] Yet the efforts of a few are seldom sufficient to generate wider awareness, to mobilize sustained pressure, or to influence tangible contributions from reluctant governments.

As a result, the level of commitment among the participants is low, even among those who previously agreed to be lead contributors. Rather than lead, Canada promptly refused to participate in a UN operation to Darfur, effectively stemming the prospect of a SHIRBRIG deployment.[70] Had the members met to discuss a SHIRBRIG contribution, it might have been sufficient to send a message, possibly deterring Khartoum from continuing to stymie UN efforts.[71]

SHIRBRIG remains a "work in progress" although the progress has been unacceptably slow and increasingly directed away from the participants' initial aspirations of a high-readiness, rapidly deployable brigade.[72] At least, the UN now has conditional access to a cohesive, standby, rapidly deployable mission headquarters. To their credit, elements of SHIRBRIG can still claim to be the only multinational mechanism devoted to working exclusively in UN peace operations and in the UN DPKO. As a partnership agreed to in the aftermath of Rwanda – one primarily designed to stop the "next Rwanda" – the SHIRBRIG arrangement and its participating members should have been ready to assume a lead role in UNMIS. Once again, it has demonstrated the extent to which it can be relied upon for rapid deployment to UN peace operations. At best, it may be helpful when the conditions are appropriate. As it continues to stand by, SHIRBRIG is far from sufficient in addressing any of the four challenges noted.

EU BATTLEGROUPS

A group of European Union (EU) nations (acting under the EU umbrella) are now preparing thirteen battlegroups for rapid, long-range deployment to robust peace operations, including enforcement to quell or contain a crisis.[73] Each battlegroup is to be composed of 1,500 elite troops, kept on standby within national defence establishments. They are supposed to be ready for deployment within five to ten days' notice and be sustainable within theatre for up to thirty days. In November 2004 the EU approved plans to develop these battlegroups, with its defence minister indicating that the first one should be operational within one year (late 2005) and others by 2007.[74] Following a recurring pattern of delays, it was subsequently announced that the first formation should be ready by 2007.

Three potential frameworks are under consideration by the EU: a participating country deploying alone; a country serving as the lead or "framework nation"; or a broadly multinational format with diverse participants. It would appear that the EU members are drawing on the British experience in helping to stabilize a tough situation in Sierra Leone in 2000, as well as the French experience in leading the EU contingent in the Ituri region of the Democratic Republic of the Congo until the Security Council could assemble a stronger UN force.[75]

The option of battlegroups initially generated guarded optimism. In the words of the UN U-S-G for peacekeeping operations, Jean-Marie Guéhenno, "the EU force would not be a standing army, but it would have a similar function. It would be built around the few countries that have a capacity to deploy troops quickly and over big distances. And its existence would lend some deterrent capacity that a light UN presence on the ground so often lacks. The concept needs to be tested to see its full measure."[76] An early test in 2005 demonstrated considerable potential, raising wider expectations, and the EU announced plans for further cooperation with the UN and a new partnership arrangement, designed specifically for more demanding, robust operations.

However, this arrangement is also conditional. Any deployment will still be subject to national decision-making processes. The troops will not be designated in advance but remain on standby within national defence establishments. Since the EU also requires a consensual decision-making process, any deployment may be delayed or blocked by an opposed member. In short, the EU battlegroups may be more rapid and effective if deployed, but their availability, as well as their reliability in another conditional arrangement, remains in question. To date, there is also confusion over whether these EU battlegroups are ready, appropriate, or inclined to help in UNMIS or any UN operation. UN Secretary General Annan endorsed this initiative in October 2004, shortly after the initial announcement that there would be EU/UN battlegroups. Yet his endorsement was followed by a subsequent discussion within the EU over the primary institutional affiliation of the proposed battlegroups; a few EU members preferred the UN, while others claimed that these new arrangements might be redesignated for NATO's Rapid Response Force. This issue has not been clarified.

Further, if the term is related to the intent, an EU "battlegroup" may not be the ideal name for UN peacekeeping operations.[77] Few governments in the south are likely to welcome a foreign battlegroup on their territory, particularly when it comes from those with a history in colonizing the south. As indicated, Sudan's president was already exploiting such fears to generate broader opposition to any UN mission.[78]

If the EU members were actually inclined to help in a demanding UN operation, the preparation of their battlegroups could have been advanced for a deployment in September 2006. There was sufficient forewarning of the need to accelerate their operational readiness. Five of these battlegroups might have made a substantive difference in rapidly augmenting other contributions to UNMIS, particularly as a complement to the AU forces. Since the choice was relatively clear by 2005, it would appear that a decision was made within the EU to forego any such effort.

Although it may be modestly premature to judge this EU option, the early indications suggest this arrangement cannot be relied upon for a prompt response to a demanding crisis. Once again, this new arrangement appears as one that may be helpful but insufficient to address the four key challenges.

NATO

With the AU experiencing predictable difficulty in Darfur by 2005, many in the West suggested that the only alternative for substantive help would be with a multinational bridging force from the North Atlantic Treaty Organization.[79] Few doubt the combined military capacity of this regional military alliance.[80] Aside from fifty years of joint training and cooperation to remain interoperable, the Allies have the most advanced military technology, extensive war-fighting capabilities, and the largest defence budgets. With a recent emphasis on force transformation and modernization, as well as rapid deployment and long-range power projection, NATO is unique in having the potential for prompt intervention worldwide.[81] Had there been a consensus among the Allies, backed by sufficient political will to make it a high priority in each government, NATO forces might have been deployed to assist at any stage of this crisis.

NATO's interest in participating in peace operations has been evident since the early 1990s. Among the Alliance members, however, there are diverse expectations over NATO's current and future role. Developed in the initial years of the Cold War as a Western response to the Soviet Union, NATO's military role became central as the Warsaw Pact expanded. As such, a long-standing focus was on nuclear and conventional deterrence to maintain "transatlantic" security, as well as the national security of its members. National and regional security for this specific community remains a high priority. Yet, with NATO expanding throughout the 1990s, new and former members also expressed interest in extending its reach to out-of-area-operations, with the prospect of a new global role.[82] Given overlapping geo-strategic and economic interests, Alliance officials also conveyed support for a focus on industrial security.[83] NATO is clearly the institutional preference of northern defence establishments, defence industries, and most, if not all, northern governments.

With the United States being the dominant member and unrivalled military power, NATO policy has reflected the official perception of threats within Washington and the Pentagon. As to be expected, following the terror attacks of 11 September 2001, counter-terrorism and counter-insurgency were elevated to the top of the Alliance agenda. The ongoing war in Afghanistan became a NATO mission (ISAF) in the early stages of the United States' Operation Enduring Freedom. With an attack on NATO's most powerful member obligating Alliance members to respond under Article 5 of the North Atlantic treaty, and with authorization from the UN Security Council, the majority of NATO members contributed troops and equipment to ISAF, albeit at various levels and often with specific conditions attached. The subsequent American-led war in Iraq proved to be the exception, attracting support from less than half the NATO members.[84] By 2006, there was little political consensus within NATO over current and future priorities of the Alliance or the leadership of the Bush administration in Iraq, Afghanistan, and the wider "war on terror."

Was NATO an appropriate arrangement for stemming the crisis in Darfur? As indicated, the NATO option had attracted public and political support in several Allied countries. But was this support premised on a reasonable assessment or wishful thinking? With two ongoing wars in Iraq and Afghanistan requiring substantive troop contributions, as well as equipment, transport, support, and financing, few Alliance members were inclined to open a third military front in Africa. Two of the Alliance's most powerful armies were already heavily engaged in both wars, suffering substantive losses in wounded and casualties. Confronted by an enormous economic cost and the possibility of losing the war in Iraq, with all the political pressure these realities entailed, neither Washington nor London was well positioned to encourage the Alliance to undertake another demanding operation.

NATO was also encountering difficultly in attracting sufficient contributions from Alliance members to maintain or expand ISAF.[85] With even a remote chance of NATO also losing the first land battle in its fifty-seven-year history, a prompt response to the Darfur crisis was unlikely to be at the forefront of Alliance priorities. The long-awaited announcement that NATO's Rapid Response Force was "fully operational and ready to go" was made at the Alliance summit in Latvia on 29 November 2006. However, no mention was made of any deployment to Darfur. Further, as reported by CNN, "allies have been reluctant to commit the necessary troops, in part because of the potential costs of participating in its missions."[86]

NATO may also be inappropriate for out-of-area operations, particularly in the southern hemisphere. For one, the NATO members are all predominantly white, almost all wealthy, and, with the exception of Turkey, all Christian. Furthermore, as an all-northern military alliance, NATO lacks wider legitimacy and political credibility outside its region. Much as the Warsaw Pact was frequently viewed as an instrument for protecting and extending Soviet power, NATO is often perceived as a similar instrument of American power. Irrespective of any intentions, these perceptions combine with former fears of colonialism and imperialism in a manner that inevitably generates scepticism and opposition.[87] A NATO military intervention in the south may now encourage hostilities and an escalation of violence. A NATO military intervention in Darfur would likely give the impression of another American-led war against another Islamic-led state. There is a high probability that NATO would be forcefully opposed, not only by Sudanese armed forces but also by others united in terms of identity, religious cause, values, and interests.

It does not help that the commitment of the NATO alliance and its members to the United Nations is now in doubt. [88] The statistics are difficult to ignore. NATO members are now among the lowest contributors of personnel to UN peace operations despite their capacity and their alleged commitments to the UN. At present, NATO has a mixed, heavily mythologized record in peace operations within its region.[89] It would also be quite difficult for the majority of NATO members to claim a long-standing commitment to the security and development of countries in the south or even previous experience in attempting to stop any genocide. Regrettably, in a world characterized by deep divisions between religious extremes, wealth and poverty, and north and south, NATO is unlikely to be widely accepted or even tolerated as an appropriate arrangement for addressing the crisis in Darfur.

SUMMING UP: SHORTCOMINGS OF EXISTING TOOLS

In short, the existing arrangements may be helpful on occasion when the conditions are conducive, but they are clearly insufficient for addressing the four challenges noted at the outset. There are numerous inherent limitations in the AU Standby Brigades, the UN system for coping with emergencies (particularly the UN Standby Arrangements System), SHIRBRIG, the EU battlegroups, and NATO.[90] All these groups still depend on national political will and the provision of national standby personnel. Frequently, these limitations stymie any response to fast-breaking crises. Repeated efforts have demonstrated that conditional arrangements seldom generate tangible contributions. Our current tools remain slow and unreliable. Worse, the stipulated conditions are unreliable and defy any remedy to obligate or bind participants.

Several of these arrangements have helped to build a wider foundation for peace operations, which remains an important objective, but few, if any, will ever provide an appropriate response to real emergencies. Given what is currently available, officials in Khartoum could plan to do as they pleased in Darfur, with the confidence – if not the assurance – that any UN or multinational intervention to stop them was exceptionally unlikely. Another horrific precedent with far-reaching implications has been established. At least for the near future, the "sovereign right to genocide" appears sufficient to impede all attempts to stop or constrain another catastrophe. Thousands more are likely to die, while millions will continue to suffer. Regrettably, Gwynne Dyer may have been correct in claiming that nothing substantive will actually be done to avert the crisis in Darfur, that the best anyone can reasonably hope for is a continuation of the AMIS operation and the current AU force. In his words, "the end-of-September deadline for putting a 20,000-strong force of United Nations troops into Darfur, including large numbers of soldiers drawn from NATO countries, was always a fantasy. The deadline has passed without any softening of the Sudanese government's total rejection of the plan, and no Western troops are heading for Sudan any time soon."[91]

Optimism, at least at this point, is increasingly difficult to sustain. One can only hope that the lessons learned from the Darfur crisis (and past crises) will prompt wider interest in something more than continued false promises. By now, most people should understand the urgent need to develop a viable alternative. Emergencies by their nature require rapid, reliable, and effective responses. To ensure an effective response, diverse services must be pre-planned, well coordinated, and immediately available. Currently, a minority of people have the option to dial 911 with some confidence in knowing that various useful services are already prepared and committed to help them quickly. Elsewhere, the majority of people seldom have such 911 access or any other decent options. If the objective is to prevent violence and protect people at risk, an operation should be deployed quickly, with a legitimate, credible presence to start providing the necessary services within days and deter the likelihood of mass murder and ethnic cleansing.[92] Increasingly, we can see a close relationship between preventing armed conflict, genocide, gross violations of human rights, protecting civilians at high risk, deploying rapidly, and addressing critical human needs. These challenges are closely linked and interdependent. Clearly, there is an evident need for a comprehensive approach to develop one integrated UN service specifically to deal with the four challenges noted, and possibly to attend to an even broader spectrum of emergencies.

What Might Work?: A United Nations Emergency Peace Service[93]

One possible innovation – a UN Emergency Peace Service – is designed to address each of the four challenges noted. As proposed, the UNEPS would be a permanent UN formation, maintained at high readiness with pre-trained, well-equipped UN personnel, immediately available once authorized by the UN Security Council. This service would be both multidimensional and multifunctional, composed of military, police, and civilian elements and prepared for rapid deployment to diverse UN operations.[94] Ideally, approximately 14,800 personnel would be co-located at a new UN base under a static operational headquarters (see organizational chart in appendix A) and two mobile field headquarters (MHQs). Each MHQ would be assigned sufficient strength to provide security and protection and law and order, as well as to address critical human needs within the mission area (see organizational chart in appendix B).

The UNEPS is primarily intended to be a dedicated "lead service," "vanguard," or "first responder." Given the nature and size of this new service, it would be reserved for emergency situations, particularly to fill the gap in the initial six months when others may be unavailable, unprepared, or unwilling to help. As a permanent UN service, composed of UN personnel, lead elements could be deployed within forty-eight hours. With immediate access to an available service, the UN would have a credible deterrent capacity. Furthermore, with a priority on ensuring an effective, preventive, and prompt response in the early stage of a conflict, it may be sufficient to offset deadly violence. This approach would help to diminish the need for subsequent efforts and the almost routine rotation into a larger, longer multinational operation. Yet the UNEPS would also include elements to establish the groundwork for well-integrated, comprehensive, and sustained efforts when necessary.

Another objective of the proposed UNEPS is to complement, rather than replace, existing UN arrangements. In fact, such a service could not operate without the support of the wider UN system and the assistance of supportive member states. In some cases, the latter may be essential to augment and rotate into an operation after the first six months. This period should be sufficient to secure and prepare national standby personnel as a replacement for the UNEPS. In accord with the UN Charter, the Security Council would retain responsibility for authorizing any deployment and for developing the mandate (in cooperation with the UN secretary general and officials of the secretariat). Once deployed, the secretary general would retain primary responsibility for the mission and UN services within it, reporting on both to the Security Council.

The permanent operational headquarters would have to be directed by a highly qualified special representative of the UN secretary general (SRSG). This individual would be responsible for the administration, oversight, and coordination of the UN base and an integrated headquarters, including those personnel assigned to plan, manage, and conduct operations, support, and training. Both MHQs would be planned and prepared to operate at a similar level of capacity for similar purposes, and each would likely be under the command of two deputy SRSGs and integrated with civilian, police, and military staffs leading their respective deployable elements. Within each MHQ, there would also be a need for political and legal advisers, translation, communication, signals, and liaison units, and a defence and security platoon.

Among the deployable civilians (in teams or companies) would be medical and public-affairs units as well as experts in civilian policing; disaster relief and humanitarian assistance; human rights monitoring and education; conflict resolution; peace-building; de-mining; demobilization; disarmament; reconstruction, reintegration, and reconciliation; and environmental-crisis response. In all emergencies, there is a common need for diverse services to address critical human needs immediately. Even at the outset of a deployment, there is a requirement for quick-impact projects and the prompt provision of incentives to restore hope, health, and law and order. Safety and security are also necessary to ensure an environment where people can live free from fear or harm.

A robust military composition is required in contemporary peace operations, particularly when the risks are high and the threats are real. The UNEPS must be capable of deterring belligerents and defending the mission, as well as civilians at risk. As noted, all recent UN peace operations have been authorized under Chapter VII. The deployable military components would include technical reconnaissance units; light armoured reconnaissance units; motorized light infantry battalions; armoured (wheeled) infantry battalions; a helicopter squadron (of utility, heavy lift, and armed scouts); an engineer battalion; a logistics battalion; and a medical unit/hospital. The military elements under each MHQ would constitute a robust brigade group of approximately 5,000 troops. When combined, the deployable military personnel of the UNEPS would total approximately 10,000 troops. While this total cannot be construed as another "force" for war fighting, each brigade group should have sufficient capacity to maintain the security and the safety of people within its area of operations. Notably, the UNEPS provides a modular formation, which allows for prompt "tailoring" or selection of elements appropriate to mission-specific requirements.

The UNEPS would be composed of individuals who volunteer for service and succeed in demonstrating dedication, professional expertise, and competence throughout a rigorous selection and training process. There would be no shortage of committed individuals with advanced skills willing to volunteer and participate in such a service on a paid, full-time basis, similar to that of UN civil servants. Applications would be encouraged from all member states to ensure universal representation. The advantages are recognized even within member states. As noted in the 1995 Canadian report *Towards a Rapid Reaction Capability for The United Nations*: "As professional volunteers develop into a cohesive UN force, they can assume responsibility for some of the riskier operations mandated by the Council, but for which troop contributors have been hesitant to contribute. UN volunteers offer the best prospect of a completely reliable, well-trained rapid reaction capability. Without the need to consult national authorities, the UN could cut response time significantly, and volunteers could be deployed within hours of a Security Council decision."[95] "No matter how difficult this goal now seems," the report states, "it deserves continued study, with a clear process for assessing its feasibility over the long term."[96] This new service would offset much of the burden and pressure on governments, which are now reluctant to prepare and deploy their national citizens at short-notice into environments of "high risk" and "low interest." Moreover, as a dedicated U N service, it would not be constrained by the need to acquire approval and meet the conditions of each participating member state. This would ensure that a reliable option was available to the U N when desperately needed.

Rapid deployment is a very demanding task, one that can be easily delayed or stymied by the absence of one component. Is it reasonable to expect success or even a cohesive unity of effort and purpose when requesting various national services with varying levels of training, preparation, and equipment to assemble promptly for the first time into a multinational formation in a foreign environment under extreme duress? The lessons learned from previous experience suggest that this may be exceptionally problematic and a slow process.

Already, there is a recognized need for more cohesive and effective personnel, particularly those with advanced preparation, prior comprehensive training, and "first-rate" equipment for assigned tasks in diverse U N operations. A U N E P S of professional volunteers, co-located and trained at a U N base, would be the optimal way to ensure a higher level of sophistication and competence, which is essential to rapid deployment. Rather than having to organize transportation out of numerous countries around the world, staging and deployment could occur promptly out of the designated U N base. By including a wider range of services within a permanent, modular formation, co-located at a designated U N base, it would be possible to provide a prompt, coherent response to various contingencies. Even small units of specialists in humanitarian, environmental, or health crises may plan and coordinate a larger meaningful effort (each tend to be needed in areas of armed conflict).

The future roles and potential tasks of the new service should include the provision of reliable early warning with on-site technical reconnaissance; rapid deployment for preventive action and protection of civilians at risk; and prompt start-up of diverse operations, including robust peacekeeping, policing, peace-building, and humanitarian and environmental assistance. The threshold criteria for any deployment would be authorization by the Security Council, just cause, right intention, proportional means, and reasonable prospects.[97] As the report of the International Commission on Intervention and State Sovereignty stresses, there is a responsibility to protect, to prevent, to react, and to rebuild, particularly when there is the potential for large-scale loss of life or gross violations of human rights such as mass ethnic cleansing.[98] These are obligations that cannot be neglected even in the early stages of a mission.

In short, a UNEPS, as a permanent UN formation specifically prepared for the four challenges identified, is designed to address the current gaps in political will and limited national capacity. By no means, however, will this service be a panacea; there will be situations where it is neither appropriate nor likely to succeed. Given its relatively discrete size and composition, there are recognized limits. There are also likely to be conflicts that are beyond its capacity to prevent or circumstances where it will be unable to deploy rapidly, protect the civilian population, or provide for critical human needs. In this respect, Nobel laureate Dr John Polanyi presents a fitting analogy: "Fire departments and police forces do not always prevent fires or crime, yet they are now widely recognized as providing an essential service. Similarly, a rapid reaction capability may confront conditions beyond its capacity to control. This should not call into question its potential value to the international community. It is a civilized response to an urgent problem."[99]

What might have been done in Darfur? There are no easy or accurate answers. At best, one can provide only informed speculation for the purpose of illustration. Under the proposal for a UNEPS sketched out here, only one of the MHQs with assigned deployable elements would be available for any specific operation. Had it been available, it might have prevented the start and the escalation of the Darfur crisis. By 2004, it would have been effective at protecting the majority of civilians in Darfur, but it would not have had sufficient capacity to maintain safety or security throughout the region. By 2005, once the violence had escalated and spread, it would have been more effective than the designated AU force but far from sufficient at stemming violence on its own. Similarly, even following the Darfur Peace Agreement in May 2006, a UNEPS deployment would have furnished the capacity to expand and reinforce UNMIS rapidly, possibly providing other troop contributors with sufficient encouragement and confidence to commit. Yet, even as a vanguard, bridging force, or strategic reserve to complement AU forces, it would not have been adequate to stop any determined mobilization or attack from the Sudanese military. At best, it would have provided a six-month tripwire that may have deterred Sudanese officials from their current campaign. And it would have required assistance from others to control the region, as well as help to ensure rapid augmentation or rapid extraction.

Costs of a UNEPS

We often hear that "an ounce of prevention is worth a pound of cure!" This common medical metaphor also applies to the issue of potential or existing armed conflict. Increasingly, it is understood that early preventive action is more cost-effective than later, larger efforts once a violent conflict has escalated and spread.[100] Aside from horrific human suffering, armed conflict wastes massive financial resources. According to the Carnegie Commission on Preventing Deadly Conflict, "the international community spent approximately $200 billion on conflict management in seven major interventions in the 1990s (Bosnia Herzegovina, Somalia, Rwanda, Haiti, the Persian Gulf, Cambodia and El Salvador), but could have saved $130 billion through a more effective, preventative approach."[101]

As with any new service, there would be additional costs in developing and maintaining a UNEPS. It would entail approximately $2.25 billion in start-up costs, as well as an annual recurring cost of approximately $1 billion. Given a zero-growth budget, this may be initially viewed as beyond the capacity of the 192 member states. However, since such a service would likely reduce the number of operations, alleviate the need to deploy as many multinational contingents, and help to prevent armed conflicts from starting, escalating, or spreading, as well as diminishing the high cost of prolonged operations, it would reduce the overall costs of UN peace operations. As such, a UNEPS should be a very cost-effective investment, one with the potential to save millions of lives and billions of dollars.

The Role of Civil Society: The Responsibility to Assist

With the majority of governments failing to act in humanitarian emergencies, the onus is now on civil society and supportive non-governmental organizations to ensure that the UN receives sufficient support to develop a UNEPS. At this point, however, it is important to realize that the development of a UNEPS is no longer "mission impossible" but an idea whose time has come. While there are risks in being overly optimistic, there are now grounds for some modest hope.

First, historically, only in the aftermath of bad wars and/or genocides has serious public and political consideration been directed towards proposals vaguely similar to the idea of a UNEPS. That interest was temporary, subsiding within a period of two years when new developments arose to capture concern and headlines. Moreover, on no previous occasion was there serious prior preparation to develop a viable alternative and a broad-based supportive constituency. Few nations, if any, were ready. Today, however, lessons learned from previous late, failed efforts at intervention have helped to clarify what might work and, equally important, what would not.[102] The crisis in Darfur has already contributed to the lingering worries over Cambodia, Rwanda, Srebrenica, Sierra Leone, East Timor, and the Democratic Republic of the Congo, as well as Iraq and Afghanistan. Increasingly, people recognize a similar pattern.

Second, once again, there is a discernible shift in attitudes and priorities, even at the political level. Looming global challenges are demanding global responses. In a far more connected and interdependent world, a deeper level of global cooperation is inevitable – or, at least, essential – for survival.

Third, a UNEPS is already more than another nice idea. It is central to a growing global initiative. In 2003 the UNEPS attracted a small supportive constituency,[103] and numerous civil society organizations are now engaged in educational outreach worldwide.[104] An executive committee, a secretariat, and an international working group of prominent scholars and practitioners are coordinating diverse efforts.[105] There are approximately forty related organizations now active in educational outreach, with approximately four hundred other organizations endorsing the initiative.

Fourth, the proposal and plans for this UN service are available and have been repeatedly reviewed and scrutinized since 2003.[106] So far, the response has been encouraging. In the words of Sir Brian Urquhart, former UN under-secretary general for special political affairs, "this venture is of the greatest importance both to the UN as a responsible institution and to the millions as of yet unknown, innocent victims who might, in the future, be saved by this essential addition to the UN's capacity to act on their behalf. There is one overwhelming argument for the United Nations Emergency Peace Service. It is desperately needed, and it is needed as soon as possible."[107] According to Sadako Ogata, former UN high commissioner for refugees, "this initiative directly responds to the widely recognized need to protect people caught in deadly conflicts. I pleaded on numerous occasions for the rapid deployment of specialized forces. Effective, trained and specialized standing forces would have been invaluable."[108]

Fifth, representatives of very diverse sectors in the north and the south have also agreed that, compared to past suggestions along similar lines, this case is more compelling, the concept is more appealing, the model is more appropriate, and, overall, the idea has more political potential.[109]

Sixth, some governments may soon be inclined to support this idea and initiative, possibly by 2008. There are a few promising indications. To cite one example, a bipartisan group of American legislators submitted H. Res 180, the United Nations Emergency Peace Service Act of 2005, to the US House of Representatives.[110] The 1995 Canadian government study *Toward a Rapid Reaction Capacity for the United Nations* acknowledged that, if all existing arrangements failed, further consideration would have to be given to the idea of a standing UN emergency group. By now, it is understood that the existing arrangements have a tendency to fail when most needed. Of course, as with Darfur, governments will not really act until some influential constituency at home and partners abroad compel them to do so. Active support at the local and domestic level will have to influence national governments to form prompt multinational partnerships.

Seventh, over the past decade, civil society has become far more adept at influencing promising change. This initiative links and expands upon the work provided by report of the Panel on UN Peace Operations, the earlier multinational efforts to enhance UN rapid deployment, the ongoing emphasis on the prevention of deadly conflict, the treaty to ban landmines, the establishment of the International Criminal Court, and the endorsement of the Responsibility to Protect. In each of the three latter examples, civil society demonstrated a capacity to mobilize support at almost every level, propelling previously stalled efforts towards successful outcomes.

The development of a UNEPS is a common-security initiative that will require ongoing, determined efforts from a global constituency. The next step in this process is to expand the network of supportive parties. Help will be needed from diverse sectors of society, particularly academe, institutes, and foundations. There will be a requirement for further efforts to ensure that the constituency is well informed and well organized, and there will be a need for ongoing research, drawing on available expertise to prepare more detailed plans and blueprints. Once organized, it will be important to engage in a wider consultative process with both member states and the UN. Finally, to avoid the long and arduous process of securing consensus from "all," it will be necessary to initiate dialogue and negotiations outside the established forums and channel them into a treaty process that can "fast-track" this initiative.

Conclusion

The crisis in Darfur continues. Repeated warnings of a rapidly deteriorating situation, marked by more violence, systemic killing, rape, and scorched-earth tactics, have not been sufficient to mobilize an effective response. Regrettably, the AU efforts in AMIS have not prevented these or worse atrocities or protected many innocent people. Despite a late but promising resolution from the Security Council, the UN has not been able to attract adequate national or regional troop contributors. There are few, if any, indications that UNMIS will be expanded rapidly or at a level of strength sufficient to protect civilians at high risk. At this point, the existing arrangements have repeatedly proven that they are not reliable, rapid, or effective in addressing any of the four challenges noted. Even with substantive reforms, there will remain too many inherent limitations in the AU Standby Brigades, the UN Standby Arrangements System, SHIRBRIG, the EU battlegroups, and NATO.

Many are already ashamed of and inclined to lament the crisis in Darfur. Yet "we the people" should also make a far more substantive effort to ensure that the promise of "never again" is accompanied by a UN capacity to enforce "never again." By now, it is widely evident that governments alone will not save succeeding generations from the scourge of armed conflict, genocide, and war. This responsibility is now shared among us. Rather than await the next crisis, prior preparation has already helped to develop a proposal and a constituency for a UNEPS. Without wider and deeper support, these efforts will also be insufficient. But at least there is now a viable alternative and some hope.

Developing a UN Emergency Peace Service will be a challenging but essential endeavour. In his seminal 1957 study, *A United Nations Peace Force*, William R. Frye provided an insight that is worth recalling: "Establishment of a small, permanent peace force, or the machinery for one could be the first step on the long road toward order and stability. Progress cannot be forced, but it can be helped to evolve. That which is radical one year can become conservative and accepted the next." Together, we might make a critical difference.

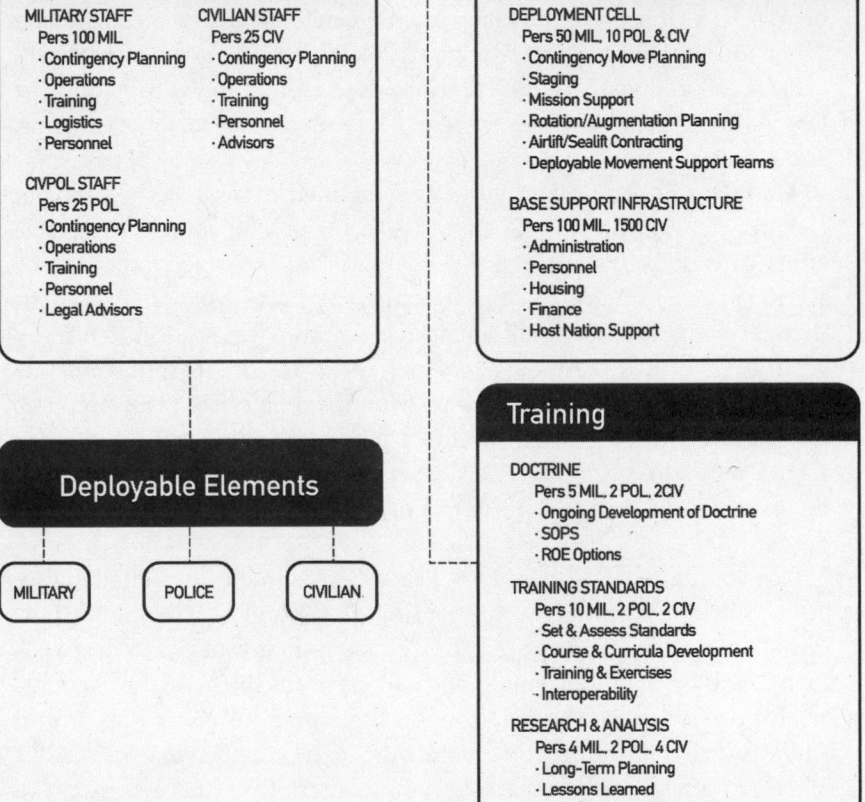

SRSG

Operational Level
UN Emergency Peace Service
Permanent Operational Level
Headquarters and Base

PERSONNEL:
MIL 270
POL 40
CIV 1540

EMC Liaison
Cell: DPA, DPKO, OCHA, UNHCR,
Field Log & National Support

Office of SRSG
Pers 3 MIL, 2 POL, 10 CIV
· Senior MILAD, POLAD & CIVAD
· Policy & Legal

Operations

MILITARY STAFF
Pers 100 MIL
· Contingency Planning
· Operations
· Training
· Logistics
· Personnel

CIVPOL STAFF
Pers 25 POL
· Contingency Planning
· Operations
· Training
· Personnel
· Legal Advisors

CIVILIAN STAFF
Pers 25 CIV
· Contingency Planning
· Operations
· Training
· Personnel
· Advisors

Support

DEPLOYMENT CELL
Pers 50 MIL, 10 POL & CIV
· Contingency Move Planning
· Staging
· Mission Support
· Rotation/Augmentation Planning
· Airlift/Sealift Contracting
· Deployable Movement Support Teams

BASE SUPPORT INFRASTRUCTURE
Pers 100 MIL, 1500 CIV
· Administration
· Personnel
· Housing
· Finance
· Host Nation Support

Deployable Elements

MILITARY   POLICE   CIVILIAN

Training

DOCTRINE
Pers 5 MIL, 2 POL, 2CIV
· Ongoing Development of Doctrine
· SOPS
· ROE Options

TRAINING STANDARDS
Pers 10 MIL, 2 POL, 2 CIV
· Set & Assess Standards
· Course & Curricula Development
· Training & Exercises
· Interoperability

RESEARCH & ANALYSIS
Pers 4 MIL, 2 POL, 4 CIV
· Long-Term Planning
· Lessons Learned
· Multidisciplinary Think Tank

© 2007 Dr. H. Peter Langille

Appendix A

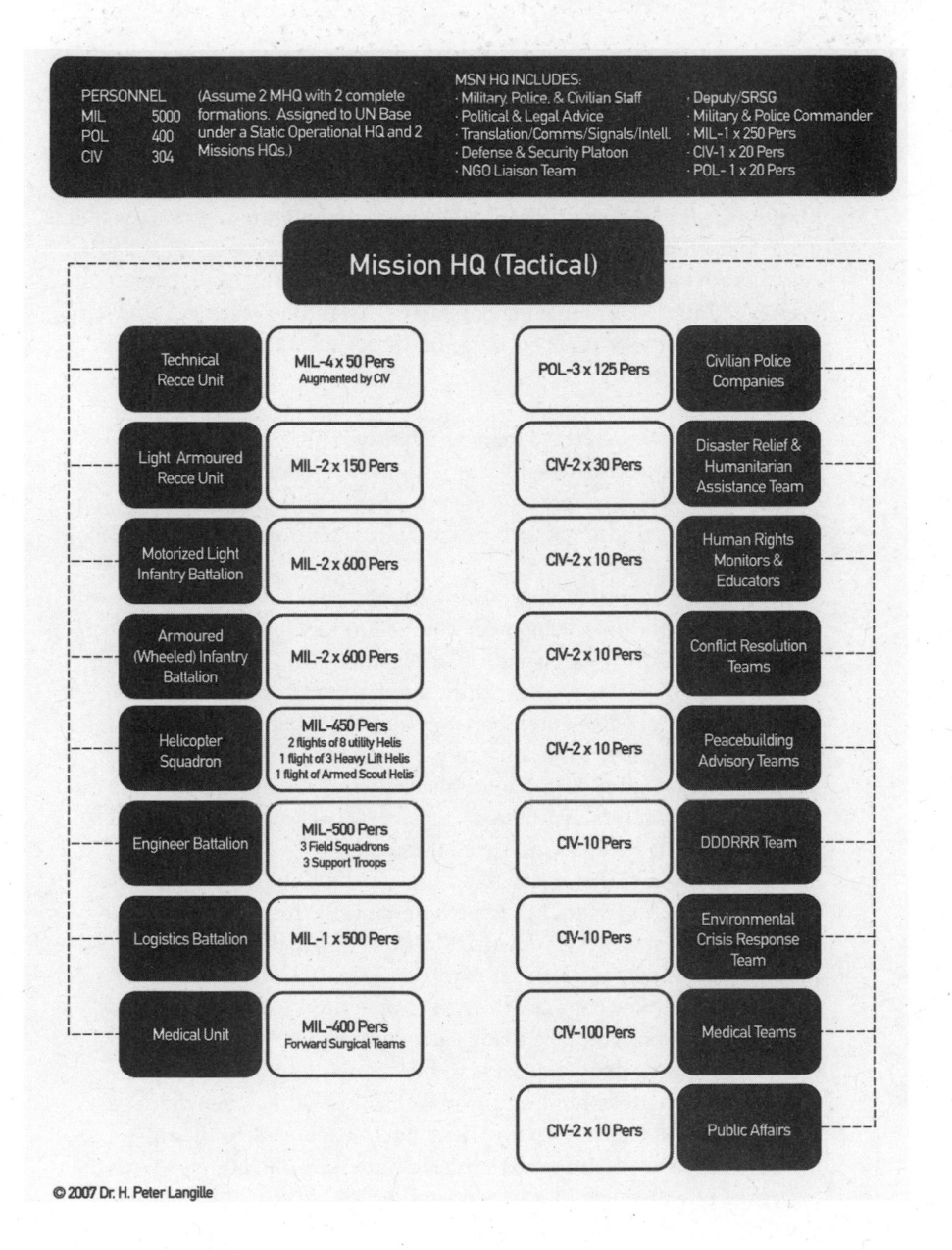

Appendix B
Composition of Deployable Elements for a UN Emergency Peace Service

Notes

* The author wishes to thank the Social Science and Humanities Research Council of Canada for a two-year fellowship, which made it possible to complete this essay and related studies. He is also grateful for the assistance of the Canadian Consortium on Human Security and a previous Human Security Fellowship, as well as the Agnes Cole Dark Award, provided by the Faculty of Social Science at the University of Western Ontario. For amazing patience, outstanding editing, and deep insight, he is also most appreciative of the editor of this volume, Dr Amanda Grzyb.

1 For a brief overview of the Sudanese offensive launched after the Darfur Peace Agreement, see Craig Timberg, "Sudan's Offensive Comes at Key Time," Washington *Post*, 5 September 2006, http://www.washingtonpost.com/wp-dyn/content/article/2006/ 09/04.

　　UN DPKO's deputy director, Hedi Annabi, provided an accurate early warning of this development. See Glenn Kessler, "UN Official Warns of Major New Sudanese Offensive in Darfur," Washington *Post*, 18 August 2006, http://www.washingtonpost.com/wp-dyn/content/ article/2006/08/17. By September, it was evident that the Sudanese government was deploying substantive forces into the Darfur region, including larger troop formations, heavier weapons, armoured vehicles, and attack helicopters. Antonov transport planes were also reported to be bombing villages at an increased frequency.

2 See, for example, H. Peter Langille, "Preventing Genocide: Time for a UN 911," *Globe and Mail*, 14 October 2004, http://www.theglobeand-mail.com/servlet/story/RTGAM.20041019.wdarfur19.

3 In hindsight, it may appear as if officials in Khartoum were the only ones who knew how complex the AMIS operation would be and how adverse conditions could be made even more daunting. By denying visas and permits, denying access to fuel, denying the use of airports at night, denying telephone and communication access, denying interpreters and translators, and denying AMIS access to the automatic weapons on their loaned vehicles, Sudanese officials effectively destroyed any prospect of AMIS operating effectively.

4 For a brief overview of this dilemma, see Lydia Polgreen, "Obstacles Test African Force in Grim Darfur," New York *Times*, 17 May 2006. Some have compared the area of operations with the size of AMIS, suggesting that it leaves one AU soldier to patrol an area the size of Manhattan, or one soldier per every twenty-eight square kilometres.

5 Among the international military resources provided to AMIS were: 12 helicopters, 105 armoured personnel carriers, 300 to 400 vehicles,

training assistance, fuel, communication, and logistic support. Few could consider this a robust, cohesive, or even competent force.

6 See "Report of the Secretary-General on Darfur to the United Nations Security Council," s/2006/591, 28 July 2006, para 8, p.3.

7 For example of a frequent critique, see "Sudan: AMIS Needs New Resources for New Responsibilities," *Bulletin of Refugees International*, 27 July 2006. Also see "No Power to Protect: Increase Troops," Refugees International, 22 September 2006, http://www.refugees-international.org/section/publications/au_troops/ &output. Eric Reeves has repeatedly documented this problem with AMIS: http://www.sudanreeves.org.

8 Further, by May 2006, the AU participants indicated that they lacked sufficient resources to continue in the AMIS operation beyond October of that year. However, in negotiating the terms for the authorized UN mission (UNMIS), African Union leaders initially stipulated that AU forces must remain the majority within the wider mission. Avoiding the perception of "failure" in Darfur remained a political priority for several AU governments.

9 For a modestly encouraging perspective, see the summary (press statement) of Brigadier-General Les Rudman's address, "The Status of the African Stand-By Force: A SADC Perspective," Africa Dialogue Lecture, Centre for International Political Studies, University of Pretoria, 20 September 2005.

10 "Costs and Steps for Establishing and Operationalizing the African Standby Force." Prepared for the Institute for Security Studies, October 2004. Also see African Union, "Issues Paper on the Establishment of the African Standby Force and the Military Staff Committee," First Meeting of the African Ministers of Defence and Security on the Establishment of African Standby Forces, Ababa, Ethiopia.

11 Further, aside from a centralized AU headquarters and planning element, they also intend to develop a continental logistics system and a continental command, control, communications, and information system, as well as a continental training system.

12 This point was raised by an officer in the South African armed forces, following a brief presentation on the AU Standby Brigades' potential on 7 November 2005.

13 These concerns arose in an informal discussion with officials in the UN Department of Peacekeeping Operations in October 2004.

14 Prior to the signing of the DPA, AU diplomats had insisted that their armed forces would remain the majority in any future UN operation. That there had been an informal agreement on the issue at a senior level was well known in sectors of the diplomatic community.

15 While the scope of UN activity is exceptionally broad, with specialization in thousands of areas, the organization is unduly vulnerable in

peace operations, particularly given its dependence on national decision making and national personnel and resources.

16 It is worth recalling that, throughout the early to mid-1990s, in a period characterized by broad cooperation, the Security Council worked relatively effectively in setting new precedents to intervene when necessary for humanitarian purposes and to maintain peace and security. Although there were horrific exceptions, the UN system was, at least, capable of responding since the P5 were inclined to avoid any use or threat of their veto power.

17 Currently, decision making in the Security Council is frequently contested as geo-strategic competition has replaced enlightened multinational cooperation for the common good. In the current political environment, the P5 members have frequently returned to bargaining over their perceived narrow national interests. Oil rights and profits from exports of weapons appear to be a higher priority for most, if not all, of the P5.

One of the more profound changes over the past twenty years has been the shift from a bipolar system in the Cold War to a cooperative multilateral system in the early to mid-1990s, a regionally divided system in the late 1990s, a hegemonic system pursuing global control after the millennium, and a contested, competitive system by 2006. Security Council decision making, particularly by the P5, appears to be directly influenced by the prevailing system. While global human security and an effective United Nations are seldom a high priority for the Permanent Five, the prospects increase with cooperative multilateralism. Similarly, the prospects decrease during periods of intense competition for resources and war. Given the relatively short lifespan of recent international systems, one may anticipate further shifts.

18 This shift has been evident in almost all UN operations since 2001. While such changes were initially recommended in the report of the High-level Panel on UN Peace Operations, A/55/305–S/2000/809 (the Brahimi Report of 2000), further elaboration on each was provided in the report of the secretary general's High-level Panel on Threats, Challenges and Change: "A More Secure World: Our Shared Responsibility, 1 December 2004, A/59/565, 2005, 58–61.

19 "A More Secure World," para 39, p.23.

20 Ibid., para 87, p.34.

21 Ibid., para 217, p.59.

22 See the report of the International Commission on Intervention and State Sovereignty, *The Responsibility to Protect* (Ottawa: International Development Research Centre 2001).

23 For an overview of a 2003 attempt to explore SHIRBRIG's potential and future requirements in protection operations, see H. Peter Langille

and Tania Keefe, "The Future of Peacekeeping," *Canadian Foreign Policy*, vol. 11, no. 1 (2004): 31–47, http://ligi.cfhosting.ca/admin/Information/73/030602future_of_peacekeeping1.pdf.

   Modest elaboration was provided in H. Peter Langille, "Rapid Deployment to Prevent Armed Conflict and Protect Civilians: New Requirements in United Nations Peace Operations," in Tami Amanda Jacoby, ed., *Transformation of War in the 21st Century: Old Lessons and New Trends* (Winnipeg: Centre for Defence and Security Studies 2004), 115–34. For a subsequent effort to address similar questions in more detail, see Victoria K. Holt, "The Responsibility to Protect: Considering the Operational Capacity for Civilian Protection," Discussion Paper, Stimson Center (Washington, D.C.), January 2005, http://www.stimson.org/pub.cfm?id=240. Also see Victoria K. Holt and Tobias C. Berkman, *The Impossible Mandate? Military Preparedness, The Responsibility to Protect and Modern Peace Operations* (Washington, D.C.: Stimson Center, September 2006), http://www.stimson.org/fopo/pdf/Complete_Document-TheImpossible_Mandate-Holt_Berkman.pdf.

24 See United Nations Security Council, Resolution 1706, S/Res/1706 (2006), 31 August 2006.

25 Key points summarized from ibid., 3–6.

26 UNMIS was initially established following UN Security Council Resolution 1590, on 24 March 2005, to support implementation of the Comprehensive Peace Agreement signed by the Government of Sudan and the Sudan People's Liberation Movement/Army on 9 January 2005; and to perform certain functions relating to humanitarian assistance and protection and promotion of human rights. See UNMIS, "Fact Sheet," 23 September 2006, http://www.un.org/Depts/dpko/missions/unmis/.

27 Among the sixty-one member states contributing military personnel to UNMIS as of 31 July 2006 were: Australia, Austria, Bangladesh, Belgium, Benign, Bolivia, Botswana, Brazil, Burkina Faso, Cambodia, Canada, China, Croatia, Denmark, Ecuador, Egypt, El Salvador, Fiji, Finland, Gabon, Germany, Greece, Guatemala, Guinea, India, Indonesia, Jordan, Kenya, Kyrgyzstan, Malawi, Malaysia, Mali, Moldova, Mongolia, Mozambique, Namibia, Nepal, Netherlands, New Zealand, Nigeria, Norway, Pakistan, Paraguay, Peru, Philippines, Poland, Republic of Korea, Romania, Russian Federation, Rwanda, Sri Lanka, Sweden, Tanzania, Thailand, Turkey, Uganda, Ukraine, United Kingdom, Yemen, Zambia, and Zimbabwe.

28 Sudanese officials might exercise their option to deny consent, but they would then be faced by the problematic decision to expel UNMIS from their territory, a move that would only increase international pressure.

29 Having become a signatory to the Convention on the Prevention and
    Punishment of the Crime of Genocide in the same year that it initi-
    ated its plans for Darfur, the Sudanese government could only be relied
    upon to remain duplicitous.

30 For further elaboration on this diplomatic tussle, see Eric Reeves, "The
    UN Security Council and a final betrayal of Darfur," *Sudan Tribune*,
    17 June 2006, http://www.sudantribune.com/imprimable.php3?
    id_article=16239. The appeals and assurances offered to President
    Omar al-Bashir appear to have encouraged worse behaviour. For one
    widely alleged to be a war criminal, it must have been comforting to
    hear that there would be no prospect of any intervention force, that
    there would be absolute respect for the national sovereignty and terri-
    torial integrity of Sudan, and that no UN operation would even happen
    without his consent. Having been given the right to veto the UN opera-
    tion, he accepted the offer and adamantly refused to accept any kind of
    robust UN force, particularly one authorized under Chapter VII of the
    UN Charter.

31 Cited by Colum Lynch, "Peacekeeping Grows, Strains U.N.," Wash-
    ington *Post*, 17 September 2006, http://www.washingtonpost.com/
    wp-dyn/content/article/2006/09/16.

32 Evelyn Leopold, "UN Scrambles for Troops for Future Darfur Force,"
    Reuters, 26 September 2006.

33 Many national officials know the limits of the current UN system and
    the temporary nature of public pressure. Among most member state
    governments, there is a shared preference for duplicitous excuses
    to justify existing arrangements, even when the tools at hand are
    increasingly recognized to be unreliable and insufficient. While some
    are intensely cynical about this system and believe it too difficult to
    change, others are simply satisfied with the way things now work since
    the system serves their national interests and can always be blamed
    for their own complacency. There are also those who see pragmatic
    incremental steps as the only option and view the gradual combination
    of reforms as a promising evolution towards a new UN system, which
    should eventually work better than the old one. A smaller number
    retain a judicious mix of realism and idealism, continuing to work with
    "what is" while striving to create the conditions that will facilitate more
    ambitious change and ultimately produce a system that functions as it
    "could" and "should."

34 United Nations Security Council, Resolution 1679 (2006),
    S/Res/1679(2006), 16 May 2006.

35 UN Under-Secretary General Jean-Marie Guéhenno quoted in a tran-
    script, "Key Challenges in Today's UN Peacekeeping Operations,"
    Council on Foreign Relations, Washington, D.C, 18 May 2006, 3,

http://www.cfr.org/publication/10766/key_chellenges_in_todays_un_
peacekeeping_operations.

36 Following a poorly conceived mission in Somalia, with multiple chains
of command and authority as well as national interference leading to
unnecessary casualties, the blame shifting commenced within the
UN's most powerful member state. For an excellent overview of the
related problems in this operation, see John L. Hirsch and Richard
B. Oakley, *Somalia and Operation Restore Hope* (Washington, D.C.:
United States Institute for Peace 1995). After failure in Somalia, the
political and institutional challenges increased with deliberate misinformation, "scapegoating," and a recurring refusal to help.

37 United Nations Charter, Article 43, para 1.

38 This comparison was initially made by Sir Brian Urquhart in "Beyond
the Sheriff's Posse," *Survival*, vol. 32, no. 3 (1990).

39 While there were indications that Washington was intent on shifting
Allied support to NATO as early as 1994, the Non-Aligned Movement's
demand for the removal of all gratis northern personnel (loaned professional officers) from the UN DPKO was the last straw for many
northern governments. The defence establishments of the latter had
a strong institutional preference for NATO and many were actively
encouraging a departure from UN peace operations.

40 For example, in 2005 the top ten contributors of troops to UN peacekeeping were: Bangladesh (9,529), Pakistan (8,999), India (7,284), Jordan
(3,703), Nepal (3,466), Ethiopia (3,410), Ghana (2,520), Uruguay (2,428),
Nigeria (2,412) and South Africa (2,010). United Nations, Department
of Peacekeeping Operations, "UN Troop Contributors," *Year in Review*
2005.

41 Increasingly, the trend for the majority of northern members is to wait
and watch for, defer, and deny UN requests for their national resources,
particularly appropriately trained, well-equipped personnel.

42 For elaboration on this dilemma, see H. Peter Langille, *Bridging the
Commitment–Capacity Gap: An Overview of Existing Arrangements
and Options for Enhancing UN Rapid Deployment* (Wayne, N.J.: Center
for United Nations Reform Education 2002).

43 United Nations, Department of Peacekeeping Operations, "Fact
Sheet," prepared in cooperation with the UN Department of Public
Information, DPI/2429.

44 For a thoughtful overview of this unprecedented surge, see "Twenty
Days in August: The Security Council Sets Massive New Challenges for
UN Peacekeeping," *Security Council Report*, Special Research Report,
no. 5, 8 September 2006, http://www.securitycouncilreport.org.

45 See Colum Lynch, "Peacekeeping Grows."

46 Cited in ibid., 2.

47 See Evelyn Leopold, "UN Tells Sudan It Is Sending Military Help to Darfur," Reuters, 26 September 2006.

48 As reported in Agence France-Presse, October 2006. Cited by Eric Reeves, "How Long Must the People of Darfur Wait for Meaningful Security," 15 October 2006, http://genocidewatch.org/SudanHowLong MustThePeopleOfDarfurWaitForMeaningfulSecurity15Oct2006.htm.

49 In 1991 there was broad official support for a UN that might finally be made to work, not only more effectively in peacekeeping but also as the collective-security institution its founders intended. Yet within the space of five difficult years – a period characterized by high demand for emergency assistance in peacekeeping – support for the UN began to dissipate in key countries. See, for example, Secretary General Boutros Boutros-Ghali, *An Agenda for Peace: Preventive Diplomacy, Peacemaking and Peacekeeping,* A/47/277-S/241111, June 1992.

50 See Boutros Boutros-Ghali, *Supplement to an Agenda for Peace: Position Paper of the Secretary-General on the Occasion of the Fiftieth Anniversary of the United Nations,* A/50/60-S/1995/1, New York, United Nations, 3 January 1995. This report was followed by three national studies which focused on enhancing the rapid-deployment capacity of the UN. See Government of Canada, *Towards a Rapid Reaction Capability for the United Nations,* 1995; the Netherlands' *Non-paper on a Permanent UN Brigade,* 1995; and the *Report of the Danish Multinational Study on Developing a Standby High Readiness Brigade for UN Peacekeeping Operations,* 1995. The *Final Report* of the Carnegie Commission on Preventing Deadly Conflict was a seminal document released in 1997. Another influential effort to revise dated practices was *The Report of the Panel on UN Peacekeeping Operations,* A/55/305-S/2000/809 (the Brahimi Report of 2000). The report of the International Commission on Intervention and State Sovereignty, with its new doctrine of the Responsibility to Protect, established a promising new norm as well as useful principles and criteria for intervention to protect human security. Two of the latest substantive contributions, combining aspects of the preceding documents, are the report of the secretary general's High Level Panel on Threats, Challenges and Change: *A More Secure World*; and the secretary general's report *In Larger Freedom: Toward Development, Security and Human Rights for All,* A/59/2005.

51 Further elaboration on what "could" or "should" be, particularly with regard to new tools or more ambitious UN arrangements to enhance collective security, is seldom encouraged, let alone tolerated by the P5 of the Security Council. After all, this is their system. As such, the most powerful share a preference for maintaining and controlling it,

competing to advance their interests within it, and occasionally even subverting aspects of it when they pose too much of a problem.

52 For an exceptionally thoughtful overview of integrated analysis and approaches, see Oliver Ramsbotham, Tom Woodhouse, and Hugh Miall, *Contemporary Conflict Resolution: The Prevention, Management and Transformation of Armed Conflict*, 2nd ed. (Cambridge: Polity Press, 2005).

53 Overall, the reforms proposed in *A More Secure World* may help address real-world needs as well as meet diverse challenges. Several proposals might even attract the support needed to firm up the foundations of UN peace operations, which also need help. This reflects the sort of modest, incremental progress pursued over the past fourteen years. As was the case with the Brahimi Report, which also focused on the minimum threshold of change necessary within the constraints of existing arrangements and a no-growth budget, the ideas set out in *A More Secure World* are worthwhile. Yet, even if adopted, this combined package would still remain insufficient to provide any assurance of a dependable capacity for the prevention of armed conflict or genocide, the protection of civilians at risk, or rapid UN deployment to address any urgent crisis.

54 As reported, Guéhenno stated that "a six-month timeline between the decision to deploy and the deployment is a more practical timeline, especially if you think of the logistical conditions in Darfur. January 2007 is a much more realistic date." Reuters, 12 June 2006. Cited by Erik Reeves, "The UN Security Council and a Final Betrayal of Darfur."

55 "Security Council Extends the Mandate of the UN Mission in Sudan, Citing 'Grave Concern,'" UN News Centre, 23 September 2006, http://www.un.org/apps/news/story.asp?NewsID+19982&Cr= sudan&Cr1.

56 "Chad Warns General Assembly That Darfur Crisis Threatens to Destabilize Entire Region," UN News Centre, 23 September 2006, http://www.un.org/apps/news/story.asp?NewsID=19991&Cr= general&Cr1=debate.

57 See Paul Majendie, "Global Protests Call for UN Intervention in Darfur," Reuters, 18 September 2006.

58 Having seen their country finally reach a new level of international stature, one year prior to hosting the Olympics, Chinese officials had to be alarmed over the prospect of being widely stigmatized for aiding and abetting genocide. Following the US elections in November 2006, and the potential for a wider shift in global politics, Sudanese officials would have less support or grounds to blame President Bush for another unwarranted crusade in his war on terror. Instead of a tempo-

rary protest, public pressure continued to increase, pushing numerous governments to affirm stronger policies towards Sudan.

59 US Secretary of State Condoleeza Rice hinted at the prospect of a worse option when she stated, "The Sudanese Government faces a clear and consequential decision. This is a choice between cooperation and confrontation." Cited in Sue Pleming, "U.S. Tells Sudan: Cooperate or Expect Confrontation," Reuters, 27 September 2006.

60 Robert F. Wirth, "Sudan Says It Will Accept U.N.-African Peace Force in Darfur," New York *Times*, 17 November 2006, http://www.nytimes.com/2006/11/17/world/africa/17darfur.html?_r= 1&scp=1&sq=Sudan%20says%20it%20will%20accept%20U.N.-African %20Peace%20Force%20in%20Darfur&st=cse&oref=slogin].

61 The member states participating in SHIRBRIG could not reach consensus on a deployment to Darfur. While there was evident support in several national capitals, others, particularly several NATO allies, were concerned about being stretched too thin with another military commitment in Afghanistan.

62 For an official perspective on this arrangement, see http://www.shirbrig.dk. For a constructively critical overview of SHIRBRIG, see Howard Peter Langille, "La Brigade multinationale d'intervention rapide des forces en attente des Nations Unies (BIRFA): est-elle perfectible?" in Jocelyn Coulon, ed., *Guide de la maintien de la paix* (Outremont, Que.: Athena Editions 2003), 111–26. For further analysis of the strengths and limits of SHIRBRIG, see Langille and Keefe, "The Future of Peacekeeping." A well-documented, more encouraging perspective is provided by Peter Armstrong-Whitworth, "SHIRBRIG: The Future of Canada's Contribution to UN Peace Operations," *Canadian Military Journal*, vol. 8, no. 2 (2007): 25–34, http://www.journal.dnd.ca/vo8/no2/army-armee-eng.asp.

63 On 15 December 1996 seven countries signed a letter of intent to cooperate in establishing and maintaining this high-readiness brigade. This initial group has expanded, as has the number of members signing the initial memorandum of understanding for observer status. Each full participant conditionally agreed, albeit on its own specific terms, to provide particular military assets, in a few cases a smaller contribution of specialists but often an infantry battalion and several officers for the headquarters and planning element.

64 SHIRBRIG is made up of three elements: a Steering Committee, which makes policy and oversees force generation and deployment; a Planning Element, which serves as the nucleus for the force headquarters and plans for individual deployments; and a Brigade Pool of Forces consisting of the troops who might be made available to SHIRBRIG by the participating countries.

65 Among the full participants in SHIRBRIG are Denmark, the Netherlands, Canada, Austria, Finland, Hungary, Ireland, Italy, Lithuania, Norway, Poland, Portugal, Romania, Slovenia, Spain, and Sweden. Argentina may soon return. Participating observers include Chile, Croatia, Czech Republic, Egypt, Jordan, Senegal, and Japan.

66 In the words of the SHIRBRIG Canadian commander, Brigadier-General Greg Mitchell, "If the political situation clears, we feel the SHIRBRIG could make a huge difference." Cited in "Despite Our Commitment in Afghanistan, the Canadian Forces Still Have the Capacity to Make a Big Difference in Darfur, Says Conflict Specialist Peter Langille," *Special to Globe and Mail Update*, 27 April 2006, http://www.theglobeandmail.com/servlet/story/ RTGAM.20060427.wcomment0427.

67 Since its inception, SHIRBRIG has made the following deployments. In 2000 SHIRBRIG deployed a headquarters, an infantry battalion, and a headquarters company to the UN Mission in Ethiopia and Eritrea (UNMEE). Three participating countries (Canada, Denmark, and the Netherlands) contributed to the SHIRBRIG deployment to UNMEE. A serious review of this deployment reveals a slow response (almost four months), low readiness, and a lack of prior training. Further, since only three members participated in that mission, it raised legitimate questions about the depth of political commitment to the partnership. Regrettably, these issues have not been adequately addressed. In March 2003 SHIRBRIG provided a planning team to assist the Economic Community of West African States in the planning of a peacekeeping mission in Côte d'Ivoire. In September 2003 SHIRBRIG deployed twenty members to assist the UN in forming the core of the interim UN headquarters in Liberia. In 2005 SHIRBRIG's Planning Element provided the core for the headquarters of the UN mission in Sudan, as well two security companies (i.e., approximately 220 troops).

68 As the crises in Darfur unfolded in 2004, UN DPKO's national military advisers confirmed that there was little, if any, discussion or consideration of SHIRBRIG being appropriate for stemming further violence. This may have been due to expectations that SHIRBRIG might be making a small contribution to the forthcoming UNMIS operation.

69 Among those raising the SHIRBRIG option in Canada were Langille ("Despite Our Commitment in Afghanistan"); Senator Roméo Dallaire ("There's No Time to Wait," *Globe and Mail*, 5 May 2006); and Linda McQuaig, "Surely We Can Spare 600 of our 18,000 Troops to Do What They Do Best – Peacekeeping, Says Linda McQuaig," (Toronto *Star*, 14 May 2006).

70 It is noteworthy that in 2005 Canada announced it would take a lead role in SHIRBRIG. Yet on 11 May, prior to any formal UN request,

Canadian Prime Minister Stephen Harper promptly declared that the Canadian Forces would not be making a substantive contribution to a UN mission in Darfur. Harper claimed to have consulted with US President George Bush and UN Secretary General Kofi Annan. In explaining his decision, he said, "It is not apparent that there's a desire to have western troops." See "Sudan: PM Rules Out Major Canadian Commitment of Troops to Darfur," *Globe and Mail*, 11 May 2006. The author relayed options to the Prime Minister's Office (PMO) in a futile attempt to encourage a Canadian contribution to a SHIRBRIG deployment to Darfur. The response from the PMO can best be described as utter confusion; it included a request for clarification of the proposed arrangement, the available resources for it, and its purpose.

71 The option of a participants meeting to discuss potential contributions was quietly proposed and promptly rejected.

72 In 2002 the members agreed to consider and prepare for robust operations. However, agreement to engage in missions authorized under Chapter VII is to be decided on only a case-by-case basis. In 2003 there was a wider agreement among the participating members that the deployment of a complete coherent brigade would remain an objective, although it was also recognized to be unlikely. As a result, the various components of SHIRBRIG would be listed within the UNSAS and each would be conditionally available on a case-by-case basis. See Lt.-Gen. (ret.) Ray Crabbe, president and chair of SHIRBRIG, "Concept Development for the Employment of the SHIRBRIG," 24 June 2003. Paper prepared for meeting of the SHIRBRIG Steering Committee and UN, DPKO, New York.

73 Aside from the evident need for further assistance, one objective was to provide tangible support to a joint EU-UN declaration on crisis management.

74 "EU Approves Rapid Reaction Force," BBC News, 23 November 2004, http://news.bbc.co.uk/go/pr/fr/-/hi/world/Europe/4034133.stm.

75 For example, the British deployed fewer than one thousand personnel, which had a calming influence on the savage violence in Sierra Leone. Roughly that number stopped further killing in East Timor. Similarly, France assumed a lead role in an EU mission (UNDOC) to the Democratic Republic of the Congo designed to stabilize the Ituri region. Confronted by direct attacks, UN peacekeepers desperately needed reinforcement as UNDOC began to sustain casualties and lose control of a volatile region. The EU presence, while not specifically designated as a battlegroup, succeeded in restoring and maintaining security as the UN increased its capacity through additional reinforcements from other troop contributors.

76 UN Under-Secretary General for Peacekeeping Operations Jean-Marie
    Guéhenno, "Rwanda Ten Years on," *Prospect Magazine*, London,
    25 March 2004, 2, http://www.un.org/Depts/dpko/dpko/articles/
    article250304.htm.

77 On an earlier occasion in 2004, the Irish foreign minister indicated
    that the chosen term "EU Battlegroups" was problematic and not his
    first preference.

78 In the week following UN Security Council Resolution 1706, President
    Omar al-Bashir referred to the proposed UN force as "an attempt to
    re-colonize his country."

79 See for example, "Darfur Needs Bolder Intervention," International
    Crisis Group, Brussels, 25 May 2005, http://www.crisisgroup.org/
    home/index.cfm?id=3468&1=1&m=1.

80 NATO currently includes the following twenty-six countries:
    Belgium, Bulgaria, Canada, Czech Republic, Denmark, Estonia,
    France, Germany, Greece, Hungary, Iceland, Italy, Latvia, Lithuania,
    Luxembourg, the Netherlands, Norway, Poland, Portugal, Romania,
    Slovakia, Slovenia, Spain, Turkey, United Kingdom, and the United
    States. Officials anticipate that Australia and Japan will be included
    in the next round of NATO expansion. The Euro-Atlantic Partnership
    Council includes those noted above as well as Albania, Armenia,
    Austria, Azerbaijan, Belarus, Croatia, Finland, Georgia, Ireland,
    Kazakhstan, Kyrghyz Republic, Moldova, Russia, Sweden, Switzerland,
    Macedonia, Tadjikistan, Turkmenistan, Ukraine, and Uzbekistan.

81 The NATO Response Force combines land, sea, air, and special forces
    components for rapid reaction to crises worldwide. Scheduled to
    reach full operational capability in October 2006, it consists of 25,000
    troops, capable of being deployed within five days. See "The NATO
    Response Force: At the Centre of NATO Transformation," NATO, July
    2006, http://www.nato.int/issues/nrf/index.html.

82 For a recent perspective on this, see Ivo Daalder and James Goldgeier,
    "Global NATO," *Foreign Affairs*, September/October 2006,
    http://www.foreignaffairs.org/20060901faessay85509/
    ivo-daalder-james-goldgeier/global.

83 See, for example, Martin Walker, "NATO Means Business to Protect
    Pipelines," United Press International, 31 October 2005,
    http://www.spacewar.com/news/energy-tech-05zzzzzzz.html.

84 Here, it is noteworthy that several NATO members actually left
    the American-led war in Iraq, despite considerable pressure from
    Washington to increase their military contributions.

85 See Gloria Galloway, "Silence Greets Call to NATO to Help Canada,"
    Globe and Mail, 14 September 2006. As reported: "A call for additional

troops to help Canadians, British, Dutch and US forces battle the violent Taliban insurgency in southern Afghanistan went unanswered as representatives of NATO countries met in Belgium." Citing NATO spokesman James Appathurai, the article noted that "every NATO country would have to put such a request to their parliament or cabinet. And every country is stretched in terms of the number of troops it has committed to operations around the world."

86 "NATO Response Force 'Ready,'" CNN.com, 29 November 2006, http://edition.cnn.com/2006/WORLD/europe/11/29/nato.meeting.ap.

87 Consuming vast global resources, NATO is often criticized as an alliance of the predators, inclined to forceful means to enhance their well-being at the expense of others less fortunate.

88 By 1994, it had become evident that the Americans wanted NATO to usurp the UN's primacy over matters of international peace and security. NATO has always been far easier for the Americans to dominate. Dan Plesch of Britain's Royal United Services Institute reported on the release of an American "non-paper" at NATO headquarters in 1993, which argued that UN authority should be replaced with NATO's. Senior defence officials within NATO planned to set the parameters for the UN, largely by denying assistance to the UN when needed. This appears to have been a deliberate attempt to deprive, slowly and steadily, the UN of support, even from traditional troop contributors like Canada. It also appears to have worked.

Military officials, as well as their counterparts in defence industries, had to be worried about keeping the old game alive. The institution of war nurtures a deep dependency and provides substantive benefits for powerful interests. Neither the UN nor peacekeeping could be relied upon to provide the bigger budgets, the advanced war-fighting systems, or the big-league professional soldiering roles. As the largest military alliance in history, NATO had set an all-time record in each respect.

89 Contrary to the notion that NATO stopped the fighting in Bosnia, the largest military alliance in history actually stood by and left the UN to cope with an unmanageable, deadly conflict until most of the fighting, ethnic cleansing, and raping was finished. The warring factions were at a stalemate when they agreed to the Dayton Peace Accords in 1995. NATO deployed only after the elusive peace agreement was in place. Similarly, the bombing of Kosovo can be cited as only a political success – deterring Slobodan Milosevic from even worse conduct than he was already guilty of – since the air campaign, conducted at 10,000-to-15,000 feet, was largely unsuccessful in destroying his military assets. Yet both operations are now frequently cited as examples of NATO success and UN failure.

90 First, as indicated, these are all conditional standby arrangements
that lack any binding commitment to participate. Second, all of these
arrangements depend upon national political will and national decision-making processes, which tend to be slow and also inclined to
assess the national interest first. Third, governments assess the depth
of public support and how this is playing in the polls, as well as in the
media. Fourth, governments assess the availability of well-trained,
well-equipped national contingents and the potential risks to national
personnel. Fifth, they also assess the mandate and the prospect of success. Then, before agreeing to join any multinational formation, they
assess their potential partners and whether they are sufficiently competent. In short, there tends to be lots of assessing prior to any
movement.

91 Gwynne Dyer, "No Genocide in Darfur," London *Free Press*,
6 October 2006, 11, http://www.gwynnedyer.com/articles/
Gwynne%20Dyer%20article_%20%20No%20Genocide%20
in%Darfur.txt.

92 A similar point was made by the Honourable Lloyd Axworthy, former
minister of external affairs, in his "Remarks to the Commemorative
Address at the United Nations on the Occasion of Rwanda+10," May
2004: "If the objective is to protect people and prevent violence you
send a legitimate credible UN presence to start a mission quickly – not
wait for 4 to 6 months – then there is far less likelihood of people being
murdered, or large scale massive ethnic cleansing. That suggests a dedicated UN mechanism including a range of services – military, police
and civilian and capable of using force – even when opposed to it – a
entity that Peter Langille has called a UN Emergency Service."

93 This section draws upon and updates the more detailed elaboration
of the initial concept, case, model, and plans for a "UN Emergency
Service" provided in Langille, *Bridging the Commitment*.

94 This option was first outlined in H. Peter Langille et al., "A Preliminary
Blueprint of Long-Term Options for Enhancing a UN Rapid Reaction
Capability," in David Cox and Albert Legault, eds., UN *Rapid Reaction
Capabilities: Prospects and Requirements* (Cornwallis, N.S.: Pearson
Peacekeeping Press 1995), 179–200. Both inspiration and ideas were
derived from Sir Brian Urquhart, "For a UN Volunteer Military Force,"
New York Review of Books, vol. 40, no. 11 (10 June 1993): 3–4. For an
early response to the Urquhart proposal, see Lord Richard Carver,
"A UN Volunteer Military Force: Four Views," *New York Review of
Books*, vol. 40, no. 12 (24 June 1993), 59, http://www.nybooks.com/
articles/2521.

95 Government of Canada, *Towards a Rapid Reaction Capability*, 62.

96 Ibid., 60. A Canadian discussion paper on the issue also acknowledges that "it would provide the UN with a small but totally reliable, well-trained and cohesive group for deployment by the Security Council in urgent situations. It would break one of the key logjams in the current UN System, namely the insistence by troop contributing nations that they authorise the use of their national forces prior to each deployment. It would also simplify command and control arrangements in UN peace support operations, and put an end to conflicts between UN commanders and contingent commanders reporting to national authorities." Government of Canada, "Improving the UN's Rapid Reaction Capability: Discussion Paper," 29 April 1995, 3.

97 This is a modified list of criteria derived from the International Commission on Intervention and State Sovereignty, *The Responsibility to Protect*, 32.

98 Ibid., xi–xiii.

99 Dr John Polanyi, co-chair, International Conference on a United Nations Rapid Reaction Capability, Montebello, Quebec, 8 April 1995. Cited by Langille et. al. in Cox and Legault, eds., *UN Rapid Reaction Capabilities*.

100 For an exceptionally rigorous assessment, see Malcolm Chalmers, "Spending to Save: An Analysis of the Cost Effectiveness of Conflict Prevention," *CICS Working Paper* 1, University of Bradford, April 2005, http://www.brad.ac.uk/acad/cics/publications/spending/working_paper_1.pdf.

101 Cited in the International Commission on Intervention and State Sovereignty, *The Responsibility to Protect*, 20.

102 For a historical review of previous efforts and their potential to guide future options, see H. Peter Langille, "UN Options for Preventing Armed Conflict, Protecting Civilians, Rapid Deployment and Modest Enforcement: A United Nations Emergency Service?" Paper presented at the International Conference on Preventing Genocide and Crimes against Humanity: The Challenge of Enforcement, under the auspices of the Nuclear Age Peace Foundation and the Simons Centre for Peace and Disarmament Studies, Liu Institute of Global Issues, University of California, Santa Barbara, 5 December 2003.

Among the lessons learned from previous related efforts was the need for a less contentious, confusing concept. A "UN Standing Force," a "UN Legion," and a "UN Army" or any form of permanent "rapid deployment force" are simply inappropriate, insufficient, and unappealing, both globally and in theatre. By now, it should also be evident that any military force alone is also insufficient, even as a rapid-deployment mechanism for emergencies. People in desperate circumstances frequently need more than a military presence. Yet most people tend to be quite receptive to receiving useful services, particularly when they come from a widely respected source. Moreover, when there is an evident, urgent need, such as a real emergency, many expect that the necessary services will be provided. Equally important, at the political level almost everywhere, the concept of a UN Emergency Peace Service should be a lot tougher to argue against.

103 For an overview of the meeting that prompted this initiative, see Justine Wang, "A Symposium on Genocide and Crimes against Humanity: The Challenge of Prevention and Enforcement," University of Southern California, Santa Barbara, 5–6 December 2003, http://www.wagingpeace.org/articles/2004/01/ 08_wang_symposium.htm.

104 For a thoughtful summary of this proposal with modest elaboration in a few areas, see Robert C. Johansen, ed., *A United Nations Emergency Peace Service: To Prevent Genocide and Crimes against Humanity* (New York: Institute for Global Policy 2006), http://www.globalactionpw.org/uneps/UNEPS_PUBLICATION.pdf.

105 For an overview, see the UNEPS website and links hosted by Global Action to Prevent War, http://www.globalactionpw.org/uneps/ index.htm.

106 As noted above, an overview of the first international conference to focus on a UNEPS was provided in a report by Justine Wang. The second conference on a UNEPS, in Cuenca, Spain, was the subject of a detailed report by Robert Johansen, available at http://www.globalactionpw.org/uneps/UNEPS%20Cuenca%20 Conference%20Report.PDF.

107 From Sir Brian Urquhart's "Preface" in Johansen, ed., *A United Nations Emergency Peace Service*.

108 From the cover to Johansen, ed., *A United Nations Emergency Peace Service*.

109 Strong support for a UNEPS was expressed by those active in the areas of development; social justice; environment; human rights; disarmament; peacekeeping; international law; genocide prevention; UN reform; cooperation; peace; conflict transformation; and common, collective, and human security.

110 Representative Albert Wyne (with eight co-sponsors), H.R. 180, The United Nations Emergency Peace Service Act of 2005, US House of Representatives, 109th Congress, First Session, Washington, D.C., 27 March 2005, http://thomas.loc.gov/cgi-bin/query/z?c109:H.RES.180.

Index

Aballa people, 8
abandonment: of Darfur, 77–8;
    intervention vs., 66; of Jews, 64,
    65; of Rwanda, 12, 15, 33, 61, 77
ABC News, 84
Abd al-Halim, Abd al-Mahmud,
    129–30
Abkam, Mawlana Mahmud, 123
Abuja accord. *See* Darfur Peace
    Agreement (DPA)
Abu Shouk camp, 239
Action against Famine, 239
activists/activism: and Beijing
    Olympics, 20; celebrity, 86;
    and complicity of West, 66;
    regarding Darfur, 80; and dis-
    semination of information, 66;
    educated Sudanese and, 134;
    and exhibitions, 216, 218, 234,
    246–7; genocide-prevention, 86;
    and international intervention,
    83; and middle powers, 32; NGO
    campaigns and, 80; and Rwandan
    genocide, 31, 66; and US, 38, 200
Addario, Lynsey, 235, 239–40
Adelman, Howard, 59n12
Adorno, Theodor, 219

advocacy groups, for Darfur, 8, 83–6
Aegis Trust. *Darfur* exhibition, 222
Afghanistan, 307; ISAF mission
    in, 298; Taliban insurgency in,
    324n85; US invasion of, 125,
    213n52; war in, 298
African Union (AU): and compre-
    hensive agreement between Sudan
    and rebels, 133; and DPA, 166;
    on genocide in Darfur, 118; GOS
    and, 127–30, 183; and interna-
    tional intervention, 206, 213n48;
    intervention by, 50–1; monitors/
    observers, 52, 201, 260, 266, 282;
    peace agreement proposed by, 154;
    Peace and Security Council, 282;
    regional economic commissions
    (RECs), 283; in Sudan, 134–5; and
    UN, 50–1, 129, 156, 313n14; and
    UNMIS, 313n8
African Union (AU) forces, 205–6;
    as ceasefire monitors, 183, 188;
    in Darfur, 127–30, 183, 184, 188,
    190, 191, 196; and GOS, 206; and
    Janjaweed, 206; NATO and,
    204–5; as peacekeepers in Darfur,
    53, 96; replacement by UN con-